Introduction to the Wisdom of Kabbalah

A Beginner's Course in the
Authentic Wisdom

Introduction to the
Wisdom of Kabbalah

Translation: Alex Zusin, Naftali Ringel, Aviram Gottfried
Proofreading of English version: Susan Gale
Editors: Gianni Conti, Markos Zografos, Gilad Shir
Content Management of English version: Gilad Shir

kabbalah.info
kabuconnect.com
KabbalahBooks.info

ISBN: 9798843388782

Table of Contents

Table of Contents

Preface

In recent years, interest in the Wisdom of Kabbalah is on the rise. Up to the late 20th century, very few studied this Wisdom, and opportunities to study were quite limited, whereas since the beginning of the 21st century, millions worldwide have been studying the Wisdom of Kabbalah one way or another and the study of this Wisdom has become much more accessible. Nowadays, the Wisdom of Kabbalah can be studied via: live lessons broadcast on television and the Internet, frontal lessons broadcast all over the world in various languages or dozens of books (original texts and interpretation of the original texts) published in recent years.

According to the Wisdom of Kabbalah, that is no surprise. Actually, according to the writings of Kabbalists, we are at the beginning of a process, at the end of which the Wisdom of Kabbalah will have a central place in the life of every person in the world as a method for solving global and personal problems, which continue to worsen all over the world.

The reason for that stems from the nature of this Wisdom. The Wisdom of Kabbalah is a science of the laws governing all of creation. These laws are concealed from us, and since we are unaware of them, we repeatedly act against them, summoning a contrary, negative reaction. As a result, the global crisis has appeared, leaving its mark on all areas of the modern person's life, both on the global and personal level. Studying the concealed laws of creation, by means of the Wisdom of Kabbalah is the solution to these problems. That is the root of growing interest in this Wisdom.

Except that the purpose of this concealed Wisdom is much higher and more sublime than solving problems being revealed in this world. Kabbalists write that just by revealing the laws of creation, which are concealed from us for now, leads to the revelation of a different reality from what is revealed in our world: A spiritual, eternal, and complete reality, the revelation of which is the purpose of all of creation, and each individual's life.

Since all of creation has a purpose, nothing happens incidentally, surely not such meaningful processes as those being revealed to us since the beginning of the 21st century. In all the Kabbalistic books written throughout thousands of years, where the Wisdom was developed, it is written that all of creation and each of its parts develop in accordance with a certain plan, whose purpose is, the revelation of spirituality, as written above. Kabbalists write that according to this plan, in our times, we have reached a particular stage, where all of humanity is ready for the revelation of the spiritual reality. That is why the Wisdom of Kabbalah is being revealed in the world after thousands of years of concealment.

About the Course "Preface to the Wisdom of Kabbalah"

"Preface to The Wisdom of Kabbalah" is a fundamental course in the study of the Wisdom of Kabbalah. The course introduces the student to all areas of study of this Wisdom, in the appropriate measure for those taking their first steps in this study.

These are some of the topics we will study: what is the Wisdom of Kabbalah, the language of Kabbalah, perception of reality, freedom of choice, structure of the spiritual worlds, the soul of the first Man (*Adam HaRishon*), the Ten Sefirot, the influence of the environment on the individual, and more.

In accordance with the unique nature of the study of the Wisdom of Kabbalah, this course's aim is not just to convey the required information to students, but rather to provide the student with the tools for the correct study of this Wisdom, as well. First and foremost, our intent in this course is to present the Wisdom of Kabbalah as a practical method, offering the path of attaining balance with the world to every person, enabling one to live one's life in happiness, security, and wholeness.

The course is based on authentic sources of the Wisdom of Kabbalah: Rabbi Shimon Bar Yochai (*RASHB"I*), Rav Yehuda Leib Ashlag, known as "*Baal HaSulam*," and on a method of studying this Wisdom for generations. While organizing the study content of the course, we set a goal of presenting the material in a light, comprehensible language, arranging the means of study and its content such that enables the student to acquire it in the easiest and most convenient way.

Course goals:

- Acquiring basic knowledge in all areas of study of the Wisdom of Kabbalah

- Acquiring the correct approach to the study of the Wisdom of Kabbalah
- Acquiring basic tools for reading original Kabbalistic texts
- Acquiring basic terminology

The course is divided into three units, which present the material gradually, from beginners to advanced. Each unit is divided into three parts. It is important to study in the order of the course units, as each unit sets the foundations for the following ones.

The course includes the following means of study:

- The Study Unit – Contains basic study content, guiding the student through the additional study tools.
- The Course Book – Advanced study content, expanding on the material presented in the study unit and a dictionary of terminology.

Each lesson begins with the study unit, which presents students with a basic, initial description of the topics to be covered. At the end of every lesson, students are directed to the Course book, to deepen and expand their study of the topics covered that lesson.

We wish you a fruitful and joyful study,
The Editing Team

Study Unit #1 - The Foundations of Kabbalah

About the Study Unit "Foundations of Kabbalah"

The "Foundations of Kabbalah" is the first unit of the "Preface to the Wisdom of Kabbalah" course, and as such, constitutes an important and essential foundation for all the following study content. Given its importance, we have paid extra attention to organizing its content and taken special care to present it in the simplest and most easily understood language as possible.

The unit is divided into 3 parts:

- What is the Wisdom of Kabbalah – What does the Wisdom of Kabbalah deal with and who is permitted to engage in it?
- The perception of reality – Ways of revealing the spiritual reality.
- The language of branches – The language of Kabbalah, introducing Kabbalistic writings.

The goals of this study unit are:

- To clarify what the Wisdom of Kabbalah deals with.
- To remove misconceptions concerning the study of the Wisdom of Kabbalah.
- To introduce the language of Kabbalah.
- To provide the correct approach to the study of the Wisdom.

Within this framework of study, we will define the following concepts: spirituality, corporeality, Creator, the created, equivalence of form, surrounding light, will to receive, will to bestow, spiritual worlds, revelation, concealment, thickness and purity.

Part #1 - What Is the Wisdom of Kabbalah?

Lesson #1 – What do we truly know about the Wisdom of Kabbalah?

In this lesson we will learn: The definition of the Wisdom of Kabbalah / Misconceptions of the Wisdom of Kabbalah / What is "Creator" according to the Wisdom of Kabbalah / How does the study of the Wisdom of Kabbalah relate to us?

From Concealment to Revelation

In order to explain what the Wisdom of Kabbalah is, what we know about it, or more precisely, what we don't know about it, we will begin with a brief summary of the Wisdom of Kabbalah's history.

The Wisdom of Kabbalah dates back thousands of years. The first person to reveal it was *Adam HaRishon* (The First Man)– a regular person, like you and I (not a mythical figure), who lived 5,780 years ago[1] and since he was the first to discover the wisdom, he was called "*Adam HaRishon.*"

The next significant step towards revealing the Wisdom of Kabbalah was another unique individual named Abraham. His uniqueness was in the method he developed for engaging in the Wisdom of Kabbalah. He gathered a group of people who learned the method from him, a group who consequently developed and became the Nation of Israel.

Engaging in the wisdom of the Nation of Israel continued to develop and reached its peak in the days of the First and Second Temples. Then, with the destruction of the Second Temple, studying the wisdom ceased abruptly. It was concealed for two thousand years and only a select few studied it.

---

[1] True to when this was written, 2020.

We will expand on the history of the Wisdom of Kabbalah and the reasons for its concealment and revelation later in this unit. Our goal for now is to understand what the Wisdom of Kabbalah deals with and what we truly know about it. That is why we have specifically chosen to first emphasize the fact that Kabbalah is being revealed today after two thousand years of concealment. That is because during that period, many rumors and misconceptions developed around it, both concerning its essence and being allowed to study it.

It turns out that many people think they know what Kabbalah deals with, whereas few truly do. Here are some examples of various common opinions concerning the Wisdom of Kabbalah: Kabbalah is Jewish mysticism, Kabbalah deals with charms and blessings, Kabbalah is related to parapsychology, Kabbalah is red strings, you mustn't study the Wisdom of Kabbalah before age 40, one can lose one's mind from studying, studying Kabbalah is only meant for the select few, and so on.

As mentioned above, all of the views appearing on this "shopping list" (along with all the other misconceptions we omitted) are not true. All the misconceptions regarding the study of the Wisdom of Kabbalah result from the intentional concealment of two thousand years; that's exactly why the first step in the study of the Wisdom of Kabbalah is to remove the misconceptions in its regard and in parallel, define precisely what it deals with.

So, what is the Wisdom of Kabbalah? The great Kabbalist of our generation, Rav Yehuda Ashlag (1884-1954), known as "Baal HaSulam" (The Ladder) named for the "*HaSulam*" Commentary which he wrote for the book of Zohar, writes that "this wisdom is no more and no less, rather the arrangement of roots cascading by means of cause and result through set and definite laws connecting and targeting one very sublime goal, which is called, revealing His Divinity to His creatures in this world."[2] In other, more simplified

---

[2] The Writings of Baal HaSulam, essay, "The Essence of the Wisdom of Kabbalah."

words: The Wisdom of Kabbalah is a method for revealing the Creator to the created in this world.

Who is the Creator? According to the Wisdom of Kabbalah, the Creator is the general law of nature governing all of reality. This law is concealed from us and the Wisdom of Kabbalah is the method for its revelation. Whereas science in our world studies the laws of nature that are revealed to us, Kabbalah studies the laws of nature that are concealed from us. In other words, the Wisdom of Kabbalah is a method of revealing the single concealed force, according to which all of creation is governed. Revelation of the Creator – The general law of nature governing creation – also called revelation of spirituality.

"Nature," Kabbalists write, "has the same numeric value as Creator."[3] Meaning, the general law of nature is that "G-d," "Creator" or "Upper force" we need to reveal. Likewise, as mentioned, this is also the goal of the Wisdom of Kabbalah, as Baal HaSulam writes: "Revealing the Creator to His created in this world."

Test yourself:
- Define what the Wisdom of Kabbalah is and explain why so many misconceptions have developed around it.

Why do we need Spirituality?

Why do we need the revelation of spirituality, you may ask, is it not enough what has been revealed to us already? Perhaps, if our daily, revealed reality was clearly understood. However, it presents us with many challenges. Perhaps we will solve them first and then engage in spirituality. The question is certainly justified. The answer to this question lies in the definition of the Wisdom of Kabbalah.

As we have learned, the Wisdom of Kabbalah is a method of revealing the concealed laws governing creation. These laws are

---

[3] Nature in *Gimatria* 86="*Elo-him.*"

clear and genuine, just like the laws revealed in our world (the law of gravity, for example), but we are not aware of them, they are concealed from us. Since we are not aware of them, we repeatedly act contrary to them and summon a negative response. Just as ignoring the law of gravity results in a painful response, so (and even more so) ignoring the concealed laws governing creation summons a painful response. Lacking knowledge of these laws is the reason for all the problems being revealed in our world. Knowing these laws will save us all the pain and sorrow we know in our life. Furthermore, as a result, a different reality will be revealed to us, a new, spiritual reality, complete and eternal.

To whom is the general rule of nature revealed? The answer to this question lies in Baal HaSulam's definition, we mentioned above: "To His creatures in this world," meaning to a person in this world. In other words: spirituality or a connection with the Creator, the single force governing all of reality is revealed to a person during his lifetime in this world. That is an important point, for one of the misconceptions about the Wisdom of Kabbalah is that the spiritual reward from studying Kabbalah is revealed to a person only after one's death, whereas the truth of the matter is that the opposite is true.

A Kabbalist – a person who has revealed the Creator – he is a scientist and not a mystic. A Kabbalist is a rational person who studies his nature and the nature of the world in which he lives. He asks questions and seeks answers, tries to understand, like each one of us, what motivates the "crazy" world we live in. Yet, whereas most of us set these questions aside and get carried away in the currents of life, Kabbalists do not relent until they reveal the secret of life.

"Understanding the word spirituality," writes Baal HaSulam,[4]"has nothing to do with philosophy at all. For how will they discuss a matter they have never seen or sensed? And upon what basis? Unless there is a certain definition with which to separate and differentiate

_____

[4] The Writings of Baal HaSulam, essay, The Wisdom of Kabbalah and Philosophy."

spiritual from corporeal, it is irrelevant, except for those who have attained the spiritual and sensed it, those being the true Kabbalists."

Test yourself:
- What is the benefit of studying the Wisdom of Kabbalah?

The Law of Love

After understanding that the Wisdom of Kabbalah is a science dealing with revealing the Creator, the general law governing all of creation, we will explain the nature of this law, mainly its implications for us.

From their research of nature, Kabbalists reveal that the Creator is a force which is all giving and loving. This force governs creation in harmony, as one body, where all its parts are connected with each other through invisible fibers of interdependence. According to this law, the existence of each part of nature is possible only in balance and harmony ('homeostasis' in scientific language) with the other parts of creation.

We, humans, as part of nature, must reach balance and harmony among us and with nature. In order to actualize our natural purpose and feel content and happy, we need to maintain balanced connections of love and mutual support among us. However, unlike the inanimate, vegetative, and animate nature, we do not feel the law of balance of nature as an obligating force and we act in complete opposition to it.

Yet, lack of knowledge of the law does not release from punishment. As explained above, that is the reason for the deep crisis leaving its mark on human society in every corner of the world.

Furthermore, if we observe the process we have been undergoing for thousands of years, we will reveal that the forces of nature have actually been "guiding" us to understand the necessity to attain the correct balance and connections among us. Apparently, there truly is a plan for us, except we don't take notice of it.

Evolution of the human species is all one of connection. If, at the beginning of human history we lived in family clans, disconnected from each other, with time we began to cooperate, the clans grew and we began to battle to gain control over other people and territories. In parallel, we developed agriculture which led to trade relations and more developed connections among people. Social, cultural, and educational revolutions connected us even more closely together and beginning with the industrial era, we took a path of accelerating the connections among people all over the world, reaching its peak towards the end of the 20th century.

We initiated battles and arguments, yet nature led us to the understanding that we can benefit much more from our combined forces and efforts. Thus, we have naturally turned into one global society, into a single human body dependent on the cooperation of all its organs. The law at the base of all natural development has been causing us to connect with each other through thousands of connections. Whereas a few decades ago we were able to exist alone, today that is no longer possible.

It turns out that globalization is not just a pretty word. It expresses a natural, incessant development advancing us towards a new life; one in which each cell and organ, or each person and country, live well only if they cooperate with each other and care for the benefit of all. On the other hand, if we choose to resist nature and live our lives isolated from others, what will happen to us is what happens to the entire body when a certain organ decides to isolate or disconnect itself from others – a cancerous growth develops.

That is exactly what is happening today in human society. Although we are interconnected, we also take advantage of one another and act only for our own – in complete contradiction to the law of balance in nature. That is why we all suffer. Unlike the other parts of nature, the necessity to maintain connections of mutual guarantee among us is concealed from us. We are capable of understanding the need for such connections, but are incapable of practicing it in actuality. The law of balance in nature is concealed from us in a much deeper way than just intellectual awareness. Something very deep, natural and innate within us prevents us from maintaining it. We will expand on the reasons for its concealment later in the study unit.

As long as we don't take responsibility for ourselves and decide that we need to connect with each other, we won't be able to attain safety or serenity. Kabbalists explain that if we do not begin to educate all the people in the world to consider nature, which is pushing us to evolve towards a heartfelt, genuine connection, rather continue to concentrate only on our own benefit, the crises will increase and we will never be able to build a happy society. The key is in the desire to reveal in our relations that same concealed force of nature, unity, love and bestowal – the Creator. The method for the revelation of the Creator is the Wisdom of Kabbalah.

Test yourself:

- What does each and every part of creation, including human beings depend on for their existence?

Summary of the Lesson

Main Points

- The Wisdom of Kabbalah is being revealed in our times after thousands of years of purposeful concealment, resulting in many misconceptions about it, whereas few truly know what it deals with.
- The Wisdom of Kabbalah is a method of revealing the Creator to the created.
- The Creator, according to Kabbalah is the general law governing all of reality. This law is concealed from us.
- All the suffering in the world stems from the fact that we do not act according to the general law of creation.
- Revealing the Creator will save us all the suffering and expose another reality to us: spiritual, eternal and complete.

- The Creator is a force which is entirely of love and giving, governing creation in harmony, as one body whose parts are connected with each other by invisible fibers of interdependence.

Definitions and Kabbalists

Wisdom of Kabbalah – A method for revealing the Creator to the created in this world.

Creator – The general force of nature.

Creator – From the Hebrew word (Bo'Reh) meaning "Come and see." It emphasizes the fact that the Wisdom of Kabbalah speaks of the Creator as He is attained by man, not as He truly is.

Kabbalist – A person who has revealed the Creator.

Adam HaRishon – A Kabbalist, the first person on earth who revealed the Creator.

Abraham – A Kabbalist. The first one to develop the method of revealing the Creator.

Baal HaSulam – Rav Yehuda Ashlag. One of the greatest 20th century Kabbalists.

Questions and Answers

Question: What is the Wisdom of Kabbalah and why are there so many misconceptions around it?
Answer: The Wisdom of Kabbalah is a method of revealing the Creator to His created in this world. Since it was hidden for 2000 years, many misconceptions developed around it.

Question: What is the benefit in studying the Wisdom of Kabbalah?
Answer: The study of the Wisdom of Kabbalah saves us from misery and pain, and reveals a spiritual, eternal and complete reality to us.

Question: What does the existence of each and every part of creation, including human beings depend on?

Answer: The existence of each part of nature, including human beings depends on balance and harmony with the other parts of creation.

Lesson #2 – Who is allowed to study the Wisdom of Kabbalah?

In this lesson we will learn: Desire – the engine of evolution/ Pleasure extinguishes the desire / The Point in the heart /The history of Kabbalah

The Point in the heart

One of the most common and intriguing questions concerning the Wisdom of Kabbalah is: Who can study it? When Rav Kook (1865-1935), a Kabbalist of great stature, who served as the first General Rabbi of Israel, was asked this question, he answered very simply, "Whoever wants to."

Whoever wants to what? You may ask. Whoever wants to reveal the purpose of his life. That is the only thing a person should check before approaching the study of the wisdom of Kabbalah – whether he has a desire to reveal the purpose of life. Do you have such a desire? You may study! A person comes to the wisdom of Kabbalah in search of a new perspective on this life. Subconsciously, one feels that the answers to gnawing questions exist on a much deeper level than what is offered in the mundane, routine life of this world.

Rav Kook's seemingly simple answer to the question of who may study the wisdom of Kabbalah contains great depth within. In order to understand the depth of his answer, even slightly, we must first relate to the crucial role that desire plays in shaping a person's life in general, specifically on the reasons leading to the ripening of the desire to reveal the purpose of life.

Desires do not simply pop up out of nowhere. Desires are created subconsciously inside of us and only float to the surface when they become defined. Before that, we do not feel the desires, or we may feel general uneasiness. We have all experienced that sensation of wanting something but not knowing exactly what. That occurs when the desire has not yet ripened.

Plato once said: "Necessity is the mother of invention," and he was right. The wisdom of Kabbalah explains that our ability to learn anything inevitably depends on our desire to learn it. Desire is the driving force. It is a very simple formula: When we want something, we do whatever it takes to attain it; we make time, muster our energy and develop the necessary skills. Hence, we can conclude that the engine for change is desire.

Furthermore, the way in which our desires evolve, defines and shapes not only the life of the individual, but the entire history of humanity. As human desires proceeded to evolve, they pushed people to study their surroundings, in order to actualize their aspirations. Unlike rocks, plants, and animals, humans evolve continuously. In every generation and individual, desires proceed to increase.

According to the wisdom of Kabbalah, the engine of change – the desire – consists of five levels from zero to four. Kabbalists call this engine "the will to receive pleasure," or in short "the will to receive." The will to receive increased, level after level, from zero to four, where in each stage it yearned for greater and higher quality fulfillment. When the Wisdom of Kabbalah first appeared in ancient Babylon 4,000 years ago, the will to receive was at level 0. Today we are at level 4 – the highest one.

What is the mechanism causing the desire to rise each time to a new degree? Kabbalists write that the reason is simple: Whenever the will to receive is fulfilled, it is actually nullified. The pleasure filling the desire cancels it. When a desire for a certain fulfillment is canceled, we can no longer enjoy it. In the Wisdom of Kabbalah this principle is called: "Pleasure cancels the desire."

For example: Think of your favorite dish. Now, imagine You're in a fancy restaurant, you get comfortable in your seat as a kind waiter serves you a large plate and sets it on your table. Ah... that pleasant and familiar fragrance! Are you already enjoying yourself? Of course! Yet, as soon as you begin to eat, the desire diminishes. The fuller we get, the more our pleasure diminishes. Finally, when we are completely full, we are no longer able to enjoy the food, so we stop eating. We don't stop because we are full, rather because it is no longer enjoyable to eat on a full stomach. That is the trap of the will to receive – the moment it receives what it wanted (filling), it no longer enjoys it and does not want it. (See Graph #1)

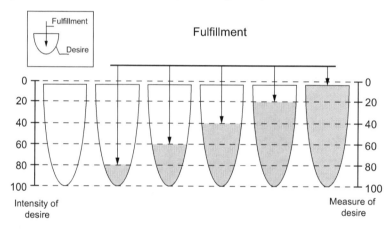

Since we are unable to live without pleasure, we have to continue seeking new and greater sources of pleasure. That is how we have developed from generation to generation, from simple desires for basic needs, such as food, sex, family, and shelter, to more complex desires for possessions, honor, control, and knowledge. At every level, new desires were revealed within us, and in the end, they too, remained dissatisfied. The more we wanted and desired, the emptier we felt. The emptier we felt, the more frustrated we became.

In our times, we are at the degree of the strongest desire to receive, hence, the inevitable conclusion is that nowadays, we are less satisfied than ever before, even though we have much more than our parents and ancestors did. The contrast between what we have, on one hand, and our increasing lack of satisfaction, on the other hand, is the essence of the crisis we are experiencing today. The greater our will to receive is, the emptier we feel and the crisis becomes tougher.

Thus, it is clear why Rav Kook set the desire to understand the meaning of life as a condition for studying the Wisdom of Kabbalah. As long as our will to receive had something to be filled with, it pushed us to fulfilling our aspirations and fill our life with meaning. Whereas in our time, after tens of thousands of years of evolution, since the will to receive has reached its final stage of evolution and no longer sees any new pleasure with which to be filled, the question concerning the purpose of life is rising in increasingly more people. This question, aimed towards a higher realm than life itself is actually the beginning of a new desire, one to reveal the spiritual, eternal and complete reality. As Rav Kook said, when this desire is revealed in a person's heart, he can already begin to study the Wisdom of Kabbalah.

The new desire to reveal spiritual reality is called "the point in the heart" in the Wisdom of Kabbalah. "Heart," in the Wisdom of Kabbalah, is all of a person's corporeal desires and the point is a new desire to reveal the purpose of life, however small for now.

Test yourself:
- Who can study the Wisdom of Kabbalah?

The History of the Wisdom of Kabbalah – The First Kabbalists

The major role of the desire in the evolution of creation in general and in the recent revelation of the Wisdom of Kabbalah in particular, can be learned from the history of the Wisdom of Kabbalah. We will devote the following sections of this lesson to that topic.

The mechanism driving the process of revelation and concealment of the Wisdom of Kabbalah is the same mechanism driving the evolution of humanity – desire. At the initial evolutionary stage of the desire, when it was still relatively small, the Wisdom of Kabbalah was revealed to a select few of people stemming from their closeness to nature. As the desire grew and Man became distant from nature and began to seek new fulfillment (possessions, honor, control, and knowledge), the Wisdom of Kabbalah was concealed. In our times, when the desire has reached the point of saturation and questions concerning the purpose of life are arising, the Wisdom of Kabbalah is being revealed again, for the last time, and this time, it is for every single person.

The Kabbalists we'll become familiar with in this historic scan revealed the Wisdom of Kabbalah during times when the will to receive shifted from one stage of evolution to another. The Wisdom was revealed to them in order for the Kabbalists to adapt it to the degree of the new desire. Indeed, so they did. It is important to mention that the history of the Wisdom of Kabbalah includes an abundance of many additional Kabbalists, who are not mentioned in this review. Surely, it is not to take away from their greatness or importance in any way; to the contrary, some reached higher attainments than the Kabbalists we will review below.

The first Kabbalist on the face of the Earth was "Adam HaRishon" (The First Man). No, it is not about the same famous biblical character who was exiled from the Garden of Eden (we will study it along with the Kabbalistic meaning of the Bible and other holy books in the second and third units.) Adam HaRishon, who attained the Wisdom of Kabbalah was an ordinary man, like you and me, who was born 5,780 years ago.[6] It is thus clear that he wasn't the first man on earth; many wandered on Earth before him. He was called "Adam HaRishon" since he was the first to reveal the Wisdom of Kabbalah, as described in Baal HaSulam's words:[7]" Adam HaRishon was the first of those who received an order of sufficient knowledge to understand, succeed and use to the end all he saw and attained with his own eyes (from the Wisdom of Kabbalah)."

The Wisdom of Kabbalah was revealed to Adam HaRishon at the time when the will to receive was at its first stage of development. As explained above, in those times, mankind was very close to nature and stemming from his closeness to nature, the blueprint of nature, the Wisdom of Kabbalah was revealed. As all the other Kabbalists who represent major and important points in the development of the Wisdom, Adam HaRishon also wrote a book in which he described his revelations. That book is called "The Angel Raziel."

The next station in the history of the Wisdom of Kabbalah is Abraham the Patriarch. During that period (approximately 4,000 years ago) humanity was concentrated in ancient Babylon and due to their closeness to nature, the law of bestowal and love, they lived in harmony as one large family. Except that then, the will to receive shifted from the first stage of development to the second, in one leap. The growing will to receive distanced people from nature and dispersed them (as described in the story of the Babylon Tower).

At the new degree of the revealed desire, man was no longer able to reveal the Wisdom of Kabbalah naturally, based on his purity, stemming from his closeness with nature. The intensifying desire raised the need for a structured method to reveal the wisdom. The development of this method is attributed to Abraham. Abraham gradually gathered a group of students around him who studied the method, and in time became the nation of Israel. Abraham wrote the essence of the method in the book called "Sefer HaYetzira" (The Book of Creation).

This is how the Rambam describes it:[8] "At the age of forty years, Abraham knew his Creator... and he would walk and call and gather the people, from city to city and kingdom to kingdom... until thousands and tens of thousands were gathered around him, and they are the people of the house of Abraham. And he planted the essence of this great thing in their heart, and wrote books with it... the matter proceeded to increase in the sons of Jacob and those accompanying them, and a nation came to the world who knows the Creator."

The group of Kabbalists, Abraham's followers, used the method of Kabbalah they learned from him over several generations, but then the will to receive proceeded to its next degree of development and the need arose to reveal the Wisdom of Kabbalah at a higher degree above the new will to receive.

That degree was revealed to Moses, the great Kabbalist alive at that time, some 3,000 years ago. The method of correction of Moses, a continuation of the method of Abraham, is called "Torah." The significance of Torah is not intended as a history book or one of ethics, as it is regarded nowadays, rather as a method and guide for revealing the Creator, the law of bestowal and giving, above the increasingly growing will to receive.

Under Moses' leadership, the people of Israel exited Egypt and reached the Land of Israel. At the time of the first and second Holy Temples, every person in Israel was in spiritual attainment. Children were educated in the ways of the Wisdom of Kabbalah and attained spiritual attainment themselves. Yet, again, according to the same plan of evolution in nature, the will to receive was revealed at a new degree, sowing separation in Israel, bringing about the destruction of the spiritual degree and leading them into exile.

Test yourself:
- What did Abraham and Moses add to the process of revealing the Wisdom of Kabbalah?

History of the Wisdom of Kabbalah – From Exile to our Times

The Kabbalist who appeared with the exit to exile (in the 2nd century, A.C.E), in order to adapt the method of Kabbalah to the new degree of the revealed will to receive was Rabbi Shimon Bar Yochai. Along with his nine students, Rabbi Shimon wrote the most important composition in the Wisdom of Kabbalah, "The Book of Zohar."

The significance of "The Book of Zohar" is directly connected to the will to receive revealed during that period. It was a desire of a completely new quality – from exile onward, the last stages in the evolution of the desire began to be revealed. To counter the desire on such a degree, spiritual magnitude was required, one which Rabbi Shimon and his students attained and encoded in "The Book of Zohar." In practice, the magnitude of "The Book of Zohar" is comparable to the will to receive at its final level of development, as is being revealed in our time. For that reason, "The Book of Zohar" was concealed throughout exile, and only now, at the beginning of the 21st century, it is being revealed.

The next stop in the history of the Wisdom of Kabbalah is Rabbi Yitzhak Luria Ashkenazy (1534-1572) known as the Holy ARI. In less than two years when he lived in Safed, between 1570-1572, until his death at the age of 38, the ARI brought about the greatest revolution in the history of Kabbalah, turning the Wisdom of Kabbalah from a method intended for a select few, to a method intended for all people.

Here, too, of course, the reason for the change was that same evolutionary plan of the will to receive, which entered its last stage of development. Many Kabbalists write that from the period of The ARI onward, the concealment period concluded. Not only is it allowed to study the Wisdom of Kabbalah, there is an obligation to do so. The ARI himself didn't write anything. His student, Rabbi Chaim Vital wrote what he had heard from him. The most famous composition from those writings is "The Tree of Life."

The evolutionary plan of the will to receive reached its conclusion at the end of the 20th century. Hence, it is not surprising that it was the most turbulent century in the history of humankind. The Kabbalist who adapted the Wisdom of Kabbalah to the new reality being revealed was Rabbi Yehuda Ashlag, known as "Baal HaSulam" (The Ladder). That is why Baal HaSulam's writings are the most suitable for studying Kabbalah in our generation. (Most of the study material in this program is based on Baal HaSulam's writings.)

To summarize, the history of the concealment and revelation of the Wisdom of Kabbalah is parallel to the process of the will to receive's growth. Every time the will to receive shifts to its next stage of development, a Kabbalist appears who adapts the Wisdom of Kabbalah to the will to receive at its new degree, and accordingly, a higher degree of connection with spirituality is attained (see drawing #2).

Two of Rabbi Ashlag's most prominent works, the result of many years are "Talmud Eser Sefirot" (Study of the Ten Sefirot) based on the writings of The ARI, and the Sulam commentary to "The Book of Zohar," which is the fullest and most extensive commentary ever written on "The Book of Zohar." In addition to these commentaries, Baal HaSulam published many articles and compositions, and even published a Kabbalistic newspaper.

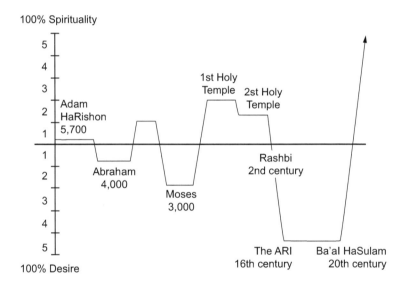

What characterizes Baal HaSulam and is his main uniqueness is his open and intensive dissemination of the Wisdom of Kabbalah to all people. A considerably difficult endeavor was required of him - to remove the barriers and disperse the superstitions and myths attached to the Wisdom of Kabbalah over the years. Above all, he developed a method for spiritual development, suitable for all people in our times.

He adhered to his mission up to his last breath and due to his devotion, succeeded in actualizing the Kabbalists' dream – Kabbalah became attainable to every person wishing to study it, with no preconditions.

This great man led a spiritual revolution, whose fruit we are harvesting today. Thanks to him, the circle which opened back in the time of Abraham was closed. The Kabbalistic books, which had been secured in the past with a thousand locks are now open to us by means of one key alone – a person's desire.

Test yourself:
- How are The ARI and Baal HaSulam different from all preceding Kabbalists?

Summary of the Lesson

Main points
- Studying the Wisdom of Kabbalah is permitted to anyone whose desire to reveal the purpose of his life has awakened.
- Desire is the force which defines and shapes the evolution of humanity.
- The more the desire develops, it reveals increasing emptiness. In our generation, the desire has reached its final stage of development, which is why more and more people are asking about the purpose of life and are naturally drawn to studying the Wisdom of Kabbalah.
- Evolution of the desire has also defined the stages of revelation and concealment of the Wisdom of Kabbalah. In the initial stages of the desire's development, the Wisdom was revealed to a person out of his closeness to nature. As man grew and developed, the Wisdom was concealed, as there was no need for it. In our times, at the end of the evolution of desire, the Wisdom is being revealed once again.

Concepts and Kabbalists

Pleasure extinguishes the desire – The mechanism causing the desire's development. Whenever the desire is filled with pleasure, it diminishes, the pleasure is extinguished and as a result, a new desire awakens- a greater one.

The Point in The Heart – The desire to reveal spirituality, which is revealed in a person.

Rabbi Shimon Bar Yochai – A Kabbalist. He wrote "The Book of Zohar" with his nine students, shortly before the Wisdom was concealed.

The ARI – A Kabbalist. He adapted the method of Kabbalah to the masses, to all whose point in the heart awakened.

Rabbi Chaim Vital – A Kabbalist. The ARI's student. He wrote most of the books attributed to The ARI.

Answers to the Questions

Question: Who can study the Wisdom of Kabbalah?
Answer: Anyone whose desire to reveal the meaning of life has awakened.

Question: What did Abraham and Moses add to the process of revealing the Wisdom of Kabbalah?
Answer: Each of them adapted the method of Kabbalah to the new desire being revealed at the new degree of development.

Question: How were The ARI and Baal HaSulam different from all preceding Kabbalists?
Answer: The ARI and Baal HaSulam adapted the method of Kabbalah to the will to receive at its final degree of development.

Lesson #3 – The Order of Development of Creation according to the Wisdom of Kabbalah

In this lesson we will learn about: The Thought of Creation to do good unto His creatures / Why the Creator is concealed / The development of desire in our world

The Good and Benevolent

In the previous lesson, we focused on the question of who may study the Wisdom of Kabbalah and we scanned the history of the Wisdom of Kabbalah. The common denominator to both issues and the undeniable star of the entire lesson is the desire, or "the will to receive" to be exact. We learned that a desire which has developed enough and begins to ask about the purpose of life is the only condition to studying the Wisdom of Kabbalah. We also learned that the history of the Wisdom of Kabbalah has been shaped by the development of the will to receive.

In this lesson, we will learn the reasons for creating the desire and deepen our understanding of the process of its development. Up to now, we spoke mainly about the reality in our world, meaning how the Wisdom of Kabbalah is revealed to a person in accordance with the development of desire in our world. Whereas, this lesson, we will start specifically from the other end of creation, the root of creation, the thought creating the desire.

According to the Wisdom of Kabbalah, the Creator – the general law of nature – is an all giving and loving force. In the language of Kabbalah, this force is called "the Good and the Benevolent," meaning a force, whose essence is good and its entirety is directed towards giving of His goodness. Kabbalists also refer to this force as the "will to bestow" (see drawing #3); Bestow comes from the Hebrew root of abundance, the desire to grant His abundance.

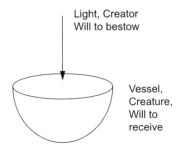

In order to actualize the will to bestow, someone needs to exist to receive the abundance. Hence, the Creator creates a creature, whose purpose is to receive the good from the Creator that He wants to give. If the Creator is the will to bestow in His essence, indeed the creature He created is the will to receive by essence. The Creator, the will to bestow, is called "Light" in Kabbalah and the creature, the will to receive, is called "kli" (vessel), see drawing #3.

Test yourself:
- What did the Creator create and why?

Resembling the Creator

The thought to create a creature who will receive the abundance is called "the Thought of creation to do good unto His creatures." Thought is the source of all; it precedes creation and all of creation cascades and evolves from it, both its revealed and concealed parts. We will now expand on the cascading.

If the Thought of creation is to do good unto His creatures, we should ask – what is the benefit promised to the creatures? That's certainly not a simple question. The following example could allude to a possible solution. Imagine you are kings, not the kind that is power drunk, abusing his subjects, rather the kings from fairy tales, those who love their kingdom and people unconditionally. All their subjects love them, and their kingdom thrives. Now imagine you have a newborn son, your only and beloved son. What would you want to give him? What is the best thing you could give him?

Think about it…

Well, the answer is: To be like you, a successful and beloved king.

That is also the answer to the question of what good the Creator wants to grant His creatures. The good that the Creator wants to give us, the creatures, is to raise us to His stature, to raise us to be like Him. This is how *Baal HaSulam* describes it in the essay "The Essence of The Wisdom of Kabbalah:" "Creation, in all its orders, in all its trails, inlets and source is set and organized all from the start, only according to this purpose, for the human race to evolve within it and ascend in attributes until trained to sense the Creator."

At first glance, that might sound exaggerated, even unfounded, yet if we think about it for a moment, we will realize that there could not be any other answer. Indeed, if the Creator is the absolute good, it is unconceivable that He would give one ounce less than what He has, the very best. And He is the very best possible, the absolute good. Accordingly, the benefit the Creator wishes to give us is necessarily to be like Him.

This is the place to stop for a moment and comment on something important: The Wisdom of Kabbalah is not philosophy. Kabbalists do not construct their explanations on all kinds of logical analogies. Everything written in Kabbalist books is based on actual attainment of the Kabbalist. In other words, Kabbalists write us about spirituality itself, as it was revealed to them and not based on what they think it is. This is a crucial point, since it also defines the correct approach to the study of the Wisdom of Kabbalah. The Wisdom of Kabbalah should be studied out of a desire to reveal spirituality in practice, in our senses and not out of the desire to philosophize about it. We will expand on this explanation throughout the entire course.

Getting back to our issues. Kabbalists have attained that the Thought of creation is to do good unto His creatures, meaning to raise the creature to the Creator's degree. The thing is that the first and basic condition to the realization of this thought is for the creature to want it on his own, to be aware of his desire and actualize it independently. The Thought of creation cannot be actualized forcefully or without awareness, because a creature unaware of his actions or who performs them through coercion does not resemble the Creator. Just as the Creator is the active and creative force of creation, so the creature needs to be, as well.

Therefore, in order to awaken the creature's own desire to resemble the Creator, he has to first feel pleasure in resembling the Creator and then, the pleasure has to dissipate. Only in such a way, can an independent desire to enjoy that pleasure again be born in the creature. The truth is that this is how all of our desires are born. For example: A desire for a certain food is born in us only after we tasted it for the first time, and its flavor dissipated – only thus a genuine desire arises in us.

Accordingly, in order to awaken the creature's own desire to resemble the Creator, the will to receive was created full of all the good intended for it, and from a state of complete resemblance to the Creator, called "the world of *Ein Sof*," the Creator gradually distanced the creature to the reality called "this world," in which the creature is completely separated from the Creator.

In this world, the creature is so separated from the Creator, that he has no contact with Him. In this world, the Creator is completely concealed from the creature. As mentioned above, only from this total concealment, will the creature be able to awaken within him an independent desire to resemble the Creator and attain all the good and abundance intended for him in the Thought of creation.

The process of distancing the creature from the Creator, from the world of *Ein Sof* to this world is divided into five stages. At each stage, the creature further loses his resemblance to the Creator and the Creator is increasingly concealed from him. Each stage in the distancing process of the creature from the Creator is called "world," in Hebrew *Olam*, from "*Ha'alama*'" or concealment (See drawing #4).

The first world, where the creature most resembles the Creator, is called *Olam Kadmon*. The second world, where the degree of resemblance to the Creator lessens and concealment increases, is called *Olam Atzilut*. The third, fourth and fifth worlds are called *Olam Briya, Olam Yetzira*, and *Olam Assiya*. Below *Olam Assiya* is this world, in which, as we've learned, the creature is completely separated from the Creator, and the Creator is completely concealed from him. The Wisdom of Kabbalah calls the border between this world and the spiritual worlds "Machsom" (Barrier).

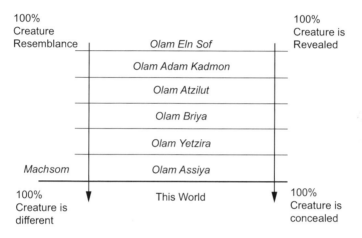

Test Yourself:

- What is the benefit intended for the creature in the Thought of creation?
- Why is it necessary for the Creator to be concealed from the creature?

Near or Far

Surely, many questions arise from what we have learned till now, and all require answers. We will answer most, if not all, throughout the entire course. Two of them will be answered now:

1. What does it mean to resemble the Creator?
2. What does it mean to be distant or near Him?

At the beginning of the lesson, we learned that the Creator is the force of bestowal and giving, governing all of creation. Hence, the question arises, what does it mean to resemble a force? A force by definition is a concept devoid of any image.

Answer: To resemble the Creator means to resemble His attribute, His inner quality – the quality of bestowal. The more the creature bestows, the more he acts without any calculation for himself and is entirely focused on the benefit of what is outside of him, thus, he resembles the Creator and feels the goodness the Creator intended for him, more intensely.

Having clarified this point, we can answer the second question: What does it mean to be distant from the Creator or near Him? After all, the Creator, as a force, is found everywhere, so how is it possible to be far or near something that's everywhere?

Answer: Closeness to the Creator or distance from the Creator is measured by the resemblance to Him. The extent to which the creature's nature (the will to receive) controls him, he is distant from the Creator. The extent to which the creature bestows, he is close to the Creator.

Baal HaSulam explains the matter of distance from the Creator in the essay "The Giving of the Torah:" "A wild ass shall be turned into man, because when one emerges from the bosom of Creation, one is in utter filth and lowliness, meaning in a multitude of self-love imprinted in him, whose every movement revolves solely around himself, without a shred of bestowal upon others.

Hence, one is at the farthest distance from the root on the other end, since the root is all bestowal without a hint of reception, whereas the newborn is in a state of complete self-reception without a hint of bestowal. Therefore, his situation is regarded as being at the lowest point of lowliness and filth in our human world."

In the process of distancing the creature from the Creator through the five worlds: *Adam Kadmon, Atzilut, Briya, Yetzira,* and *Assiya,* the will to receive gradually becomes aware of its nature to receive and as a result, it proceeds to grow distant from the Creator, until it reaches the final stage in the process, this world, where its nature, the will to receive, completely controls him and conceals the Creator from him.

The process of distancing the creature from the Creator doesn't end in the descent of the creature down to "this world." In some way, from this point on, it's just the beginning. In this world, the will to receive goes through a process of evolution as well, whose goal is to lead the creature to an independent desire to actualize the Thought of creation. In the previous two lessons, we mentioned several significant stepping stones and tendencies in the development of the will to receive in this world. In the following part of the lesson, we will expand and complete the picture.

Test yourself:
- How is the resemblance to the Creator measured and how is closeness to the Creator measured?

A New Beginning

After the will to receive completes its distancing from the Creator till this world, it begins to grow within the framework of this world. The purpose of this development is to continue distancing the creature from the Creator until the nature of the creature is revealed to its fullest degree, being completely opposite the nature of the Creator, for only from total concealment of the Creator, can the creature desire to resemble the Creator on his own. We learned about the distancing of the created from the Creator in the previous part of this lesson. In this section we will review the evolution of the desire within the framework of this world.

For billions of years, matter developed on the face of the Earth from relatively simple forms of the still to more complex forms of the vegetative, animate, and finally, human (which is called the "speaking degree" in the Wisdom of Kabbalah.") In essence, all of the abovementioned forms constitute matter called "the will to receive" and the process of their development is the process of the desire's development. In the essay "Preface to the Wisdom of Kabbalah," *Baal HaSulam* writes that all parts of creation - those revealed to us and those to be revealed are only different levels of the will to receive being revealed to us in degrees of the still, vegetative, animate, and speaking. In this brief review, we will focus on the development of desire in man, the speaking degree.

In general, we can identify two outstanding trends in the development of desire in man.

1. The desire continuously increases; it desires more and longs for greater qualitative and intangible fulfillments.
2. The developing desires become more dependent on the environment, more aware of it, and take advantage of it for their own benefit.

The first level of the speaking degree is called "physical desires:" desires for food, coupling, shelter, and family – basic desires necessary for man's existence. The next desire that develops is the desire for possessions. Following, comes the desire for honor and control, and then, the desire for knowledge. It is assumed that the more one knows, the better one's life will be. The desire for possessions, respect and knowledge are defined as "social desires" because they are aroused in a person and fulfilled by the social surroundings.

The development of desire in people is the force driving all of humanity's development from ancient times to now. In pre-historic times, people sufficed with fulfilling their physical desires and their entire world was restricted to the limits of one's cave and the hunting grounds around it. At a later phase, desires for possessions and control began to awaken; thus, a primitive-tribal society became an agricultural society, and later – an urban society and man's limits expanded accordingly. The final stage in the development of desire at the speaking degree is the desire for knowledge. This desire was expressed in the expansion of the education circle in the 18th and 19th centuries, especially in the 20th century, when the internet revolution turned people into a "global citizen" of the "global village."

Towards the end of the 20th century, the desire to receive exhausted its development on the speaking degree of this world. It is evident in two fashions:

1. A person is no longer satisfied with fulfilling his bodily and societal desires. A general sense of restlessness is now felt in increasingly more people around the world.
2. The will to receive, human nature, is being revealed at its fullest extent. People have mastered their ability to exploit others for their own benefit to perfection. The world operates according to the approach of "I, and I alone."

The last stage of the development of the will to receive in our world started manifesting at the beginning of the 21st century, in a deep crisis affecting all areas of life: education, family, culture, ecology, security, and so on. However, crises aren't necessarily negative. They simply point to the fact that the current situation has exhausted itself and that it is time to advance to the next stage. The "negative" forces being revealed in the world are actually like labor pains pushing us towards a new birth.

We are very lucky to be living at a time in which a prolonged process of billions of years – beginning before time itself, in the Thought of creation – is reaching its peak. For the first time in human history, conditions for a conscious evolution of man towards actualizing the Thought of creation are formulating. The will to receive has grown to its maximum, concealing the Creator from mankind. However, specifically from the concealment, can a person develop his own desire to reveal the Creator, the force of love and bestowal governing the world and receive the good the Creator has intended for him.

Although the evolution of the will to receive has reached its end, the end only symbolizes a new beginning. Increasingly more "points in the heart" are awakening in people worldwide. The desire for spirituality, the final stage in the development of desire is beginning to be revealed in the world. (See drawing #5).

The way of actualizing the desire for spirituality, in the ascent from below upwards, is different from anything we are familiar with. That is why we need the Wisdom of Kabbalah. Through the study of the Wisdom of Kabbalah we will proceed and five spiritual worlds, which will then become degrees of revelation, until we reach full resemblance to the Creator, sensing the good and the benevolent, up to a state called "Gmar Tikun" (end of correction), (See chart #5)

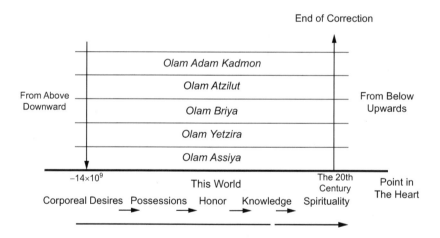

Test Yourself:

- What is unique about the development of the will to receive in our times?

Lesson Summary

Main Points

- The Thought of creation "to do good unto His creatures" is to raise the creature to the degree of the Creator.
- The basic condition for actualizing the Thought of creation is for the creature to want it on his own.
- In order to develop an independent desire to become like the Creator in the creature, the Creator needs to be concealed from the creature.
- The creature has continued being distant from the Creator over a long process, through the five spiritual worlds and throughout its development in this world, reaching a state of complete concealment.
- In our times, the process of developing the will to receive has reached its end, hence the Wisdom of Kabbalah is being revealed.

Terms

Will to bestow – The Creator, the force of love and giving.

Olam Ein Sof – A state in which the will to receive is filled with all the good intended for it in the Thought of creation.

World – A degree of concealment from the Creator. (In Hebrew, *Olam* – world, from the word *He'alem* – concealed). (There are five spiritual worlds: *Adam Kadmon, Atzilut, Briya, Yetzira, and Assiya*.)

This world – The reality in which the will to receive completely conceals the Creator from the creature.

Barrier – The border between this world and the spiritual worlds.

Physical desires – Basic desires which are not dependent on society.

Societal desire – Developed desires, awakened and fulfilled by society.

Speaking degree– The will to receive at the degree of man.

End of Correction – Full resemblance to the Creator

Answers to the Questions

Question: What did the Creator create and why?
Answer: The Creator created the will to receive in order for it to receive the good He wants to give.

Question: What is the good intended for the creature in the Thought of creation?
Answer: To resemble the Creator.

Question: Why is it necessary for the Creator to be concealed from the creature?
Answer: The creature can attain the purpose of creation only from an independent desire; an independent desire is possible only from concealment.

Question: How is resemblance to the Creator measured and how is closeness to the Creator measured?
Answer: Resemblance to the Creator is measured by the degree of resemblance to the quality of bestowal. Closeness to the Creator is measured by the degree of resemblance to the Creator.

Question: What is unique in the development of the will to receive in our times?
Answer: In our times, the will to receive is at the end of its development in this world, and a desire for spirituality is beginning to awaken in it.

Part #2 - Perception of Reality

Lesson #1 – Reality or Imagination?

In this lesson we will learn: Different approaches to the perception of reality / The connection between the desire to receive and the perception of reality / The Law of Equivalence of Form

We were as dreamers

It was just an ordinary morning in the Italian town of Monza. The waters of the Lambro streamed gently, as they do every day, crossing the town from North to South, on their way to the Ganoa Bay. No one could have predicted what was about to happen next.

Around midday it occurred: The City Council passed a new and alarming decree, according to which – pay attention now! –citizens would no longer be able to keep goldfish in round glass bowls. Yes, life can be cruel at times.

Given all the puzzled looks, the Council spokesman, Giampietro Musca, was asked to shed a little light on the unusual decision. In an orderly message to the press, Musca explained that life inside of the round aquariums make the helpless fish miserable, for the bent glass walls force them to see the world in a distorted way – animal abuse.

Many waters have flowed in the Lambro River since then. The fishes' quality of life improved beyond recognition. And yet, one question remained hanging in the air: Although the reality perceived by goldfish in the round aquarium is different from ours, who can assure us that it is less real? Moreover, generally speaking, how are we so sure that the picture of reality we perceive is the genuine one?

Welcome to Part 2 of the course "Preface to the Wisdom of Kabbalah." The topic we'll be clarifying in this section is, without a doubt, the most interesting and challenging one in the study of the Wisdom of Kabbalah – perception of reality. Not to worry, it is not about a philosophical analysis, as it may sound. On the contrary, if we understand how we perceive reality, we will be able to face some of the more crucial questions in life realistically, finding solutions, and applying them practically.

To make it easier to understand the Wisdom of Kabbalah's approach to the issue of our perception of reality, we will briefly review how the scientific approach on the subject has developed over the years.

According to the classic approach represented by Newton, the world exists by itself, with no connection to man and its form is set. Later, Einstein discovered that the world is much more expansive than we perceive. Our perception is relative and dependent on our senses; hence we cannot say with precision what the world outside our "aquarium" is. It all depends on the observer perceiving that reality.

The modern scientific approach to the perception of reality, based on quantum physics asserts that the observer impacts the world, and as a result, changes the picture he perceives. The picture of reality is a certain mean between the observer's attributes and those of the object or phenomenon he is perceiving.

What is this all about? Physicists have discovered that the tiny particles composing all details in reality have no defined location, speed, or even time. Surprisingly, all of these factors are defined only when someone is measuring them, and all of the measurements are valid to the same extent.

Confusing? Listen to what the Wisdom of Kabbalah has to say about it: According to the Wisdom of Kabbalah, the world outside of us is in fact, an illusion. In actuality, it has no shape of its own. In the essay, "Preface to the book of Zohar,"[5]

Baal HaSulam explains that the entire vast and wonderful world, which we seem to see outside of us is actually an inner image that is only depicted inside us.

---

[5] Letter 21

Here is how it sounds in the words of *Baal HaSulam* himself: [6]

"Take our sense of sight, for example: we see a wide world before us, wondrously filled. But in fact, we see all that only in our own interior. In other words, there is a sort of a photographic machine in our hindbrain, which portrays everything that appears to us and nothing outside of us. "

To illustrate these things, let's compare man to a closed box with 5 entrance channels: eyes, ears, nose, mouth, and hands. (See drawing number 6).

These organs represent the five senses: sight, hearing, smell, taste, and touch, through which man perceives whatever seems to be found outside of him.

Through the five openings in the box, all kinds of stimuli enter. They all collect inside and go through various processes, relative to the information found in that person's memory and in relation to his desire. The outcome is a certain image of reality, which is projected on a type of "movie screen" found in the hinds of the brain. The image depicted in the hinds of the brain is our image of reality. In other words, according to the Wisdom of Kabbalah, man is the one who determines his perception of reality. What exists in actuality outside of us? We don't know.

We see a world with infinite details before our eyes, but we cannot know what those details are themselves, their essence. All we know is how we perceive them. Even the Creator the Wisdom of Kabbalah speaks of is the Creator as we perceive Him (under very particular conditions, to be detailed later in this unit) and not as He is. The Creator as He is, is called in the Wisdom of Kabbalah "His Essence," which the Wisdom of Kabbalah does not deal with.

---

[6] Preface to the Book of Zohar, section 34

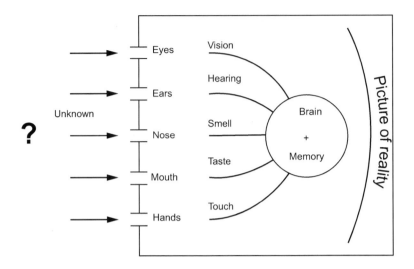

We will briefly summarize the three approaches to the perception of reality we have reviewed and the approach of the Wisdom of Kabbalah: According to classic physics, reality has an objective existence outside of us. According to Einstein, the picture of reality is a relative matter, which depends on the observer. According to quantum physics, the picture of reality is a mean between the qualities of the observer and whatever is outside of him. According to the Wisdom of Kabbalah, the reality outside of us has no image. The person is the one who determines his picture of reality.

Why is this information that a person is the determinant of his image of reality so important to us? Because the conclusion from all this is that a person's inner change inevitably leads to a different perception of reality. Indeed, that is how the spiritual reality is revealed to us – out of an inner change taking place inside of us.

Test yourself:

- According to the Wisdom of Kabbalah, how is the image of reality created in a person?

Who Gave the Order?

The Wisdom of Kabbalah is the root of all sciences. That is what *Baal HaSulam* writes in the essay "The Teaching of Kabbalah and its Essence." So, there is no wonder that after thousands of years of development, science is proceeding to draw near the Wisdom of Kabbalah and many of its conclusions are aligned. Thus, for example, as we explained at length in the previous section of the lesson, the approaches of modern science and the Wisdom of Kabbalah to the perception of reality are rather close. However, a significant difference is apparent between the two: Although science explains how we perceive society, it still does not explain what the purpose is of perceiving reality specifically in that way. The Wisdom of Kabbalah, on the other hand, focuses on studying the purpose.

According to the Wisdom of Kabbalah, the force behind the mechanism of our perception of reality is the will to receive. The will to receive operates according to a simple program: Receiving what benefits it and distancing from what harms it. Clearly, according to that precise logic, the will to receive also manages the way we perceive reality. All of our sensory organs and mechanisms for decoding information, including the "movie screen" at the back of our brain, upon which the picture of reality is projected are all "agents" of the will to receive, serving its desire: to receive what is beneficial for it and distance from what harms it.

In other words, we see what we want to see and do not see what we don't want to see. The desire is what arouses needs in us and determines what we will or will not see around us. Likewise, for instance, a new parent begins to notice the presence of baby shops at every corner. The stores were there before as well, of course, but since there was no need for them, their existence wasn't noticed.

Naturally speaking, our desire directs us to perceive only what benefits us (or whatever might harm us.) As the desire evolves, in parallel with the intellect, we understand more, perceive more, control more and accordingly, our perception of reality expands.

But – and this is an important "but" – as long as we perceive reality through the "lens" of the will to receive, our perception will remain limited to a very specific part of reality – to the corporeal part alone. That is because the concealed, spiritual level of reality cannot be perceived by means of the will to receive.

In order to understand more deeply why we are incapable of perceiving the spiritual reality by means of the will to receive, we need to become familiar with one of the basic laws in the Wisdom of Kabbalah, the "law of equivalence of form." According to the law of equivalence of form, in order for us to perceive anything in corporeality or in spirituality, we need to develop within us sensitivity to that thing. In other, more scientific words: the sensory tool that is to perceive a particular object needs to contain within it something of the quality of that object it is to perceive.

A relatively simple example will help us understand the matter. Outside of us, numerous sound waves, in endless frequencies are all around. In order to receive a certain frequency, say, a certain radio station, we tune the radio to that frequency. (We turn the selecting knob.) In actuality, we are generating an equivalent frequency in the radio and according to equivalence of form, we receive the station we'd like to listen to.

Similar to corporeality, so it is in spirituality. In order to perceive spirituality, we need to generate within us a spiritual "frequency," to insert within the desire to receive something of the quality of bestowal. How is that done? We will learn that in the following lesson. For now, it suffices for us to understand that as long as the desire is entirely immersed in receiving and has nothing of the quality of bestowal, it is impossible for us to understand what bestowal is and impossible for us to perceive spiritual reality.

In summary, we perceive reality through the five senses, which act according to the program of the will to receive. If we distort or interfere with the action of one of the senses, or God forbid, one of them is damaged, we will perceive reality in a completely different way. Even if we sharpen the senses (by means of an aiding device), we will perceive reality differently.

We can change the ranges of our reception of our senses, and accordingly expand or restrict our image of the world. Yet, in any case, we will never exceed the boundaries of our image of the world. Why? Because at the end of the day, we will always perceive reality according to the inner program of the will to receive and as we learned in the previous lessons, the will to receive limits us to only a partial perception of reality, to perception of the corporeal reality. Corporeality according to the Wisdom of Kabbalah is everything we perceive through the "lens" of the will to receive.

If we wish to begin to advance from our current situation, expand our reality, know where we exist and for what purpose, we need to tend only to what is within us – the desire. Deep inside sits the desire, the one managing all of our perception vessels, as well as the intellect and thought. How will we be able to perceive the more expansive, spiritual reality, which is not limited by our will to receive? In order to do that, we need to change the program, according to which the will to receive works. How is the program according to which the will to receive changed? The Wisdom of Kabbalah deals precisely with that.

Test Yourself:
- What do we need to do in order to perceive the image of spiritual reality?

Lesson Summary

Main Points
- According to the Wisdom of Kabbalah, the reality outside of us has no form of its own. The person perceiving reality gives

it its form. In other words, man is the one who creates his image of reality.

- Even the Creator the Wisdom of Kabbalah speaks of is a Creator as **we** perceive Him and not as He truly is. The Creator as He is Himself is called "His Essence," and the Wisdom of Kabbalah does not deal with that.

- The will to receive is the inner program managing the mechanism of our perception of reality. We see what we want to see. In order to perceive spiritual reality, we need to change the inner program, according to which we perceive reality, meaning the will to receive.

- According to the law of equivalence of form, in order to perceive the spiritual reality, we need to develop within the will to receive sensitivity for spirituality, or in other words, imbue it with something from the attribute of bestowal.

Definitions

Law of equivalence of form – In order to perceive something, we need to develop sensitivity to it. In order to attain spiritual reality, we need to contain within us the attribute of bestowal, since spirituality is bestowal.

His Essence – The Wisdom of Kabbalah deals only with the way we perceive the Creator and not with the Creator Himself. The Creator as He is Himself is called "His Essence" in the Wisdom of Kabbalah.

Answers to the Questions

Question: According to the Wisdom of Kabbalah, how is an image of reality created?

Answer: A person perceives the information outside of him by means of five senses, processes it by means of the intellect and as a result, an image of reality is received in the back of the brain.

Question: What do we need to do in order to perceive an image of spiritual reality?

Answer: We need to change the "program" that manages the mechanism of our perception of reality, meaning to change the will to receive, from receiving to bestowing.

To expand and delve into the study material, go to page 252 of the Course Book.

Lesson #2 – True Reality

In this lesson we'll learn about: desire and intention / intention in order to receive and intention in order to bestow / perception of the "I" and the external world / what is bestowal?

What exactly is your intention?

This tiny particle galloping forward at the speed of light is on the path of collision. Our microscopic friend is about to crash into a plutonium atom, split its nucleus and release an immense amount of energy. There's going to be quite an explosion, an atomic explosion.

Yes, that is how it happens, more or less. An innocent neutron meets a nucleus of uranium or plutonium at the speed of lightning, the nucleus splits and releases massive atomic energy from within–energy that can be used for terrible and devastating purposes, as witnessed during the Second World War, or for beneficial purposes, as used for the needs of research and medicine. The nucleus can split in order to kill, and it can split in order to revive – all depends on the intention.

Intention, my friends, is the whole story! So buckle your seatbelts. It is time to delve into the depths of creation – to the place where the most delicate, abstract, concealed and powerful forces of reality operate. Welcome to the world of intentions.

Life in our world teaches us that the more abstract a certain force is, the greater the power it contains within. Think, for example, of a big wooden baton – how much damage, or how much benefit can be drawn from it, in comparison to the damage or benefit that can be drawn from a tiny atom of uranium. The invisible atom is charged with immeasurably greater force than the very tangible baton. So just imagine how much energy is contained in the abstract forces even greater than the atom – our thoughts and intentions. As we said, "buckle your seatbelts," there's going to be an explosion…

In order to understand what intention is according to the wisdom of Kabbalah, we need to first clarify an important point regarding the matter of creation – the will to receive. In the previous lesson and throughout the entire course, we learn that our nature, the will to receive, is what conceals us from the Creator. The will to receive only wants to receive; the Creator only wants to give, and this oppositeness is what prevents us from revealing the Creator. Kabbalists write that concealment or revelation of the Creator is measured by our resemblance to Him. The more the creature bestows, the more the Creator is revealed to him. And vice versa, the more the creature is under the control of his force of reception, the more concealed the Creator is from him.

The natural conclusion from the abovementioned is that we need to correct the will to receive. It would seem that if we shift our nature from receiving to bestowing, the spiritual reality will be revealed before us, along with all the goodness of creation. However, the will to receive is not the source of the problem and not what needs to be corrected. The will to receive is not bad or good. The will to receive is the matter of creation – matter and no more. The fault requiring correction is not the will to receive; rather, our use of the will to receive. Correction, according to the wisdom of Kabbalah is changing the usage of the will to receive from reception to bestowal.

The way the will to receive is used is called "intention" in the wisdom of Kabbalah. According to the wisdom of Kabbalah, the will to receive can be used in two ways:

1. For self-benefit.
2. For the benefit of others.

Using the will to receive for self-benefit is called "receiving **with the intention** of in order to receive." Using the will to receive for the benefit of others is called "receiving **with the intention** of in order to bestow" in the wisdom of Kabbalah. The intention of in order to receive – the calculation "what is in it for **me**" – is what conceals spirituality from us. In order to feel spirituality, we need to shift the intention of in order to receive with the intention of in order to bestow.

An action with the intention of in order to bestow means an action that has not even a trace of thought for self-benefit. Just as the Creator is all bestowal and has no trace of self, so should be the creature's action of bestowal. The issue is that as long as we exist in our world, every action is inevitably infected, in one way or another with self-benefit. Even a mother giving of herself to her children does it from a calculation of self-benefit.

In the essay "The Giving of the Torah"[7]

Baal HaSulam writes:

"Any movement that a person makes to love another is performed as a result of some reward that will eventually return to him and serve him for his own good…. Although to perform any action or exert any force, from a complete love of others, meaning without any hope for any reward that may return to him, it is completely impossible in our nature."

There is no example in our world of the work with the will to receive with the intention of in order to bestow. Everyone in our world acts with the intention of in order to receive. In order to understand what the intention of in order to bestow is, we need to attain it practically, through the study of the wisdom of Kabbalah, to learn how to work with the will to receive not for self-benefit, but rather for the benefit of all. Until we are able to do that, we will not be able to understand what the intention of in order to bestow is.

In summary, it is not the will to receive that is faulty, but the intention, the intention of in order to receive, to be precise. When Kabbalists write

---

[7] Letter 13

that the will to receive is what requires correction, it is to be concise. Just like any other matter in creation, the will to receive cannot be good or bad. The values of good and bad can only be judged by the way a person uses the will to receive, meaning our intention in using it.

It turns out that in spirituality (like in anything else) we attain through the will to receive, but in the desire which has been corrected with the intention of in order to bestow. As we learned in the previous lesson, we cannot speak about anything as is, rather as we perceive it in our will to receive. We also perceive the Creator (spirituality) in the will to receive, but only in the desire which has been corrected with the intention of in order to bestow.

If you're asking yourself how all this relates to the perception of reality, here is the answer: the intention of in order to receive is the program, according to which the will to receive operates in our world and it is what is concealing spiritual reality from us. In order to reveal spiritual reality, we need to correct our intention: to change it from in order to receive to in order to bestow. The condition for the transition in our perception of corporeal reality to the perception of spiritual reality is correction of the intention.

The wisdom of Kabbalah is called the hidden wisdom, among other reasons, because it deals with the inner levels within a person, those revealed only to him, and hidden from others. The wisdom of Kabbalah deals with the thoughts, desires, and intentions of a person. We need to focus ourselves inside. There, in our desires and intentions, is where we work, and that is where spirituality will be revealed. No external action, be as it may, will reveal the spiritual reality to us, as long as it was performed with the incorrect intention, the intention of in order to receive. The shift we need to undergo is internal: a change of our inner attributes, a change of the intention.

Test yourself:
- What is the intention of in order to receive and what is the intention of in order to bestow?

56

A Whole World Out There

Huge. Everything in the United States is huge – vastly spacious, its sky scrapers touch the skies, the opportunities it provides to all who stand at its gates are boundless.

There is something heartwarming in this longing for grandeur. Perhaps it is just very fundamental, or because at the end of the day, it reflects the space in each one of our hearts. After all, the American greatness craze is no more than another example of the constant and purposeless chase of all humanity after something better. As the Manhattan elders say: "It doesn't matter how tall your skyscraper is, it is never tall enough."

According to the wisdom of Kabbalah, it is natural for us to desire more. The truth is that there is nothing more natural than that. Indeed, the Creator (nature) created us to enjoy all the goodness in creation. Yet, instead of receiving everything, we only receive a little. Instead of the vast and complete picture of reality, only a restricted and partial image is revealed before our eyes. Think about it; we don't even know what will happen to us in a moment! It is no wonder that deep inside, a deep feeling that there is something more dwells. It is no wonder that throughout history, we have been trying to reveal additional parts of the full picture, understand our reality in further depth.

Rather, the drive to reveal more with our regular sensory system is leading us to a dead end. It doesn't matter how much our picture of reality will expand; it will eventually remain very limited. Why? Because the mechanism of our perception of reality is managed by our selfish intention, the intention of in order to receive. We are constantly focused on ourselves, our benefit from all actions, which is why our perception of reality is restricted to our own limits.

Since our desire and memory work according to the intention of in order to receive, we are limited like lone cells to a narrow and restricted image from all of reality. In order for us to feel all of reality, spiritual reality, we need to expand our vessels of perception. We need to emerge from the selfish and narrow calculation of "self-benefit" and connect to the desires of others (see drawing 7).

The issue is that "connecting to the desires of others" is not trivial. In order to do that, we need to feel their desires as if they were truly ours. The only way to do that is to shift the intention that rides our desire's back – from an internal intention-egoistic, in order to receive, to an intention of in order to bestow. Only in the intention of in order to bestow, will we be able to feel the eternal desire. Only in the connection to the desires of others, will we be able to reveal the true picture of reality.

According to the wisdom of Kabbalah, the law of "Love your neighbor as yourself" is not a law of ethics whose purpose is to obligate us to treat others nicely, rather a law of nature we need to keep in order to reveal the complete spiritual reality. Just as the Creator governs creation as one body, whose parts are interconnected with invisible ties of love, so do we need to connect with each other, according to the law "love your neighbor as yourself." Correcting the intention from in order to receive to in order to bestow is actually correcting our approach to others, from an object I use for my own benefit to a genuine part of me. As we said, correcting the approach to others is the condition for revealing spiritual reality.

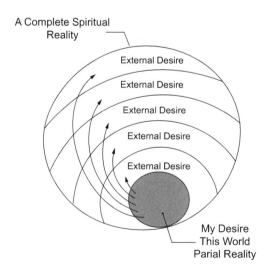

Now we can understand the benefit in the way we perceive reality. It is specifically the picture of reality separating our "I" from whatever is external to us that enables us to perform the work of connection and resemble the Creator.

If we were created in a picture of reality where there is only "me," we wouldn't be able to perform the necessary correction, whereas if we were created in a picture of reality where we were already connected in one mutual desire, our independent desire to shift the intention would be lacking.

In summary, in order for us to perceive the genuine reality, the world of truth, we need to emerge from ourselves outward and begin to become familiar with what truly exists. Then we will find that life does not depend on the human body, our senses, our internal egoistic desire, or its memory; life depends only on the extent to which a person absorbs, connects himself and all that supposedly exists outside of him, the foreign desires.

Baal HaSulam writes about that in one of his letters [8] to his students: "You lack nothing except to go out to a field that the Lord has blessed, and collect all those flaccid organs that have drooped from your soul, and join them into a single body. In that complete body, the Creator will instill His Divinity incessantly, and the high streams of light will be as a never-ending fountain."

Test yourself:
- What is the connection between the desires of others and the perception of spiritual reality?

Who is Righteous?

"I wish it were possible to assemble all of humanity into one body, so I could embrace everyone." Those warm and wise words of Rav

---

[8] The Writings of Baal HaSulam, "Letters," letter 4.

Kook – beyond being a tiny sample of the ocean of wisdom of a great Kabbalist, sum up the entire process of correction we need to perform. In the end, each one of us needs to acquire the intention of in order to bestow, to feel the desires of others as if they were his own and assemble all of humanity into one body. In the single body, the one Creator is revealed.

The issue is that in such a selfish and intensive world as ours, it is difficult to see how we can draw close to such degrees of connection, not to mention actually living them. In the meantime, at every passing moment, it seems that the train is specifically galloping in the opposite direction. The Homosapien of the 21st century is engaged with himself, obsessively. One woman in Taiwan surpassed when she bought a wedding dress, rented a wedding hall, and… married herself (unbelievable, but true.)

Well, you're probably smirking uncomfortably, "what is this totality?!" We just need to switch the dark glasses with the rose ones and reveal that not everyone is so deeply involved with themselves. The fact is that there are those who care for the weaker ones, those who help the sick with no reward and those who care for the welfare of new immigrants. And we have also given of our money, time and energy, more than once or twice. In short, the spirit of volunteering has not passed from the world."

Such claims only emphasize the different and realistic outlook of the wisdom of Kabbalah. According to the wisdom of Kabbalah, there is no individual in our world who isn't driven in every act he performs by calculating his own benefit. Each one of us, each person on the face of the Earth operates according to the internal program obligating him to care for his own benefit. At times, the calculations are complex and it is difficult to identify the true motive behind an action. However, even in those cases, the incentive is the same one – self-benefit.

For example, a person who gives charity in secret may do it with a thought that one day he or his family could find themselves in a similar situation. In the kindness of his heart, he calms himself by believing that if, God forbid, he finds himself in a similar situation, someone will give him, as well. Not to speak of the pride accompanying such action – it is also a worthy reward for the will to receive. Every action of giving in our world is driven by an interest in reception. In this matter (and not only in this one), the Kabbalists' distinction is razor sharp: either you are working with the intention of in order to receive or you are working with the intention of in order to bestow. In our reality, in this world, we are all working with the intention in order to receive.

The intention is the main thing. It doesn't matter what action we perform – we can tear the heavens in prayer for world peace, save the dolphin population from extinction, protect refugee rights – if the intention underlying this action is "what will **I** get out of it," it is not an action of bestowal. The wisdom of Kabbalah does not mean that kind of giving and bestowing.

We need to correct the intention, the innermost, deepest approach to others. We need to emerge from the calculation for self- benefit and live according to the calculation of benefit of all; to reach a state in which we feel the desires of others as if they were truly our own desires. That is bestowal according to the wisdom of Kabbalah. Only when we attain that, will the picture of the spiritual world open up to us. It is not a trivial change. We need to change our nature. Of course, we are incapable of doing it ourselves. For that purpose, we have been given the wisdom of Kabbalah.

From this, we can understand the difference between the wisdom of Kabbalah and the ethics doctrines. Throughout history, many have pointed to the ego as the source of all problems. One does not need to be a Kabbalist to realize that if we learn to cope with the ego correctly, our life will be much better. However, unlike the wisdom of Kabbalah, the solution suggested by the various methods of ethics is direct action against the ego: diminishing it, locking it up in a box, not letting it erupt.

Except that the ego is stronger than any human intellect. There is no box to lock it up in and there is no method that can diminish it. According to the thought of creation, the ego needs to grow – and it is growing. The example, perhaps the most successful one of our inability to restrain the ego and the helplessness of the methods of ethics is the educational system. For years, the educational system has been trying to force children to behave properly and the children's distress has begun to boil slowly like hot lava. Today, the volcano is erupting.

According to the wisdom of Kabbalah, there is no point in direct action against the ego. Instead of trying to diminish or restrict the ego, Kabbalists teach us how to use it correctly, how to acquire a different intention above it, the intention of in order to bestow. In this intention, we attach the desires of others to us, expanding our vessels of perception and attaining spiritual reality.

Test yourself:
- What is bestowal according to the wisdom of Kabbalah?

Summary of the Lesson

Main Points
- The desire to receive in itself is not good or bad; it is the matter of creation. Good or bad are measured only regarding our use of the will to receive, for our own benefit or for the benefit of others.
- Using the will to receive for self- benefit is called the "intention of in order to receive." Using the desire for the benefit of others is called the "intention of in order to bestow."
- Every person in our world operates according the intention of in order to receive. In order to change the intention of in order to receive, we need to study the wisdom of Kabbalah.
- In correcting our approach to others from the intention of in order to receive to the intention of in order to bestow, we

connect the desires of others to ourselves, expand our vessels of reception and perceive spiritual reality in the corrected vessel.

- The difference between the wisdom of Kabbalah and the ethics methods is that in the wisdom of Kabbalah the will is not oppressed, rather the intention is corrected.

Concepts

Intention – The way the will to receive is used.
Intention in order to receive –Using the will to receive for self-benefit.
Intention in order to bestow – Using the will to receive for the benefit of others.
Correction – Changing the use of the will to receive from the intention of in order to receive, to the intention of in order to bestow.
Bestowal – A state in which we feel the desires of others as if they truly were our own.

Answers to the Questions

Question: What is the intention of in order to receive and what is the intention of in order to bestow?
Answer: The intention of in order to receive is using the desire for self-benefit. The intention of in order to bestow is using the will to receive for the benefit of all.

Question: What is the connection between the desires of others and perceiving spiritual reality?
Answer: In order to feel spiritual reality, we need to expand our vessels of perception. We need to emerge from the selfish and narrow calculation of "self-benefit" and connect to the desires of others.

Question: What is bestowal according to the wisdom of Kabbalah?
Answer: A state in which we feel the desires of others as if they were actually our own.

Logical Sequence
(Order of course development)

We learned that the wisdom of Kabbalah is a method for revealing the Creator to the creatures in this world.

We learned that in order to reveal the Creator, we need to shift our intention from in order to receive to in order to bestow.

In the next section we will learn how we change the intention.

Part #3 - The Language of Kabbalah

Lesson #1 – The Law of Roots and Branches

In this lesson we will learn: The practicality of the wisdom of Kabbalah / The law of roots and branches / The language of branches

Abstract or Realistic?

One of the most popular adventure books of all times is "The Neverending Story," which tells of Bastian Balthazar Bux's life; a young boy, who, from reading a book of tales suddenly finds himself living within the magical reality described in the book. Surprising as it may sound, reading Kabbalah books is somewhat similar to that experience. In Kabbalah books a force is embedded, enabling the reader to break through his own reality into the wondrous reality described in the books – spiritual reality.

The third and final part of the study unit of "Foundations of Kabbalah" deals with the language of Kabbalah and the books of Kabbalah. In the first part of the unit, we learned that spirituality is a method for revealing the Creator, the general law of nature. In the second part, we learned that the condition for revealing the Creator is changing the method of working with our will to receive. Indeed, in this part we will learn how to do it practically; how it is possible to change the method of working with the will to receive by means

64

of reading Kabbalah books. We will first learn about the language of the books, called the "language of branches" and afterwards, we will expand on the spiritual force embedded within Kabbalah books.

In the essay "The Essence of the Wisdom of Kabbalah" Baal HaSulam writes, "Many believe that all the words and the names in the wisdom of Kabbalah are somewhat abstract names." Indeed, an effort to understand what is written in Kabbalah books without proper guidance might lead us to the same conclusion. One who is not knowledgeable in the wisdom of Kabbalah will find it difficult to attribute the words and names in Kabbalah books to his tangible and substantial reality. Both the words in the books and the content itself will sound abstract to him.

For example, here is a quote from "The Tree of Life" by the ARI:[9]

"Know that before the emanated were emanated and the creatures were created, there was simple Upper light that filled all of reality." Although the words are familiar to us, and putting them together "makes sense," yet it is not at all clear what it means: what simple Upper light is, what reality it is speaking of before creating the creatures, and so on.

A person making his first steps in the study of the hidden wisdom might think that Kabbalah books deal with abstract issues, but the truth is that Kabbalah books do not contain as much as a single word without practical meaning. One of the fundamental laws in the wisdom of Kabbalah is: "Whatever we do not attain we cannot define by name or word." Meaning, Kabbalists write only of their spiritual attainments they have attained in practice, in their senses and whatever they have not attained, they do not write about.

The spiritual reality a Kabbalist attains is no less real than the corporeal reality we attain in our world. In actuality, if we consider the fact that the image of the corporeal world is a temporary illusion,

---

[9] Tree of Life, Gate A, Branch B

being revealed in the will to receive as long as it is not corrected, indeed particularly the eternal spiritual reality, being revealed with the correction of the desire, is actual and true.

Here we should reiterate and emphasize an important principle regarding the perception of spiritual reality: the Creator Himself, as He is in His essence is not perceived by Kabbalists. That is similar to not being able to perceive the essence of our world. That is because a person always perceives reality through the will to receive and never knows what reality is itself; rather how he is impressed with it, whatever is external to him.

Thus, for example, just like we do not know what the inner essence of electricity is or what the paper we are looking at right now actually is, Kabbalists also do not perceive the Creator as He is in His essence, rather only as He is perceived in their will to receive. Yet, these limitations in perception do not interfere with their perception of a clear and sufficient image of the spiritual reality and description of it in their books.

Test yourself:
Explain why is the spiritual reality a Kabbalist perceives no less genuine than the corporeal reality?

Roots and Branches

Six thousand nine hundred and nine – If you have ever asked yourself how many languages exist in the world, indeed this is the most currently updated number[10] 6,909 – 7,151 languages, including 122 sign languages and languages of primitive tribes. A lot of languages. Except that all of them, without exception, describe only a very limited part of reality – the part we perceive within the constrict of time, motion and space in our world – corporeal reality.

---

[10] According to https://www.ethnologue.com/

Unlike corporeality, spirituality is above time, motion and space. Consequently, there is no language in our world capable of describing spirituality. The attempt to describe spiritual reality with corporeal language is somewhat similar to an attempt to describe the color red to a person who is blind from birth. We clearly will not succeed, because the object we wish to describe is not perceived in his senses.

Still, most of the Kabbalah books are written in Hebrew. Furthermore, some of the words appearing in Kabbalah books, such as coupling or kissing, are such "earthly" words, that it is surprising to come across them in books dealing with spirituality. Hence the question arises: How could it be?

In order to answer this question, we need to become familiar with one of the fundamental laws in the wisdom of Kabbalah: The "Law of roots and branches." According to the law of roots and branches, everything taking place in our world is a copy of what is taking place in the spiritual world. The spiritual world is called "the world of roots" in the wisdom of Kabbalah and according to the law of roots and branches, each "branch" in our world has a single and unique "root" of its own, from which is cascades to this world. (see drawing #8). As our sages said: "There is not a single blade of grass without an angel from Above, who strikes it and tells it 'Grow'" (Breshit Raba, 10: 6.)

This is how it sounds in the words of Baal HaSulam: [11]

The entire lower world is an imprint of the world Above it. Hence, all forms existing in the Higher World in all their quantity and quality are copied fully and appear so in the lower world. In a way, where there isn't a single detail in reality, or occurrences in reality that exist in the lower world, that would not be found as such in the world Above it, in an equal manner like 2 drops of water. And are called 'root and branch'. Meaning, that the same detail, which exists in the lower world, is scrutinized as a branch, with the value of its example, which is found and stems from the Upper world, which is

---

[11] Baal Hasulam, "The Essence of the Wisdom of Kabbalah"

the root of the lower detail. For, from that place it is stamped and materializes, in the lower world."

Complicated? Here is an example to help us understand what it's all about. Picture any computer in your mind. Let's allow ourselves to become sentimental for a moment and imagine that in the picture, we see our beloved mother-in-law. She is dressed in a blue button style shirt, Mao Zedong style, with a livid expression for some unknown reason. Is the picture actual reality? Luckily, no. The picture is a result of a few coded lines from the depths of the computer and given the command, they are presented as information on the computer screen as an image. If we wanted to play around with it and change the color of our mother-in-law's shirt from Mao Zedong blue to radiant orange, or spread a smile on her face, what would we do? We'd turn to the code lines of course and arrange them differently, since the image on the computer screen is only the result, and the coded lines are the cause.

According to the law of roots and branches, the image of reality revealed before our eyes is only the result – a "branch" of a spiritual cause. Since every branch in our world has a spiritual root of its own, Kabbalists can use the names of branches in our world to describe the spiritual roots. They name the branch and it is clear to them which spiritual root it speaks of.

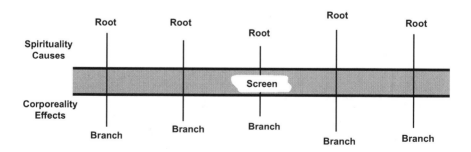

The language the Kabbalists created, based on the law of roots and branches is the language in which all Kabbalistic books are written and is called "the language of branches." In the next section of the lesson, we'll explain it further.

Test yourself:

- Briefly define the law of roots and branches.

The Language of Branches

Biologists have developed a microscope in order to identify bacteria. Astronomers have built telescopes in order to increase their scope of vision. Kabbalists, on the other hand, are people who have developed a unique sense enabling them to feel the spiritual reality.

Attaining the spiritual world places a special challenge before Kabbalists: To convey their attainments to each other, despite it being impossible to describe them in words. In order to solve that problem, Kabbalists developed a special language, based on the law of roots and branches, called "the language of branches." The next part of the lesson is dedicated to a brief, initial familiarization with this language.

When we observe a certain phenomenon taking place in our world, we are unable to point to its spiritual root, since the world of roots is concealed from us. On the other hand, a Kabbalist, who has ascended to the feeling of the Upper world clearly sees the connection between both worlds; between the corporeal branch and its root. The ability to connect between the spiritual root and its unique corporeal branch enables Kabbalists to point to the spiritual roots by means of the matching corporeal branches and describe their spiritual attainments through them.

Indeed, that is what they do. In their books, Kabbalists describe the spiritual world by means of the corporeal branches. The books that Kabbalists composed tell only of the spiritual world, yet they use words from our world to describe the roots and the occurrences in the Upper world.

Baal HaSulam writes in the essay "The Essence of the Wisdom of Kabbalah": "Kabbalists have found a set and annotated vocabulary, sufficient to create an excellent spoken language. It enables them to converse with one another of the spiritual roots in the Upper Worlds. Meaning, by merely mentioning to their friends the lower, tangible branch in this world that is well defined to our corporeal senses.

The listeners understand the Upper root to which this corporeal branch points because it is related to it, being its imprint."

The necessity to interpret the words in the spiritual sense presents a significant challenge, since a large portion of the words in the books of Kabbalah are very familiar to us from the Hebrew language and it is very easy to be tempted to interpret them in their familiar, corporeal sense. Indeed, one of the major problems causing misunderstanding of the wisdom of Kabbalah stems from the tendency to actualize the wisdom, although not even a single word describes the corporeal reality of our world.

Many of the misconceptions about the wisdom of Kabbalah originate from misunderstanding the written word. For example, several sections in the "Book of Zohar," with a detailed description of different combinations of the lines on the palm of our hand and facial features have inevitably led to a mistaken conclusion that the wisdom of Kabbalah is connected to palm reading and interpreting facial features. Actually, the detailed description of the lines on the palm of the hand and of facial features is nothing but a description of spiritual states, according to the law of roots and branches and that is the only correct way of reading it. Any other interpretation is considered going against the rule "You shall have no other gods before me."[12]

An important part of the initial stages of the study of the wisdom of Kabbalah is acquiring a new dictionary of terms, helping the student remember the correct, spiritual meaning of words in Kabbalah books. Here are a few examples of terms from the language

---

[12] Book of Exodus, Chapter 20 Item 3

of branches; All the concepts were taken from Baal HaSulam's book "Study of the Ten Sefirot," part 1, "Answer chart for word meanings":

Light: Everything accepted in the worlds from the aspect of existence from existence, which is all-inclusive, except for the matter of the vessels.
Time: A certain sum of aspects cascading from one another intertwined with one another in an order of cause and effect.
Darkness: The fourth phase of the will to receive, which doesn't receive the Upper Light into it from the force of restriction.
Place: The will to receive in the emanated is the "place" for all the abundance and Light in it.
Head: That same part of the emanated which is most equivalent to form of the root called head.
Spirit: The Light of *Hassadim* (Mercy) is called *Ruach* (Spirit)
Light: The force of bestowal governing and filling all the souls.

Test yourself:
- What should we be strict about when reading Kabbalah books and why is it so difficult to do?

Summary of the Lesson

Main Points
- All of the Kabbalah books were written based on actual attainment of the spiritual reality, according to the rule: whatever we do not attain, we will not define by word or name.
- A person attains reality (spiritual or corporeal) through the will to receive and never knows what reality is in itself, rather only how one is impressed with it.
- According to the law of roots and branches, each "branch" in this world has its own single and unique "root," from which it cascades to this world.

- The language of branches describes the spiritual roots by means of names of the "branches" in our world.
- When we encounter words in Kabbalah books that are familiar to us from our daily life, we need to remember that they are directing us towards the spiritual roots, rather than the occurrences of this world.

Concepts

Root – Cause.
Branch – Result.
World of roots – The spiritual world.
World of branches – The corporeal world.
The Language of branches – A language which describes the spiritual reality by means of the names of the "corporeal" branches.

Answers to Questions

Question: Explain why the spiritual reality the Kabbalist attains is no less real than the corporeal reality.
Answer: The Kabbalist attains the spiritual reality in his senses, the will to receive, just like we perceive the corporeal reality.

Question: Briefly define the law of roots and branches.
Answer: According to the law of roots and branches, each "branch" in this world has its own unique "root," from which it cascades to this world.

Question: What should we heed while reading books of Kabbalah and why is it so difficult to do?
Answer: We should heed the correct meaning of the words in their spiritual sense. It is difficult for us to do because a large portion of the words in the Kabbalah books are very familiar to us from the

Hebrew language and it's very easy to be tempted to interpret them in their corporeal sense.

Lesson #2 – The Light that Reforms

In this lesson we'll learn: How to study the wisdom of Kabbalah in the correct manner / The Light that Reforms / The four holy languages

The Lower Learns from the Upper

In our chaotic world, it's nice that there are a few definite, consistent truths which always help one get organized anew after getting dizzy on the carousel of life. The sun, for example, always rises in the East, your wife is always right, and what is bound to go wrong will always do so. Similarly, when a person comes to study the wisdom of Kabbalah and is slightly confused with the barrage of new and unfamiliar concepts and with new directions of thought, at least he can take comfort in that if he studies well, after some time, he will begin to master the material and understand what is written. However, that's not the case.

As strange as it may sound, the wisdom of Kabbalah isn't studied with the intelligence, but with the desire. The wisdom of Kabbalah isn't studied the way of any other wisdom. In the wisdom of Kabbalah, one is not required to accumulate knowledge and piece bits of information correctly to one clear picture. In the wisdom of Kabbalah, in order to understand, you need the desire – the desire to change, the desire to be corrected.

Spirituality can only be understood from the desire corrected with the intention of in order to bestow. The wisdom of Kabbalah is not theoretical the condition for understanding it is to live it, meaning, to feel spiritual reality in practice.

Only from the feeling of spirituality, can one understand what spirituality is. That is what we learned in the previous lesson…

In order to understand what is written in Kabbalah books, first, it is necessary to rise to the spiritual degree the books describe. Only through attaining the spiritual root, can we understand the language of branches. As long as we exist in the reality of our world, the Kabbalah books are sealed to us; we do not understand what is written in them.

Not only are the books sealed from us. As long as we exist in our world, the entire spiritual reality is closed and sealed from us.

Take a pen or pencil and highlight the following sentence: We are unable to understand what spirituality is from our world. That is a very important principle in the study of the wisdom of Kabbalah, because it clearly defines what we are and are not capable of doing in order to attain spirituality. In order to attain spirituality, it is necessary to heed to the advice of Kabbalists, for they are in spirituality. There's no other choice. From the reality of our world, it is completely impossible to understand, imagine or even guess what the path to attaining spirituality is.

Furthermore, even if we desire to understand what is happening here, in our world, we need to first rise above this world, to the world of causes. For, only out of attaining the spiritual world, can we understand the reason for all that takes place in this world. As Baal HaSulam writes: "The lower will learn from the Upper."[13]

Even the limits of our understanding in this world are similarly defined. Thus, for example, the degrees of evolution below us – the still, vegetative, and animate – we can research and understand. We also have sufficient understanding of everything connected to the functioning of the human body. The questions start coming up when we speak of the internality of man. We lack clarity regarding the set of laws determining the connection among us, if any even exist. Even the inner-psychological structure of each and every one of us isn't

---

[13] The Writings of Baal HaSulam, "The Essence of the Wisdom of Kabbalah" essay.

sufficiently clear to us. In this regard, the concealed is more than the revealed. Why? Because we are incapable of studying our essence and understanding it from our current degree. In order to understand who we truly are, we need to observe ourselves from an external point of view, a higher one. In other words, in order to understand who we are, we need to elevate to a higher degree of existence – to spirituality.

Test yourself:

- What is the condition to understanding the wisdom of Kabbalah?

A Wonderful Remedy

Like rain in mid-summer, an elephant in the center of Manhattan, Gustav Mahler in the middle of a marketplace – one question is prominent in the explanation of the language of branches, requiring an answer. The question is simple: If we do not understand anything in Kabbalah books, why study them?

In truth, it's an important question and no wonder it is so charged, because in the answer to this question we find the key to entering the spiritual world – the only means for shifting the method of working with the will to receive; the secret separating us from spiritual reality – that same secret Kabbalists have been keeping for thousands of years.

Sounds interesting?! Allow us to leave you in a bit of suspense. The answer to the question will be revealed in a few paragraphs. In the meantime, in order to sharpen this point further, we'll briefly summarize the main points of the previous chapter. We learned that spirituality can't be described in corporeal language. That is why Kabbalists write their books in the language of branches. Since every corporeal branch cascades from its own unique spiritual root, Kabbalists can use the names of branches in our world in order to describe the spiritual roots. That is what they do- use the language of branches. It follows that the fundamental condition to understanding the language of branches is attaining the spiritual root of each corporeal root.

In other words, in order to understand the language of branches, spiritual attainment is essential. In the essay, "The Essence of the Wisdom of Kabbalah," Baal HaSulam writes that the language of branches needs to be studied from a Kabbalist and understanding it is possible "only if the listener is wise himself, meaning that he knows and understands the relations between branches and their roots," which means one who has attained spirituality.

Actually, Kabbalists wrote their books for those who have already attained spirituality, to convey to each other information about the spiritual world. When one Kabbalist reads what another Kabbalist wrote, he can recreate what is written within himself and feel exactly what his friend intended, just as a musician recreates the sounds of a composer from 500 years ago (using notes), or as we express the language of math in numerals.

Our opening question is relevant here. What is the purpose of a person who is not in spirituality to read Kabbalah books? Baal HaSulam himself answers this question in the essay "Preface to The Study of the Ten Sefirot":[14]

"Indeed, there is a great thing in it, worthy of being publicized: There is a wonderful, invaluable remedy to those who engage in the wisdom of Kabbalah. Although they do not understand what they are learning, through the yearning and the great desire to understand what they are learning, they awaken upon themselves the Lights that surround their souls.... which bring him much closer to achieving perfection."

In simple words, as Baal HaSulam writes, a special spiritual force is embedded in Kabbalah books. If we read these books out of a desire to understand, we awaken the spiritual force embedded in them and it acts upon us, drawing us closer to spirituality, to our perfect state.

---

[14] Letter 155.

How does it work? According to the wisdom of Kabbalah, we already exist in our perfect state, full of all the good and pleasure promised to us. All that remains is for us to reveal it. As long as we do not feel our perfect state, the Light does not shine within us, rather outside of us. The lights shining outside of us are called "Surrounding Lights" in the wisdom of Kabbalah. As Baal HaSulam writes, when we awaken the Surrounding Lights upon us, they draw us closer to our completion.

How are the Surrounding Lights awakened? Baal HaSulam writes that we awaken the Lights out of our desire to understand what is written; except that our intention is not understanding, as common in our world. Understanding in spirituality is possible only from the desire to change and in the end, from attainment, the inner change of the desire and feeling spiritual reality in practice. Only that way, can we understand what is written in Kabbalah books; only from attaining the sense of the spiritual world. That is why when we read Kabbalah books, we should yearn to reach a feeling of spirituality. Only this way, can we awaken the Surrounding Lights. The correcting light is called "Torah" in the wisdom of Kabbalah; Torah comes from the word *Orah* (*L*ight). Studying Torah, according to the wisdom of Kabbalah is studying with the intention of drawing the Light that Reforms, so as to bring us to the feeling of spirituality.

The following paragraph is dedicated to all those for whom the explanation of the Surrounding Lights and lights in general, sounds somewhat "up in the air," mystical and not at all scientific. According to the wisdom of Kabbalah, two forces are at the base of creation: the force of bestowal and the force of reception, Light and vessel. The Light, the desire to bestow. The vessel, the desire to receive. The relationship between them is simple: if the vessel wishes to receive what the Light wishes to bestow unto it, the Light will shine instantly. It is a law of nature. As such, when we read Kabbalah books with a desire to shift from receiving to bestowing and reach spiritual attainment, meaning reach the abundance the Light wishes to illuminate in us, we inevitably summon a response from the side of the Light, which draws us closer to spirituality.

From this point, we begin to understand the meaning of the word "Segula," a unique power, which Baal HaSulam mentioned. Indeed, according to the wisdom of Kabbalah, all parts of creation are interconnected by strict laws, according to a predetermined program, which is why there is no room in creation for mysticism and miracles. Rather in our current state, most of the connections among the parts of creation are concealed from us. That is why we don't always know how to discern the connection of cause and effect in different phenomena and cannot explain them. We call this lack of connection "Segula."

Imagine a person from a remote tribe, standing for the first time in his life in front of the doors of a neighborhood supermarket which open on their own. He immediately drops to his knees in an attempt to please the supernatural force being revealed to him. As far as he is concerned, it is a wonder which cannot be explained. The sequence of cause and effect events causing the doors to open is concealed from him. Similarly, we are unable to understand the connection between reading the books and the effect the Light has upon us.

That is actually totally fine. We are not required to understand. To the contrary; attempts to explain the influence of the Surrounding Lights on a person rationally, actually misses the goal. As we end this section, it is important to reiterate and emphasize that the wisdom of Kabbalah is not learned in order to accumulate knowledge, philosophize and become smarter. The wisdom of Kabbalah is studied with a desire, the desire to be corrected. The desire is the determinant factor - remember that.

Spirituality is attained only from the desire to be in spirituality. The correct desire draws the Light that Reforms to it, which acts upon the desire and changes it. Each time the desire changes, even slightly, and is further aimed towards spirituality; we draw closer to understanding spirituality. That is what is called "the heart understands."

Test yourself:
- What are the Surrounding Lights and how can they draw us closer to spirituality?

Four Languages

If you received a religious upbringing, you may have had a teacher who dutifully explained the Bible stories in a simple and consistent manner. "What do you mean you do not understand how a whale can swallow a person, who emerges intact after three days and three nights?! It is as simple as it sounds."

Simple, it isn't. We knew it then and we know it today. What we still don't know is what exactly the author meant, meaning what is the correct way to understand the stories. See what is written in the "Book of Zohar" on the Torah: "Woe unto one who says that the Torah comes to tell literal tales….And if the Torah indicates to mundane matters, even the rulers of the world have among them better things, so let us follow them and turn them into a law in the same way. However, all the words of the Torah have the uppermost meaning."[15]

The truth is that it isn't only the Torah not telling us literal tales. All of the Jewish holy books hold upper secrets. The Bible, writings of the sages, Talmud, legends and of course the writings of Kabbalah – were all written by Kabbalists and in their inner, deeper sense, they only describe spiritual reality. Hence, the inner meaning embedded in the books is concealed from us.

Kabbalists use Four Languages:

The language of Torah – Describes the Upper world in story language.
The language of *Halacha* (Laws) – that of the *Talmud* and *Mishna*.

---

[15] The Book of Zohar with The Sulam Commentary, *BeHa'alotcha*, When you Mount, 58

The language of Legend – A very deep language, difficult to understand.

The language of Kabbalah – A very precise and practical language.

All of those languages (excluding the language of Legends) use the language of branches and each language exhibits advantages and disadvantages: one of them describes spiritual reality in general and the other –in detail. One is comprehensible and the other is difficult.

Here are a few examples of the internal meaning embedded in the holy languages.

Language of Torah:

Genesis 1, 1: "In the beginning, God created the Heavens and the earth."

The wisdom of Kabbalah teaches us that the Creator created reality composed of two forces: the will to give and the will to receive – the ego. In the story of creation, they are called "Heaven and earth." In order to actualize the thought of creation, the creature needs to use both forces rather than only one of them. If we only had the will to bestow in us, meaning 'Heaven,' we would be like angels, giving and that's all, with no choice. If we only had the will to receive within us, meaning "earth," we would only want to receive, like babies. Through different languages, the wisdom of Kabbalah explains to us how to integrate both forces correctly.

The language of Halacha: "Two hold a *Talit*(garment)...One says 'It is all mine' and the other says 'Half is mine.' The first gets three parts and the other gets the fourth." Bava Metzia, 2:71.

Kabbalists who composed the *Gemarah* explained extensively how to use the will to receive and the will to bestow correctly. In this example of the language of Halacha, the creature is called "Talit." When a person begins his spiritual path, both forces – the will to give and the will to receive – have a 'hold' on him, meaning control him. One moment he wants to unite with others and give, and the next moment he is suddenly being controlled by the other desire, only wanting to derive pleasure from others and take advantage of them. While advancing in spirituality, one learns to control both forces and determine in each and every situation the correct integration and relations between them.

The language of Legends:

> "When she passed by the entrances of Torah of Shem and Eber, Jacob would run and struggle to come out; when she passed the entrance of idolatry, Esau would run and struggle to come out." (RASH"I, Genesis, 25:22)

Kabbalists chose the language of legends in order to explain spiritual states which were difficult to describe in other languages. 'Jacob,' in this case, is the positive force helping the creature ascend to the degree of the Creator and be loving like Him. 'Esau' in the story is the force seeming to hinder the creature from attaining this goal. In this story, it is explained how to determine the relationship between the forces; which one of them will operate within you. Everything depends on the people you choose to be with. There is a society which will help you advance in spirituality and turn you into a person who loves others, and there is a society which will distance you from spirituality, making you feel that the whole world is obliged to you.

The language of Kabbalah: This association of *Malchut* in *Bina*… a new *Sium* (End) on the Upper Light was made on it, that is, in *Bina*'s place." (Baal HaSulam, Preface to the Wisdom of Kabbalah, letter 59)

As in other sections, the above quote also speaks of the two forces operating in creation: the will to receive and the will to bestow. "Malchut" in the language of Kabbalah is the will to receive, and "Bina" is the will to bestow.

Reading any one of the holy books with a desire to reach spiritual attainment awakens the influence of the Surrounding Lights. The most successful language for studying the wisdom of Kabbalah is the language of Kabbalah. Why? Because in all the other languages, there is great danger of materializing matters. Reading the Bible or *Shulchan Aruch*, for example, may mislead a person to think it speaks of ethics or tales about this world. Whereas the language of Kabbalah describes spiritual reality in the language of *Sefirot*, (Spheres) making it easier for us to keep the correct intention throughout the study and awaken the influence of the Surrounding Lights.

Test Yourself:

- What is described in the holy books and which type of holy books is the most suitable for studying the wisdom of Kabbalah?

Lesson Summary

Main Points

- The wisdom of Kabbalah is not theoretical. The condition for understanding it is to live it, to feel what spiritual reality is in practice.
- The lower learns from the Upper. It is impossible to understand spirituality from corporeality.
- Kabbalah books are embedded with a special spiritual force called the Light that Reforms, which has the ability to draw us closer to spirituality.
- The condition for drawing the Light that Reforms is reading the books out of a desire to attain the feeling of spiritual reality.
- Kabbalah books are the most successful for studying the wisdom of Kabbalah.

Terms

Upper: Next degree
Lower: Current degree
Surrounding lights: The Lights illuminating outside of us for as long as we are not yet corrected.
The Light that Reforms: The force correcting the egoistic nature and elevating it to the attribute of bestowal.
Torah: The correcting Light. Torah from the word Orah (Light)

Questions and Answers

Question: What is the condition for understanding the wisdom of Kabbalah?
Answer: The condition for understanding the wisdom of Kabbalah is reaching spiritual attainment. The wisdom of Kabbalah is not theoretical. The condition for understanding it is to live it, to feel spiritual reality in practice.

Question: What are the Surrounding Lights and how can they draw us closer to spirituality?
Answer: The Surrounding Lights shine outside of us for as long as we are not yet corrected. There is a remedy within them, drawing us closer to spirituality, on condition that we read Kabbalah books with the desire to reach a feeling of spiritual reality.

Question: What is described in the holy books and which type of holy books is the most suitable for studying the wisdom of Kabbalah?
Answer: On the inner, concealed level of the holy books, Kabbalists describe spiritual reality. Kabbalistic books are the most suitable for studying the wisdom of Kabbalah, because while reading them, the danger of materializing what is written is diminished.

Lesson #3 – Kabbalah Books

During this lesson we will learn about: The Writings of Rav Yehuda Ashlag – Baal HaSulam / The Writings of Rav Baruch Shalom Ashlag – Rabash

Let's Open the books!

Those were the days of austerity, the early 1950's in the Land of Israel. In the center of a large room in an old and raggedy building about to collapse stands an old printing press. A person in his 60's is hunched over the printing press and arranging letters on it. The room is filled with a heavy and bitter smell of lead. The person laboring as he arranges the letters is Rav Yehuda Ashlag; he had just completed writing his most prominent composition, which would later be revealed as one of the most important writings in the history of the wisdom of Kabbalah – "The Sulam Commentary" on the Book of Zohar. At that point in time, he was working on publishing it.

Since he has no means to pay a professional printer, Rav Ashlag spends hours bent over the printing press and given the immense importance he sees in publishing the "The Sulam Commentary," arranges the letters for print on his own. That is what he does, despite his old age. Rav Ashlag spent so many hours arranging its printing, that much later, it turned out that the lead had damaged his health.

It is hard not to be impressed by the great importance Baal HaSulam saw in printing his books. If we understand the unique value of Kabbalah books in general and the unique value of Rav Ashlag's books in particular, we can also understand the extreme importance Baal HaSulam saw in publishing his books.

Kabbalah books are the only connection between our world and the spiritual world, thus, they are the most important means to actualizing the purpose of our lives. Through these writings, Kabbalists connect between the spiritual system they have attained and the common person living in our world, who for now lacks understanding and awareness, yet desires to reach spiritual attainment.

Not only Baal HaSulam saw great necessity in publishing his writings, many Kabbalists throughout history have left us with books, such as "The Book of Creation" of Abraham our Patriarch, "The Book of Zohar" of Rashbi, "The Tree of Life" of the ARI, or "The Creator's Path" of the Ramchal. The following lesson will be devoted to explaining about Kabbalah books in general and the books designated to be studied in our generation, in particular.

One of the outstanding characteristics of Kabbalah books is the extraordinary and often mysterious circumstances of the time they were written and revealed. For example, many Kabbalah books composed over the years were hidden or partially burned after being written, only to be revealed anew years later. Many of the Kabbalists did not write their own books, rather one of their students put into writing the things they had heard from their Rav. An eminent example of that is the "Book of Zohar," written by Rabbi Abba, a student of Shimon Bar Yochai, which was hidden after being written and revealed centuries later under obscure circumstances we do not yet understand. Another example is the writings of the ARI, which were written by his student Rav Haim Vital, who ordered for the writings to be buried with him and hidden. However, his tomb was broken into and the writings removed.

Underlying such a strange phenomenon is the necessity to reveal the wisdom and keep it hidden simultaneously. As long as humanity was not ready for the wisdom of Kabbalah, the wisdom was revealed to few chosen ones, who adapted it to their generation. In parallel, they had to conceal it from the rest of the people, who were not yet ready to reveal it. Those Kabbalists acted according to the rule "Disclosing a portion and covering two," meaning they revealed the wisdom only to the necessary measure and simultaneously made sure to conceal it – either in the way they had been written, or by actually hiding or burning them.

As abovementioned, throughout history many books were written by Kabbalists. In the essay "The Teaching of Kabbalah and Its Essence," Baal HaSulam explains why: "The wisdom of truth… must be passed on from generation to generation. Each generation adds a link to its former, and thus the wisdom evolves. Moreover, it becomes more suitable for expansion in the public." We expanded upon that in chapter 1. We'll briefly state that the wisdom of Kabbalah is revealed in parallel to the development of the will to receive and Kabbalists write their books in order to adapt the wisdom of Kabbalah to the degree of the new desire being revealed in their generation.

Hence, it is clear why the books of Baal HaSulam are the most appropriate for studying the wisdom of Kabbalah in our generation. Baal HaSulam wrote his books for the will to receive, which has been revealed at its last stage of development at the end of the 20th century; times when every person is allowed – and more precisely, obligated – to study the wisdom of Kabbalah. Accordingly, what is most prominent in all of Baal HaSulam's writings is the clearly arranged method for studying the wisdom of Kabbalah described in his books, suited to all.

Test Yourself:
- Why it is so important for Kabbalists to write Kabbalah books and publish them?

The Writings of Baal HaSulam

The different and revolutionary point of view of the wisdom of Kabbalah has repeatedly caused the ex-communication of Kabbalists from communities where they operated, or at the very least being outright ignored by their community. Like many of his predecessors, Rav Ashlag and his writings weren't accepted amicably, either. When he passed away in 1954, few were familiar with his compositions and even fewer continued studying them.

In the preface to the book "The Last Generation," Professor Eliezer Shweid (winner of the Israel Price for Jewish Thought) described with great sensitivity the circumstances of anonymity imposed upon Rav Ashlag throughout his life:

"Neither the difficulty to understand the depth of his ideas nor cumbersome of expression caused that. To the contrary – Rav Ashlag was gifted with a rare ability to decode secrets. His words are crystal clear to the point that every reader attains the truth he presents through them. Rav Ashlag made an effort to be known to the public, in order to bring salvation to the world, yet spoke as an individual person and directly addressed all his people as the individuals they were, beyond parties and without the intervention of any party. Belonging to a specific Jewish community did not make him a representative of interests of any establishment, hence, no establishment supported him.

It was thus the price Rav Ashlag paid for his integrity, openness, freedom of thought and boldness of spirit. However, due to all of the above, his words were not enslaved to the shortness of vision of establishment ideologies of the time. They seem relevant and convincing as they did in their time, and perhaps even more so, since much of what he had foreseen is happening in our time and his explanations are still valid as a worthy tool for coping with the challenges of the future of humanity, the Jewish people and of the State of Israel."

Indeed, from the year 1995 onwards, as foreseen by Baal HaSulam himself, interest in his writings and teachings continues to increase. The global world being revealed to us, along with the new challenges it is presenting highlight even further the relevance and importance of the writings of Baal HaSulam as the sole means for solving the difficult problems being revealed in our times, both on the individual level and the collective level.

Baal HaSulam wrote a great deal. Throughout his life and after his death, dozens of his articles were published. Among his writings,

Rav Ashlag wrote interpretations to writings of other Kabbalists and even published a newspaper called "The Nation." Two of his most prominent writings, after many years of labor, each of which span over thousands of pages are "The Sulam Commentary" which he wrote to the "Book of Zohar" and "The Study of the Ten *Sefirot*," which is the interpretation he organized to the writings of the ARI.

Baal HaSulam invested immense efforts in writing the commentary on the "Book of Zohar." His students reported that he would sit and write for long hours every day, until he'd fall asleep with his pen in hand and they could hardly free the pen from his clutched fingers.

The importance Baal HaSulam saw in publishing the "Commentary to the Book of Zohar" stemmed, first and foremost, out of the importance of the "Book of Zohar" itself. The spiritual force embedded in the "Book of Zohar" is unique as no other; there is none like it in all the Kabbalah books. That is because it is intended for the correction of the will to receive at its last and greatest degree of development, the one being revealed in our times. That is why Baal HaSulam labored so much in the writing of "The Sulam Commentary" on the Book of Zohar.

The "Book of Zohar" is mostly written in Aramaic and is abundant with corporeal allegories. As a result, it is very easy to mistake its interpretation and mislead others, as has indeed happened many times over history. In order to remove such an obstacle from us, Baal HaSulam translated the "Book of Zohar" from Aramaic to Hebrew and interpreted all the corporeal allegories into the language of *Sefirot* in a way that cannot be misinterpreted. Except that Baal HaSulam's work on "The Sulam Commentary" did not end there. From attainment of the highest spiritual degree, the same degree from which the "Book of Zohar" was written, Baal HaSulam arranged his interpretation of the "Book of Zohar" so that the words of the "Book of Zohar" would operate upon our souls most effectively.

As abovementioned, another one of Baal HaSulam's most significant writings, parallel to "The Sulam Commentaries" is "The Study of the Ten Sefirot" – his interpretation to the writings of the ARI. Similar to "The Sulam Commentary," "The Study of the Ten *Sefirot*" is also a comprehensive and expansive composition, spanning over thousands of pages. The book describes in great detail the structure of the spiritual worlds and their cascading from the thought of creation to this world. As in "The Ladder," in "The Study of the Ten Sefirot," Baal HaSulam took particular care in interpreting the original text, so there would be no danger of their actualization.

Talmud Eser Sefirot (Study of the Ten Sefirot) was written as a proper study book. It spans over 16 volumes, which are divided into chapters and subchapters. At the end of each section is a special chapter to summarize the entire study unit, at the end of which a dictionary of terms and questions and answers are found. Arranging "The Study of the Ten Sefirot" as a study book signifies Baal HaSulam's approach to the study of the wisdom of Kabbalah as the study of any other science.

In addition to "The Sulam Commentary" and "The Study of the Ten Sefirot," Baal HaSulam wrote dozens of additional articles. Among the most prominent of them are the articles published in the book "Matan Torah" (Giving of the Torah), as well as the four prefaces he wrote to "The Sulam Commentary" on the Book of Zohar: "Preface to the Wisdom of Kabbalah", "Introduction to the Book of Zohar" and "Preface to the Sulam Commentary." In the articles of "Matan Torah" and others, Baal HaSulam describes man's spiritual path from beginning to end. In these compositions, Baal HaSulam presents a clear and practical method for attaining spirituality, accessible to all.

Test yourself:
- Name three important characteristics of "The Sulam Commentary" on the Book of Zohar." What does "The Study of Ten Sefirot" deal with?

The Last Mohican

Rav Baruch Ashlag (The Rabash) (1907-1991), the son and successor of Baal HaSulam, Rav Yehuda Ashlag, was a concealed Kabbalist in the fullest sense. Despite his immense spiritual height, he was a very humble man who shied away from fame and spent all his time studying and writing. Nevertheless, there are few words to describe, even slightly, the enormous contribution of this great Kabbalist to our generation and to generations to come.

In a certain sense, Rav Ashlag was "the last Mohican." He was the last link in the glorious chain of the greatest Kabbalists, beginning with the first great Kabbalist, Abraham and continuingup to his father, Rav Yehuda Ashlag. The role of the Rabash in this chain is perhaps the most significant one in our times – to connect all of the greatest Kabbalists with man in our world and suiting the method of Kabbalah to the souls being revealed in our generation.

Although the Rabash himself stood at the top of the spiritual ladder, his feet never disconnected from the ground, even momentarily, and all his writings are aimed towards the common person who wants to reveal if there is something higher than what this world has to offer. From his sublime spiritual attainment, Rav Baruch Ashlag understood the necessity of a person living at the end of the 20th century to reveal the secret of life and succeeded in adapting the wisdom of Kabbalah to that need in the simplest and most convenient way.

In 1983, there was a turning point in the life of Rabash. Until that period, he had only taught a few students who accompanied him over the years. All of a sudden, 40 new students came to his group; young and secular from all over the country, who had longed to discover the secret of life. They came from all walks of life and were very different from the students the Rabash had met until then.

In his unique work with the new students, the Rabash developed the most suitable spiritual method for our generation. He wrote a weekly essay for them, in which he described in great detail and very simple language each and every step of a person's internal work on one's path to spirituality. The essays the Rabash wrote serve as a cornerstone in the study of the wisdom of Kabbalah in our generation. Recently, all the articles have been compiled into the series of books called "The Writings of Rabash."

Test yourself:
- What is the role of the Rabash in the chain of the great Kabbalists?

Lesson Summary

- Kabbalah books are the only connection between the spiritual world and our world.
- Many of the Kabbalah books were written and hidden, because the will to receive was not sufficiently developed to reveal the wisdom of Kabbalah.
- The writings of Baal HaSulam are most suited for the study of the wisdom of Kabbalah in our generation, because he wrote them for the will to receive being revealed in our generation.
- The two most significant compositions of Baal HaSulam are "The Sulam Commentary" on the Book of Zohar and "The Study of the Ten Sefirot."
- The writings of Rav Baruch Ashlag (Baal HaSulam's son) represent the connecting link between us and the chain of great Kabbalists, beginning with Abraham and concluding with Baal HaSulam.

Terms

Disclosing a portion and covering two: Revealing the wisdom of Kabbalah to the desired measure, accordingly, its concealment to the desired measure.

The Sulam Commentary on the Book of Zohar: Baal Hasulam's interpretation on the "Book of Zohar" of Rabbi Shimon Bar Yochai.

The Study of the Ten Sefirot: Baal HaSulam's interpretation on the writings of the ARI.

Answers to the Questions

Question: Why is it so important to Kabbalists to write and publish Kabbalah books?

Answer: Kabbalah books are the only connection between the corporeal world and the spiritual world. Through these writings, Kabbalists connect between the spiritual system they have attained and the common person living in our world.

Question: Name three important characteristics of "The Commentary on the Book of Zohar."

Answer: a) Translation from Aramaic to Hebrew; b) Explaining the corporeal allegories in their spiritual meaning, so that it is impossible to actualize them. c) Arranging things so that the words of "The Book of Zohar" would operate upon our soul most effectively.

Question: What does "The Study of the Ten Sefirot" deal with?

Answer: Explaining the structure of the spiritual worlds.

Question: What is the role of the Rabash in the chain of great Kabbalists?

Answer: Connecting between all of the greatest Kabbalists and the common person in our world along with adapting the method of Kabbalah to the souls being revealed in our generation.

Logical Sequence
(The order of course development)

We have learned that the wisdom of Kabbalah is a method for revealing the Creator to the creatures in this world.

We have learned that in order to reveal the Creator, we need to change our intention of in order to receive to in order to bestow.

We have learned that Kabbalah books are embedded with a special spiritual force called the Light that Reforms, which has the power to change our intention from in order to receive to in order to bestow.

In the next study unit we'll expand our explanation on the conditions for studying Kabbalah Books.

Study Unit #2 - Freedom of Choice

About the Study Unit "Freedom of Choice"

The study unit "Freedom of Choice" deals with one of the most important topics in the study of the wisdom of Kabbalah and in a person's life: Free choice. Throughout this unit, we will clarify whether we have free choice, and if so, what our free choice is.

The unit is divided into three parts:

- Receiving and giving - The connection between man and society as a condition for revealing the Creator.
- Free Choice – The influence of society upon a person and choosing a society.
- Souls and worlds – Spiritual roots of the connection between man and society.

The goals of this study unit are:

- Introducing the issue of free choice.
- Providing extensive knowledge on the importance of society in spiritual development.
- Giving an initial explanation of the method of correction according to the wisdom of Kabbalah.
- Introducing additional basic concepts in the wisdom of Kabbalah.
- Reviewing basic concepts which were learned in the first unit.

Within the study framework, we will define the following concepts: Providence, *Torah* and *Mitzvot* (precepts), nature, giving, receiving, love, love of the Creator, angel of death, The Soul of *Adam HaRishon* (The First Man), worlds and shattering.

Part #1 Receiving and Giving

Lesson #1 – Good and Evil in Creation

In this lesson we will learn about: The wisdom of Kabbalah as a science / The question of good and evil in creation / The law of receiving and the law of bestowal/ Globalization and the obligation of bestowal

What's New in Science?

One of the unique experiences of studying the wisdom of Kabbalah is encountering its non-conventional perspective. This wisdom knows how to pull rabbits from its hat, surprising you anew every time. With every topic it covers, new directions of thought are opened. It is somewhat like living in a Hitchcock movie: many turning points in the plot, except that fear and anxiety are replaced with joy and a sense of rejuvenation.

Take for example the issue of science and Kabbalah. As "Kabbalah bloomers" who have already completed the first study unit in the course, you have surely noticed that the Kabbalistic approach is closer to science than to religion. However, if we were to ask a person who is not familiar with the wisdom of Kabbalah whether it is religion or science, he would choose the first option with no hesitation. Would that be correct? – Wrong!

The wisdom of Kabbalah is science. In truth, the wisdom of Kabbalah is the root of all sciences. Baal HaSulam states that in several of his essays. For instance, he describes one of his most prominent essays, "The Peace," as "scientific research by the critique of empirical reason regarding the absolute necessity to assume the work of the Creator." Although the research topic (the necessity to assume the work of the Creator) is not popular with scientists, to say the least, the format is scientific from every aspect: research.

Moreover, the study is not philosophical-theoretical; rather, as Baal HaSulam writes, it was conducted empirically.

The following lesson will be dedicated to understanding the research on the matter of the necessity to assume the work of the Creator, as is described in the essay "The Peace." We will affirm that the concept of "work of the Creator" is a definite law of nature and the necessity of heeding to it is no different from the necessity to heed to any other law of nature.

Kabbalah is a science which studies the concealed part of reality. Just as scientists study the world around us by means of their five physical senses and devices that expand the scope of their sensitivity, similarly, Kabbalists study the spiritual world by means of an additional, spiritual, sense called "screen" or "soul." This sense is actually the will to receive corrected with the intention of in order to bestow.

Rav Kook writes about the scientific nature of the wisdom of Kabbalah in his book "Treasures of the Ra'aya": "Just as a person needs to become accustomed to corporeal nature and its forces, similarly and even more so, does he need to and have to accustom himself to the spiritual laws of nature, that control the entirety of reality, which he is a part of." Likewise, in the essay "The Essence of the Wisdom of Kabbalah," Baal HaSulam writes: "As the emergence of the living species in this world and the conduct of their lives are a wondrous wisdom, the appearance of the Divine Abundance in the world, the degrees and the conduct of their actions unite to create a wondrous wisdom, far more than the science of physics."

Thus, Kabbalah is a science which studies spiritual reality. Through their research, Kabbalists have found that a single law operates in the entirety of reality – the law of bestowal and love. This law connects all parts of creation together and activates them as one body, so that each action of one of the body parts projects onto all the other parts of the entire body. The actions of human beings project onto all the most, for they are the most evolved parts of creation.

According to the law of bestowal, each one of us is obligated to work in bestowal towards all, meaning to maintain the correct balance between oneself and the other parts of creation, so that one's actions do not harm the general body. This work, to which we are all obligated (and not doing for the meantime, since its necessity is concealed from us) is called "work of the Creator" in the wisdom of Kabbalah. This is also the work Baal HaSulam proves the necessity of engaging in, as written in his essay, "The Peace." In fact, all of the wisdom of Kabbalah is scientific research concerning the necessity of work of the Creator, which is the work of bestowing unto others.

The Good, The Bad and Creation

If we believed all soccer fans, the Creator exists, but only on Saturdays when their team wins; when it loses, His existence is doubtful. Since the beginning of time, humanity has been searching for the formula of connection between existing "good" and "bad" events and the existence of an Upper force, or at least some sort of order or justice, according to which it is clear when we are rewarded and when we are punished. It is our nature to want to know that there is a certain order and search for a clear answer to the question: Why do "good" events take place alongside "bad" ones? However, such an order is hard to find.

A person viewing reality discerningly reveals two opposite phenomena. The first reflects that nature is good and miraculously managed in perfect, wondrous order. For example, let's take the wonder of creating life. Out of one miniscule cell, a body is constructed, containing billions of cells, composing hundreds of sophisticated systems beyond measure, and all of them together operate in perfect harmony for the existence of the fetus. Whoever studies how the body develops, beginning with the single cell and ending in birth, will undoubtedly be in awe of the miraculous order by which the body develops, according to an initial clear and defined plan, catering to all the needs of the fetus, eventually passing the newborn into the hands of loving parents.

In contrast, as the "jewel" grows and matures, it is as if he has been thrust mercilessly into a war of survival in an unjust and chaotic world. There do not seem to be any rules. Everyone builds his success on the ruins of the other, the evil thrive, and the good-hearted are trampled under their feet.

Over history, many explanations have been given regarding the unperceivable gap between the good supervision of nature throughout the initial developmental stages of creatures and the cruel war for survival, where they are thrust immediately after growing up. In each generation, humans have tried to understand how it could be that evil emerges from a Creator who is all good. Indeed, the Creator can extend only that which exists within Him and if He is the absolute good, there is no evil in Him.

Some have solved the problem by a theory of "division of work" between two authorities: one Creator responsible for the good and another Creator responsible for the bad: "Elokim," who creates the good and maintains it, and "Satan," who creates the evil and maintains that. Others enhanced the method and assigned an Upper force to each and every action: one force responsible for wealth, another one for beauty, a third force for food and additional forces responsible for death, lies, and so on. The best example of that is Greek mythology.

As long as man's familiarity with the world surrounding him was limited, it was possible to live with the thought that there was more than one "landlord" managing matters. However, as science developed and as it became clear that creation operates as one body, in accordance with a single plan which connects all its parts together as one entity – the claim that creation is managed by more than one force has lost its validity.

A new explanation was needed concerning the contradiction between the existence of good and evil and it did not take long to come into being. The realization that creation operates as one body led people to the conclusion that the single force creating creation is indeed complete benevolence that created the world with great wisdom. Yet, particularly because of His greatness, He has no consideration for our world and it is of no interest of His to take care of our insignificant matters. That is why He has abandoned us and everyone does that which is right in his own eyes, resulting in all the evil in the world. Such ideas are expressed in the teachings of the German philosopher, Frederich Nietzsche.

Nevertheless, despite all the explanations of the contradiction between good and evil, "nothing is new under the sun," as Baal HaSulam writes in his essay, "The Peace, "not only was that great and horrible tear (between good and evil) not mended; rather, it continues to grow and expand before our eyes into a terrible chasm, without seeing or hoping for a way out of it."

The chasm is expanding because we seek a solution distant from us, whereas it is set right under our noses. Instead of attempting to solve the contradiction between good and evil by understanding the nature of Providence, we need to understand that the root of the problem is within us, in our nature and its solution is found there. The problem is not in the supervisor. The reason for the open chasm between good and evil is human nature and therein a correction of this great gap is found.

Test yourself:
- What is the main difference between the approaches to solving the question of good and evil in creation, and the approach of the wisdom of Kabbalah on this issue?

A Hard-and-Fast-Law

Laws are meant to be a serious matter. At times, legislators might be much more serious than necessary and when that happens, the whole story becomes amusing. In Tennessee, USA, for example, a law was passed prohibiting the shooting of any animal from a moving vehicle, except for a whale (an especially interesting prohibition, considering the fact that the state is not located at the shore of any ocean.) In France, you will be brought to court if you call your piglet "Napoleon," and in California every citizen is allowed to enjoy the sun, by law. It's good they have a law.

Enough said regarding state laws. The laws of nature are a completely different story. They are simple, practical and the mechanism of their reinforcement is much more efficient. If, for instance, you went for a stroll through the window of the fifth floor, it would not end well. The law of gravity does not support such actions. Any action contrary to the laws of nature automatically summons a negative response, and even the greatest lawyer would not be able to help you in that matter.

As we stated before, the wisdom of Kabbalah teaches us to be familiar with the general law of nature, the law of bestowal and love, from which stem all the other laws of nature in our world. The general law of nature, the law of bestowal and love is called "Elokim" (Creator) in the language of Kabbalah. Obeying the law of bestowal and love is called "keeping the *Mitzvot*" (Commandments from the word command) in Kabbalah. The work of keeping the law of bestowal is called the work of the Creator, as mentioned above. "It is best for us to meet halfway," Baal HaSulam writes in the essay "The Peace," "and accept the words of the Kabbalists that *HaTeva* (the nature) has the same numerical value (in Hebrew) as *Elokim* (God)—eighty-six. Then, I will be able to call the laws of the Creator «nature's *Mitzvot* (commandments),» or vice-versa, for they are one and the same."

Both science and the wisdom of Kabbalah speak of a world governed by laws, which we are commanded to follow. The difference is that according to science, we have to keep these laws out of necessity, rather than for a certain purpose and according to the wisdom of Kabbalah, we have to keep these laws for a certain purpose – actualizing the thought of creation.

Either way, we should be familiar with the laws within the framework of our life, because when we act contrary to the law, we are punished. We know the laws operating in nature around us very well. We know how to live by them and even harness them for our needs. The issue is that similar to nature around us, our relationships among people in our world are arranged according to strict laws. The problem is that we are not aware of that.

In the essay "The Peace", Baal HaSulam states three fundamental laws according to which human society is organized. We will describe them briefly:

Law #1: A person is obligated to live a social life.

Every species in nature has a typical social structure: Some creatures live as lone individuals, others live in pairs and there are creatures living as a huge swarm of millions of individuals. Humans also have a natural social structure and it is the communal form. People are commanded to live together according to the law of nature.

We constantly strive to improve our financial, security, and social situation and live as pleasantly and happily as possible. All that is possible, only when a number of people live together in cooperation. If a person chooses to live alone, he indeed sentences himself to a life of meagerness, hard work and boredom. It is the punishment for not heeding to the law, which obligates people to live a social life.

Laws #2 and #3: Within our social life, we are commanded to keep two additional laws of nature: receiving and giving.

The law of receiving obligates every person to care for his personal prosperity and welfare. The law of giving obligates every individual to care for the prosperity of society and its welfare. (This law is also called the "law of bestowal.")

We are naturally motivated to keep the law of receiving. It is a fact that people are willing to invest endless hours for their individual success. If we do not keep the law of receiving, we will immediately feel the resulting damage. For example, a person who stops working will very quickly find himself in financial deficit, which will obligate him to be concerned with his sustenance. Life itself obligates us to follow the law of receiving.

Our biggest problem is that we do not heed to the law of bestowal. We lack a strong desire and motivation to invest and care for the prosperity of society, because the punishment for not keeping that law is not revealed before us. The will to receive, our nature, conceals it from us. On the contrary, it seems to us that if we succeed in avoiding giving to society, we actually benefit more. Out of all the laws of nature, the law of bestowal is that which is concealed from us.

We learned about the necessity to conceal the law of bestowal from us in the previous study unit and we will expand upon it in this unit. In short, we will add that unlike any other law of nature, we are to keep the law of bestowal not only out of obligation, but rather in order to resemble it, actually be like it. Resembling the law of bestowal is possible only from an independent desire, and an independent desire can be aroused in us only from a reality where the need to bestow is concealed from us.

Either way, lack of knowing the law does not free us from punishment. "Thus," as Baal HaSulam writes with razor-sharp precision, humanity is being fried in a heinous turmoil, and strife and famine and their consequences have not ceased thus far."[16]

The cause of all evil in the world is that we are not keeping the law of bestowing to society. It's as simple as that. That is also the cause of the gap between good and evil upon which we expanded at the beginning of this lesson.

---

[16] The Writings of Baal HaSulam, the essay "The Peace."

From everything said thus far, the obligation of 'work of the Creator' also becomes clear, or in other words, the obligation to heed to the law of bestowal. If we learn to bestow, we will save ourselves all the pain and suffering. Not only will we arrange the relations among us in our world, but we will attain the spiritual world.

One of the forces operating upon us in order to reveal and eventually also follow the law of bestowal is globalization. We will expand upon that in the next section of the lesson.

Test yourself:

- What are the three laws according to which human society is arranged?

What's the Connection?

Mohamed Bouazizi, a young Tunisian with a B.A. degree in computer science made his living by selling fruit at an illegal booth in one of the Tunisian markets. One day in December 2010, the authorities closed Bouazizi's booth. In response, Bouazizi set himself on fire and burned to death, which in turn caused a wave of riots all over Tunisia and eventually led to the fall of the government.

The fall of the Tunisian government aroused a chain reaction in a number of other Arab countries. In Yemen, Bahrain, Egypt, Syria, and Libya, uprisings against the governments took place. As a result of political instability in the Arab countries, oil prices shot up. As a result of the rising cost of oil, a sharp rise in the cost of basic products, a harsh blow to millions of people worldwide became apparent. The rise in prices was "the last straw" for thousands of Spanish youths, who left their homes and being inspired by the uprising in the Arab world, moved to tent camps on city squares all over Spain.

The snowball that began rolling in a fruit booth in Tunisia traversed through Arab countries, accelerated on the squares of Spain and inevitably proceeded and will proceed to pass through additional stations as you read this text, is just one example of many in our global world. Tightening cultural and economic ties between countries, societies, and people are becoming so apparent in the 21st century, that at times, it seems possible to actually hear the rustle of thousands of connections being formed.

Sociologists who study the phenomenon of globalization point to technological, financial and political developments as the main causes of its expansion. The wisdom of Kabbalah points to a completely different reason. According to the wisdom of Kabbalah, increasing multiplication of connections among countries and people around the world are not forming, rather they already exist. They are simply being revealed.

Kabbalists write that the world is global and integral in essence; meaning that it operates as one body whose organs are interconnected with dense and tight connections of mutuality. Up to now, we have revealed these connections on the degrees of the still, vegetative, and animate. Breaching the balance of various parts on those degrees has led to harsh results. The most prominent example is Earth's warming. These days, similar connections on the degree of man are also beginning to be revealed to us as a predetermined evolutionary stage in the process of correcting the desire.

As the wisdom of Kabbalah explains, the revelation of global integral ties, which connect us together as a human society, is actually the revelation of the laws of nature. Globalization is an external expression of all the laws we described in the previous part of this lesson, concerning the necessity to live a social life and the need to receive from society and give to it.

As already stated, we have no problem with everything dealing with the need to receive. Each one of us knows how to take whatever we need. The problem is that we do not know how to give and revealing the mutual interconnection among us in the global world only highlights this problem. A particularly good example is the great global financial crisis of 2008. The tight mutual ties among world economies on one hand and the selfish calculations of economists on the other hand caused the collapse of world economies like a house of cards.

Life in the global world village highlights two important, parallel aspects:

On one hand, it is becoming clear that all of us (all over the world) are interdependent. On the other hand, as a result of the growing ego, it is becoming apparent that we are incapable of bearing it.

Both of these contrary forces which proceed to be revealed intensely, further emphasize the need for a method, by which we will be able to correctly maintain the network of connections among us. We already exist in this network, inter-connectedly, yet since everyone is concerned with one's own benefit, we feel our interconnectedness negatively.

If until now, we could afford to decry the law of bestowal and evolve only by means of the law of reception, indeed in the integral world, where we are all parts of one body and interdependent, it is no longer possible to disparage this law. In the past, any damage caused in a certain area was limited to that area, whereas these days, any problem could spark a global, chain reaction. We have become interdependent; we have become an integral system.

We have no choice. Nature is stronger than us. It is constructed in such a way that we cannot escape it. We have no other choice but to obey the law of bestowal. All of the world crises humanity is experiencing – crises in education, economy, over-consumption leading to the exhaustion of natural resources with no control – all of those will disappear only if we strictly obey the laws of nature; if we learn how to integrate the law of reception along with the law of bestowal.

Test yourself:
- What is the connection between the law of bestowal and the revelation of global-integral ties among us?

Lesson Summary

Main Points

- In order to maintain a proper social life, we need to heed to two commandments (laws). Receive from society what is necessary for our survival and give to society what is necessary for its survival.
- Human nature conceals from us the necessity to give to society what is necessary for its survival.
- The cause of all evil in the world is that we do not follow the commandment of giving to society whatever is necessary for its existence, or in other words, we do not heed to the law of bestowal.
- The revelation of global-integral connections among us is actually the revelation of the law of bestowal in our world. Revealing these ties highlights the need for the wisdom of Kabbalah as a method of correctly maintaining the network of connections among us.

Concepts

- Commandment: From the word command, keeping the law of bestowal and love.

Answers to the Questions

Question: What is the main difference between the approaches to solving the question of the good and evil in creation, and the approach of the wisdom of Kabbalah on this issue?

Answer: The wisdom of Kabbalah searches the answer to the question of good and evil in human nature, whereas the other approaches described in this chapter seek the solution in the nature of Providence.

Question: What are the three laws according to which human society is arranged?

Answer: 1) A person is obligated to live a social life. 2) A person is obligated to receive from society in order to assure one's existence. 3) A person is obligated to give to society in order to assure its existence.

Question: What is the connection between the law of bestowal and the revelation of global-integral ties among us?

Answer: The revelation of global-integral connections among us is actually the revelation of the law of bestowal in our world. Revealing these ties highlights the need for the wisdom of Kabbalah as a method of correctly maintaining the network of connections among us.

Lesson #2 – From Love of the Creatures to Love of the Creator

In this lesson we will learn: The difficulty in working directly towards the Creator / The advantages of working with others / The difference between Kabbalah and Ethics

A False Picture

A famous joke says that if you want to make the Creator laugh, all you need to do is tell Him your plans. I say, assuming there is a grain of truth in that and the Creator would truly laugh – in retrospect, most of my plans make me laugh as well – the question is how exactly do I tell Him about them?

The wisdom of Kabbalah teaches us that we need to attain a connection with the Creator. The question is how that's done. In the previous lesson, we learned that correcting the connection between a person and his human environment -meaning, a person's ability to receive from society and give to it in a balanced way, is the solution to all afflictions in the world. In this lesson, we will learn that correcting a person's approach to society is not only the recipe for solving the suffering and misery in the world, but also the condition for revealing the connection with the Creator.

To be honest with ourselves, communication with the Creator isn't all that great. Whenever we attempt to talk to Him, He is not available and the few times we succeed to somehow understand Him, it turns out that He has got completely different plans for our life. In truth, it isn't clear why we deserve such treatment. What do we want, after all?! Enough money to pamper our family, a little respect when we hang out in the neighborhood and if possible, for everyone to listen to us. That's simple, isn't it?!

With such elementary requests, it is not clear what the problem is. Isn't the Creator supposed to be nice and considerate?! At least let Him come and explain why, what does He want in exchange; we are willing to be flexible.

Rav Baruch Ashlag, the elder son of Baal HaSulam and his successor, brings an allegory in one of his essays, which illustrates our situation very well. A father and son are walking down the street. The son bursts out crying and his bitter weeping is heartbreaking. Every once in a while, the child falls down and refuses to get up. For some reason, his father ignores his son's wailing, grasps his hand and drags him along behind him. Someone on the street, who can no longer bear the father's cruelty, approaches him to clarify the matter. "Why are you being so cruel to your son?" he asks. "My beloved son wants a pin and I refuse to give it to him, that is why he is crying," the father explains. "If so, give him the pin, so he calms down," the man suggests. "The problem is," replies the father, "his eyes itch and he wants to use the pin to pick at his eyes."

So much for the allegory and here is the meaning. The Creator is the absolute good; that is how he is attained by Kabbalists. The good that the Creator wishes to give us is to become like Him, to be similar to him, for He is the absolute good. The problem is that the Creator wants us to bestow and we want to receive – the total opposite. Hence, whatever seems good to us is similar to the aspect of "a pin to pick at our eye." We and the Creator broadcast on two different frequencies. In order to be in contact with Him, understand Him even in the slightest and feel the good He wishes to give to us, we need to learn how to bestow, to be similar to Him at least to some extent.

At this exact point, meaning in our study of how to become similar to the Creator, there is an obstacle, which could distract us from the goal and it is important for us to become aware of it.

If the goal is to become similar to the Creator, we need to find some kind of scale, with which we will be able to measure the extent of our similarity to Him, if at all. It would seem that what we need to do is depict the Creator and bestowal in our eyes and check how similar we are to that image. However, that is precisely the problem! If we set an image of the Creator before us, an image of bestowal as we imagine it and try to examine ourselves directly according to that, we will inevitably err. Our scale will be mistaken.

We are incapable of examining ourselves directly towards the Creator and enter into direct connection with Him. Why? Because the Creator is concealed from us, and who can assure us that we aren't imagining Him incorrectly. Particularly since He is concealed, it is very easy to err and think that we are already connected with Him, while the truth of the matter is that we do not know who He is. In proof, our world is full of people who are certain they are already in close contact with the Creator.

Since there is no Creator in our reality, nothing stops us from imagining Him as we see fit and live with the illusion that we are in contact with Him – instead of actually drawing closer to Him, we grow more distant from Him.

How can we check ourselves correctly regarding the attribute of bestowal? That is the topic of the next section of the lesson.

Test yourself:

- Why can't we depict the Creator (the attribute of bestowal) correctly?

The Path of Truth

Have you ever asked yourself where the border lies between truth and falsehood? It's an interesting question. Take a few minutes and think about it; where is the place where falsehood ends and from which truth begins; how long do we live in falsehood and at what point do we reach the path of truth? Each one of us would surely be happy to know the answer. Or perhaps not...

Rav Baruch Ashlag (The Rabash) has a simple and eye-opening answer. The border between truth and falsehood, he writes, passes through a place where a person begins to become aware to the fact that he is in falsehood. In other words, the awareness of falsehood is also its exit point. From the moment a person begins to become aware of the fact that he is in falsehood, he reaches the path of truth.

Now, after becoming a little more knowledgeable on the matter of truth and falsehood, please read the following excerpt from the Writings of Rabash: "We should know that there is a virtue to love of friends: one cannot deceive himself and say that he loves the friends...But with love of the Creator, one cannot examine oneself as to whether his intention is the love of the Creator, meaning that he wants to bestow upon the Creator, or his desire is to receive in order to receive."

Do you remember the question with which we ended the first lesson: How can we know if we are truly in bestowal? The answer to that question is found in the words of Rabash:

In order to understand the words of Rabash, we first need to explain the Kabbalistic definition of "love." Love, according to the wisdom of Kabbalah is bestowal, giving without a trace of personal benefit. When Rabash writes of love of the Creator, he means bestowal to the Creator. Each and every one of us has to attain that sublime degree. However, as we learned in the previous section of the lesson, the problem is that in direct work towards the Creator, we are incapable of examining ourselves. If we try to work in bestowal directly towards the Creator, we will inevitably be lying to ourselves and think that we are already in contact with Him.

A lie is not a superfluous matter. In general, nothing is superfluous in our world; everything in the world was created with great wisdom in order to bring us to actualize the purpose of our lives. A lie, as we've just learned, is a necessary step onto the path of truth. The thing is that in order for the lie to lead us to the truth we need to be aware of it.

The main problem in directly working towards the Creator is that a person might think he is already in contact with the Creator and be unaware of the fact that he is in falsehood. It is a type of honey trap. Everything looks so wonderful, so much so that there is no chance of escaping that state.

As long as we have not corrected ourselves and not yet acquired a certain measure of the quality of bestowal, the Creator is a completely abstract concept for us, which is why we are incapable of examining ourselves and checking – are we truly bestowing to Him? What is our approach towards Him? Are we truly clear of any turning to self in our connection with Him, in bestowal to Him?

On the other hand, in "Love of Friends," meaning in the attempt to bestow unto people around us, there is great virtue: we are unable to deceive ourselves. Unlike the Creator, people around us have a genuine and physical presence. They have their own desires, their own opinions and feelings. We can check in actuality, whether we are truly working with their desire as our own, if we are truly clear of turning to ourselves in relating to them and only want the best for them. As Rabash writes, we cannot deceive ourselves and think that we are bestowing unto them if it isn't really the situation.

This vital aspect in a person's spiritual work– examining our attitude towards others as a scale of our approach to the Creator, to the attribute of bestowal – is called "from love of the creatures to love of the Creator." Only out of the attempt to bestow unto others is it possible to attain revelation of the Creator. It is impossible to reveal the Creator directly. In order for us to learn to bestow unto Him, the Creator concealed Himself and left us in the company of other people like us, so that in the correction of our regard of them, we will reveal Him.

At this point, it is important to emphasize that correcting our attitude to others does not mean that we begin smiling to whomever we see, helping the needy or paying our taxes on time. The correction the wisdom of Kabbalah speaks of is internal, correcting the intention. No external action will help, as long as the intention behind the action is faulty.

Only in the work with others, can we check the extent to which we are in bestowal. If we discover that we are not in bestowal, rather that we are still acting out of the intention of self-benefit, we are already aware of the falsehood in which we exist and can turn to the Light that Reforms with a strong and scrutinized request for correction, acquiring the attribute of bestowal, connection with the Creator.

From now onwards, the path of truth begins.

Test yourself:
- What is the benefit in the work towards others instead of working directly towards the Creator?

"No-no"

Correcting the attitude towards others as a condition for revealing the Creator leads many students who are taking their first steps in the study of the wisdom, to think that the wisdom of Kabbalah is the teaching of ethics. We will devote the final part of the lesson to clarifying the difference between teachings of ethics and the wisdom of Kabbalah.

The world is a dangerous place to live. One doesn't need to be Albert Einstein to understand that. Yet, when the genius physicist was asked why, in his opinion, the world is a dangerous place, his answer shone with his unique brilliance and sharpness: The world is dangerous, Einstein said, not because of the people doing evil, but because of those who do nothing about it.

There is no point arguing with such wise and simple truths. It is clear to all that in order to eradicate evil, it is necessary to act against it. It does not matter how high we raise the fence around the villa, or how strongly we bar the windows; if we do nothing against the evil rampant out there, it will eventually reach our own living room.

Up to this point, everything is clear. The question is: what are we to do?

Seemingly, the answer is simple: We need to learn how to restrain our ego (the will to receive). Any logical person can see that. Indeed, throughout human history, many have pointed to the ego as the source of evil in the world. In fact, all of the various methods of ethics are based upon this perception. The more the ego proceeds to be revealed, thus it becomes increasingly clearer that it is the cause of all our afflictions. Allegedly, if only we knew how to restrain and limit it, we would be able to build a healthy society and live in a much better world.

However, human experience has taught us that the methods of ethics simply don't work. The method of correction according to the wisdom of Kabbalah is significantly different from all methods of ethics. If we know to distinguish the uniqueness of the method of Kabbalah, we will save ourselves unnecessary mistakes in studying the wisdom and know exactly what we need to do in face of the world's growing dangers.

According to methods of ethics, the solution to the growing ego is its suppression, mainly by mechanisms of punishment and societal opinion. It begins almost immediately from our birth – with the inevitable "no-no" of Mom and Dad – continuing until our dying day. Whoever steals, lies, hits, or acts against the general interest of society is punished, and "earns" a negative attitude from society. Simply put, that is the logic behind all methods of ethics.

The thing is that nothing we do to restrain the ego works. To the contrary, as time passes, the ego only proceeds to grow and the more we try to restrict it, it proceeds to intensify. It's just like the mythological monster whose beheading causes it to grow two new heads from within.

The reason for that is simple: According to the thought of creation, the desire to receive has its own plan of evolution and we have no way of stopping it. That is why the wisdom of Kabbalah, cascading down to us from the thought of creation does not deal at all with correcting the desire to receive itself. According to the wisdom of Kabbalah, it is impossible and unnecessary to correct the desire. The problem is not our nature, of receiving; rather the way we use it, for our self-benefit alone. In other words, the problem is not the desire, but the intention and that intention is what we need to correct.

In actuality, the Kabbalistic approach to working with man's will to receive is completely opposite from the approach of methods of ethics. Whereas methods of ethics speak of suppressing or diminishing the desire, Kabbalah specifically speaks of increasing the desire. A person studying the wisdom of Kabbalah feels his desire increasingly growing. He learns to recognize it in its full stature, intensity and glory, and in parallel, learns how to use it correctly and receive within the abundance promised to it at the thought of creation (see drawing #1). The more one reveals an increased will to receive with the goal of correcting it, one thus accelerates one's process of spiritual development, in accordance with the words of our sages: "He who is greater than his friend, his inclination is greater."

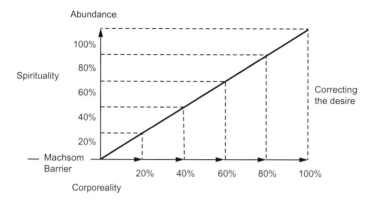

In summary, although the wisdom of Kabbalah speaks of correcting the relations among us, the Kabbalistic method of correction is completely different from methods of ethics. Kabbalah does not believe in punishment or suppression. According to the wisdom of Kabbalah, we will only be able to correct the relations among us by changing the intention and for that purpose, we have been given the wisdom of Kabbalah. No external solution will help.

There is yet another difference between the wisdom of Kabbalah and various methods of ethics: the wisdom of Kabbalah is a method for revealing the Creator to the creatures in this world. Unlike methods of ethics, it is not a method of correcting human society. The wisdom of truth has been given to us in order to elevate us to a much higher degree of existence than that of our world. According to the wisdom of Kabbalah, correcting the attitude to others is only a condition for revealing the spiritual world and not the goal itself.

There are other differences, as well. We'll touch upon them later in the course.

Test yourself:
- What is the main difference between methods of ethics and the wisdom of Kabbalah?

Lesson Summary

Main Points

- The Creator (the attribute of bestowal) is concealed from us. Hence, we are incapable of depicting what the attribute of bestowal is and become similar to it. For that purpose, we need another scale, one which is not concealed from us.

- The only way to check the extent of our similarity to the attribute of bestowal is our attitude towards others. People around us have tangible and actual presence. They have their own desires, their own opinions and feelings. Accordingly, we can examine in practicality if we are truly working with their desire as if it were our own.

- The expression "from love of the creatures to love of the Creator" describes the condition for revealing the Creator. Only in correcting the attitude of one to others, will the Creator be revealed.

Terms

Love – Bestowal, giving without a trace of calculation for self-benefit.
Love of the Creator – Bestowing unto the Creator.

Answers to the Questions

Question: Why can't we depict the Creator (the attribute of bestowal) correctly?
Answer: The Creator is concealed from us; hence, we can imagine Him as we please. We have no way of knowing if we have depicted Him correctly.

Question: What is the benefit in the work towards others instead of working directly towards the Creator?
Answer: In working with others, we cannot deceive ourselves. Unlike the Creator, people around us have tangible and actual presence.

They have their own desires, opinions and feelings. We can check in actuality, if we are truly working with their desire as if it were our own, if we truly love them and want only the best for them.

Question: What is the main difference between methods of ethics and the wisdom of Kabbalah?

Answer: The methods of ethics suppress the ego (the will to receive) and try to restrain it. In the study of the wisdom of Kabbalah, we learn to recognize the ego in all its intensity and formulate our corrected attitude towards others above it.

Logical Sequence
(Order of course development)

We have learned that the wisdom of Kabbalah is a method for revealing the Creator to the creatures in this world.

We have learned that in order to reveal the Creator, we need to shift the intention from in order to receive to in order to bestow.

We have learned that there is a special spiritual force embedded within Kabbalah books called the Light that Reforms, which has the power to shift our intention from in order to receive to in order to bestow.

We have learned that only through scrutinizing our attitude towards others, can we create within us a genuine request for the Light that Reforms.

In the following section, we will learn what the conditions are for scrutinizing the attitude towards others.

Part #2 - Free Choice

Lesson #1 – Do we have free choice?

In this lesson we will study the following: Do we have free choice? / The "Program" of the will to receive / The influence of environment on a person

Mind Boggles

Marcos Peter Francis Du-Sautoy is a professor of mathematics in the University of Oxford. In 2008, Du Sautoy went on his own televised journey. Accompanied with BBC television channel cameras, the professor underwent a series of various and strange brain tests, with the purpose of studying the limits of his consciousness and solving the simple yet unexplainable question, once and for all: Who truly is Professor Du Sautoy?

In one of the experiments, the professor was connected to a brain-wave scanner and asked to randomly press one of the two buttons placed in his hand. The scanner registered when the decision was made in the professor's brain and the computer registered when the button was actually pressed. The purpose of the experiment was to check how much time passes, if at all, from the time a decision is made in the brain until it is actively executed.

The results stunned the professor. No less than six seconds had passed between the moment the decision was made in his brain regarding which button to press and his hand actually pressing that same button. "Knowing that John (the researcher conducting the study) is looking into my brain and knows 6 seconds before me what I am about to do, before I am even aware of it myself," said the professor to BBC cameras in well-orchestrated shock, "is utterly shocking."

No less shocking and perhaps even more so is the following question, which also arose from the experiment: If the decision to press the button was made subconsciously, without asking for the professor's opinion, 6 seconds before he decided to actively press it, who actually pressed the button? In other words, do we have free choice, or perhaps we are the consequence of predictable neurological responses?

The Bookkeeper

In the second section of this study unit, we will deal with the issue of free choice. It is a topic of utmost importance in the study of the wisdom Kabbalah and in every person's life. Even if at first glance the topic seems philosophical or distant from our daily reality, we will soon realize that the opposite is correct.

A newborn baby has no free choice. He can only perform simple actions, such as eating, sleeping, eliminating waste, all of which are performed automatically. If he is hungry, he cries; if he is tired, he falls asleep. He is governed with no awareness of his own, by a system of internal attributes, with which he was born (with no choice of his own) in a predetermined and predictable way.

When the baby grows, he acquires new abilities. He can crawl and after some time also walk; he wants certain toys and isn't interested in others. It seems that he is already beginning to make conscious choices. However, looking deeper into the matter, we find that in actuality, nothing has changed. The toddler, who is still growing, is governed by a system of inner qualities with which he is born (with no choice of his own). Since he has begun to become aware of his surrounding, it begins influencing him as well (which is also with no choice of his own).

What about adults? Intuitively, we tend to think that adults have free choice, that one has one's own desires and thoughts. Yet, here as well, when we take a deeper look, we discover that the adult is also governed exactly the same way as the baby. The only difference is that his decision-making system is much more complex and that complexity creates in him an illusion of choice.

None of us chose when to be born and to whom. None of us chose our genes, according to which our inner qualities were determined, defining our character and inclinations, which inevitably greatly affect our decisions. None of us chose the environment in which we were raised and educated; the environment, which actually shaped us as adults, according to our inner qualities. It turns out that the answer to the question of what we choose is not at all clear.

If that weren't enough, surely none of us chose to be born with the nature of the will to receive, which actually governs us from within with decisiveness, according to a simple calculation: maximum pleasure at minimal effort. Like a hand in a glove, the will to receive does as it pleases with us. By its nature, it wants to be filled with pleasure and without asking us, it will always choose an action that will guarantee it maximum pleasure at minimal effort.

When we were in basic training we were told: "Whatever you're given, take it; if they hit you, run." Although it's a cliché, as all clichés, there is a grain of truth to it. Chasing pleasures and avoiding pain are the two basic attributes of all human beings. Although it may sometimes seem that there are people who run after pain, or that no pleasure interests them, it is only superficial.

Within each and every one of us sits a little bookkeeper, called "he it always calculates the profit and loss: the extent of investment needed (pain) compared to the extent of expected profit (pleasure). Whenever the calculation is positive, the bookkeeper will order taking action; whenever the calculation is negative, the bookkeeper will order not taking action.

At times, the calculations can be complicated; sometimes the bookkeeper will be willing to take a loss into account for a certain amount of time in exchange for future profit. For example, he will order a person to go and study engineering at the university for four years, work odd jobs, and live in student lodgings. However, upon completing his studies, he will have a respectable profession, and in the future – high income and honor for the rest of his life. All in all, it seems like a worthy deal.

An intermediate summary: We did not choose our inner qualities; we did not choose the environment in which we grew up; our nature, the will to receive, which governs us from the inside was also not our choice. As Baal HaSulam writes in his essay "The Peace: "This concept, expressed in that word, "freedom," remains unclear, and if we delve into the meaning of that word, there will be almost nothing left."

Yet, a person without freedom of choice is a like a bird without wings. There must be a point of choice; otherwise what is the purpose of all this commotion called "life?!" If a good and benevolent force created us – as Kabbalists who attained it write – it can't be that He created us as puppets on a string, without the ability to break free. That is not benevolence.

In short, the story is not so simple, or as the famous Jewish author Isaac Bashevis Singer expressed beautifully when he said: "We have to believe in free choice; we have no other choice."

Test yourself:
- Name three factors that influence our decision-making unknowingly.

Tell Me who your Friends are and I will Tell You who You are

Street musicians offering their musical merchandise to all interested are a common scene. We usually do not give them much thought. We seldom throw a coin in their box as a sign of gratitude. So it happened at the underground metro in Washington D.C. one January morning in 2007, when a young man wearing a cap, stood at the entrance to the metro and played the violin. Thousands of people passed by him, rushing to work. Most of them paid no attention at all. A few stopped for a moment to listen to the tune. Several of them put their hand into their pockets and threw a coin into the open violin case.

Not one of those thousands passing through the train station knew that the guy playing the violin was Joshua Bell, one of the best violin players in the world. His yearly income from playing violin is tens of millions of dollars. The value of the violin he held in his hands is approximately more than three and a half million dollars. Several days before the "concert" he gave at the subway, a crowd had filled one of the most prestigious halls in town in order to hear Bell play. Throughout the concert, the crowd gave Bell several long standing ovations.

The attitude towards Bell at the subway station was completely different. Over the hour Bell played at the subway station, there were $32 and a few cents in his violin case. No one applauded him, although the compositions he played were of the most complicated violin compositions.

Joshua Bell's performance at the metro was part of a social experiment conducted by one of the "Washington Post" journalists, in order to discover the extent to which public opinion affects our attitude towards high-grade art. The answer was clear: influence of public opinion is decisive. Bell's performance at the subway is also a good example of the topic we will clarify in this section of the lesson: influence of the environment on a person within the context of free choice.

In the previous section of the lesson, we learned that a person is a product of his innate qualities and the environment where he grew up and was educated. We also learned that the will to receive is a sort of inner program, which governs a person according to a simple calculation: maximum pleasure at minimum effort.

A person cannot choose his qualities; he cannot choose the environment where he is born; surely, he cannot choose whether to be governed by the will to receive, which will always prefer maximum pleasure at minimal effort. We cannot choose any of those, but at least, we can decide what pleasure is for us; what is good and what is bad. Is that our free choice?

In order to answer that, let's again remember how a baby develops. Parents lay the baby on his belly, so he develops his muscle tone. Then they place toys in front of him to tempt him to crawl. When he stands up, they clap with excitement to encourage him. Parents use a variety of aids to continually develop the baby. Without them and other environmental stimuli, the baby would not develop his capabilities.

The parents are the ones who decide for the baby what is good and bad for him. Although the baby makes his own effort to crawl and learns to stand by himself, without the intervention of the environment, without its encouragement and support, the baby would not develop properly.

And the adult, how does he develop? How does he determine values of good and bad? Exactly in the same way, by the environment. If the environment values a certain thing as good, we will also value it as good. If the environment does not value something as good (even the very same thing), we won't value it as good, either. Definite proof for this (one of many) is the attitude of the masses to Joshua Bell's violin playing at the subway.

Baal HaSulam explains [17] that human society to a person is like earth to a seed of grain. Just as the seed contains within it all the possible qualities of the plant and the earth is what determines how it will grow, so the genetic code of a person contains within it all the person's qualities and tendencies and it is the society, or more precisely, the values of society which determine how a person will develop his qualities. For example, a person with an inclination to paint, who was born in an environment that does not respect painters, is likely not to grow up to be a painter. A person develops his inclinations in accordance with the values of good and bad in society.

Likewise, a person has no choice in determining values of good and bad, either. The human environment in which a person lives is what determines the values of good and bad (see drawing #2). Baal

---

[17] The Writings of Baal HaSulam, "The Freedom" Essay.

Ha'Sulam explains it very well in the article "The Freedom:" "I sit, I dress, I speak, I eat, all of that – not because I want to sit in such a way, or dress in such a way, speak in such a way, eat in such a way. Rather, it is because others want me to sit, dress, speak, and eat in such a way. All of that is according to the desire and taste of the society – and not my free will. Moreover, I mostly do all of those against my own will, because it is more convenient for me to behave simply without any burden, except that I am enslaved in all my movements and chained in iron shackles, in the tastes and values of others, which are the society."

1. Innate attributes

Input

2. Environment
(Values
  of good
  and bad)

Output

3. Maximum pleasure
at minimal effort
(The program)

New studies show that the influence of the environment on a person is much greater than we imagine. In the book "Connected,"[18] Professor Nicholas A. Christakis and Professor James Fowler, senior researchers from Harvard University and California University described a tight and expansive system of connections among all the people around the world. It is a system that obligates us, without our knowledge, to behave, think, and act in a certain way.

Among other things, both researchers studied health and behavioral phenomena, within networks of social connections and found that the likelihood of a person gaining weight is very high if one's close friend gains weight. The researchers found that the decision to start smoking through a friend of a friend of a friend, meaning a person we don't know at all, raises our chances to start smoking by more than ten

---

[18] Connected: The surprising power of our social networks and how they shape our lives Nicholas A. Christakis, James H. Fowler, "Matar" Publishers

percent. Another examination revealed that happiness is contagious as well: when a person is around happy people – his happiness level rises.

Following those findings, the researchers proceeded to larger networks, consisting of millions of people and reached a conclusion taken from the animate world: humanity as a social network behaves like a super-organism, as one creature that grows and develops, within which different and various content flows and influences all members of the network. It turns out that our environment has a definitive influence upon our development and decision-making.

In conclusion: on the surface, it seems that a person in our world has no choice. We do not choose our innate qualities; we do not choose the environment where we are born and educated; we do not choose our will to receive, which governs us from the inside according to the calculation: maximum pleasure at minimal effort (see drawing #2). Moreover, we do not even choose the values of good and bad. The environment does that for us.

Test yourself:
- What is the comparison Baal HaSulam brings concerning the influence of the environment on a person and why?

The Irony of Fate

Before we expand our explanation on where exactly we do have free choice, we will clarify one more important issue concerning free choice in our world – the issue of fate.

The feeling that all of our life events are predetermined seems to have accompanied humanity from the beginning of time. The question of fate has engaged philosophers, the clergy, science, and culture throughout all generations, and much has been written on the subject. Some claimed that each person's fate is predetermined and cannot be changed, and others asserted that man was given the option of determining his fate, at least at certain points of choice.

What does the wisdom of Kabbalah have to say on the matter? Overall, in a few words:[19] "All is foreseen and freedom of choice is granted." Although for many, Rabbi Akiva's famous saying specifically highlights the contradiction between predetermined fate and free choice, the wisdom of Kabbalah explains to us that the words of Rabbi Akiva, a huge Kabbalist himself, describe the correct integration of the two with great precision. To further understand what is meant, we will first explain the Kabbalistic interpretation to the words "All is foreseen" and afterwards, we will clarify Rabbi Akiva's intention regarding "and freedom of choice is granted."

According to the wisdom of Kabbalah, the whole of creation, including our world as well, is integrated within one thought, which effected creation – the thought of creation to do good unto His creatures. Every creature, thought, or event that has happened, is happening, or will happen in our world and in the spiritual worlds – all cascade and stem from the thought of creation, as a part of the plan for its actualization.

All stages of the desire's cascading from the thought of creation to our world are predetermined. All stages of the evolution of desire in our world over billions of years are predetermined, as well as all stages of ascending from below upwards, in correcting the intention up to the end of correction. None of the stages can be skipped. It is taken for granted that the final goal is also predetermined and there is no other goal (see drawing #3).

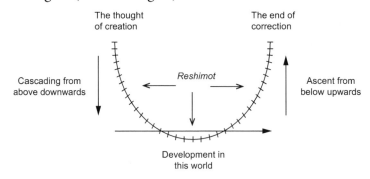

19 Talmud Bavli, Ethics of the Fathers, 3:15

The Creator, unlike us, does not need time in order to actualize His plans. That is why, as strange as it may sound, when the thought of creation to benefit His creatures emerges, it is instantly actualized. Kabbalists write that in actuality, we already exist in the end of correction and all we need to do is reveal that. In addition, not only the final state already exists, even all the stages up to its actualization are in existence at this very moment; we only need to reveal them.

Here's an explanation from a different angle to that same phenomenon: we are accustomed to perceiving our world in chronological order. For instance, I suddenly get an urge to cross the room to the other side; soon I will go to the other side and then I will stand on the other side. The perspective of the wisdom of Kabbalah is different, in essence. According to the wisdom of Kabbalah, the state where I am standing on the other side of the room already exists and it is what arouses the desire in me to cross the room and stand on the other side.

Another example: We are used to thinking that our Mom and Dad met each other, got married, decided to have kids and here we are. According to the wisdom of Kabbalah, the state in which we exist in the world as our parents' children already exists and since it must actualize, that is what caused our Mom and Dad to meet, get married, and bring us into the world.

All states of development from the thought of creation until the end of correction are predetermined. It only seems to us that we make something happen. In fact, the predetermined plan of development is what causes the different conditions to be revealed one after the other.

The sum of all our states of development, organized and revealed one after the other according to a predetermined plan are called "*Reshimot*" by Kabbalists. In other words, "*Reshimot*" are informative data, in which the individual plan of development of each and every one of us is defined. Each "*Reshimo*" determines a certain state of development we must go through. At every given moment, a new "Reshimo" awakens, causing a new emotion. Our entire life and all of reality are "*Reshimot*" traversing through us and materializing, in accordance with the thought of creation.

In summary: All events of reality are predetermined as stages in a plan that must be actualized. They already exist; we only need to reveal them. Every event that has happened in our lives or in the lives of others, every thought or desire which has aroused in us or in any other creature are all predetermined and will inevitably materialize as a part of the plan to actualize the "*Reshimot.*" In Rabbi Akiva's words: "All is foreseen."

If so, what is "and freedom of choice is granted?" The answer is simple: All our stages of development up to the end of correction are predetermined. What isn't known is the way in which we will experience them; will we do so slowly and through suffering, or quickly and joyfully? That is the authority given to us. It is at this point that our free choice is found.

How exactly is the development hastened and switched from a military stretcher journey to a joyful adventure? More on that in the next lesson.

Test yourself:
- According to the wisdom of Kabbalah, what is predetermined and what is our free choice?

Lesson Summary

Main Points
- Our innate qualities, the environment where we were born and educated and the will to receive that will always prefer maximum pleasure for minimal effort influence every decision we make, without us being aware of it.
- Society's value system influences the person without his awareness, in determining his personal value system, consequently also influencing his decision-making.
- All stages of the development of desire are predetermined. Every thought, desire, or occurrence happening in our world

is written in a predetermined plan of development in a predetermined order. The authority given to us is to choose how our stages of development will be revealed, upon the ascent from our world to the spiritual world: through suffering and slowly or joyfully and quickly.

- The total states of our development, arranged and revealed one after the other according to a predetermined plan are called "*Reshimot*" in the wisdom of Kabbalah.

Concepts

Reshimot - informative data in which the personal plan of each and every one of us is defined. Each "*Reshimo*" determines a certain state of development we must go through.

Answers to the Questions

Question: Name three factors that influence our decision-making unknowingly.
Answer: 1) Our innate qualities; 2) The environment; 3) The calculation of the will to receive: maximum pleasure at minimal effort.

Question: What is the comparison Baal HaSulam brings concerning the influence of the environment on a person and why?
Answer: Baal HaSulam compares the influence of the environment on a person to the influence of the quality of soil on the growth of a plant. Just as the quality of the earth determines how the plant will develop, so the society's value system determines how a person will develop his innate qualities and actualize his desires.

Question: According to the wisdom of Kabbalah, what is predetermined and what is our free choice?
Answer: All stages of the development of the will to receive are predetermined, in its cascading from above downwards, development

in our world and ascent from below upwards to the end of correction. We have the freedom to choose how we will develop in the ascent from below upwards: through suffering and slowly or joyfully and quickly.

Lesson #2 – Choosing an Environment

In this lesson we will learn: The factors shaping our development / The importance of the environment in a person's spiritual development / How to choose an appropriate environment for spiritual development / What "freedom from the angel of death" is.

Four Factors

After learning that our free choice is in the way we participate in our process of development – through suffering and slowly or joyfully and hastened – it is time to be even more precise in describing the point of choice and explaining how we hasten our development in practice and turn it into an adventure.

In order to describe where the point of our free choice is found with further precision, we will first clarify the four factors dictating the development of every creature, as depicted by Baal HaSulam in the article "The Freedom." The model of development mentioned above is true for all forms of existence in reality: still, vegetative, animate, and man. Becoming familiar with these four factors will help us understand where exactly we have free choice.

First Factor – The Source, the First Matter. In our world, nothing can be created from absence. Our world is a world of consequences (the spiritual world is a world of causes), accordingly, everything in our world takes its form from something else. Ice is formed from water molecules, a plant stems from a seed, and we are a product of our mother and father.

The formation of something from something else is actually a process in which a particular essence sheds its previous form, and assumes a new form. Hence, for example, a molecule of water (the essence) turns from liquid (water) into solid (ice). The essence that strips its previous form and dresses in a new form is a type of unit of information, containing within all of the information on the creature's future stages of development, which develops from within up to its final state. For example, a tomato seed contains within all the information of the plant and fruit which will develop from it. This essence, at the base of every process of development, defining it, we will call "source."

Our source as human beings is the genetic burden we received from our parents, grandparents and ancestors. The "package" we were bestowed from our ancestors defines not only our external form, but our personality as well. All ideas, thoughts, opinions and knowledge our ancestors acquired, strip off their previous form and appear in us as potential, awaiting realization, as inner tendencies that will also become, with time, our perception of life.

Second Factor – Unchanging Attributes. Any source is actually a collection of certain attributes intended to emerge from the potential into practice. Some of these attributes are unchangeable. Their plan of development is predetermined and precisely defines the future form they will obtain. For example, a seed of wheat will grow and inevitably become wheat and never oats; a giraffe's fetus will develop into a giraffe and never become a lion.

Similar to the still, vegetative, and animate, our internal tendencies inherited from our ancestors will also inevitably develop into a matching perception of life and not into any other direction. For example, a person born with a tendency to write music will not develop into a politician out of that tendency. He may grow up and, in the end, become a musician, and he may not. He might be a successful musician or not, but one thing is clear, his tendency for music will not push him towards a career in politics.

The development of a certain attribute into a way of life mainly depends on the environment where a person grows up and develops. It is similar to a seed of wheat planted in the ground: It is clear to all that only wheat can grow from it, yet the quality and quantity of the wheat inevitably depend on the environment in which the seed develops, meaning the quality of the ground. We are like the seed. Our innate attributes will only develop in one direction. A tendency for concessions, for example, will develop in a person into a moderate and forgiving perception of life, except that its development directly depends on the environment where we are raised and educated. This dependency leads us straight to the third factor.

Third factor – Changing Attributes. Just as in every source there are attributes, with a plan of development which is predetermined and unchangeable, there are also attributes, in which the plan of development is not predetermined and they may change throughout their development, according to the influence of the environment upon them. For example, the height or quality of the wheat to develop from a seed of wheat could change, according to the environment where the plant develops; meaning according to the quality of soil, amount of water, sunlight, etc.

As abovementioned, the tendencies we inherited from our ancestors could develop in different measures or not develop at all, as a result of the influence of the environment upon them. For example, if a certain person is born with a tendency for stinginess, the environment in which he is brought up may develop the quality of stinginess at different measures and shape him as a stingier or less stingy person.

Except that a human being is capable of more than that. Unlike any other creature, a person can even completely uproot a certain tendency from within. For example, that same person born with a tendency for stinginess can uproot it from within, on the condition that the environment where he is raised grants him enough security for his existence and does not value stinginess as a positive quality.

Fourth Factor – Alien Factors. An additional factor dictating the development and stages of development of every creature is the influence of alien factors upon the development of the source. Every source develops in a certain environment which directly influences its development. That is what we learned when we detailed the previous factors. Rather, the immediate environment of the developing source also exists within a broader environment influencing it, and consequently also influencing the development of the source. Accordingly, for example, climate changes caused by global warming could damage the proper development of the seed of wheat.

Likewise, we, human beings, surely exist under the influence of our immediate environment, which is also under the influence of a broader environment indirectly influencing our development. For example, the state of global economy or various fashions popular with the public could influence the development of tendencies we inherited from our ancestors. The tendency for stinginess that we brought as an example could be enhanced during times of financial crisis.

Those are the four factors dictating the development and stages of development of every creature. In everything regarding the first factor, the source, we have no freedom of choice. Our source is embedded in us even before our birth and no one asks us if we would like it or not. In the other three factors, which are all based on the choice of the correct environment for development, we have freedom of choice. We can choose the suitable environment for our development and turn it from the path of suffering to a fascinating adventure.

How exactly do we choose an environment and under what conditions? More on that in the following sections.

Test yourself:

- List the four factors which shape the development of every creature.

The Path to Pleasure

It was in the early evening hours, as darkness began to cover the east coast of the United States. Those were the golden radio days – the end of the 1930's. The voices heard that evening from the CBS radio station sounded at first like just another dreary broadcast, transmitted according to the ceremonious rules, in a slightly over-dramatized voice. It was seemingly an ordinary evening, but as the newscaster continued with his reports, fear and trepidation spread across the United States and the apparent innocent evening became one of the most defining events in the history of the American nation.

What happened that night? The CBS radio station broadcast a staged radio play of a violent invasion of aliens from Mars. The radio play was broadcast as a series of news flashes sounding so credible, that the listeners were convinced of their accuracy. The result was mass panic. Many citizens suffered from anxiety attacks in fear of the unexpected invasion and began running from their homes. Women fainted upon hearing the news. In many cities, residents took to the streets and screamed desperately for help. In New York, a rumor was spread that the aliens were about to attack the city with gas and the entire city was horrified. Not an hour had gone by and the hysteria had spread like wildfire throughout the continent. Even when the radio announced (according to the prewritten script) that the aliens were destroyed by bacteria, the storm did not fade. Only hours later, when it turned out that the news had been fabricated, did life gradually return to its routine.

The fabricated news flashes that had been broadcast by Orson Welles in the framework of a radio play based on the book "War of the Worlds" is brought to this day as an example of the power of mass media and the contagious influence of the environment upon a person. If the environment we live in communicates anxiety, we will also be anxiety stricken. And the other way around, if the environment creates a joyful atmosphere, we will be "sentenced" to happiness, as well.

We have expanded a great deal on the strength of the environment in this study unit. The influence of the environment upon a person has determinant importance in one's spiritual development. Actually, our free choice is the choice of the environment. Only through that, will we be able to change the process of development in which we exist, from the long path of misery to a challenging and enjoyable path. All the rest is predetermined and there is no room for free choice. That is what we learned in the previous lessons.

As long as a person's point in the heart has yet awakened, one is governed down to the level of the atom by the will to receive and with no awareness: chasing pleasures the environment has defined as valuable. Only after the point in the heart has awakened in a person and one begins developing within the desire for a connection with the Creator, will an opening appear to begin the work on actualizing free choice.

With the awakening of the point in the heart, a person discovers an empty space which he cannot fill. All the pleasures the will to receive chased no longer satisfy him. He is seeking something beyond it. What exactly? It's not clear to him yet. Although the feeling of emptiness discovered along with the point in the heart is not pleasant, it is specifically there that the opportunity to actualize one's free choice for the first time is embedded, breaking free from the will to receives' control.

The point in the heart eradicates all of the former values that society has inculcated in a person. Whatever around him was valued as good is not good enough for him. In a sense, he is like a newborn, a "clean slate," ready to absorb within new values from the environment. Except that now, for the first time in his life, as opposed to whatever had happened in the past, he has an opportunity to determine the values according to which he will act, by **himself**. His only possibility to do so is to choose an environment, for which attaining spirituality is its supreme value. Hence, it is clear why our free choice is in choosing the environment.

In a society which determines that receiving=pleasure and bestowal=pain, we have no control over our lives, because that is exactly what our will to receive claims. There is nobody to object to these determinations. In such a society found in endless pursuit after corporeal pleasures, people exchange one pleasure for another and pursue every pleasure determined by the society, with no awareness.

When the society asserts that bestowal = pleasure, a disagreement arises between the will to receive, that objects to this assertion and the values of society. That is a good disagreement, for now a person has two options. The individual, who had been enslaved to his will to receive now faces another option: to prefer bestowal over reception. This conflict creates our place of independence, the place of free choice. In this space, each one is free to express his desire to bestow from within.

Imagine you have received a new car. You get on the road and begin to drive. On the road, there are signs directing to "Pleasure" or "Emptiness," naturally, you only choose the roads leading to "Pleasure." It doesn't occur to you to visit "Emptiness." All the other cars on the road also choose to drive to "Pleasure." No car takes the turnoff to "Emptiness."

After years of driving following the signs of "Pleasure," you reach the conclusion that there is no genuine pleasure there. You seek a solution. But since all the other cars on the road continue to choose the road "Pleasure" and since you don't see any other direction you can drive to, you must choose theirs. You are at a dead end. In "Pleasure," there isn't really any pleasure and you are incapable of driving to "Emptiness."

The only way to break through the dead end is to change the environment. If you could exist in an environment where other drivers turn to "Emptiness" and explain to you that the signs directing to "Emptiness" are an illusion and in actuality, they direct you to a wonderful, new and unique place, unlike any other, a place of endless pleasure, indeed you would also have the option of arriving there.

Test yourself:
- When does the option for free choice open before a person? Explain why.

Since we are in an Environment

Though the allegory concluding the previous section clearly illustrates the state of being with the awakening of the point in the heart, it could be misleading with regard to choosing the environment. From the allegory, it seems that a person should change his existing environment and choose a new one. The truth is – and in this case it is very important to emphasize that we are not required to change anything externally.

In order to choose the correct environment, we are not required to move elsewhere, or detach ourselves, God forbid, from our immediate environment. All our work in choosing the environment is in parallel, to build an environment, parallel to the one we live in, where spirituality is the most important value.

Just as a piece of iron is attracted to a magnet, so a person whose point in the heart has awakened is attracted to an environment of additional people who want spirituality as he does, drawn to the correct books and a teacher who will guide him how to study. He hasn't yet chosen this environment and surely doesn't engage in building it; he was led to it without being asked. Only now, after he has reached the place where he can develop, he is given the option of building his spiritual environment and raising it, out of free choice.

The work in building the spiritual environment is divided into two areas:

1) Building the environment in one's internality.
2) Building the environment in one's externality.

Just like in any other area in the study of the wisdom of Kabbalah, the work in internality is more important than the work in externality, but the external work is necessary in order to succeed in the internal work. First, we will describe the work we have to do in building an environment internally and afterwards we will describe the work in externality.

According to the wisdom of Kabbalah, every person in essence is a will to receive and our social environment no more or less than a collection of desires. Our goal in building the spiritual environment is to increase our desire for spirituality. The greater our desire for spirituality is, so we will be able to raise the importance of spirituality over corporeality. The issue is that each one of us begins the spiritual journey with a point in the heart, which as it is called, is a small point, a small desire. In order to increase it and build within us the importance and longing for spirituality, we need to acquire others' desires; to build inside us a spiritual environment, which prefers the spiritual to the corporeal.

It is delicate work, requiring great attention. We need to locate the inner desire leading our friends to the spiritual path and be impressed with that, in particular, raising the importance of that desire above the external image perceived in us through our five senses. This work is done completely within us. In order to perform it, we are not required to carry out any external action, rather great sensitivity is needed, which proceeds to be acquired along with the study of the wisdom of Kabbalah.

In summary: We need to accumulate within us a great desire for spirituality and we build it through connecting to our friends' desires for the spiritual path. We thus construct the spiritual environment within us and choose the correct environment.

There is also work in choosing the external environment as well. We can also acquire additional desire for spirituality through the organized study of the wisdom of Kabbalah in any Bnei Baruch framework for studying, from reading Kabbalah books, self-paced courses on KabU, or surfing the kabbalah.info website. The books and websites are also a part of our spiritual environment. In our free time, we have the option to choose them.

Regarding the importance of choosing an environment, Baal HaSulam[20] writes in unambiguous words: "The one who exerts during his life, and chooses each time in a better environment – then he is worthy of praise and reward… not because of his thoughts of good deeds, that come to him without his choice, but because of his effort to gain himself a better environment which brings him the better thought, and deeds. And this is what Rabbi Yehosha Ben Parchaya: Make yourself a Rav, and buy yourself a friend."

Another way to build a spiritual environment is participating in the dissemination of the wisdom of Kabbalah. It is written "In the multitude of people is the King's glory."[21] The larger our spiritual environment will be in quantity of people, so its influence upon us will grow and in parallel, the importance we have for spirituality will increase. Participating in the dissemination of the wisdom of Kabbalah as a means for spiritual advancement is unique to our generation, for it is the first time in history that all of humanity needs to begin ascending to spirituality.

We will expand on the importance of disseminating the wisdom of Kabbalah as a means for spiritual development at the end of the third study unit.

---

[20] The Writings of Baal HaSulam, "The Freedom" essay.
[21] Proverbs 11:28.

Test yourself:
- Briefly describe the work of choosing an environment, in its internal and external sense.

On Life and Death

To conclude this lesson, a few words on our famous friend, whose head is a hollow skull, hands hold a scythe, with a hood over his head – it turns out that he is also connected to freedom of choice.

In order to avoid unnecessary misunderstandings, we will begin straight from the end: "The angel of death" according to the wisdom of Kabbalah is no more or less than the "will to receive." The famous character coming to claim our lives, dressed in a long robe may exist in horror movies, but has no place in the wisdom of Kabbalah.

An "angel," according to the wisdom of Kabbalah is a force through which the Creator governs creation. "Life," according to the Wisdom of Kabbalah is feeling spirituality and "death" which separates us from feeling genuine life, is as abovementioned, the will to receive, or more precisely, the intention of in order to receive.

What is the connection between the intention of in order to receive (the angel of death) and freedom of choice? The connection is simple: our true freedom to choose exists in emerging into freedom from the control of the intention of in order to receive. In other words, our true freedom is in becoming free of the angel of death. As long as we are under the control of the intention of in order to receive, it governs us from within, without asking us, like a hand in a glove and we have no free choice.

Correcting the intention of in order to receive and acquiring the intention of in order to bestow directly depend on the choice of environment, meaning on the spiritual environment we need to build. It clearly follows why our free choice is in the choice of environment. In actuality, throughout the study of the wisdom of Kabbalah, we will discover that choice of the environment is not only a condition for attaining spirituality; rather it is the spiritual work itself. For, it is in the choice of the environment where are free choice exists.

It is correct to interpret the words "freedom from the angel of death" literally, as ascending above the temporary and lost existence in our world to a degree of eternal existence. What does that refer to? Baal HaSulam writes that the method of working with the will to receive in our world, with the intention of in order to receive for ourselves causes pleasure that is received within the desire to cancel the desire. The best example of it is food (pleasure) which cancels the appetite (desire). Yet, even pleasure obtained after much exertion, such as the pleasure from a new car or a respectful position, dissipates after some time, since the pleasure cancels the desire, and without the desire, pleasure cannot be felt.

This constant pattern of pleasure entering a desire and canceling it eventually leads to general desperation from the pursuit after pleasure. As a result, the will to receive gradually diminishes and we diminish with it, until it dies and so do we along with it.

As children, we are full of curiosity, charged with unending energy to discover the world. Everything is new, everything is exciting. As teenagers, we want to devour everything, climb every mountain top, reach every destination, change the world. Yet, as a person matures, he fulfills a portion of his desires and gives up reaching others. Spiritually speaking, he ages, meaning his desires are weakened and gradually disappear, until no desire is left in him.

This is how it sounds in the words of Baal HaSulam:[22] "However, when half a person's life is through, begin the days of the decline, which, by their content, are his dying days. This is because a person does not die in an instant, just as he did not receive his life in an instant. Rather his candle, being his ego, withers and dies bit by bit… For he begins to relinquish many possessions he had dreamed of in

---

[22] The Writings of Baal HaSulam, "The Freedom" essay, Freedom from the Angel of Death.

his youth… until in his real old age where the shadow of his death is hovering above him, exists a person in days he did not desire at all, for his desire to receive, meaning his ego, diminishes and leaves."

Freedom from the angel of death, meaning the work with the intention of in order to bestow instead of the intention of in order to receive changes the picture completely. Instead of the desire being filled momentarily with pleasure and the pleasure extinguishing the desire, the pleasure traverses through the desire with the intention to bestow it unto others. In this form of work, we can convey through us all the pleasures existing in the world, and the desire won't ever be extinguished. We can receive limitlessly and the flow of light within us raises us to a state of eternal life.

A person who has corrected his intention to receive and is in spirituality does not identify his existence as the existence of his corporeal body. He continues to exist in the corporeal body, yet the spirituality he attains constitutes a much higher degree of existence for him, which is not dependent on his corporeal body, and he identifies with that. He continues to live in that, even after corporeal death. Rav Baruch Ashlag used to say that death is like changing a shirt, one takes off one's used shirt (the corporeal body) and puts on a new shirt (if one's soul needs to reincarnate into this world in a new body).

Test yourself:
- What is "freedom from the angel of death?"

Lesson Summary

Main points
- Four factors dictate the development of every creature; source, unchanging factors of the source, changing factors in the source and external factors.

- Our freedom of choice is choosing an environment that will influence our development positively (development of the source).
- The option of free choice opens before a person when the point in the heart is revealed. The new desire for spirituality eradicates all former values society inculcated in a person, enabling him to determine for himself, through the environment, a new scale of values where bestowal is more important than reception.
- Choosing an environment means increasing the desire for spirituality from the impression of others' desires for spirituality, along with setting a study framework, reading Kabbalah books, watching TV programs on the topic, and so on.
- Our true free choice is in choosing to escape from the control of the will to receive. Escaping the control of the will to receive directly depends on the environment where we choose to be.

Concepts

Life – Feeling the light in the vessel.

Angel – A force through which the Creator governs creation

Angel of death – The intention of in order to receive, which prevents us from feeling spirituality – genuine life.

Answers to the Questions

Question: List the four factors which shape the development of every creature.

Answer: a. The source– The informative part defining all the stages of a creature's development; b. Unchanging Attributes – Attributes in the source which are unchangeable; c. Changing Attributes – Attributes in the source that are changeable; d. Alien Factors – Influence of the distant environment on the development of the source.

Question: When does the option for free choice open before a person? Explain why.

Answer: The option for free choice opens before a person with the awakening of the point in the heart. The new desire for spirituality eradicates all former values that society inculcated in a person and enables him to start determining for himself, through the environment, a new scale of values where bestowal is more important than reception.

Question: Briefly describe the work of choosing an environment, in its internal and external sense.

Answer: Choosing the environment in the internal sense is increasing the desire for spirituality from one's impression with others' desire for spirituality. Choosing the environment externally means determining a set study framework, reading Kabbalah books, watching a TV programs on the topic, etc.

Question: What is "freedom from the angel of death?"

Answer: Freedom from the intention of in order to receive. The intention of in order to receive is what prevents us from the feeling of genuine life, the spiritual life, which is why it is called "angel of death" in the wisdom of Kabbalah. Correcting the intention from reception to bestowal thus releases us from the grip of the "angel of death" and grants us the feeling of spiritual life.

Logical Sequence
(Order of Course development)

We learned that the wisdom of Kabbalah is the method for revealing the Creator in this world.

We learned that in order to reveal the Creator, we need to change our intention from in order to receive to in order to bestow.

We learned that in Kabbalistic books, a unique spiritual force is embedded within, called the Light that reforms, which is able to change our intention from in order to receive to in order to bestow.

We learned that only through scrutinizing our attitude towards others, can we create within us a genuine request for the Light that reforms.

We learned that only by choosing the correct environment for spiritual development, can we scrutinize our attitude towards others with precision.

In the next section, we will learn what the spiritual roots of choosing the environment are.

Part #3 - Worlds and Souls

Lesson #1 – The Five Worlds

In this lesson we will learn: The four phases of Direct Light / The five spiritual worlds / Where the spiritual worlds exist

Light Creates the Vessel

In the previous sections of this study unit, we dealt with the question of free choice. We clarified the topic from the reality of life in our world, from the wisdom of Kabbalah's unique angle. In the third and last part of this study unit, we will set aside the reality of life in our world for a moment and delve into the structure of the spiritual worlds. Becoming familiar with the structure of the spiritual worlds and the process of their formation will enable us to understand in greater depth the reality in which we operate and the issue of free choice.

We will start from the beginning – the thought of creation is to do good unto His creatures. Stemming from correcting the desire, Kabbalists attain that the Creator is the will to bestow; a force of giving, whose sole purpose is to grant others with the goodness within Him. That is why the Creator creates a created being, a will to receive that will receive His goodness. Hence, the beginning of creation is in the Creator's thought to do good unto His created beings. This thought is the cause and the plan for all of creation.

The will to bestow is called **"Light,"** the **will to receive** is called **"vessel."** The will to receive was created by the will to bestow in a developmental process of four phases, called "four phases of Direct Light." In these phases, the Light builds the vessel so that it will be worthy of receiving the abundance.

The process begins with phase 1 – a point where the vessel is created and filled with Light and ends at phase four – with the desire of the created being to ascend to the Creator's degree and attain the greatest pleasure existing in creation (see drawing #4). At each of the developmental phases, the vessel acquires and adds acertain discernment, up to the fourth phase, where it becomes a worthy vessel for receiving the Light.

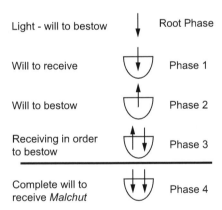

Light - will to bestow		Root Phase
Will to receive		Phase 1
Will to bestow		Phase 2
Receiving in order to bestow		Phase 3
Complete will to receive *Malchut*		Phase 4

Before the four phases, there is an operational plan, called "the thought of creation to do good unto His created beings." It is the thought existing at the root of creation; hence it is also called the "Root phase." The root stage is actually the will to bestow, which proceeds to emit from itself the will to receive in these four phases of development.

The first phase of the will's development is called "Phase 1." At this phase, the will to receive is full of Light. The Light creates a vessel, the will to receive (see drawing #4), which completely matches the Light that created it, so that the Light fills the vessel and brings it pleasure.

When the will at phase 1 feels that the Light reaching it, is from someone giving it the Light, it realizes that true pleasure is not found in receiving, rather in bestowing. As a result, it begins to desire to give. This is a new phase in the development of the desire, called "Phase 2" (see drawing #4). At phase 2, the will to receive wants to receive pleasure from giving rather than from receiving. At phase 1, the will to receive was created, whereas in phase 2, the will to bestow was created.

The will to receive at phase 2 wants to bestow. The question is, can it bestow? The answer is no, since it has nothing to bestow, nothing to give. The only source of abundance in creation is the Creator. The created being can only receive the abundance, but is incapable of giving anything of oneself. Thus, the will to bestow at phase 2 is mere desire; it isn't clear how it may be actualized.

The solution to the problem rests within the Creator's nature. The Creator wishes to give and in order to actualize His desire to give, He created the will to receive – because without the desire to receive, the Creator could not bestow. It follows that the will to receive of the created being is essentially what the creature can give to the Creator. The only way for the created being to bestow is to receive from the Creator the goodness He wishes to give him. Except, that he has to receive not for his own sake, but for the Creator's sake, in order to enable the Creator to actualize His desire to bestow.

And so he does. The will to receive receives from the Creator in order to bestow unto Him and this receiving is called "Phase 3" (see drawing #4). At phase 3, the will to receive receives, thus bestowing back unto the Root phase, the Creator. At this point, a perfect circle is created, where all bestow: the Root phase (The Creator) bestows unto the will to receive (phase 1), and the will to receive, after going through phases 1,2 & 3, bestows back unto the Creator by receiving from Him. At phase 3, the action is receiving, as in phase 1, yet its intention is to give, as in phase 2.

At phase 3, the will to receive bestows in practice and feels for the first time what it is to be like the Creator, what it is to bestow. Remember, "Creator" in the wisdom of Kabbalah is "will to bestow" and the only way for the creature to feel the Creator, to become familiar with Him and understand Him is to perform an action of bestowal, like Him. Such an action is performed for the first time at phase 3.

Phase 3 feels what it is to be like the Creator and as a result, a new desire awakens in it, it wants to receive the pleasure being revealed at the stature of the Creator; it wants to enjoy all that exists and the Creator, Himself. This new desire is called "Phase 4" and it is the final desire created (see drawing #4).

Unlike phase 3, the desire at phase 4 does not wish to bestow and does not calculate its steps concerning the degree to which it can bestow. It is interested in one thing only, to derive pleasure, and from everything – including, and mainly from the Creator Himself, the pleasure being revealed from being at His stature.

Imagine that an opportunity opened to you to know all of the secrets of creation, all the connections connecting different parts of reality, to control every single detail and direct all of creation to your benefit. The first lottery prize would be "small change" compared to the opportunities opening up before you. Who wouldn't agree to that?

That is how, from the limited angle of perception of our world, we can depict the pleasure of being like the Creator. In spirituality, things are surely felt completely otherwise; only when we attain them, will we know what it is about. However, this imaginary example can help us somewhat understand what the desire revealed at phase 4 actually is.

To conclude, we will briefly review the entire process: Root phase, the will to bestow emits from itself phase 1, the will to receive and fills it with Light. Phase 1 feels that there is a Giver of the Light and wants to become similar to Him and bestow, thus creating phase 2. In order for phase 2 to actualize its desire to bestow, it receives at phase 3, only in order to enable the Root phase to actualize Its desire to bestow. When phase 3 feels in practice what it is to be like the Creator, it also wants to receive within it all of the pleasure revealed in the stature of the Creator. This new desire is phase 4, also called "Malchut."

Phase 4 is the will to receive that was created. All of the previous phases are not considered the will to receive, rather discernments in the Light preceding the emergence of the will to receive. The will to receive at phase 4 is the creation that the Creator created: within it we see the still, vegetative and animate of our world, along with the still, vegetative and animate of the spiritual worlds. Every detail in our world and every detail in the spiritual worlds is the will to receive in essence (see drawing #5).

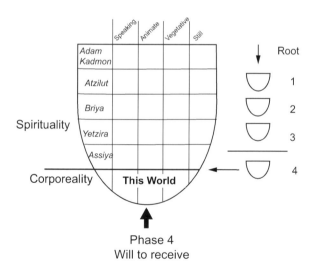

Phase 4
Will to receive

At this point, it is important to clarify that the will to receive at phase 4 is not yet the created being that can correct itself and attain adhesion with the Creator. It still has to go through many stages of development in order for such a created being to be created from it.

Test Yourself:

- Briefly summarize the five phases of creating the will to receive.

Five Worlds

The primary condition for creating a created being that will be able to receive the goodness the Creator wants to give him is the created being's independent desire to receive the goodness. Indeed, it is impossible to do good unto someone forcefully, without his will. The will to receive needs to want the goodness the Creator wishes to give it on its own. It would seem that such a desire was created in phase 4; however creating the desire in phase 4 (as the entire process of development of the will to receive) is done without the creature's awareness of it. Over the 4 phases of Direct Light, the Light emits from itself the will to receive mechanically, with no participation of the will.

The created being's independent desire is possible only in a reality where the Creator is concealed from the created being. As long as the Creator is revealed to the created being, one will annul oneself before Him. The matter is similar to the parent-child relationship in our world – as long as the children are under their parents' authority, they cannot be truly independent.

There is yet another way to describe the necessity for concealment. In order to awaken within the created being an independent desire for pleasure promised to it with the thought of creation, the feeling of pleasure needs to fill it once and then dissipate. Only under such conditions, can a desire for pleasure be formed. Even in our world (according to the law of roots and branches) similar conditions exist.

For example, in order for a desire for a certain type of food to arise in us, we must feel its flavor once and only after the taste dissipates, will our own desire for that flavor arise in us.

Accordingly, after the emergence of the will to receive at phase 4, the Creator distances the will to receive from Him, through a system of five worlds. The system of worlds gradually conceals the Creator from the will to receive. The word "World" (*Olam* in Hebrew) is from the word Concealed (*He'alem* in Hebrew). Thus, down to the reality of this world, where the will to receive has no feeling of the Creator; the Creator is completely concealed from it.

The five worlds emerge according to the structure of the 4 phases of Direct Light. Opposite the Root phase, the world of *Adam Kadmon* emerges; Opposite phase 1, the world of *Atzilut* emerges, opposite phase 2, the world of *Beria* emerges; opposite phase 3, the world of *Yetzira* emerges and opposite phase 4, the world of *Assiya* emerges(see drawing #6). Below the world of *Assiya* is our world.

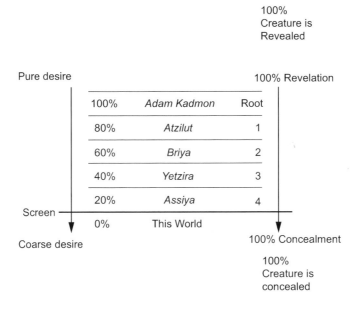

The five worlds are, as abovementioned, five phases of concealing the Creator's Light (pleasure) from the will to receive. In the world *Adam Kadmon*, the will to receive feels 100% of the pleasure; in the world of *Atzilut*, it feels 80% of the pleasure; in the world of *Beria*, it feels 60% of the pleasure; in the world of *Yetzira* it feels 40% of the pleasure; in the world of *Assiya* it feels 20% of the pleasure and in this world - 0%. In our world, we don't feel the Creator at all, and particularly from this state can an independent desire be created within us for connection with Him.

It is important to emphasize that the Light itself does not change, as Kabbalists write to us, "the Light of *Ein Sof* is in the state of absolute rest."[23] Only the vessel – the will to receive is what changes and accordingly, it feels one simple light in different forms.

In the cascading of the five worlds from Above downwards, the will to receive reveals more and more the extent to which its nature is opposite the Light. Light is the will to bestow, whereas he is the will to receive. This opposition, being revealed more and more with the cascading of the worlds, conceals the Light in increasing measures, up to complete concealment. In the whole world, the will to receive becomes coarser, thicker and submersed deeper into the receiving nature. Upon reaching this world, the nature of receiving controls it completely, totally concealing the Light from it. (see drawing #6).

As abovementioned, the emergence of the five worlds takes place according to the structure of the 4 phases of Direct Light. In fact, every part of creation is constructed according to the four phases of Direct Light. The four phases and the root phase preceding it are a type of fundamental model, according to which all of creation and all its parts are constructed.

Accordingly, each world is also divided into five internal parts, called "*Partzufim*" (Faces) and each *Partzuf* is divided into 5 parts as well, called *Sefirot*. It follows that the spiritual worlds are divided into 125 parts, according to the following calculation: five worlds times five *Partzufim* in each world, times five *Sefirot* in each *Partzuf*. These 125 steps are the 125 spiritual steps, cascading from Above downwards, upon which we will ascend on our way back up, from below upwards.

---

[23] The Writings of Baal HaSulam, TES, part 1, Inner Light, p.9, letter 2

Test Yourself:

- Describe the structure of the spiritual worlds and write what caused the emergence of the worlds.

Everything is Internal

One of the greatest concerns of people studying the wisdom of Kabbalah, especially new students, is that spirituality is unattainable, that its pursuit is like the endless pursuit after the perfect fairy tale princess. However, spirituality is much closer to us then we imagine. Particularly since it is so close to us, we do not see it. It is like a speck of dust on our glass lens, hidden from our eyes, precisely because it is so close to us.

The truth is that the spiritual worlds are much closer to us even than that speck of dust. In order to attain spirituality, we don't need to drive anywhere, not even walk, stretch out our hand or make the tiniest motion outwards. The spiritual worlds simply do not exist outside of us. Just like any spiritual discernment and spirituality itself, the spiritual worlds exist inside of us.

There is no world outside. Even the corporeal world is actually an internal picture depicted within us (as we learned in the first unit). Each of the five spiritual worlds is an inner discernment in our desire, a state in which we exist to a higher or lower measure of connectedness with others and connection with the Creator. To the extent that we connect to others in ties of true love, we reveal the spiritual worlds and ascend through the worlds of *Assiya*, *Yetzira*, *Beria*, *Atzilut*, and *Adam Kadmon*, up to the end of correction. Without man revealing the worlds, there are no worlds.

"We aren't saying anything new," stated the great Kabbalist of the 18th century, Rav Menachem Mendel of Kotzk, "all our work is in illuminating what is embedded within man." All degrees of the corrected connection with others, from the smallest to the greatest, already exist as potential in each one of us. They are only awaiting being revealed. Similar to a baby, who, in accordance with his development reveals his concealed abilities: sitting, walking and speaking, similarly a person developing in spirituality reveals at each stage of his development tighter ties of bestowal between him and others, and accordingly he ascends the spiritual steps and attains within him the connection with the Creator more intensely.

Kabbalists have written that we all already exist in the corrected state. All that remains for us is to reveal it. It is difficult for us to understand, but the Creator is not limited by time, space or motion; hence there are no limitations upon Him in order to actualize His thought of doing good unto His creatures. The moment the thought of doing good to His creatures appeared, it was also actualized. We already exist in the corrected state, yet in order to reveal for us to reveal it in all intensity and glory, it has been concealed from us.

All the stages of development in creation have been summarized by Kabbalists in three main stages: stage 1- The thought of creation: stage 2 - correction of creation; stage 3 – the end of correction, the purpose of creation (see drawing #7). At the end of correction, we are connected to each other in ties of love and bestowal, and in the single mutual desire, when connected together, the Light of the Creator shines. In order for us to attain this state to its fullest depth, it is concealed from us and we need to reveal it from concealment, in what is called the correction of creation.

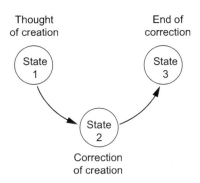

Thought
of creation

End of
correction

State 1

State 3

State 2

Correction
of creation

The Kabbalist Baruch Shalom HaLevi Ashlag, Baal HaSulam's eldest son, portrays a fine allegory on this matter. Imagine, he writes, that a rich uncle from overseas has deposited one million dollars in a bank account under your name, but has requested to hide that important information from you, until the conditions ripened to notify you of it. You live your life with no knowledge of the money. And then, one fine day, you get a phone call from the bank, informing you of the hidden treasure. The money had been there all along, the only thing that changed is your knowledge. Similar to the money, (though very different) is the end of correction – we are already there, only we are not aware of it. We need to reveal it.

Revealing our corrected state occurs gradually, in our ascent from world to world, from this world up to the world of *Adam Kadmon*. Ascending the spiritual steps is done by correcting the will to receive, from using it with the intention of in order to receive, to using it with the intention of in order to bestow. In correcting the desire, we acquire a suitable vessel for receiving the Light.

Time after time, we correct another part of the desire, until the entire desire is corrected and all the pleasure the Creator intended for the created being in the thought of creation shines within. The correction of the intention from receiving to bestowal occurs by drawing the Light that reforms during the study of the Wisdom of Kabbalah (We will expand on that in the third study unit.)

In summary, in order to develop within us an independent desire that is as large and refined as possible, the Creator conceals Himself behind the five spiritual worlds. To the extent the desire is corrected from in order to receive to in order to bestow, by means of the Light that reforms, we ascend back up through the spiritual steps and merit spiritual pleasure.

Test yourself:

- Where do the spiritual worlds exist and how does a person ascend their steps?

Summary of the Lesson

Main Points
- The light creates the will to receive in a four-step process, called four phases of Direct Light.
- Phase 4 in the 4 phases of Direct Light is the will to receive that was created, and all its preceding stages are discernments in the Light.
- In order to enable the created being an independent desire, the Creator distances the will to receive from Him through five spiritual worlds (*Adam Kadmon, Atzilut, Beria, Yetzira* and *Assiya*) until this world, a place where the Creator is completely concealed from it.
- All the spiritual worlds are within a person. The spiritual worlds are revealed to us in the correction of the will to receive with the intention of in order to bestow. In correcting the desire, step by step, we climb through the spiritual steps of the spiritual worlds up to the end of correction.

Concepts

Light- Will to bestow
Vessel- Will to receive
4 Phases of Direct Light- The process of creating the vessel from the Light.
Malchut- The will to receive that was created in the four stages of direct Light.

Answers to the Questions

Question: Briefly summarize the five phases of creating the will to receive.
Answer: Root phase: The desire of the Creator to bestow unto the created beings. Phase 1: Will to receive. Phase 2: Will to bestow. Phase

3: Will to receive in order to bestow. Phase 4: Desire to enjoy from the stature of the Creator.

Question: Describe the structure of the spiritual worlds and write what caused the emergence of the worlds.

Answer: The uppermost world is the world of *Adam Kadmon,* after which emerges the world of *Atzilut,* and after it the worlds of *Beria, Yetzira* and *Assiya.* Below the world of *Assiya* is this world. What caused the emergence of the worlds is the necessity to conceal the Creator from the created being. The five spiritual worlds are actually the increasing degrees of the Creator's concealment from the created beings.

Question: Where do the spiritual worlds exist and how does a person ascend their steps?

Answer: All the spiritual worlds exist within a person. The spiritual worlds are various degrees of the corrected desire with the intention of in order to bestow. In correcting the desire step by step, we ascend the steps of the spiritual worlds.

Lesson #2 – The Souls in the Worlds

In this lesson we will learn: The Soul of *Adam HaRishon*(The First Man) / The Sin of the Tree of Knowledge

The Soul of *Adam HaRishon* (The First Man)

In the previous lesson, we learned how the Light yields the will to receive in four phases of Direct Light. We also learned how, according to the structure of the four phases, the five spiritual worlds cascaded from above downwards, concealing the Light from the will to receive.

The picture seems to be clear: The Creator conceals Himself through the five spiritual worlds, so that the created being in this world will reveal Him, while ascending those same worlds. The thing is that the reality of the created being in this world, yearning for spirituality, inevitably obligates a reality of a spiritual creature opposite it. Opposite the corporeal branch in our world, expressed as a desire for spirituality, there has to be a spiritual root. This root has yet to be revealed in the emergence of the four phases of Direct Light and the five spiritual worlds. This lesson is on the emergence of this spiritual root, called "The Soul of *Adam haRishon.*"

In the creation of the vessel out of the four phases of Direct Light, there is no reality of a created being, as yet. In the four phases of Direct Light, only the will to receive was created, which is the matter of creation. The created being himself has yet to emerge from it. In the cascading of the worlds from above downwards, there is no reality of the created being, either. In the emergence of the five spiritual worlds, only the suitable environment for creating a created being was formed, for him to be able to correct himself by means of the study of the wisdom of Kabbalah. The created being himself has yet to be created. The five spiritual worlds are no more than an inanimate environment, where it would be possible to create the created being.

Indeed, following the emergence of the spiritual worlds, the created being was created. Of course, it is not about a human being in our world, rather a spiritual discernment - a particular part of the will to receive, whose purpose is to reach equivalence of form with the Creator. He was created in the world of *Atzilut* and is called "The Soul of *Adam haRishon*" (see drawing #8).

At this stage of studying, where our knowledge in the wisdom of Kabbalah is not expansive enough, we will not be able to understand what the inner essence of *"Adam haRishon"* is; from which part of the will to receive he was created and under what conditions. For now, we will have to suffice with the following definition: "The Soul of *Adam haRishon*" is a certain part of the will to receive, in which all of its parts are connected together in ties of bestowal and love, working together, as one body.

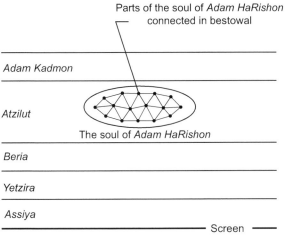

This World

In simpler words, the Soul of *Adam haRishon* is a desire that works in bestowal. It is a desire whose parts are all interconnected with the intention of in order to bestow and they operate as unified parts in one system. In this single system, in the connection of all its parts, the one single Light is revealed - The Creator.

The best example in our world of a similar system is the human body. The human body, like the Soul of *Adam haRishon* is also comprised of many parts, cells and organs, all of which are connected together and work according to the calculation of the general benefit of the body. In the human body, the connection among all its parts also creates wondrous perfection, which is not found in each separate part.

The Soul of *Adam haRishon* is actually our corrected state; a state in which all human beings are connected together as a single body, in ties of bestowal and love. The question arises: if the desire already exists in its corrected state, in the Soul of *Adam haRishon*, why is the existence of man in this world necessary, one who needs to correct his desire by means of the study of Kabbalah? For what purpose has our flawed state been imposed upon us, if we already exist in the corrected state?

In order to answer this question, we need to backtrack a little, to phase 1 in the four phases of Direct Light. In phase 1, similar conditions to those revealed in the Soul of *Adam haRishon* were also revealed, and the same question arises in that regard. When we are more familiar with the state revealed at the first phase, we will be able to understand why, with the emergence of the Soul of *Adam haRishon*, the process of correcting the desire does not end.

At the first phase, the will to receive was created. The root stage emits from within, phase 1 as the will to receive, in order to be able to fulfill its desire to bestow. It fills the desire to receive with Light, thus realizing its own desire to give. Similar to the Soul of *Adam haRishon*, at phase 1, all the conditions for realizing the thought of creation also seem to exist: there is a Creator Who wishes to bestow goodness and there is a created being to receive His abundance. What else is missing?

The answer is simple: Independence is missing. The will to receive in phase 1 was created in a unique state; it was created with the Light within. The deficiency and fulfillment are revealed simultaneously and as a result, the fulfillment cancels the feeling of deficiency. It is similar to the feeling of satiation we feel in our world when a meal (the fulfillment) extinguishes the feeling of the appetite (deficiency).

In other words, at phase 1, there isn't really a feeling of deficiency, of desire. The Light cancels the vessel, thus the will to receive does not feel its reality. It is unaware of itself and is certainly unaware of the Creator external to it. In such a state, the thought of creation cannot be actualized, for there is no independent desire to receive the Light, yet. As we learned, such a desire is the basic condition for actualizing the thought of creation.

The goodness that the Creator wants to give the created being is to elevate him to His degree, to the highest possible level of awareness: to be like Him, to know the general plan of creation in all its details, the thought of creation itself. However, the will to receive at phase 1 is in a completely opposite state; it is not aware of itself, at all. The pleasure fulfilling it also cancels it and it has no sense of its reality. That is not being like the Creator. Therefore, the process of developing the desire continues.

As abovementioned, a state similar to phase 1 is revealed in the Soul of *Adam haRishon*, too. The Soul of *Adam haRishon* was created into a state of bestowal, being full of Light. It never felt what the state opposite to bestowal is, and as such, it cannot feel what true bestowal is. In a sense, it is also as in phase, unaware of its state.

The purpose of creation is, as we've stated is to elevate the created being to the degree of the Creator; meaning for him not only to be in a state of bestowal, but to attain the thought underlying this state and know how to maintain it himself. In order for the created being to be able to reach that high degree, the soul of *Adam haRishon* shatters in a process called "The sin of *Adam haRishon*." When we connect all its shattered parts together, we do not only reconstruct the corrected state of connection where we already existed, rather we acquire the intellect that maintains this state, the thought of creation itself.

We will expand on the shattering and its results in the following part of the lesson.

Test Yourself:
- What is the Soul of *Adam haRishon*?

Six Hundred Thousand Souls

Man is the only creation in the world that is not in bestowal. All of the still, vegetative, and animate abide completely to the one law of nature governing creation. They all act in total harmony as one body, always for the benefit of the single body - all except man. Man is the only creature in the world operating counter to the laws of nature. That is why he suffers.

That's strange. Why us, in particular? What is the purpose in creating such a developed creature as us and throwing him into our world, only for him to get on the highway with his worn-out vehicle time after time, having to drive against the direction of traffic; Who derives pleasure from all that?!

Not me, that's for sure. It is very likely that it's not you, either. However, if we stop for a moment and try to understand the logic behind this absurd theatre, we will find that things could not have been arranged otherwise. Only from this oppositeness, can all the goodness promised us in the thought of creation be revealed.

Though the still, vegetative and animate in our world exist in bestowal and total harmony, they are not aware of it. Just like puppets on a string, the Creator governs them from the inside, according to the laws of creation and they do not ask why. "Angels," so they are called in the wisdom of Kabbalah - forces with which the Creator governs creation. The still, vegetative, and animate have no independence and have very little awareness of their state, if at all.

"Man was created to raise the skies," said Rabbi Menachem Mendel of Kotzk. Similar to other Kabbalists, the words of Rabbi of Kotzk are also deeper than any ocean and in order to truly understand them, we need to attain his degree. However, we will not be mistaken if we conclude from his words that we were not created to be puppets on a string.

Man is the only creation that is opposite in nature to the attribute of bestowal, because particularly from this oppositeness, is it possible to ascend to the highest degree of creation. If we learn to ascend from a state of separateness to a state of bestowal, not only will we be in bestowal and harmony with all of creation, rather on our path to the corrected state, we will also acquire the intelligence governing creation and be able to maintain that state on our own.

The purpose of creation is to do good unto the created beings and the goodness intended for us is to ascend to the degree of the Creator, know the plan of creation down to its finest details and maintain it. In order to attain that, we need to contain within us the entire chasm between complete receiving and complete bestowal. Only through the study of the separateness, is it possible to attain the whole. Hence, man has to be born in our world under the control of the will to receive and particularly from this oppositeness, ascend from separation to connection, from receiving to bestowal.

In order to enable these conditions, the soul of *Adam haRishon* was created in the world of *Atzilut* in its corrected state and then shattered. Each one of us human beings, is a result of the shattering of the soul of *Adam haRishon*. In each one of us, there is a Divine spark, a small part of that same shattered soul and our mutual mission is to reconnect all those "sparks" into one soul, as we were connected together in the soul of *Adam haRishon*.

With the shattering of the soul of *Adam haRishon,* the connection of bestowal and love was broken, which connected all of its parts. As a result, in our world, connection among us is broken, as well. We live in a reality of separateness and from this reality, by means of the study of the wisdom of Kabbalah, we need to attain the connection we once had. Rather, this time, we need to attain it consciously, out of an independent desire.

In order to understand in greater depth the work we need to perform in the ascent from our world to spirituality, we will expand our explanation some more, regarding the spiritual process called the "shattering of the soul of *Adam haRishon*." We will begin with an important clarification: *Adam haRishon,* created in the world of *Atzilut* is not the same first man who lived in our world 5,772 years ago and was the first to reveal spirituality. Those are two completely different discernments. The Soul of *Adam haRishon* in *Atzilut* is a spiritual discernment, who, G-d forbid, has no corporeal form. The first man in our world was a live human being.

Adam haRishon, created in the world of *Atzilut* is that same first Adam appearing at the beginning of the Book of Genesis. All *Torah* (Bible) stories, as all the other holy writings, are actually descriptions of spiritual discernments. The sin of the Tree of Knowledge mentioned in the Torah and the exile from the Garden of Eden essentially describe the spiritual process called the "shattering of *Adam haRishon*."

As abovementioned, with the shattering of *Adam haRishon*, the connection of bestowal which connected all its parts was broken. Consequently, Kabbalists write, *Adam haRishon* was divided into six hundred thousand shattered parts of the soul, which fell from the world of *Atzilut* to the worlds of *Beria, Yetzira*, and *Assiya* (see drawing #9). Each shattered soul in the spiritual worlds is also divided into several sparks of the soul, which fell to our world. These sparks of the soul are the points in the heart, awakening in each and every one of us.

Each one of us has a sliver of a spark of desire from the soul of *Adam haRishon*, which desires to return to unity, connection with the Creator, spirituality. We need to reconnect these desires into a single desire, as we were once connected before the shattering. Since in the ascent from below above, we will connect out of our own conscious free will, we will attain the connection with the Creator in all its depth.

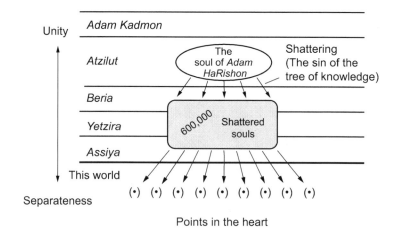

Points in the heart

This is how Rabash put it: "Each of them had a spark of love of others, but the spark could not ignite the light of love to shine…so they agreed that by uniting, all the sparks together would become one huge flame… And when one has great strength, he can execute the love of others. And then he can achieve love of the Creator."[24]

Test Yourself:
- Why was the soul of *Adam haRishon* shattered?

From Above Downwards and Back

As promised, we will conclude this study unit putting together all the "parts of the puzzle" we have studied into one broad and comprehensive picture. One to one, we will put all the main parts comprising the reality in which we operate in their place, in the ascent from below upwards. It is all with a particular emphasis on the importance of the environment and the matter of free choice.

In the essay "The Essence of the Wisdom of Kabbalah," *Baal HaSulam* writes: "The wisdom of Kabbalah is a sequence of roots, which cascade by way of cause and consequence, by fixed, determined rules, interweaving into a single, exalted goal described as "the revelation of His Godliness to His creatures in this world." Meaning, the Wisdom of Kabbalah is the wisdom of the sequence of development of creation from beginning to end. It teaches us what the thought of creation is, how it is realized and how we take part in its realization.

Kabbalists are people who have corrected their intention from receiving to bestowal and as a result have attained spiritual reality. They write for us, out of their attainment that the thought at the foundation of creation is

"to do good unto the created beings." They also write that this goodness is expressed in a state called "*Dvekut*," (adhesion) when the

---

[24] The Writings of Rabash, part 1, "One Should Always Sell the Beams of His House," Essay No. 9, 1984, "According to What Is Explained Concerning "Love Thy Friend as Thyself," Essay No. 7, 1984

created being equalizes his form to the form of the Creator and they both become as one.

Indeed, the goodness promised us in the thought of creation is to ascend to

Indeed, the goodness promised us in the thought of creation is to ascend to the degree of the Creator, to become like Him.

The basic condition to actualizing the purpose of creation is for the created being to have an independent desire to actualize it. It might seem to be a simple matter, except that such an independent desire is possible only in a state where the created being is free (seemingly) from the control of the Creator. That is why, in order to enable such a reality, the Creator distances the created being from Him through a system of five Worlds, called "Adam Kadmon," "Beria," "Yetzira" and "Assiya" up to the reality of this world, where the created being no longer feels the presence of the Creator.

In the process of being distanced from the Creator, the created being comes to recognize his own nature as opposite the Creator and this recognition is what distances him from the Creator. In each world cascading from above downwards, the will to receive becomes increasingly coarser and thicker, until it is revealed in this world in its coarsest and thickest form, furthest from the quality of bestowal. Only from this oppositeness, the created being is able to develop a desire of his own for *Dvekut* (adhesion) to the Creator.

The control of the will to receive and the feeling of separateness in our world is the corporeal result of the spiritual process, called "The shattering of the soul of *Adam haRishon*." The soul of *Adam haRishon* is the spiritual root of the created being in our world. It was created in the world of *Atzilut*, as a desire whose parts all work in bestowal, and then shattered. The connection of bestowal and love that connected all of its parts shattered. As a result of the shattering, the soul divided into six hundred thousand souls, which fell to the worlds of *Beria, Yetzira*, and *Assiya*.

Out of every shattered soul in the worlds of *Beria, Yetzira*, and *Assiya*, the sparks of the soul fell to our world. Those sparks are the points in the heart, the desire for connection with the Creator embedded within every person in our world. Throughout tens of thousands of years, the points in the heart were awakened in relatively few people; those are the Kabbalists of past generations. In our days, when the will to receive has exhausted all of the stages of its development in our world, the point in the heart is starting to awaken in many people, leading them to the study of the wisdom of Kabbalah.

The entire process of evolution of creation, from the thought of creation up to the awakening of the point in the heart takes place mechanically, according to a predetermined plan and of no choice from the side of the person. Throughout this entire complex process, the Creator arranges all the conditions for the person's spiritual development. He does that without asking us.

Then, when the point in the heart awakens in the person, it leads him to a place where the wisdom of Kabbalah is studied. At this point, the rules of the game change completely. From this point on, the Creator will not advance a person even one step forward, without desire from the side of the person, himself. For the first time, a point of free choice opens before him. (See drawing # 10).

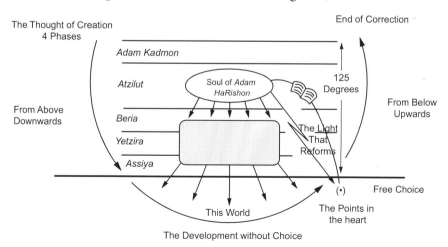

The Development without Choice

167

Until the awakening of the point in the heart, we do not have choice. As long as the desire for spirituality has not awakened in us, we are governed from within by the will to receive, which will always prefer maximum pleasure at the least effort, and always for one's own benefit. This cold and "financial" calculation is done by the will to receive according to two factors, which are also forced upon us without our choice: our inherent tendencies along with the scale of values of good and evil determined for us by society.

When the moment arrives and the point in the heart awakens within a person, the equation changes. The values society has defined for him as good are no longer good enough for him. He finds inner emptiness. He is no longer drawn to the goals society considers as good and worthy. The new desire for spirituality awakened in him cannot be fulfilled within the framework of this world and the other desires being awakened in him will no longer satisfy him.

This emptiness entails great tidings. It is this feeling in particular that enables a person to redefine the values of good and evil and this time out of free choice. From now on, he can choose between corporeality and spirituality; meaning, whether to be in an environment that raises the value of internality and spirituality or to be in an environment that worships the opposite values.

Our free choice is in choosing the suitable environment for spiritual development. Our work in this environment is to connect to the other points in the heart comprising it and together compose one great collective desire for spirituality.

Connecting all the points in the heart to one *Kli* (vessel) is performed by the Light that Reforms (see drawing #10). A person cannot rise above the calculation of self-benefit on his own and connect to the desire of others as if it were his own. Only the Light that created the *Kli* can correct it. In the words of our sages: "I have created the evil inclination (the intention of in order to receive), I have created the spice of Torah."[25]

The Light that Reforms influences us when we read Kabbalah books describing our corrected state in the Soul of *Adam haRishon*. However, It influences us only on the condition that we demand the right correction: connecting us for the sake of revealing the Creator in the shared *Kli*.

In the connection of all the points in the heart together, we ascend the 125 spiritual steps (see drawing #10). At each step, we correct another part of the will to receive with the intention of in order to bestow and connect further, until we renew the shattered connection of the soul of *Adam haRishon*.

Within the renewed connection, we reveal the Creator, the quality of bestowal. The single Light shines within the single *Kli*.

Test Yourself:

- Describe three main pivots in the actualization of the thought of creation.

Lesson Summary

Main Points

- The spiritual root of the will to receive awakened in us in this world is called "The soul of *Adam haRishon*." It was created in the world of *Atzilut* in a state where all of its parts are united in bestowal, connected to each other in ties of bestowal and love as one body.
- In order to attain the corrected state of the soul of *Adam haRishon* and the thought of creation behind it, the soul of *Adam haRishon* shatters and our work in ascending from our

---

[25] Talmud Bavli, Kidushin 30:72

world to the End of Correction is to reconnect all its shattered parts in ties of bestowal and love.

- The thought of creation is to do good unto the created beings. In order to realize it, the Creator conceals Himself from the created being by means of five spiritual worlds and shatters the soul of *Adam haRishon*. As a result of the concealment and shattering, we exist in this world in a reality of separateness, without any connection with the attribute of bestowal. When the point in the heart awakens in a person, he is ready to begin reconnecting the shattered connection with the other parts of soul of *Adam haRishon*. He does that by drawing the Light that Reforms, while studying Kabbalah books, until all the shattered parts of the soul are unified in one connection, where the Creator is revealed.

Concepts

The soul of *Adam haRishon* - a spiritual discernment- a particular part of the will to receive, where all the parts of the soul are connected in ties of bestowal and love. *Adam haRishon* was created in the world of *Atzilut*.
The Sin of the Tree of Knowledge – the shattering of *Adam haRishon*. The disconnection of ties of bestowal which connected all its parts.
Six hundred thousand souls - the shattered parts of the soul in the worlds of *Beria, Yetzira*, and *Assiya*.
Torah - the Correcting Light.
Mitzva (precept)– the correction of a part of the desire is called "performing a Mitzva."

Answers to the Questions

Question: What is the Soul of *Adam haRishon*?
Answer: The Soul of Adam Rishon is our corrected state; a state in which all people are connected together, as one body, in ties of bestowal and love.

Question: Why was the soul of *Adam haRishon* shattered?

Answer: The soul of *Adam haRishon* was shattered in order to enable us to build the connection among its parts anew and attain our corrected state out of an independent desire.

Question: Describe three main pivots in the actualization of the thought of creation.

Answer: a) The cascading from above downwards. In order to enable the will to receive to actualize the purpose of creation, the Creator distances himself through a system of concealment of five worlds: *Adam Kadmon, Atzilut, Beria, Yetzira,* and *Assiya.*

b) Development in our world. The will to receive in our world proceeds to develop, up to the revelation of the point in the heart, the desire to renew the connection with spirituality, with the Creator.

c) The ascent from below upwards. The ascent through 125 steps of the spiritual worlds, while correcting the will to receive from the intention of in order to receive to the intention of in order to bestow, in the connection of all shattered parts of the soul of *Adam haRishon.*

Logical Sequence
(Order of course development)

We have learned that the wisdom of Kabbalah is a method of revealing the Creator to the created being in this world.

We have learned that in order to reveal the Creator we need to change our intention from in order to receive, to in order to bestow.

We have learned that in Kabbalah books a special force called the Light that Reforms is embedded, which has the power to shift our intention, from in order to receive, to in order to bestow.

We have learned that only by scrutinizing our attitude towards others, can we create within us a genuine request for the Light that Reforms.

We have learned that only by choosing the correct environment for spiritual development, can we scrutinize our attitude towards others.

We have learned that the points in the heart are the shattered parts of the soul of *Adam haRishon* and that by creating a spiritual environment with other points in the heart, we create the request for correction, for connection of the shattered parts and summon the Light that Reforms.

In the following unit, we will clarify in detail how to create the request for correction.

Study Unit #3 - The Work of Man

About the Study Unit "The Work of Man"

The study unit "The Work of Man" deals with clarifying one's inner-spiritual work. In this work, all components of studying the wisdom are combined together: the purpose of the study, the correct attitude towards studying, perception of reality, Kabbalah books, the attitude towards states being revealed on the spiritual path, structure of the spiritual worlds and more.

The unit is divided into three sections:

- There is none else besides Him - the connection between man and the Creator. Clarifying the states being revealed on the spiritual path.
- The path of Torah and the path of suffering - the work with the will to receive in the scrutiny of the request for correction.
- Israel and the nations of the world - the order of correcting the will to receive.

This study unit aims to:

- Provide an in-depth explanation of man's spiritual work in internality and externality.
- Grant a deeper understanding of the importance of the environment in spiritual development.
- Introduce additional basic concepts in the wisdom of Kabbalah.
- Review concepts that have been covered in the previous study units.

Within the framework of study, we will define the following concepts: faith, *Shechina* (Divinity), recognition of evil, the path of

Torah and the path of suffering, Israel and the nations of the world, purity and coarseness, the Land of Israel and the Soul of *Adam haRishon*.

Part #1 - There is None Else besides Him

Lesson #1 - One Force

In this lesson we will learn about: Coalescing and attributing all events in reality to a single source / How to correct the desire

A Text Message from the Creator

We will open the third study unit with a joke.

Imagine an exceptionally hot and humid day in the middle of August. It's hot, very much so, enough to drive someone crazy. A person is driving around in his car in the streets of a big city; he's been looking for a parking space for half an hour already and hasn't found one. The a/c in the car is broken. His shirt is soaked with sweat and he is late for an important meeting. He's about to explode.

In torment, the driver raises his eyes to the sky and prays: "Creator, if you get me a parking spot, I'm willing to do whatever you want: donate to the poor, contribute to the synagogue, fast on Yom Kippur. Anything, whatever you want."

The moment he completes his sentence, a parking spot opens up right in front of his office. He immediately raises his eyes back to the sky and says: "It's ok, I managed."

One of the basic principles in the study of the wisdom of Kabbalah is called "There is none else besides Him." According to this principle, the initial and essential condition for every action on a person's spiritual path is to coalesce and attribute all occurrences in reality to one source, the Creator. The main aspects of this important work are detailed expansively in the essay also titled "There is none else besides Him," one of the most prominent of Baal HaSulam's essays. The first part of the third study unit is based entirely on this important article.

Kabbalists are people who have corrected their vessels of receiving and as a result, attain the spiritual world. They attain that there is a single force governing all of creation, one of giving and love and they call this force, "Creator." In their books, Kabbalists write us that the Creator's will to do good unto His created beings is what generates all of creation and leads it step by step, according to a predetermined program, until His will to do good unto His created beings actualizes.

The process of the created being's development up to attaining the thought of creation to do good unto His created beings is divided into three parts (see drawing #1):

The cascading of the spiritual worlds from above downwards, from the world of *Ein Sof* to this world.

The development of the will to receive in this world over six thousand years, until the point in the heart awakens.

The ascent from below upwards in the spiritual worlds, until correcting the entire will to receive and actualizing the thought of creation.

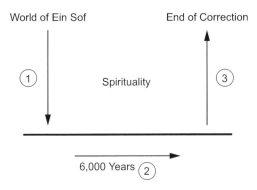

The three stages described above and all the infinite occurrences revealed as they manifest in the order of cause and consequence - all cascade from the single thought to do good unto His created beings, from the one Creator governing creation. There is nothing incidental in reality. All occurrences in reality, whatever they may be, cascade directly from the thought of creation with the purpose of drawing the created being closer to actualizing the purpose of creation.

To sum up, all occurrences in reality stem from one source and direct towards one goal, to do good unto the created beings. It might seem that there is no big discovery here, as for hundreds of millions of believers around the world, this perception is a way of life. However, if we delve deeper into the matter, we will find that there is a message concealed behind the words, which is not at all easy to digest, almost unbearable.

What is meant by that? According to the principle "There is none else besides Him," the source of all occurrences in reality is the Creator. Rather, "all occurrences in reality" mean the bad events as well and even the most horrific and terrible ones - and this truth is difficult for us to accept: robbery, stealing, rape and murder. Ahmadinejad -from the Creator, war and destruction - from the Creator, Stalin - from the Creator. Every horror scene presented to us on the stage of history for tens of thousands of years in history is all from the Creator.

Clearly, such a perception of reality sets some complications before us (an understatement). How could we justify such an attitude!? It is simply unperceivable.

Not only that, but Kabbalists write that this entire horror show has been performed from the Creator's will to do good. How can such a claim be perceived?

Now, we can understand to a certain extent, how the work of "There is none else besides Him" is not easy. "There is none else besides Him," according to the wisdom of Kabbalah, means to attain in practice the feeling that a single good and benevolent force governs the entire creation. No "lip service" will help here. According to the wisdom of Kabbalah, the feeling in the heart is our inner truth, and as long as we feel bad, we are convicting the Creator instead of justifying Him.

In other words, in order to actualize the words "There is none else besides Him" in practice, we have to achieve a distinct feeling that a single force governs all of reality, and all His deeds are absolute goodness. We don't need to dig into the depth of our heart to realize how far we are from that feeling. It is enough to open the evening news and be forever surprised (if indifference hasn't overtaken us yet) at the horror movie we live in - it is not "the good and benevolent."

Rather, the difficulty in attributing all the evil in creation to the good and benevolent Creator is not the only challenge in the work of "There is none else besides Him." In fact, if we examine ourselves, we will find that we even have trouble attributing the good occurrences in creation, not to mention all those countless moments that are neither good nor bad, all of those meaningless moments comprising the routine of our life.

Attributing every occurrence to a single source, the Creator, is the primary foundation of the world perception called "There is none else besides Him." According to the wisdom of Kabbalah, whenever we don't do so, we are worshiping other gods - idol worshiping. Who are the idols we are worshiping? The answer is incredibly simple: All those we blame for the evil revealed to us. Be it the driver at the intersection, the boss at work, or the enemy from a hostile country.

If the driver in the intersection honks me and in return I yell at him instead of attributing the situation to the Creator, I am an idol worshiper. Who is the idol I am worshiping? The driver honking me. He ruins my mood and it seems to me I have something to settle with him. Another example: if the boss at work makes my life miserable and deep inside I wish he got fired, instead of attributing this situation as well to the single force governing reality, I am worshiping idols. What idol am I worshiping? My boss. I am confined within the illusion that he is making my life miserable.

"Nature is not forsaken in its march," writes Rav Kook[26] "neither is history widowed in its entanglement. Within it lives a mighty Redeemer, Master of all deeds, the Righteous in all the generations. The moves are set and orderly, and everything grows ever brighter." Every occurrence taking place in our life, whatever it may be comes to us from the Creator in order to draw us closer to Him. Our work in "There is none else besides Him" is to attribute everything to the single source governing all of creation, even the events that seem to distance us from the spiritual path.

Every thought popping up in our mind, every desire awakening in our heart, every event taking place in our life, are actually a call from the Creator to re-establish the connection with Him. In renewing the connection with the Creator, we are instantaneously rescued from the blinding routine to the place where we truly live. As long as we live without asking about the purpose of our life, we are like puppets on a string; being led through the paths of life without having been asked. The thought of the Creator, the purpose of creation and where I am in relation to it, is an invaluable precious gift, an opportunity to emerge into genuine life. The Creator is sending you a text message every moment, won't you answer?

Test yourself:
- What is the work in "There is none else besides Him" and what are the difficulties revealed in this work?

I am the First and I am the Last

In the initial stages of studying the wisdom of Kabbalah, most of the student's effort is invested in connecting the numerous parts comprising the wisdom into one meaningful image. First and foremost, we would simply like to understand what it is all about.

---

[26] "*Orot*" (Lights), 28

Then, after a clear image begins to more or less be depicted, (which will change again countless times), we stretch back a bit, cross our arms in satisfaction and ask: "Okay, so what needs to be done? Tell me how to attain this spirituality."

The answer, as you have probably already noticed from other cases, catches us off- guard here, as well: we do not need to do anything! The Light does all the work. We only need to desire, request the Light to change us and the Light will do what It knows how to do. The Light that created the vessel is the One to correct the vessel and fill it with Light. The understanding that the Light is what corrects the desire and we only need to desire to change is an inseparable part of the work in "There is none else besides Him" and we will focus on this aspect of the work in "There is none else besides Him" in this part of the lesson.

We are told that we need to change the intention; we are taught that we need to restrict the desire and acquire a screen. "Excellent," we say, "now we want to know how to do all that. Teach us and we shall do." It is difficult for us to grasp that indeed "There is none else besides Him, and as Maimonides writes, He "did, does, and will do all the deeds."[27] The will to receive in us wants to control the process, perform an action and see a result accordingly. Except that we need the Light's help, for as it is written "We haven't deeds within us.[28]

The Creator is the force behind all occurrences and actions in reality, and the corrections we need to perform on our way to actualizing the thought of creation are also performed by the Creator. In all of creation and all of the developmental stages of desire in our world and the spiritual worlds, the Light is what acts upon the *kli* (vessel). What is our part in this whole story? It is simply to want to be corrected.

---

[27] Maimonides, Thirteen Tenets

[28] Litany

We can learn of the essence of the connection between the Light and vessel already from the initial stages of development of creation. The Light, also called the "will to bestow," emits from Itself the will to receive, called "*kli*," (vessel), existence from absence. It turns out that the Light precedes the vessel and Light is what builds the *kli*. That is the sequence of things in the thought of creation and the order of development over all of the stages of creation's development up to the end of correction. Throughout the entire process, the Light is the active and creating force, and it is the force building the *kli*.

Just as the Light, the creating force in creation develops us throughout our life, from infancy to adulthood, so it develops us on our spiritual path, when we study the wisdom of Kabbalah. There is great similarity between the processes. In a sense, the study of the wisdom of Kabbalah is a natural process, just like the way a baby learns to walk and talk. Similar to the baby, all our future stages of development already exist within us. Likewise, similar to the baby, we need only to want to reveal them. In all cases, the Light is what performs the work. "There is none else besides Him."

And yet, there is a significant difference between the baby's development in our world and a person's spiritual development. Although both the baby and the point in the heart are developed by the Light and according to the desire, the desire of the baby is revealed naturally without asking him, according to his predetermined plan of development, whereas we need to build the desire for spiritual advancement ourselves. This is a very important point, because our free choice exists within that exact point.

Throughout all stages of the desire's development, from its emergence from the thought of creation, through the cascading of the spiritual worlds, concluding in our world, and over the billions of years of development in our world, up to the awakening of the point in the heart, we developed with no awareness, according to a predetermined plan. Each time, the Light revealed to us a new desire within us and filled it with Light.

From the moment the point in the heart has awakened in us, the rules of the game changed. Even though the Light is also what is operating upon the desire now, It is what will correct us and It is what will fill us, as it is written "There is none else besides Him;" from now on the Light will do nothing unless we ask. Kabbalists call this condition "half a shekel:" we have to give our half-shekel and then the Creator will complete it with His half-shekel.

In the entirety of creation, there is nothing but Light and vessel, pleasure and desire. If we develop a strong enough and focused enough desire within us, the Light will inevitably be revealed and teach us what restriction is, what a screen is and what the intention in order to bestow is. In order to reach such a strong focused request, we need to attempt to re-establish the connection with the Creator at every opportunity. It clearly follows why it is so important for us to coalesce and attribute all occurrences in reality to the Creator.

Test yourself:

What is the connection between the work in "There is none else besides Him" and correcting the desire?

Truth and Faith

Similar to all well-known sayings, the pith of "There is none else besides Him" is embedded in its simplicity. We don't need to add a word; the message is brief and to the point: There is no other force besides the Creator, everything comes from Him. That is the popular meaning of this statement and seemingly its meaning in the wisdom of Kabbalah, as well. Yet, there is a big difference between the common meaning of "There is none else besides Him" and "There is none else besides Him" in its Kabbalistic meaning. The last part of the lesson will be devoted to clarifying this difference.

In order to discern the difference between both approaches: the Kabbalistic and the common one, first, we need to clarify the meaning of the concept of "faith" according to the wisdom of Kabbalah. That is because both in the wisdom of Kabbalah and in its common meaning, the words "There is none else besides Him" actually express the faith in a single force, except that the meaning of the term "faith" in Kabbalah is completely different in essence from the common and familiar meaning. That is the source of the difference between both approaches.

In its common meaning of the word, "faith" means to accept a certain assumption as truth, despite not having attained its truthfulness in practice. Someone told us something and we believe him. Thus, for instance, for years we believed that the sun revolved around Earth. Likewise, although on a different level, we believe in the Creator's existence.

Faith, according to the wisdom of Kabbalah is the complete opposite from faith as its common meaning. Faith, according to the Wisdom of Kabbalah is attainment of the matter in practice. The wisdom of Kabbalah does not require us to blindly believe in the Creator's existence, rather to attain His existence in practice, to sense Him. It is written "Taste and see that the Creator is good."[29]

According to the wisdom of Kabbalah, we need to reach a direct connection with the Creator, sense Him, as real as a flavor diffusing in the mouth. Faith in its common meaning has no place in the wisdom of Kabbalah.

Now we will also be able to understand the difference between the common "There is none else besides Him" and "There is none else besides Him" in its Kabbalistic meaning. According to the wisdom of Kabbalah, we need to reach a feeling that one good and benevolent force governs creation, that all occurrences in creation stem from a single source, which is entirely good, and its goal is to do good. We need to feel that in our senses. Simple faith won't help here, not to mention things that are stated as "lip service."

---

[29] Psalms 34:8

According to the wisdom of Kabbalah, as long as we don't actually sense the Creator as good and benevolent, we will not be able to say, "There is none else besides Him." The common, simple faith in one good and benevolent Creator is to be respected. It does have its own purpose. However, it will not suffice a person within whom the point in the heart has awakened and is beginning his spiritual path. It will not bring him to fulfilling the new desire being revealed in him to attain connection with the Creator.

The work in "There is none else besides Him" according to the Wisdom of Kabbalah drives a person towards correcting his desire, since the condition for revealing the Creator is correcting the desire with the intention to bestow. As the desire proceeds to grow and another portion of it is revealed each time, the work is constantly renewed. The effort to coalesce and attribute all occurrences in creation to a single, good and benevolent source develops a person, not allowing him to suffice with the simple faith of "There is none else besides Him."

Test Yourself:
What is faith according to the wisdom of Kabbalah?

Lesson Summary

Main Points

- The main work of a person is to coalesce and attribute all occurrences in reality - the good, the bad and the insignificant - to one source, the Creator. If we attribute a certain occurrence to another source other than the Creator, we are called "idol worshipers."

- An important part of the work with "There is none else besides Him" is the understanding that only the Creator can correct the desire. A person cannot correct the desire on his own;

he needs the help of the Creator for that. All our work is to request the correction.

- According to the wisdom of Kabbalah, we need to attain the Creator in practice. Only out of complete attainment of the Creator, will we be able to attribute all events of reality to one good and benevolent force and live the words "There is none else besides Him" in practice. As long as we don't feel the Creator as good and benevolent in practice, we will not be able to say, "There is none else beside Him."

Concepts

Idol Worshiper- An inner state of a person. Attributing the bad or the good which is revealed to another source other than the Creator.

Half a Shekel- The request for correction, as the person needs to build within him from understanding that the correction itself will be done by the Creator, is called "half a shekel." Half of the work (discerning the desire) is on the individual and the other half (correction of the desire) will be done by the Creator.

Faith- Attainment in practice of the force of bestowal.

Answers to the Questions

Question: What is the work in "There is none else besides Him" and what are the difficulties revealed in this work?

Answer: The work in "There is none else besides Him" is to coalesce and attribute all occurrences in life to one force. The difficulties in this work are: 1) attributing the severe events to the Creator, as well. 2) attributing every occurrence to Him, with the emphasis on "every."

Question: What is the connection between the work in "There is none else besides Him" and correcting the desire?

Answer: Throughout the entire development of the desire, from creation to the end of correction, the Light is what develops the *kli*(vessel). Just as the source of all occurrences in reality is the Creator, so the correction of the desire comes from the Creator. We only need to request to be corrected. If we do that, the Creator will correct the desire.

Question: What is faith according to the Wisdom of Kabbalah?
Answer: According to the wisdom of Kabbalah, faith is the practical attainment of the quality of bestowal. Attaining the quality of bestowal is possible only by correcting the desire from the intention of in order to receive to the intention of in order to bestow. Only by correcting the desire, will we be able to justify the Creator and attribute all occurrences in life: the bad as the good, to the single good and benevolent force.

Lesson #2 - The Landlord and I

In this lesson we will learn about: Desire and intention / Pleasure and Giver of the pleasure / "If I am not for me, who is for me" and "There is none else besides Him"

Adhesion and Independence

The Creator created the created being for him to grow and develop up to the Creator's degree. Kabbalists call this state, which we need to attain, "adhesion." In a state of adhesion, the Creator and the created being are truly adhered to each other as one, and one does not cancel the other's existence.

Sound complicated? Rightfully so. The definition of the state of adhesion entails an inner contradiction. It is not clear how two separate and opposite entities, the Creator and the created being could adhere to one another, truly as one body, while maintaining each one's existence.

On one hand, the created being has to be similar to the Creator and truly adhere to Him. On the other hand, in order to be as great as the Creator, the created being has to maintain its independence. Thus, it is not clear how it is possible to maintain both of these opposite states simultaneously. Indeed, if the created being is independent, something inevitably distinguishes him from the Creator. How is it possible to be similar to the Creator and at the same time maintain the created being's independence?

Dealing with the question of adhesion and independence leads us to discerning one of the central points in one's inner spiritual work – discerning how a person relates to the Creator as an inseparable part of the work in "There is none else besides Him." We will devote the lesson to discerning this point.

We will begin from a somewhat surprising direction, with an allegory from the world of car passengers. Fasten your seatbelts and think of the following question: What is more important in the car, the gas pedal or the steering wheel? It's okay, there is no need to respond; the answer is on its way. The steering wheel is more important. That is clear. If we cannot control the car's direction, the gas pedal is useless.

The allegory is clear. And what is the moral? The wisdom of Kabbalah discerns between the will to receive, which is the nature of creation, and the intention, to receive or to bestow, which is the way the will to receive is used. The desire is the driving force, the matter making up all of creation and all its details. Intention directs the will to receive to receive or bestow (see drawing #2). It turns out that according to the abovementioned allegory, the will to receive is the gas pedal and the intention is the steering wheel, which is the more important of the two.

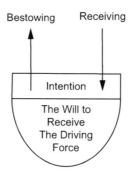

We will set aside the topic of the importance of intention for a moment. The main thing for us now is to understand that the will to receive does not change, rather the intention does. The intention can be in order to bestow or receive, yet the will to receive will always remain the will to receive, as it was created. Even if we want to cancel the will to receive (even though there is no reason to do that), we will not be able to. We were born with the will to receive and will ride upon it all the way to the end of correction. Even then, it will not be canceled. We are incapable of changing our created nature and have no reason to change it. The will to receive is the matter of creation; simple and shapeless matter. Only the way we work with it can be good or bad; hence, we can only change the intention.

After understanding the relationship between the will to receive and the intention riding upon it, we will now be able to understand the answer to the question of adhesion and independence. The work with the will to receive with the correct intention is what enables the created being to adhere to the Creator and still remain independent, distinct from the Creator. The will to receive, the essence of the created being remains unchanged. He wants to receive and actually receives all the goodness of creation (see drawing #3). The intention of in order to bestow with which the created being works, meaning his calculation to receive all the goodness of creation only in order to bestow to the Creator is what brings the created begin to a state of adhesion. In his essence, the created being remains the will to receive and in his action of in order to bestow, he becomes similar to the Creator.

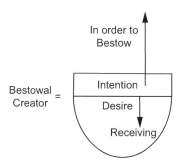

Just like a sculptor who gives shape to a slab of marble, so the intention gives the form of bestowal to the will to receive. The material remains unchanged, only its form has changed, from the form of receiving to the form of bestowal. Stemming from the equivalence of form, a person reveals the quality of bestowal within him, the Creator.

The will to receive is the driving force, just like the gas pedal in a car. If we add more of it, we advance faster. The question is to where we will advance. That is certainly an important question. If we'd like to reach a certain destination, it is important to make sure we steer the wheel in the correct direction. None of us wishes to floor the gas pedal while the steering wheel is aimed towards an abyss. We will not reach our destination that way.

The intention is the directing force, just like the car's steering wheel. If we work with it in the correct direction, we will reach the correct destination. The more parts of the will to receive with the intention of in order to bestow we correct, the more we will strengthen our connection with the Creator. The will to receive is the matter upon which we establish a connection with the Creator and the intention to bestow is the form of our connection with the Creator.

It turns out that if our work in "There is none else besides Him" is to coalesce all the occurrences of reality and attribute them to a single force, that is good and benevolent, governing all of creation, indeed the shift of intention from in order to receive to in order to bestow is the only way to do it in practice.

When we have connected with the quality of bestowal, when we are aimed outside of ourselves to giving, we are in equivalence of form with the quality of bestowal, and as a result, feel the Creator as good and benevolent. If we are not connected with the attribute of bestowal, if we are aimed internally, within ourselves to receiving, we are in oppositeness of form from the Creator, and as a result, we feel His Providence as a series of blows, whose purpose we cannot understand.

In summary, everything depends on the intention, on our connection with the Creator. Correcting the intention upon the will to receive is what leads us to become similar to the Creator, to equivalence of form with Him and finally to adhesion with Him. The will to receive remaining unchanged enables us to be in adhesion with the Creator and still maintain our independence.

How is the intention to bestow constructed upon the desire? We will address that question in the following section of the lesson.

Test yourself:
- What is the correct work with the desire and intention in creating the connection with the Creator?

What a Pleasure

A cup of tea is generally no big deal for us. We drink it and that's all. What if, for instance, one day, completely by chance, the Queen of England served us tea? That is a cup of tea we'd never forget, for sure. We would sip the tea very slowly, so it lasts and we'd save the cup as proof for our grandchildren... Unless the Queen of England isn't our "cup of tea" (in that case, feel free to switch the server of the tea; to each one, his own "Queen of England").

The will to receive which was created at the thought of creation is a desire to receive pleasure, a cup of tea for example. However, immediately at its emergence (as we learned in the previous study unit) a person feels that there is someone who is giving him pleasure and he begins to develop an attitude towards the giver of the pleasure, as well. Discerning the connection between these two feelings: the pleasure and the giver of the pleasure, is the heart of a person's inner work in the study of the wisdom of Kabbalah and has a decisive role in constructing the desire to change the intention.

The connection between the pleasure and the giver of the pleasure is actually the connection between the will to receive and the intention riding upon it. That is because the pleasure is felt in the will to receive and the connection with the giver of the pleasure depends on the correction of the intention from in order to receive to in order to bestow (see drawing #4). At this point, it is important to mention that when we speak of spirituality, the pleasure is not a cup of tea, of course, rather spiritual pleasure, and the giver of the pleasure isn't a person flesh and blood, rather the Creator.

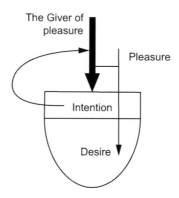

In our world, we do not feel the giver of the pleasure; we act according to the intention of in order to receive pleasure and that conceals the giver of pleasure from us, due to a disparity of form. However, we sense pleasure or the lack thereof, and how! Actually, in our world, we are enslaved to the feeling being revealed to us in the will to receive. It is what governs us.

When the will to receive is filled with pleasure, it feels good and so do we. When the will to receive is empty of pleasure, it feels bad and so do we. All of us, all human beings on the face of the Earth - the richest and the poorest, the most famous and the unknown, the smartest and most foolish - all of us, without exception, are governed by the feeling in the will to receive. It seems to us that we are sophisticated and intricate creatures, yet, at the end of the day, one very simple mechanism governs us from within: feeling filled or empty in the will to receive.

In the spiritual world, the picture is completely different. When we emerge to spirituality, with the acquisition of the intention of in order to bestow, we enter a connection with the Creator, the Giver of the pleasure and the connection with Him is infinitely more important to us than the feeling in the will to receive. We are no longer enslaved to our will to receive; rather, we use it as a means to establish a connection with the Creator. Every feeling in the desire is attributed to the Creator, as written, "There is none else besides Him" and it serves as a reminder to renew and expand the connection with Him.

After crossing the "barrier" and entering spirituality, neither the will to receive nor the feelings within it are canceled; rather the feeling in the will to receive awakens the person to establishing a connection with the One sending us the feeling, the Giver of the pleasure. From here on, a person can already begin to discern his attitude towards the pleasure and the Giver of the pleasure. Instead of being governed by the feeling in the will to receive, one governs the will to receive and the feeling being revealed in the will to receive, oneself.

Even while preparing to enter the spiritual world, once the point in the heart has awakened in us, we can begin working on establishing the connection with the Giver of the pleasure and rise above the feeling in the will to receive. We are able to do that, since the point in the heart which awakened in us is actually a desire to connect with the Creator, Giver of the pleasure.

The point in the heart is a small part of the desire for spirituality, potential awaiting fruition, like a flower bud. We begin to enlarge the point in the heart to a complete desire, meaning a sufficiently large and clarified desire, like the flower blooming from the bud, through the study of the wisdom of Kabbalah. Our work is in exerting effort to connect all the events happening to us, feelings, thoughts and desires awakening in us, to the single force sending them to us. Everything comes from Him. There is none else besides Him.

The moment we remember that, we are no longer led mindlessly. We begin to take part in realizing the thought of creation. Although we are yet to have an overt connection with the Creator, as the intention of in order to receive conceals Him from us, we can already somewhat rise above the feeling in the will to receive and begin to discern why it is awakening in us, what is the purpose of all these occurrences happening to us.

The moment a thought is awakened in us about "There is none else besides Him," it is a magical one, an exit door from the narrow, corporeal world into a vast, spiritual world. It is an escape door from the prison of the will to receive to the freedom and independence in bestowal unto others. In a single thought of the source of all occurrences, we become aware of our situation and cease being led mindlessly through the tides of life.

An opportunity opens up for us to stop and think of the purpose of what we do and why things happen as they do. A single force sends us all the occurrences and has a goal. Now we can begin to check ourselves in relation to that goal, examine where we are in relation to it and create a longing within us in its direction.

How can we awaken within us the thought of "There is none else besides Him" as frequently as possible? By means of the environment. To the extent that we build an environment which raises the importance of spirituality and the importance of the connection with the Creator, so we will remember the cause of all causes more frequently and take another step towards a genuine connection with Him.

Test Yourself:
- How should we use the will to receive in order to strengthen the connection with the Creator?

If I am not for Me, Who is for Me

One of the special challenges in the study of the wisdom of Kabbalah is to settle the numerous contradictions we find within. So, for example, it is difficult for us to understand how a good Creator emits evil from within Him, or how one can attain adhesion while maintaining one's individuality. The source of these contradictions (and those yet to be revealed) is the oppositeness between the two forces operating in creation: the will to receive and the will to bestow. Only when we bring them to unity at the end of correction, will all doubts unravel.

Until then, here is another challenging contradiction: Kabbalists write that "There is none else besides Him" - that the will to bestow, the force creating creation is what has done, is doing and will perform all of the actions. If so, what did the great Kabbalist, Hillel, the Elder mean when he said "If I am not for me, who is for me?"[30]

Meaning, what is the point in acting as if everything depends on me and there is none else but me in the world, when "There is none else besides Him?" If all the occurrences in reality inevitably descend down to us from the thought of creation according to a predetermined plan, what is the point in making any effort? Let's just sit and wait for whatever will happen.

In order to understand how this contradiction may be resolved, first we need to understand the meaning of "If I am not for me, who is for me" according to the wisdom of Kabbalah. As we have repeatedly emphasized, the wisdom of Kabbalah only deals with a person's spiritual development. The person's spiritual development is comprised of predetermined stages, obligated to be revealed one after another. Similar to a baby who will sit up at around the age of six months, walk approximately at a year and begin speaking around a year and a half, so our stages of spiritual development are revealed naturally one after another, according to the order of the emerging *Reshimot* (Reminiscence). It may seem to us that we only need to sit and wait for the stages to be revealed. However, in actuality, nothing will be revealed unless we make every effort we can in order to reveal it. That is what Hillel the Elder meant by "If I am not for me, who is for me."

---

[30] *Pirkei Avot* (Chapters of the Fathers) 1:13

Before revealing any new point of connection with the Creator, we have to do everything in our power in order to reveal it. We cannot sit around and wait for things to happen by themselves, just because "There is none else besides Him." If we wait for something to happen, nothing will ever happen. In order to reveal the next step in our spiritual development, we need to invest in building the spiritual environment, within which we develop, and keep to a strict, permanent framework of Kabbalah studies. Only after we have invested effort and revealed whatever was revealed, should we say, "There is none else besides Him" and attribute whatever happened, including our efforts, to the single force governing all of reality.

In our effort to do whatever we can with the approach of "If I am not for me, who is for me" and after the action, to justify whatever is revealed in "There is none else besides Him," we actually express our desire to reveal that everything comes from the Creator; that a single force, good and benevolent, manages all of creation as one body, where all occurrences and parts are interconnected with invisible fibers of bestowal and love.

Thus, specifically the work in "If I am not for me who is for me" accentuates and highlights the effort to coalesce all the parts of reality and attribute them to "There is none else besides Him." Actually, without this work, we would not be able to work in "There is none else besides Him." Only the effort to do everything we can do enables us to then coalesce all the actions and attribute them to the source of all causes. Just as everything else in reality is attained through its contrast, so is "There is none else besides Him" is attained only through the work in "If I am not for me, who is for me."

Baal HaSulam writes[31] about the correct combination of both these approaches in corporeality, as well: "Before one goes out to make one's daily bread, he should remove his thoughts from private

---

[31] Writings of Baal HaSulam, Letters, Letter 16.

Providence and say, "If I am not for me, who is for me?" He should do all the tactics applied in corporeality to earn his living as do others.

But in the evening, when he returns home with his earnings, he must never think that he has earned this profit by his own novelties, but rather that even if he stayed all day in the basement of his home, he would still have earned his pay, for so the Creator contemplated for him in advance, and so it had to be."

That's the way it is in corporeality and all the more so in spirituality, as explained above.

Integrating both these approaches is unique to the wisdom of Kabbalah and distinguishes it from any other method. The various religious methods cancel man and glorify the Creator. The various scientific methods cancel the Creator and glorify man. The wisdom of Kabbalah in particular, connects the two opposites and combines them together. By that means, a person reveals the complete picture where all the parts of reality connect together.

From the unique integration of these two opposite approaches, which complete one another, we can understand, however slightly, how in the end, all the opposite parts of reality will be integrated into one complete image, without canceling one another.

Test Yourself:
- What is the correct relationship between "If I am not for me, who will be for me" and "There is none else but Him?"

Lesson Summary

Main Points
- The work with the will to receive with the correct intention enables the created being to adhere to the Creator and at the same time remain independent, distinct from the Creator. The will to receive, the essence of the created being remains unchanged. He wants to receive - and receives in practice- all

the goodness of creation. The intention of in order to bestow, with which the created being works, meaning his calculation to receive all of the goodness of creation only in order to bestow unto the Creator is what brings the created being to a state of adhesion. In his essence, the created being remains the will to receive and in his action of in order to bestow, he becomes similar to the Creator.

- The feeling in the will to receive, whether it is a feeling of emptiness or a feeling of fulfillment and satisfaction is nothing other than a means of renewing the connection with Him, Who sends us that feeling. In the ascent through the spiritual steps to the end of correction, we need to rise above the feeling in the desire and use it to renew the connection with the Creator.

- The work in "There is none else besides Him" obligates a person to do whatever he can in order to reveal unity with the Creator. Only by preceding with our effort to renew the connection with the Creator, will the quality of bestowal be revealed to us. Specifically, the work in "If I am not for me who is for me?" accentuates and highlights the effort to coalesce all the parts of reality and attribute them to "There is none else besides Him."

Answers to the Questions

Question: What is the correct work with the desire and intention in creating the connection with the Creator?

Answer: The will to receive is the matter upon which we create a connection with the Creator and the intention to bestow is the form of our connection with the Creator. The more we correct more parts of the will to receive with the intention of in order to bestow, will we strengthen our connection with the Creator.

Question: How should we use the will to receive in order to strengthen the connection with the Creator?

Answer: In all feelings within the will to receive, the feelings of fulfillment and the feelings of emptiness, we need to use as reasons to renew the connection with the force awakening those feelings within us, with the Creator. In other words, the will to receive and what is felt in it are used as means to attain the renewed connection with the Creator, the knowing that all comes from Him.

Question: What is the correct relationship between "If I am not for me, who will be for me" and "There is none else but Him?"

Answer: Only out of our effort to do everything we can in order to reveal the quality of bestowal in what is called "If I am not for me, who is for me?" will we finally be able to reveal the connection with the Creator in practice, in what is called "There is none else besides Him." The obligation to do everything we can in order to reveal the next degree of connection with the Creator is an imperative condition for uniting with Him in "There is none else besides Him."

Lesson #3 – An Individual Organ of Shechina (Divinity)

In this lesson we will learn about: The Soul of *Adam HaRishon* / What *Shechina* is/ The Uniqueness of Man and his Freedom

Assembling the Parts of the Soul

"There is none else besides Him" is the foundation underlying all of a person's spiritual work. Everything begins and ends with arranging our attitude towards the Creator. At the beginning of every action, we should attribute each event to the source of all events and at the end of every action we should attribute all the events to the source of all, to the single, good and benevolent Creator.

The question then arises, if the work in "There is none else besides Him" focuses entirely on arranging a person's attitude towards the Creator, how is the work of correcting a person's attitude towards others connected to that? Indeed, we learned that we construct our attitude towards the Creator through correcting our attitude towards others.

The key to understanding the connection between correcting the attitude towards others and setting the attitude towards the Creator is embedded in understanding the spiritual structure called "The Soul of *Adam HaRishon.*"

The wisdom of Kabbalah explains that we are all parts of one great soul, called "The Soul of *Adam HaRishon.*" In the spiritual state called "The Soul of *Adam HaRishon,*" we are all connected together in our desires through ties of bestowal and love. In a sense, the Soul of *Adam HaRishon* resembles the human body: both are composed of numerous parts, which are interconnected and work together for the benefit of the general body and not for their own benefit, and all the parts together comprise a much higher degree of existence than the degree of existence of each part separately.

It is amazing that Kabbalists write that we already exist in this state, connected together as parts complementing each other in one spiritual body. Yet, this connection is concealed from us. It seems to us that we are actually separate from one another and that each one of us can create success upon the ruins of one's friend. However, that is an illusion, albeit a powerful one; so powerful that it even seems true to us. Yet, in the end, we will reveal that it is untrue and the reason for all suffering we experience in our world.

Nothing is superfluous. We exist in an illusion of separation, since only from there, both within that state and against it, will we be able to reveal the connection. As we learned in the previous study unit, the reality of separation in which we exist is a result of a spiritual process called the "shattering of The Soul of *Adam HaRishon.*" What was shattered? The spiritual connection among us. The connection that connected us together as one soul was shattered, in order to enable us to renew it and maintain it with awareness, out of our desire to know the connection among us in all its depth.

We are all shattered parts of The Soul of *Adam HaRishon*. In the connection of all the shattered parts, we renew connections of love and bestowal among us and ascend the spiritual steps up to the complete renewal of connection (see drawing #5). Thus, we reveal the Creator, the quality of bestowal connecting us together. In practice, as we've already mentioned, it is more precise to describe the process as the renewal of connection, rather than its revelation, since the connection already exists. It is only concealed from us. The shattering of *Adam HaRishon* and the reality of separation in which we live are only our temporary state, essential in order for us to ascend from it, back to the spiritual degree from which we descended.

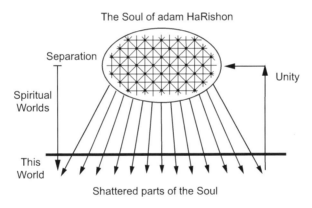

You are surely asking what the point is in losing our spiritual connection and renewing it once more. Our construction of the connection enables us not only to exist in it, but also to understand it in all its depth, attain the reasons for its existence and maintain it on our own. Through renewing the connection between us, we attain its underlying thought, the thought of creation to do good unto His created beings. By that, we reach the end of correction.

It is similar to a child, whose parents buy him a puzzle to put together. Although the picture is broken into separate pieces, once the child reassembles the picture, he gains much more than just another pretty picture. Particularly through the process of putting it together, the child becomes smarter and learns to cope with complex challenges even more.

This was all about The Soul of *Adam HaRishon*. How is it connected to "There is none else besides Him?" That will be addressed in the next part of the lesson.

Test yourself:

- What is the added value in connecting all the shattered parts of The Soul of *Adam HaRishon?*

One Light, One Created Being, One Vessel

A person proceeding along the spiritual path, encountering difficulties seeming to distance him from spirituality needs to know that everything is purposeful. All events of reality, particularly those that seemingly distance one from spirituality are sent to one in order to strengthen one's desire for spirituality and build within him greater yearning to attain spirituality. One should understand that all obstacles come from one source, from the good and benevolent Creator and their purpose is to advance a person towards spirituality. As it is written, "There is none else besides Him."[32]

All those alleged obstacles revealed on the spiritual path are in precise measure for each person, according to the root of his soul and according to his unique path towards actualizing the thought of creation. Yet, none of us can understand why a specific person receives a certain obstacle. There is no point delving into it, as we are incapable of comprehending it. All of our work is to rise above the obstacles, coalesce them all- the good and bad and attribute them to

---

[32] Deutoronomy 4:35

the single Creator, Who sends us all occurrences. That is the work in "There is none else besides Him."

In the work of "There is none else besides Him," we gradually exchange the value scale of "bitter-sweet" for a value scale of "truth–lie." What does that mean? In the value scale of bitter and sweet, we measure everything in relation to the will to receive: if it is pleasant to the will to receive, meaning sweet, we consider it to be good and if it is bitter to the will to receive, we consider it to be bad. With the value scale of truth or lie, we rise above the will to receive and measure everything in relation to the spiritual goal: does it draw us closer to connecting with the Creator or not? If it does, it is true and if not, it is a lie.

By coalescing all events of reality and attributing them to a single force, we actually gradually rise above the will to receive (we do not cancel it and whatever is felt in it, rather we rise above it), until we finally begin gaining control over it. With all our force, we try to "lock" ourselves on "There is none else besides Him," above all emotions, both the good and the bad and constantly focus ourselves on connecting with the Creator, even when confusion or weakness attacks us. We praise the bad as the good and in the recurring thought of "There is none else besides Him," we neutralize ourselves from the control of the will to receive and gradually rise above it up to the entrance of spirituality.

However, rising above the will to receive is only a condition to entering spirituality. Now, after we have acquired control over the will to receive, we can begin spiritual work, itself: connecting external desires to us and working with them as if they were truly ours. In other words, after overcoming the will to receive, we need to begin developing the will to bestow, examining the extent to which we bestow unto others, work with their *Kelim* (vessels), construct their image within us, feel how much they derive pleasure from us. Only through this work, will we attain the state called "There is none else besides Him" in all its depth.

The Creator's vessels, which we need to begin to connect to ourselves after rising above the will to receive, are the sum of all the parts of The Soul of *Adam HaRishon*, which we learned about in the previous section of this lesson. Indeed, the Creator the wisdom of Kabbalah speaks of is the quality of bestowal and love that we attain within us in our corrected desires. The corrected desires are the ones that connect together into the spiritual construct called "The Soul of *Adam HaRishon*."

We cannot say a word about the Creator Himself. Our study in the Wisdom of Kabbalah is entirely about the way we attain the Creator. The way in which we attain the Creator is through the sum of all the desires connected together in ties of bestowal and love, in which the Light of the Creator shines. Our connection with the Creator is constructed through correcting our attitude to the parts of The Soul of *Adam HaRishon*. Only in the single vessel, which unites all the soul's shattered parts in ties of love and bestowal, will we be able to feel the Creator, the quality of bestowal. We are unable to build our connection with the Creator directly, rather only through correcting our attitude towards others. To the extent of correcting our attitude towards others, we thus reveal the Creator.

In the essay "There is none else besides Him," which serves as the basis for a person's spiritual work, *Baal HaSulam* writes that a person should take care not to attribute his success and failure in the work of "There is none else besides Him" to himself, rather tie them to the spiritual body of The Soul of *Adam HaRishon*. If he is remote from connection with the Creator, he should feel regret that he is causing sorrow to The Soul of *Adam HaRishon* and if he draws near to the connection with the Creator, he should be joyful that he is reviving the spiritual body of The Soul of *Adam HaRishon*.

The Soul of *Adam HaRishon* is also called "*Shechina*" (Divinity). That is because within the connection of all its parts, the Creator dwells,

(*Shochen* in Hebrew). As abovementioned, our work in "There is none else besides Him" as an inseparable part of the *Shechina* is described by *Baal HaSulam* in the essay "There is None Else besides Him:" "When he (a person) regrets that the Creator does not draw him near, he should also be careful that it would not be concerning himself, because thus he becomes a receiver for his own benefit, and one who receives is separated. Rather, he should regret the exile of the *Shechina* (Divinity), meaning that he is causing the sorrow of Divinity."

To sum up, in the work in "There is none else besides Him," we need to unite all events of reality and attribute them to the single force governing all of creation. In doing so, we rise above the will to receive and begin working with desires external to us, with all the parts of The Soul of *Adam HaRishon*, also called "The Holy *Shechina*." We must take care not to attribute to ourselves all our success and failure in renewing the connection with the Creator, rather to that same spiritual body, which remains lifeless or enlivened, according to our efforts.

In our present state, when we are at the beginning of our spiritual path, our work in "There is none else besides Him" is to exert efforts as much as possible to coalesce all the events of reality and attribute them to the single force and tie this work as best we can to our corrected state, which for now is concealed from us and in which we are connected among us in ties of bestowal and love.

Uniting all the aspects of reality and attributing them to a single source is actually connecting all the shattered parts of The Soul of *Adam HaRishon* to one common desire. The single Creator, maintaining a single created being, all of whose parts operate as one body, can be revealed only in a single vessel, by connecting all of the souls together. We need to exert efforts to hold those three parts together: I, who yearns for the Creator, the single vessel in which the Creator is revealed and the Creator Himself – at every moment and every phase on our spiritual path (see drawing #6).

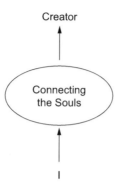

Test yourself:

- What should one feel regret or joy about in the work of "There is none else besides Him"?

The One and Only

Imagine five monkeys in a cage. A bunch of bananas hangs from the cage's ceiling with a ladder beneath it. After a while, one of the monkeys climbs the ladder and attempts to reach for the bananas. At that very moment, a jet of cold water is sprayed on the rest of the monkeys in the cage. The wet monkeys are upset, but after a while, they calm down.

A few moments pass and another monkey climbs the ladder to take a banana. Again, the rest of the monkeys are sprayed with a jet of cold water; they are upset once more and again calm down. Similarly, time after time, one of the monkeys climbs the ladder and a cold shower repetitively surprises the rest of the monkeys. After some time, the monkeys in the cage learn to stop every monkey that wants to climb the ladder. They are not interested in the unwanted surprise of the cold shower.

Now, after all the monkeys have been "educated" not to climb the ladder, a new monkey enters the cage that has never been there before, instead of one of the current monkeys. After some time, the new monkey also attempts to climb the ladder on his way to the bananas, and to his surprise, the other monkeys prevent him from doing so. After several attempts, it also learns that in this cage, the ladder is not to be climbed.

Another monkey that has never been in the cage replaces one of the "senior" ones. It also attempts to climb the ladder, and this time as well, the other monkeys prevent it from doing so. Even the new monkey that entered previously joins them with joy, yet, unlike the other monkey friends, it does so because the others are doing it, without knowing why, without ever having experienced the cold water.

Thus, one after another, all the monkeys in the cage are replaced with monkeys who had never been in the cage before, until finally there are five monkeys left in the cage that will not climb the ladder. Why not? Because as far as they know, this is how things have always been carried out in this cage.

The "supposedly scientific" script (based partly on a scientific experiment)[33]which we chose as the opening to the last part of the lesson nicely illustrates the psychological phenomenon called the "herd effect." No one would like to be a part of a herd, losing one's independence and acting mindlessly, only because all those around us act similarly. Each of us would like to be special and it is very important to each one to maintain one's uniqueness.

The necessity to maintain our individuality gets accentuated when we encounter the wisdom of Kabbalah. We approach the study with the most developed will to receive and accordingly, the need to maintain our individuality is strongest. After all, a person comes to the wisdom of Kabbalah with the question "Who am I?" and since the answer is found in the wisdom of Kabbalah, the question echoes within him more intensely. We will devote the last part of the lesson to clarifying that question and its solution.

---

[33] Stephenson, G. R. (1967). Cultural acquisition of a specific learned response among rhesus monkeys.

In the previous section of the lesson and throughout this entire course, we learned that the Creator is revealed by us rising above the will to receive and connecting to the desires of others, as if they were truly our own desires. The Creator is the quality of bestowal and He is revealed to us in accordance with the equivalence of form, meaning when we are connected to each other in ties of love and giving, and bestow unto the other parts of The Soul of *Adam HaRishon*.

The issue is that having the connection to others as a condition to attaining spirituality challenges a person in a way that isn't so simple: on one hand, the connection is an imperative condition and on the other hand, doubts arise in him whether in connecting to others, he will be forced to cancel his individuality and annul himself, just as a tiny part of the sum of all parts comprising the joint, spiritual vessel. His strong desire to discern his uniqueness further highlights the gap which seems impossible to bridge, between the inevitable assimilation with the collective and the need for self-definition.

However, these fears are unfounded. Actually, the opposite is true. As we said previously, the answer to the question "Who am I?" is specifically found in the wisdom of Kabbalah and particularly in the connection to others, a person acquires his individuality and expresses his uniqueness.

In order to understand what that actually refers to, we need to briefly review the main points from the lesson on free choice. A person in our world has no free choice. He is governed down to the atom level by the will to receive, according to the calculation of "maximum pleasure for minimum effort" and develops according to the genetics he received from his parents and the influence of the environment, which he also did not choose. It turns out that in our world, there is not even a single action we perform, for which we can take credit; there is no action in which we can express our uniqueness.

So where is a person's free choice? In one's rising above the narrow calculation of the will to receive and connecting oneself to The Soul of *Adam HaRishon*. In connecting to others, at the exact point of connection – that is where each and every one of us can express one's individuality. Each one of us is a unique part of The Soul of *Adam HaRishon*. There is no person like any other in the universe. There has never been one like him and there never will be. In his connecting back to The Soul of *Adam HaRishon,* he adds to the whole, collective picture, a special shade of color, unique to him, which only he can add. His point of connection to the other parts of The Soul of *Adam HaRishon* is the point of his free choice and it is what distinguishes his uniqueness from all the other parts of The Soul of *Adam HaRishon*.

Rav Kook wrote in his personal journal[34] about the feeling of true life, which is revealed in the connection with the other parts of The Soul of *Adam HaRishon*:, "Listen to me, my people. From the depth of my soul do I speak with you…from the depth of the bond of life that binds me to all of you…only you, only all of you, your entirety, all of your souls, all of your generations, only you are the content of my life. In you I live, in you, in the bloc that comprises all of you does my life have that character that is called life. Without you I have nothing. All hopes, all aspirations, all the value of the worth of life, all of it I find within myself only with you. And I need to bond with all of your souls; I must love you with an infinite love."

In the connection of all parts in eternal unconditional love, when each one adds his unique shade of color to the one complete desire for spirituality, the Creator is revealed in all His glory and depth. There is none else besides Him.

Test Yourself:

- What is the connection between discerning a person's point of uniqueness and connecting the shattered parts of The Soul of *Adam HaRishon*?

---

[34] "Eight Files," Notebook A, par. 163

Lesson Summary

Main Points

- In order for us to realize the purpose of creation and ascend to the degree of the Creator, The Soul of *Adam HaRishon* was shattered into numerous separate pieces. In connecting all the parts together, we copy the action of the Creator, out of which we acquire His intelligence, the thought of creation.

- Our connection with the Creator is built by correcting our attitude to the parts of The Soul of *Adam HaRishon*. Only in the single vessel, which unites within all the parts of the shattered soul in ties of love and bestowal, will we be able to feel the Creator, the attribute of bestowal. We are unable to construct our connection with the Creator directly, rather solely by correcting our attitude towards others. To the extent of correcting our attitude towards others, we reveal the Creator.

- Specifically in connecting to The Soul of *Adam HaRishon*, we express our uniqueness and independence. The point of a person's "I" is the point of one's connection to the other parts of The Soul of *Adam HaRishon*. All of a person's actions besides that connection are predetermined, with no room for the created being's free choice or independent action.

Concepts

Shochen (Dweller)– The Creator. The force of bestowal, which is revealed in the connection of the shattered parts of the soul of *Adam HaRishon*.

Shechina (Divinity) - The spiritual vessel (*Kli*) within which the *Shochen* is revealed, composed of the shattered parts of The Soul of *Adam HaRishon*.

Answers to the Questions

Q: What is the added value in connecting all the shattered parts of the *Soul of Adam HaRishon?*

A: In connecting the shattered parts of *Adam HaRishon* together, we do not only exist in bestowal and connection, we also acquire the knowledge of how to carry out that connection on our own. The purpose of creation is to elevate the created being to the degree of the Creator. Only connecting all the shattered parts of the soul of *Adam HaRishon* provides us the Creator's intelligence and elevates us to the degree of the thought of creation.

Q: What should one feel regret or joy about in the work of "There is none else besides Him"?

A: Coalescing all events of reality and attributing them to one source is possible only by connecting all the parts of The Soul of *Adam HaRishon* into one spiritual vessel. That is why one should regret that failure in the work of "There is none else besides Him" delays the connection of the single spiritual vessel, called the "Holy *Shechina*" or "The Soul of *Adam HaRishon*" and rejoice in success in the work that draws its connection near.

Q: What is the connection between discerning a person's point of uniqueness and connecting the shattered parts of The Soul of *Adam HaRishon?*

A: Each person's uniqueness is revealed in his connection to the other shattered parts of The Soul of *Adam HaRishon*. In his connection back to The Soul of *Adam HaRishon*, he adds a special shade of color to the complete, general picture, unique to him, which only he can add.

Logical Sequence
(Order of development of the Course)

We learned that the wisdom of Kabbalah is a method for revealing the Creator to the created beings in this world.

We learned that in order to reveal the Creator, we need to change the intention from in order to receive to in order to bestow.

We learned that in the books of Kabbalah, a special spiritual force called the Light that Reforms is embedded, which has the power to change our intention, from in order to receive to in order to bestow.

We learned that only in discerning our attitude towards others, can we formulate within us a genuine request to the Light that Reforms.

We learned that only in choosing the correct environment for spiritual development can we discern our attitude towards others with precision.

We learned that the points in the heart are the shattered parts of The Soul of *Adam HaRishon* and that in building the spiritual environment with the other points in the heart, we formulate the request for correction, for connecting the shattered parts and summon the Light that Reforms.

We learned that the basis for a genuine request of the Light that Reforms is "There is none else besides Him," meaning to attribute all revealed situations to the one Creator - the source of all causes.

In the following section, we will learn how to formulate the request within us.

Part #2 - The Path of Torah and the Path of Suffering

Lesson #1 - Two Paths

In this lesson we will learn about: The end of an act is in the preliminary thought / The developmental mechanism of creation / The path of Torah and the path of suffering

There is None as Wise as the Experienced

When considering mosquitos not letting us sleep, continuing with neighbors throwing garbage out of their window, all the way up to a tsunami burying half a country under a downpour - something doesn't fit what Kabbalists have determined, that absolute benevolence governs creation. "If **this** is good," you ask yourself, as you are shocked once again by the daily news broadcast, "then what is bad?!"

The Creator is absolute benevolence. That is how Kabbalists have attained Him from correcting their vessels of reception, and what they have written us in their books. Yet, a completely different image is depicted before our eyes. Life itself leads us to the conclusion that if there is a benevolent force governing creation, at best He has simply turned His back on us.

What is the reason for the contradiction between teachings of the Kabbalists and our reality? Are we doomed to live in a reality in which evil overshadows the good? How can we cause the Creator to turn His face towards us? Perhaps we are the ones who need to turn our faces towards Him? In this study unit, we will deal with these questions, along with others, thus clarifying the lesson's main topic: The major benefit in studying the wisdom of Kabbalah.

Ever since creation of the world, the universe has existed in continuous evolution. Everything changes. Nothing remains constant. Earth changes, life on it changes and people also constantly change. The force of development or "Guidance," as Kabbalists define, governs the world and pushes life towards evolution, traversing from one state to another, according to a predetermined and well-arranged plan. Still matter in the universe evolves into galaxies, suns, and planets; vegetative and animate matter on Earth evolve into a wide variety of plants and animals.

Kabbalists have revealed that the evolution of creation is not coincidental or to no avail, rather purposeful and "goal oriented." There is a final goal towards which the force of development is directed. Every detail in creation, as well as creation as a whole undergoes a gradual developmental process, through cause and effect, until the purpose is fulfilled. Thus, for instance, Earth underwent an evolutionary process until it became a suitable place for creating life; fruit on the tree undergo a developmental process before ripening and becoming suitable to eat and caterpillars undergo a developmental process until they become butterflies.

It turns out that the good purpose is revealed only at the end of development and not before, whereas the different developmental stages, not only do they not teach us of the final, purposeful and good state, rather as if intentionally to the contrary, they are specifically revealed in a form that seems completely opposite to the final goal. For example, as long as the apple on the tree hasn't ripened, it is bitter, green and unattractive and the caterpillar hatching from its egg is clumsy and charmless, before becoming a butterfly. This gap between lacking developmental stages, compared to their perfect, final state is revealed in the phases of development of each and every creature. The more the creature has evolved, the greater the gap.

The most outstanding example of that is the difference between the developmental stages of man and those of animals. A newborn calf stands on its feet a few moments after birth and knows how to guard itself from all harm. On the other hand, a newborn human being is a helpless creature, completely dependent on the grace of his parents. Many years must pass before he knows to operate his body properly and find his way around his environment. If a friend from another planet were to land in our world, he would surely think that the calf is destined to greatness, whereas the baby has no future.

In summary: Creator's Guidance over creation is purposeful and the benevolent purpose of evolution is only revealed at the end of the process, in the actualization of the purpose of development. Purposeful Guidance does not at all take the developmental states into account, which tend to deceive us and conceal the benevolent purpose from us.

Baal HaSulam writes about that in the essay "The Essence of Religion and its Purpose:" "It is about such matters that we say, "There is none so wise as the experienced." Only one who is experienced has the opportunity to examine Creation in all its phases of development, all the way through completion, and can calm things down, so as to not fear those spoilt images that the Creation undergoes in the phases of its development, but believe in its fine and pure end."

From everything said thus far, we can answer the question (at least partially) with which we opened the lesson: if the Creator is the absolute goodness, why do we feel His Guidance as bad? Even though the Creator is the absolute good, yet, since His Guidance upon creation is purposeful, His benevolence is revealed only at the end of development, with the actualization of the final purpose.

Test yourself:
- What characterizes the Creator's Guidance over creation?

The Good in the Bad

The general Guidance which develops humanity has a set pattern, according to which it pushes humanity to traverse from one state to another. Each and every state evolves by two forces. The first is a constructive force – a force that changes a bad state and turns it into a better one. The other is a destructive force - a force that turns each and every state into a worse one, until it obligates humanity to emerge from the bad situation and build a new and better one.

Humanity exists under the influence of both these forces and through their influence, proceeds and changes, proceeds and develops, repeatedly shifting from one state to the next, building a better one upon the ruins of the bad one.

An example of that is the development of feudalism in Europe. The Roman Empire, which brought immense financial prosperity to the world, began crumbling in the 6th and 7th centuries. As a result, wars increased, the financial situation declined, and the laypeople had no personal security. In response, a social system developed, according to which the farmers received protection and agricultural land and in return, they paid taxes and pledged their loyalty to their benefactor.

At the beginning, this was the best method for all, but the nobility began to gradually enslave the farmers more and more, the farmers' situation worsened and they were stifled under the nobility's rule. A war of classes began, which came to a very violent end, known as the French revolution. The age of Feudalism ended and upon its ruins, the democratic age began to form.

This pattern of development from opposites ("dialectic development") is set, since at the end, human desire responds to two types of basic stimuli: it is willing to invest effort for future gains or to escape misery. The force causing the will to receive to chase future gain is called "the pulling force," since it seems to pull the will to invest efforts in order to emerge from one's current state and shift to a new, better one. The force causing a person to escape misery is called the "pushing force," since it pushes the will to receive against its will to emerge from the existing state, to a better one, as well.

Both these forces obligate a person to emerge from one state, shift to another, and thus evolve. The pulling force does it in a way which a person feels as good and pleasant, whereas the pushing force does it in a way which a person feels as bad an unpleasant. However, if we view the process from the point of view of the final goal, we see that both forces are essential and act towards a good cause; they both act towards revealing the perfect, final and purposeful state of development, since both draw a person closer towards that end.

As illustration, let's imagine the evolution of all of creation as a horizontal axis, whose left end represents the beginning of development and the right end represents the conclusion of development and revelation of the good state (see drawing #7). We will divide the entire axis into X phases of development creation needs to go through until it reaches completion at its final state. Traversing from one developmental phase to another (and as a result, nearing the good, complete, final state) is possible only by revealing the evil in the current state. If we do not reveal the evil in our present state, or in other words, as long as we feel good in our current state, there will be no reason to leave it and move on to another, more advanced developmental phase. It turns out that the revelation of evil, in particular, is what pushes evolution forward towards the good.

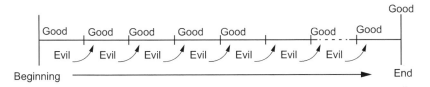

In the article "Critique of Marxism,"[35] Baal HaSulam describes that same process within the context of the development of political theories. And so he writes: Each movement and phase that humanity has taken in the political government is but a repudiation of its preceding state.

The duration of every political phase is just the time it takes to unveil its shortcomings and evil. While discovering its faults, it makes way for a new phase, liberated from these failings. Thus, these impairments that appear in a situation and destroy it are the

---

[35] Published in the Newspaper "The Nation" (1940)

very forces of human evolution, as they raise humanity to a more corrected state.

In addition, the faults in the next phase bring humanity to a third and better state. Thus, persisting successively, these negative forces that appear in the situations are the reasons for the progress of humanity. Through them, it climbs up the rungs of the ladder. They are reliable in performing their duty, which is to bring humankind to the last, most desirable state of evolution, purified of any ignominy and blemish."

Understanding that the revelation of evil advances us towards the good, draws us one step closer to settling the contradiction between the bad revealed in creation and the absolute good governing it. In the first section of the lesson, we learned that the good, benevolent Creator oversees creation with purposeful Guidance and that is why His goodness is revealed only with actualization of the goal, at the end of development. In this section of the lesson, we realized that the different states of development are not bad in essence; rather they all draw us closer towards the final, benevolent purpose. Accordingly, they are also good, in essence.

Test yourself:
- How does the transition from a certain developmental state to the next one occur?

Path of Torah and Path of Suffering

After becoming familiar with the mechanism driving the development of creation and of each and every one of us as parts within it, we can understand how to take part in the development so that it brings us contentment and we experience it as pleasure. The following section of the lesson is devoted to that topic.

When a person begins to study at the university, he receives the program he has to complete; he knows exactly which courses he needs to take, how many years he will need to study and he can even calculate how much his studies will cost him; he realizes that he is about to invest efforts and money in return for a certificate which will enable him to receive a higher income in the future and provide him with a more honorable status in society.

A person goes through the development on the academic course with awareness; he knows what he will gain and how much he will need to invest, thus he decides whether is prepared to invest or not. The course of studies is likely to be difficult and challenging, but it can be overcome, since the person sees the goal before him and knows that his efforts are for a limited time. Such a development is called development with awareness.

When a baby learns to crawl, his parents place him on the floor, spread toys around him and wait for him to move his arms and legs. The baby is not at all aware that he is developing. He might cry, refuse to crawl, but his parents will continue placing him on the floor, until he has learned to crawl.

At times, this process might be very frustrating for the baby, but in the end, he will have no choice but to develop, without knowing that he has shifted to another phase in his life. Such a development is called development with no awareness.

The difference between both types of development is apparent. In development with awareness, whoever is developing knows where he is going, does so at will and experiences the difficulties on the path as challenges he needs to undergo. In development with no awareness, whoever develops does not understand what he should do, despises the difficulties on the path and may even experience pain and frustration. Development with no awareness can be very long at times, if the person developing refuses to carry out what is required of him.

Until recently, humanity has evolved with no awareness. Throughout tens of thousands of years, we have shifted from one developmental phase to the next, without knowing where the development is leading us or what its purpose is. The difficulties that have been revealed on the path have brought us sorrow, suffering, and much frustration.

From now onward, as the point in the heart awakens in increasingly more people, a new possibility is opening before us to develop with awareness, save ourselves precious time and misery. Developing with awareness turns the suffering we feel under the pressure of development into sweet pangs of love - and that is the entire wisdom, to know the mechanism driving the process of development and develop with awareness, without unnecessary suffering.

We learned about the mechanism driving the process of development at length in the previous part of the lesson. We learned that the evil revealed at a certain degree of development is what inevitably drives us to move to the following stage of development. This is an extremely important point, because the only difference between developing with awareness and developing without awareness comes down to the form of recognizing the evil.

In developing with no awareness, we are unaware of the process of development; the evil is actively revealed, "on our flesh" and forces us unknowingly to move on to the next stage of development. On the other hand, in developing with awareness, we recognize the evil in advance, in thought, before it is actively revealed and it is enough for us to recognize the evil in order to move on to the next stage of development. In developing with awareness, we do not have to actively feel the evil.

We have two options: 1) Wait for the evil to come (and it inevitably will) and push us unknowingly to the next developmental stage. 2) Recognize the evil in advance, be aware of it before it is actively revealed and develop with awareness.

It turns out that developing with awareness has two significant benefits: It is quicker and does not involve sorrow and suffering. If we wish to accelerate our process of development, we need to expedite recognition of the evil in all states of development. Instead of waiting for the evil to be revealed, we will locate it in advance and accelerate our development. Furthermore, if we scrutinize the evil in thought, before it is actually revealed, not only will we expedite the process, we will also save ourselves the actual feeling of pain as suffering in our world.

It is similar to a person who is ill, with an illness that hasn't yet been discovered, but it is already incubating within him, awaiting to break out. A good doctor can detect the disease in advance, give the patient appropriate medicine and save him all the suffering he'd be destined to suffer if the illness were not treated in advance.

Baal HaSulam writes on the difference between the path of Torah and the path of suffering in the article "Peace in the World: "There are two authorities here, acting in the above-mentioned conduct of development: the one is the authority of Heaven, which is sure to turn anything harmful and evil to good and useful, but that will be in due time, in its own way, in a floundering manner and after a long time. And then there is the authority of the earth. And when the "evolving object" is a living being, it suffers horrendous torments while under the "press of development," a press that carves its way ruthlessly.

The "authority of the earth," however, is comprised of people who have taken this above-mentioned law of development under their own government and can free themselves entirely from the chains of time, and who greatly accelerate time, the completion of the ripeness and correction of the object, which is the end of its development."

When the point in the heart awakens in a person, he is drawn to follow to a place where he can study the wisdom of Kabbalah. The questions arising in him about the purpose of his existence no longer allow him to be led unknowingly on the trails of life. Reading Kabbalah books and drawing the Reforming Light help him scrutinize what the purpose of his life is and what the "evil" is, preventing him from attaining the purpose (we will expand more on recognition of the evil in the following lesson). Hence, out of the recognition of the evil revealed at each necessary phase of development, he hastily and joyfully traverses to the next developmental stage, on the path of revealing the good purpose at the end of development.

Developing with awareness is called a "path of Torah" in the wisdom of Kabbalah. Developing unknowingly is called a "path of suffering." We undergo the path of suffering with great misery and lengthily, as its name suggests. The "path of Torah," the path of developing with awareness from studying the wisdom of Kabbalah expedites the process of development and turns the suffering into sweet pangs of love, which amplifies one's longing for the promised good at the end of the path. This is the main benefit in studying the wisdom of Kabbalah - shifting from a path of suffering to a path of Torah.

Either way, our plan for development is known in advance, as are all the stages of development. We cannot skip any one of them; they are all necessary in order to bring us to the end of correction, to the feeling of the good and the benevolent. The only thing we can do is accept the process and hasten it.

Test Yourself:
- What is the difference between the path of suffering and the path of Torah?

Lesson Summary

Main Points
- The Creator's Guidance over creation is purposeful and the good purpose of development is revealed only at the end of the process, with the actualization of the goal of development. The purposeful Guidance does not at all take into account the states of development, whose purpose is specifically to deceive us and conceal the good purpose from us.
- The different states of development are not evil in essence; rather they all draw us closer to the final, benevolent purpose. Accordingly, they are also good, in essence.

- There are two possibilities for development: developing with awareness (path of Torah) and developing with no awareness (path of suffering). Developing with awareness has two significant benefits: it is quicker and does not involve sorrow or suffering. If we wish to accelerate the process of our development, we need to hasten the recognition of evil in all states of development. Instead of waiting for the evil to be revealed, we can locate it in advance and accelerate our development. Moreover, if we scrutinize the evil in thought before it is actually revealed, not only will we hasten the process, we will also save ourselves the actual feeling of pain as suffering in this world.

Concepts

Guidance - The force of development. The plan, according to which the Creator governs creation.

Pulling force - A force that causes the will to receive to run after future benefit.

Pushing force - A force that causes the will to receive to escape misery.

Path of suffering – Advancing with no awareness of the stages of development; a long and difficult path.

Path of Torah – Advancing with awareness of the stages of development, up to the goal of creation. A short and easy path.

Answers to the Questions

Question: What characterizes the Creator's Guidance over creation?
Answer: The Creator's Guidance over creation is purposeful. Meaning, every part of creation, and all of creation undergo a gradual process of development, by means of cause and effect, until they attain actualization of their purpose. The benevolent purpose of development is revealed only at the end of the process, with the actualization of the goal of development and not beforehand.

Question: How does transition from a certain developmental state to the next state occur?

Answer: Transition from each stage to another occurs as a result of feeling that the current stage is bad or at least not good enough. As long as the will to receive feels good in its current state, it will do nothing to change it.

Question: What is the difference between the path of suffering and the path of Torah?

Answer: On the path of suffering, we advance unknowingly; the evil revealed forces us to shift to the next developmental stage unknowingly. On the path of Torah, we advance knowingly, with awareness, by recognizing the evil in advance before it is actually revealed and stemming from the recognition of evil, we traverse to the next stage of development. The path of suffering is a long and painful one, whereas the path of Torah is a short and easy one.

Lesson #2 - Recognition of Evil

In this lesson we will learn about: Recognition of Evil / The Means for Revealing the Evil / Kabbalah and Ethics

What is Good?

In the previous lesson, we learned that the force driving us to advance forward to our next stage of development is the feeling that we are not content with our current state, or more optimistically, the feeling that the future could be much better (or with more awareness- the feeling that things are bad in our current state).

One way or the other, the deficiency - feeling emptiness or lack of satisfaction is the force that develops us and all of creation to advance, step after step, along the thought of creation's plan of correction. Baal

HaSulam writes[36] that without the feeling of deficiency, we would not make a single movement; we would leave our arms on the table for the rest of our lives without moving them at all- content with our state. The feeling of deficiency or something bad being revealed in our current state is what pushes us on to the next state.

The likely conclusion from all of the abovementioned is that if we want to accelerate the process of our development, we need to hasten the revelation of evil at every state. Instead of waiting for the evil to be revealed - for us to reveal it on our own. Except that this is no simple matter. First, we have to discern what the evil is that we need to identify (a complex matter itself) and then we have to discern how exactly it can be identified. When we know the answer to both of these questions, we will be able to shift from developing on the path of suffering to developing on the path of Torah. We will clarify these questions throughout this lesson.

In order to discern what evil is, we first need to understand what good is. Good, according to the wisdom of Kabbalah, is the final state of our development, meaning complete equivalence of form with the quality of bestowal, called "adhesion" (*Dvekut*) in the wisdom of Kabbalah. Simply put, good, according to the Wisdom of Kabbalah is a feeling of the harmonious connection with all parts of creation as one body. Good is connecting with love, stemming from the correction of the intention from in order to receive to in order to bestow.

If good is the feeling of connection, indeed the evil is the feeling of separation, or more precisely, the force that causes us to feel separated. We have been learning about this force expansively throughout the entire course - it is the intention of in order to receive, the program governing the will to receive in such a way that any work with it aims inward, only for self-benefit.

In all of his writings, Baal HaSulam repeatedly explains that the reason for all the evil in the world is our method of working with

---

[36] Writings of Baal HaSulam, "The Peace" Essay, Proof of His Work by Experience.

the will to receive, meaning solely for one's own benefit, with no consideration of others and completely against the laws of nature. The lack of equivalence of form between us and the quality of bestowal, as a result of working with the will to receive in order to receive is what prevents us from experiencing the true, good reality, governed by the single Creator, the good and the benevolent.

He writes of an example in the "Introduction to the Book of Zohar[37]: "Come and see, when all human beings agree to abolish and eradicate their will to receive for themselves, and have no other desire but to bestow upon their friends, all worries and jeopardy in the world would cease to exist. And we would all be assured of a whole and wholesome life, since each of us would have a whole world caring for us, ready to fulfill our needs. Yet, while each of us has only a desire to receive for ourselves, it is the source of all the worries, suffering, wars, and slaughter we cannot escape. They weaken our bodies with all sorts of sores and maladies."

The intention of in order to receive can be identified in our attitude towards others and whatever appears external to us. The intention of in order to receive directs our will to receive such that its only calculation regarding whatever appears external is: to what extent it may be used for self-benefit. As we have learned in previous sections of the course, even if it seems to us that there are actions we perform with no hint of self in them, when we examine our motivation in depth, we also find the same intention of in order to receive in those actions, with that same calculation of sole self- benefit.

Thus, the evil we need to identify is the intention of in order to receive, or in other words, our faulty attitude towards others. First, we need to recognize that we are indeed governed by the intention of in order to receive and then feel it as "evil," meaning to consider the value of connection, its inversion, as good. Hence, whenever we identify a part of the intention of in order to receive, we will

---

[37] Letter 19

inevitably recognize it as evil and inevitably shift to the next stage of development, until the complete good is attained at the end of correction.

This inner work of discerning the intention of in order to receive as the evil keeping us from spirituality is called the "recognition of evil" in the wisdom of Kabbalah.

The recognition of evil is actually the correction of evil. All we have to do in order to cancel the intention of in order to receive is to identify it as evil. It is like those monsters in fairy tales that vanish into thin air once peered at sternly. Correcting the intention of in order to receive begins and ends with our awareness of it. If we think about it, we will find that indeed, nothing else is necessary. If we identify the intention of in order to receive as a force preventing spirituality, the good from us, a desire to correct it instantaneously begins to form. As we have learned throughout this entire course, the only thing required of us is the desire for correction.

The work in recognition of the evil is somewhat similar to testing the quality of water. Instead of drinking the polluted water, becoming ill and suffering, we check the amount of bacteria in the water in advance with a microscope and save ourselves unnecessary suffering. Similarly, in the work of recognizing the evil, we also save ourselves the feeling of suffering "on our flesh." Instead of walking the path of suffering, we can use the wisdom of Kabbalah to identify the evil a priori, before it actually materializes and shift from the path of suffering to the path of Torah.

Either way, as long as the intention of in order to receive is embedded within us, governing us with no awareness, it is impossible for us to correct it and draw one step closer towards our corrected state. Baal HaSulam writes about it in one of his letters to his students[38]: "I do regret though, and complain, about the corruptions that still haven't appeared, but which are destined to appear, for a

---

[38] The Writings of Baal HaSulam, "Letters," Letter 5 (1921)

hidden corruption is hopeless, and its surfacing is a great salvation from heaven. The rule is that one does not give what he doesn't have. So if it appears now, there is no doubt that it was here to begin with, but was hidden. This is why I'm happy when they come out of their holes because when you cast your eye on them, they become a pile of bones."

That will suffice for now, regarding the question of what the evil is that we need to reveal. In the following part of the lesson we will learn how we can identify it.

Test Yourself:

What is the evil we need to identify?

Connecting to the Good

Well, let's recap! We have learned that the Creator created us in order to do good unto us and that on the path to the good, seemingly bad situations will be revealed. We realized that if we relate to the "bad" states being revealed as advancing us towards the goal, we will find that they are also good. We have said that particularly the evil revealed at every state is what advances us to the next stage and if we reveal it in advance, we will be able to hasten the stages of our spiritual development. After all of that, we only need to discern what the evil is, so we know how to recognize it and hasten development. We found that the intention of in order to receive is the evil preventing us from revealing the good.

In this part of the lesson, we will discern how to reach the "recognition of evil," meaning what actions we actually need to perform in order to identify the evil preventing us from attaining the good state. Before rolling up our sleeves and getting to work, it is important for us to understand one of the basic principles in a person's inner work in the study of the wisdom of Kabbalah, through which we will be able to understand more clearly what we need to do.

In one of his articles[39] Rav Baruch Shalom Ashlag (The Rabash), Baal HaSulam's eldest son and successor, brings a short and beautiful allegory that exemplifies the principle we would like to clarify. The Rabash writes that when a house is dark, no dirt can be seen in it. Only when the light is turned on, can the dirt be seen. A simple allegory for a simple principle: In order to identify the evil, we need to direct ourselves towards the good. We are unable to see the evil (dirt) without a little good (light).

As in Rabash's allegory, we are also in a dark room and also need to turn on the light in order to reveal the dirt in the room. Similar to a black hole, sucking in all of reality around it into its complete darkness, so the intention of in order to receive draws all of reality outside of us towards the black vacuum within us. In order to recognize the intention of in order to receive governing us from within, preventing the good from us, we need to draw a ray of light into us. Only in relation to the light, will we be able to notice the opposite intention.

Two powerful tools have been given to us in order to illuminate the darkness within us: The Light that Reforms and the influence of the environment. The Light that Reforms is actually the good shining upon us in our corrected state in spirituality. However, as long as we are not corrected, it shines outside of us and acts upon us in various ways, in order to draw us closer to correction. This is the light The Rabash means when he writes that we need to turn on the light in order to see the dirt.

When we read about our corrected state in Kabbalistic books and yearn to reveal them, feel them in practice, our yearning to reveal spirituality draws a unique illumination to us from spirituality, showing us how far from it we are. It seems to us that we have lost out; we wanted light and we got darkness. Yet, as explained extensively in the previous part of the lesson, revealing the darkness opposed to the

---

[39] Writings of Rabash, Part 1, "Concerning Above Reason" Essay, 1986

light is specifically what advances us to the next state in the process of "recognition of evil," on the path towards revealing the good.

Hence, we should have no fear if the study leads us to recognize the evil, a feeling of distance from others, doubts and disagreement, for particularly above all these obstacles, we build a greater and stronger yearning for spirituality. Kabbalists write that if a person studies Kabbalah and his study brings him to a state of satisfaction, he isn't truly studying Kabbalah. The light that shines upon us while studying should develop us, awaken within us new deficiencies for greater connection with the attribute of bestowal. Remember: A new deficiency is an opportunity for renewal, development, and revelations. All that is required of us is the correct deficiency, a request for connection.

Rabash writes[40], "The beginning of one's work is the recognition of evil. This means that a person asks of the Creator to feel how bad he is, meaning the will to receive. Knowing it—that the will to receive is called "evil"—is something that only the Creator can make him feel…Afterwards, he can ask for the will to receive to be replaced and to be given the desire to bestow in return for it."

Another important tool for the work in "recognition of evil" is the spiritual environment in which we operate, or more precisely, the environment's influence upon us. The good we need to draw to our condition in order to discern the evil in relation to it is not only the Light that Reforms, but also the importance we attribute to the quality of bestowal. Only if we raise the quality of bestowal to the top of our value system, will we be able to evaluate separation as evil. To the extent we appreciate the quality of bestowal we will recognize separation as evil.

The most efficient tool for raising the importance of the quality of bestowal is the environment. We are all "social creatures" and are

---

[40] Writings of Rabash, The Rungs of the Ladder, Essay "What is Holiness and Purity In The Work" 1991

all influenced by society's opinion. If we arrange an environment around us that raises the value of the quality of bestowal, we will have no choice but to value it. We are innately prepared for that. If our surroundings appreciate something, we too, according to our nature, will inevitably appreciate it. That is precisely the way advertising agencies influence us: A new product comes to the market, no one has a need for it, yet everyone begins talking about it. At first, you hear about it and laugh, then you hear about it and are silent, afterwards you begin to take interest in it and in the end, you buy it.

As in corporeality, so in spirituality. Only our spiritual environment can raise the importance of spirituality as a value above corporeality. None of us can do that on our own, and especially when spirituality (the attribute of bestowal) is opposite our nature and often felt as darkness.

To end this section, we will discern the connection between "There is none else besides Him" and the recognition of evil. If you've asked yourself where the work in recognition of evil encounters the work of "There is none else besides Him," here is the answer. Whenever spirituality is revealed as darkness, a lack of desire to study the wisdom of Kabbalah, indifference for the spiritual idea, or a corporeal disturbance preventing us from engaging in the wisdom of Kabbalah, before anything else, we need to attribute the obstacle to the single force that sends us all occurrences in our life, since "there is none else besides Him." If we remember where everything comes from and stabilize ourselves correctly towards the goal, which is the reason the disturbance was sent to us, we will be able to discern more deeply what exactly is disturbing us (recognition of evil) and formulate the appropriate request for correction within us.

Thus, we proceed and discern our desire for spirituality. The entire work is performed inside us, stemming from the recognition of evil. As we learned in the previous section of the lesson, in this work, we do not need the actual revelation of evil in practice in order to shift from one stage to another.

In summary, in order to reveal the evil, we need to direct ourselves as much as possible towards the good, by means of the Light that Reforms and the environment. Except that what may sound simple and trivial, might be revealed as difficult to perform. There is something in our nature that draws us to specifically deal with the evil, especially when we take our first steps in the study of the wisdom of Kabbalah. There is something in the feeling of suffering that awakens pride within us, and as long as we are not corrected, we are not able to refuse tasting it. It is not always simple to cleave to the good and raise the value of spirituality above all obstacles; however, if we wish to advance on the spiritual path, that is the action we need to perform.

Test Yourself:

What are the two means for revealing the evil?

Morality Squad

James "Sonny" Crockett and his partner Ricardo "Rico" Tubbs, a pair of the Miami Police Vice Squad's detectives were what we would call, "good guys." On television screens, within the fictitious world invented for them by the screenwriters of the show "Miami, Vice," the two have made most strenuous efforts to keep their hairdos and style as they attempt to instill some order on the streets of Miami and beat some morality into its criminals.

They succeeded in keeping their hairdos and style, but much less with the morals, ... and that's fine, those are also more or less the same results we achieve in the real world. It is much easier to keep the hairdo than the morals. Actually, it is much easier to keep anything other than morals.

Many people compare the wisdom of Kabbalah to Ethics. This misunderstanding of the wisdom of Kabbalah leads them to think that its purpose is to make us more moral, turn us into better human beings in this world. They are mistaken. The wisdom of Kabbalah is far from Ethics, as east from west.

We referred to the difference between the wisdom of Kabbalah and methods of Ethics in the second study unit[41], where we clarified the way the wisdom of Kabbalah relates to the work with the will to receive. Questions on the difference between ethics and Kabbalah also rise from the explanation of the work in "recognition of evil" and they constitute a good opportunity to further sharpen the difference between the two approaches.

The wisdom of Kabbalah and the methods of ethics seem to share the same goal: To eradicate the evil within us and instill within us a different, corrected approach towards others in our environment. As a result of this similarity, some conclude that the wisdom of Kabbalah is also a method of ethics. A deeper understanding of the essence of the wisdom of Kabbalah leads us to the conclusion that what seems to us as a commonality is imaginary and nothing else. Actually, both approaches are completely different from each other, from every aspect.

We make three main distinctions between the wisdom of Kabbalah and the methods of ethics. We will detail and clarify them one by one:

The foundation upon which both methods are based - different.
The reward each method promises - different.
The purpose of both methods - different.

The first difference between the methods is their underlying foundation, as noted above. From this point of view, the gap between the wisdom of Kabbalah and ethics is no less abysmal than the gap between the Creator and the created. This is because the wisdom of Kabbalah imbibes its strength and knowledge from the thought of

---

[41] This book, part 1, lesson #2, chapter 3.

creation, whereas the method of morality is entirely based on the thoughts of mortal human beings.

Ethics is a method based on our life experience as human beings. When life shows us that a certain behavior of the individual harms the collective good, we exert pressure on the individual to not behave that way. Generally speaking, that is the method of ethics. Hence, for example, we reproach acts such as lying and theft, and when necessary issue laws that prevent us from lying and stealing.

The Wisdom of Kabbalah is not based on our life experience as human beings. The wisdom of Kabbalah cascades to us from the height of creation, from the thought of creation to do good unto His creatures, and unlike the method of morality, which is limited by the human frame of thought, the wisdom of Kabbalah opens before us a complete picture of reality, independent of our limitations of perception as human beings.

This significant difference inevitably defines a completely different perception of "good" and "evil" (which we described extensively in the previous parts of the lesson.) According to the method of ethics, the values of "good" and "evil" are measured in accordance with the good of society, whereas according to the wisdom of Kabbalah, the values of "good" and "evil" are measured according to a completely different measure, in accordance to realizing the thought of creation. As explained in the previous lessons, according to this point of view, even what seems "evil" turns into "good."

The second main difference between the methods is the promised reward to those engaging in it: the wisdom of Kabbalah promises a person a reward, which is above the nature of this world; whereas the method of ethics promises a person a reward within the framework of this world.

Engaging in the wisdom of Kabbalah changes a person's nature from receiving to bestowal and raises him above the limits of this world, to attain spirituality and eternality. However, the highest reward the method of ethics can offer a person is a corrected society, within the framework of this world – a worthy reward agreeable with all, except that as long as we remain within the framework of this world, we are incapable of attaining it, since it is not within our power to forego our own benefit for the benefit of society.

It doesn't matter how much we limit the individual or deter him from acting against society; in the end, his "corrected" attitude towards others will only be lip service and no more. Deep inside, he will still only think of self- benefit and at the first opportunity he gets, will actively tend to his own benefit at the expense of society. Being concerned with the benefit of all at the expense of self-benefit is an action above human nature and in order to be actualized the promised reward also has to be above man's nature.

When we detailed the former differences, we mentioned the third main difference between the wisdom of Kabbalah and ethics, which is the purpose of both methods, yet it is worthy of being highlighted in its own right. The purpose of the method of ethics is to establish a corrected society in our world. The purpose of the wisdom of Kabbalah is to elevate man to the degree of the Creator.

The Wisdom of Kabbalah has not been given to us in order to turn us into better people within the framework of this world; rather to raise us above the limitations of this world.

Test Yourself:

What is the foundation underlying the method of ethics and what is the foundation underlying the Wisdom of Kabbalah?

Lesson Summary

Main Points

- The "evil" we need to reveal in order to proceed on the path of Torah is the ruling of the will to receive. The cause of all evil in the world is the way we work with the will to receive, meaning solely for self- benefit, with no consideration of others and in complete opposition to the laws of nature. The lack of equivalence of form between us and the quality of bestowal, as a result of our work with the desire with the intention of in order to receive is what prevents us from experiencing the genuine and good reality, governed by the single Creator, the good and the benevolent.

- Two powerful tools have been given to us in order to illuminate the darkness within us: the Light that Reforms and the influence of the environment. The Light shows us the extent to which the will to receive distances us from spirituality; the environment gives us importance for spirituality, in relation to which we identify the will to receive as evil. Recognizing the ruling of the will to receive on one hand and the importance of spirituality on the other hand creates within us a longing for spirituality and a desire for correction.

- The wisdom of Kabbalah and the methods of ethics are as distant from each other as east from west. They are based on different underlying foundations: ethics is based on our life experience as human beings whereas Kabbalah cascades to us from the thought of creation and is not bound by the limitations of our perception as human beings. The promised reward to a person in both methods is completely different in essence: ethics promises a person a reward within the framework of this world (a corrected society), and Kabbalah - a reward above this world (spirituality). The reward ethics offers a person is not enough for one to forgo one's self-benefit for the benefit of others, since such a sacrifice is beyond one's capability. The purpose of the method of ethics is a corrected society; the purpose of Kabbalah is spirituality, and since the purpose of both methods is different, the values of good and evil of both methods are also different.

Concepts

Recognition of evil - Discerning the intention of in order to receive as evil, preventing us from spirituality.

The Light that Reforms - The light that shines upon us externally, as long as we are not corrected. In the correct study of the wisdom of Kabbalah, the Light that Reforms acts upon us and draws us closer to correction.

Answers to the Questions

Question: What is the evil we need to identify?
Answer: The evil we need to identify is the intention of in order to receive, or more precisely, the fact that we are governed by the intention of in order to receive, which directs us to exploit others instead of connecting with them and bestowing unto them.

Question: What are the two means for revealing the evil?
Answer: The two means for revealing the evil are the Light that Reforms and the influence of the environment. The Light that Reforms, which shines upon us while reading Kabbalah books with the correct intention to correct the desire, shows us how distant we are from spirituality, meaning deep in the nature of the will to receive. The feeling of distance (revelation of evil) awakens in us the desire for correction. We receive importance for the quality of bestowal from the spiritual environment in which we operate, in relation to which we evaluate the ruling of the will to receive and the distance from spirituality as evil.

Question: What is the foundation underlying the method of ethics and what is the foundation underlying the Wisdom of Kabbalah?
Answer: The method of ethics is based on our life experience as human beings in this world. When life shows us that a certain behavior of an individual harms the benefit of others, we exert

pressure on the individual to not behave in such a way. The wisdom of Kabbalah imbibes its knowledge from the thought of creation and is not bound to the limitations of our perception as human beings in this world.

To expand and delve into the course material, go to the Course book, page 382.

Logical Sequence
(Order of Development of the Course)

We learned that the wisdom of Kabbalah is the method for revealing the Creator to the created in this world.

We learned that in order to reveal the Creator, we need to change our intention from in order to receive to in order to bestow.

We learned that a special spiritual force is embedded within Kabbalah books called the "Light that Reforms," which has the power to change our intention, from in order to receive to in order to bestow.

We learned that only in the discernment of our attitude towards others, can we formulate a true request within us to the Light that Reforms.

We learned that only in choosing the correct environment for spiritual development, can we precisely discern our attitude to others.

We learned that the points in the heart are the shattered parts of the Soul of *Adam HaRishon* and that in constructing a spiritual environment with other points in the hearts, we create the request for correction, to connect the shattered parts and summon the Light that Reforms.

We learned that the basis for a genuine request of the Light that Reforms is "There is none else besides Him," meaning to attribute all the states being revealed to the single Creator, the source of all causes.

We learned that in attributing all the states being revealed to the Creator, we are hastening the process of correction and saving ourselves sorrow and suffering.

In the next section we will learn about the order of correcting the desire.

Part #3 - Israel and Nations of the World

Lesson #1 - Aiming Straight to the Creator (Yashar- El)

In this lesson, we will learn about: Israel and the Nations of the World / Purity and Coarseness / The Purpose of Creation and Correcting Creation

Near And Far from the Light

Just like any other concept in the wisdom of Kabbalah, "Israel" and the "Nations of the world" are first and foremost inner discernments of desire and similar to other inner discernments, they are also expressed in corporeal reality, as the people of Israel and the other Nations of the world. The benefit of exploring this expression of inner discernments through their projection into our world is that it can help clarify the relationships among our own inner qualities.

There is an aspect of "Israel" and the "Nations of the world" in the internality of the world and the individual. In addition, there is the aspect of "Israel" and the "Nations of the world" in the externality of the world and the individual. The externality is a consequence of the internality; hence, if we wish to grasp the true nature of Israel and the Nations of the world in externality, we must first understand their spiritual nature. We will do just that in the first part of the lesson.

The will to receive is the matter comprising all of creation and each of its parts. The will to receive can be divided into two main parts: one purer part, closer in its nature to the light, to the attribute of bestowal, and another, coarser part, farther in its nature from the light. The part closer in its nature to the light is less complicated to correct and the part farther from the light is more complicated to correct.

The pure part of the desire, closer in its nature to the light, is called "Israel" in the wisdom of Kabbalah, from the words "*Yashar-El*" (straight to the Creator). Meaning, it is a desire that is aimed straight to the Creator, a desire that has innate preparation for correction and renewing the connection with the Creator. The part of the desire farther in its nature from the Creator and coarser in essence is called the "Nations of the world" in the wisdom of Kabbalah (see drawing #8).

In the entire world and within each one of us, both of these parts of the desire can be discerned- a desire closer to the attribute of bestowal and a desire closer to the attribute of receiving. The wisdom of Kabbalah refers to these two types of desires, when it speaks of "Israel" and the "Nations of the world."

Will to Receive

Both types of the desire, "Israel" and "Nations of the world" can be found in every section of creation. For instance, if we examine human development over tens of thousands of years, we will find that the desires revealed in humanity in its first days were purer and closer in their nature to the light, and as humanity developed, coarser desires have been revealed, farther from the light (this is also the reason why in ancient times, correction was more natural, whereas in our times a special method for man's correction is necessary.)

One of the basic laws in the wisdom of Kabbalah is called "the general and the individual are equal." According to this law, every individual or part of creation contains all parts of creation within it. Accordingly, even in people of our generation, we can discern both parts of desire - pure and coarse, closer to bestowal or closer to receiving. People, whose point in the heart has awakened, regardless of religion, race or sex, who are drawn to the study of the wisdom of Kabbalah and correction of the desire constitute parts from the purer desire, called "Israel." People who are not yet drawn to correction are coarser parts of the desire, called "Nations of the world."

In summary, "Israel" and the "Nations of the world" are two types of desire – a purer desire and a coarser one- which can be distinguished at every layer of creation. Rather, the division between both types of the desire is not so simple or clear. In actuality, both aspects are intermingled with each other in endless combinations. There are desires from the aspect of Israel, within which different measures of parts of the desire from the aspect of the Nations of the world are mixed. And vice versa, there are desires from the aspect of the Nations of the world, within which different measures of the desires from the aspect of Israel are mixed. It is specifically this mixture that enables working with both types of the desire and correcting even the coarsest desires.

Test Yourself:

What are Israel and the Nations of the world, according to the wisdom of Kabbalah?

Israel within a Person

So, what does it mean when Kabbalists use the term "Israel" in regard to a person? In the previous part of the lesson, we learned that "Israel" is a discernment within the desire, a part of the desire that is closer in its attributes to the light. We also learned that opposite the aspect of

Israel in the desire, we also discern another part, farther in its nature from the light, called "Nations of the world." In the world in general, both of these discernments manifest in the division of people into two main groups: those closer in their nature to correction and those farther in their nature from correction.

As in the world, so in a person. We can also divide the desires within us into two major groups: desires in the aspect of "Israel" and desires in the aspect of "Nations of the world." Within us, we also have coarser, thicker desires, which seemingly distance us from spirituality and there are purer desires, which draw us closer to spirituality. Thus, for instance, the desire with which we are now sitting and reading this study book is a pure desire among our desires and is called "Israel" within us. Of course, we also have other desires within us, which seemingly distance us from the study of the wisdom of Kabbalah. Those are the coarser desires within us, called the "Nations of the world" within us.

From studying thus far, you surely know already that desires which seem to deter us from spirituality actually have a very important role on our spiritual path. Without the aspect of the Nations of the world in a person, without the delays and obstacles revealed to us on our spiritual path, we wouldn't attain the entire depth of spirituality. It is precisely the difficulties revealed on the path that enable us to renew our connection with the Creator in all His glory. We are familiar with a similar principle from the reality of our corporeal life. In our world, too, difficulties revealed on the path of actualizing a certain goal are later discovered to have been like "spice" adding its unique flavor to the whole dish.

We need to learn how to work with both parts of the desire being revealed within us, "Israel" and "Nations of the World" and increase our desire for spirituality as much as possible, using them both. Just like a man who falls in love with a woman to the extent that love does not let him rest, so we should use the aspect of Israel within us, our longing for connection with the Creator, in order to raise the importance of spirituality. Similarly, just like a woman concealing herself from the man in order to arouse his love, so we should use the aspect of "Nations of the World" within us, the desires which seem to distance us from the Creator, in order to arouse in us a stronger longing for spirituality, up to the required measure.

So, what does it mean when Kabbalists call a person "Israel"? According to the wisdom of Kabbalah, being Israel means to arouse the longing for a connection with the Creator within us. "Israel," from the words *Yashar- El* (straight to the Creator). Whoever's desire is aimed towards the Creator, to renewing the connection with the Creator is called "Israel" in the wisdom of Kabbalah, no matter what the person's nationality or religion is.

Rav Baruch Shalom Ashlag (The Rabash), Baal HaSulam's eldest son writes of such in his essay "One who strengthens one's heart"[42]: "One who wishes to go by the path of the Creator is called Yashar-El, which is considered Yashar[straight] LaEl [to the Creator], meaning that he wants everything he does to rise straight to the Creator, and does not wish to have any other aim."

Meaning, from a spiritual perspective, "Israel" is whoever yearns for the Creator. It doesn't matter if one is American or Russian, African or Asian, Moldovan or Cambodian, Iraqi or Israel- it doesn't matter the color of one's skin, sex, or religion - if the point in the heart has awakened in a person, if a desire to renew the connection with the Creator has awakened, one is called "Israel."

In our times, when the single desire created at the thought of creation is awakening for the first time in order to actualize its purpose of existence, millions of students around the world, regardless of religion, race, or sex, are joining the wondrous adventure of studying the wisdom of Kabbalah. Tens of thousands of people around the world are already studying Kabbalah in an organized fashion, within

---

[42] Writings of Rabash, Rungs of the Ladder, "One who Strengthens One's Heart" Essay, 1985.

the official framework of "Kabbalah for All" and millions of others around the globe access contents of the organization at different times. New study groups, opening frequently invite everyone and anyone to study the wisdom of truth.

Test Yourself:
According to the wisdom of Kabbalah, who is Israel?

Two that Are One

A famous legend[43] tells that prior to the giving of the Torah at Mount Sinai, the Creator went around with the Torah to the Nations of the world and offered It to them first. One by one, the Creator passed among the nations and asked them if they accept the Torah upon themselves and each time He received a negative response, until He came to the people of Israel. That is the legend and from there on, the story is already more or less well-known…

At first glance, what seems like an ambiguous allegory or folk tale is actually a deep description of the most inner forces at the base of creation. This legend explains to us how we are to arrange within us the correct relationship between both sides of the desire, called "Israel" and "Nations of the world" and how we need to correct them, by means of the wisdom of Kabbalah, called "Torah."

We learned about the correct relationship between both parts of the desire and their correction in the previous parts of the lesson. In order to understand the legend with which we opened the lesson, we need to further expand upon this important matter.

According to the wisdom of Kabbalah, there is no good or evil in the popular sense accepted in our world. Whatever is revealed in our world, both in internality and externality is a part of the plan of

---

[43] From the writings of Rabbi Yishmael, Jethro

creation to bring us to the end of correction; hence, in its essence, it is good. It only depends on how we relate to it, and how we use it.

The wisdom of Kabbalah distinguishes between two different, complementing trends in the thought of creation:

The correction of creation

The purpose of creation, as we know well, is to do good unto the created, meaning to fulfill the will to receive that was created with the pleasure the Creator wishes to grant it. The issue is that we are incapable of receiving this goodness directly into the will to receive. If we receive it directly, a feeling of shame will be aroused in us - shame of the free gift. In order to avoid that shame, we need to "pay" for the gift, exert efforts in order to receive it. The effort we need to exert is to correct the desire, so that it operates in the form of love and giving to others. Correcting the desire is also called correcting creation.

In order to actualize the purpose of creation, which is to derive pleasure, we need the coarsest parts of the desire. The more we use a coarser and greater desire, so will we be able to receive more of the pleasure the Creator wishes to grant us. Furthermore, using the greater and coarser parts of the desire is a condition for receiving all the abundance. Only when all the coarser parts of the desire are filled, will we receive all the goodness the Creator wishes to grant us (see drawing #9).

On the other hand, in order to actualize the correction of creation, as a condition for receiving the abundance, we need the purer parts of the desire, those closer in their nature to the light. Only through them, will we be able to acquire the quality of the light and learn to love, resemble the Creator and receive all the abundance promised to us at the thought of creation.

It turns out that from the perspective of correcting creation, the most important vessels are vessels of bestowal, called the "aspect of Israel" and from the perspective of the purpose of creation, the most important vessels are vessels of receiving, the coarser ones, called "Nations of the world." It is not complete without one of the two parts. Both are necessary and equally important and each one's value is measured according to its respective specific value in the correction of creation.

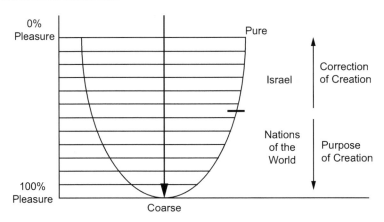

It follows that we can also understand the legend opening the lesson. The Creator, with the Torah, turns to the Nations of the world first, since from the perspective of the purpose of creation, they are more important. Only when the coarsest parts of the desire are filled with light, will the purpose of creation be fully actualized.

In order to better understand what this is all about, we will bring an example from our daily life, familiar to us all. Every mother is filled with joy when she sees her child eating well and much more so when he eats the food she has prepared. Just imagine the following situation: It is Friday evening in Mom's kitchen. The table is abundant with all the best, all of your favorite dishes, except that to your surprise and sorrow, you are simply not hungry. You only eat the green salad with great effort and out of the desire to please your mother.

Now you tell me: on a scale of 1-10, how pleased is your mom? 1, At best, actually, she's quite sad, since from her perspective, you didn't eat a thing. However, had you come with a huge appetite and eaten everything she prepared, she would be beyond joyous. Thus, similar to Mom's kitchen, although extremely different, if we want to bring contentment unto the Creator and receive all of the goodness He wishes to grant us, we need to come to Him with the greatest and coarsest desire. Only with that, will we be able to receive all the goodness the Creator wishes to give us. It turns out that from the perspective of the purpose of creation, the coarsest desire is the most important.

However, from the perspective of correcting creation, the purer desire is the more important one, or, in other words, the intention to bestow that rides upon the desire is the more important one. As with all the delicacies on the table, we eat only to please Mom, who prepared them for us, thus, although vastly different, we will receive all the abundance the Creator prepared for us, only in order to bestow unto Him.

Now, we can understand our opening legend in greater depth. Although the Creator "turns" to the Nations of the world – that is how it needs to be according to the order of actualizing the purpose of creation, However, the coarser desires are not ready to receive the Torah (the method of correction for shifting the intention) as a condition for receiving the goodness. In the meantime, only "Israel," the purer part of the desire, is ready to receive the Torah and correct itself. In correcting itself, it will eventually enable the light to fill all the parts of the desire, even the coarsest ones. Hence, only Israel receives the Torah.

In summary, "Israel" and the "Nations of the world" are two essential parts for actualizing the purpose of creation, and both parts exist within a person. From this aspect, one is not better than the other. We need to remember that, both in the inner work in correcting the desires that are revealed within us and in the order of correcting the world, as it manifests in corporeal reality in the relations between those who have a Point in the Heart and those who are not yet ripe for correction, which will be detailed in the following lessons.

Test Yourself:

What is more important: the pure part of the desire called "Israel" or the coarse part called the "Nations of the world?"

Summary of the Lesson

Main Points

- The pure part of the desire, closer in its nature to the light, is called "Israel" in the wisdom of Kabbalah, from the term *Yashar El* (straight to the Creator). Meaning, it is the desire aimed straight to the Creator, a desire with innate preparation for correction, for renewing the connection with the Creator. The part of the desire farther in its nature from the Creator and coarser in its essence is called the "Nations of the world" in the wisdom of Kabbalah. In the entire world and in each one of us, we can discern between both of these types of the desire - the desire closer to the attribute of bestowal and the desire closer to the attribute of receiving. The wisdom of Kabbalah refers to these two types of desire when it speaks of "Israel" and the "Nations of the world."

- We can also divide the desires within a person into two main groups: "Israel" and "Nations of the world." Within us, there are also coarser desires, thicker ones, which seem to distance us from spirituality, and purer desires, drawing us towards spirituality. We need to learn how to work with them both: using the aspect of Israel within us, in our longing for connection with the Creator, in order to raise the importance of spirituality, and using the aspect of the "Nations of the world" within us, in the desires that seem to distance us from the Creator, in order to arouse in us a stronger yearning for spirituality, up to the required measure.

- From the perspective of correcting creation, the most important vessels are the vessels of bestowal, called the "aspect of Israel."

From the perspective of the purpose of creation, the more important vessels are the vessels of receiving, the coarser ones, called "Nations of the world." There is no completion without one of the two parts. Both are equally necessary and important and the value of each one of them is measured according to its respective specific value in the correction of creation.

Concepts

Pure - Closer in its nature to the light, the attribute of bestowal. It is simpler to correct.

Coarse - Far in its nature from the light, the attribute of bestowal, is more difficult to correct

Israel- The purer part of the will to receive.

Nations of the World- The coarser part of the will to receive.

The law of "The general and the individual are equal" - **Every** individual or part of the parts of creation contains within it all the parts of creation. Just as in all of creation we can discern purer desires and coarser ones, so we can discern them within the individual, as well.

Answers to the Questions

Question: What are Israel and the Nations of the world, according to the Wisdom of Kabbalah?

Answer: Israel and the "Nations of the world" are two discernments in the will to receive. Israel is the purer part of the desire, closer in its nature to the light, hence, less complicated for correction. The Nations of the world are the coarser part in the desire, farther in its nature from the light, and for that reason, more complicated to correct.

Question: According to the wisdom of Kabbalah, who is Israel?

Answer: According to the wisdom of Kabbalah, "Israel" is whoever's point in the heart has awakened and longs for connection with the

Creator to reveal spirituality, regardless of the person's sex, race, nationality or religion - if the point in the heart has awakened, one is considered the aspect of Israel and can begin studying the wisdom of Kabbalah in order to actualize one's desires for spirituality.

Question: What is more important: the pure part of the desire called "Israel" or the coarse part called the "Nations of the world?"

Answer: From the perspective of correcting creation, the aspect of Israel is more important, and from the perspective of the purpose of creation, the Nations of the world are more important. In order to receive all the abundance the Creator prepared for us at the thought of creation, we need to use all parts of the desire. Only with a great will to receive, will we be able to receive the great abundance. Except that in order to receive all the goodness in creation, we need to first correct the will to receive with the intention of in order to bestow.

Lesson #2 - From Babylon to the State of Israel

In this lesson we will learn about: The history of the nation of Israel according to the wisdom of Kabbalah / The exile of Israel into the Nations of the world

The Nation of Israel - Instruction Manual

In the previous lesson, we learned about the aspects of Israel and the Nations of the world, as they are expressed in the internality of the desire. This lesson will be devoted to the way both of these attributes are expressed in the corporeal world as the Nation of Israel and the Nations of the world.

According to the law of roots and branches, each corporeal outcome in our world has a spiritual root. The spiritual root of the Nation of Israel and the other Nations of the world is the two parts of the desire, upon which we expanded in the previous lesson. The purer part of the desire, closer in its nature to the Light, also called the "will to bestow" is the spiritual root of the Nation of Israel in corporeality. The coarser part of the desire, also called the "will to receive" is the spiritual root of the Nations of the world in corporeality.

The relationship between both these types of desires in the spiritual world dictates the development and correction of the Nation of Israel and the Nations of the world in corporeality, as well. In spirituality, the purer desire is corrected first and then the coarser desire; the same order of correction is maintained in our world, too: first Israel and afterwards, the Nations of the world. In spirituality, the will to receive and the will to bestow need to mix with each other, in order to enable the correction of the will to receive as well, hence, takes place in the corporeal world as well; the Nation of Israel goes into exile and mixes with the Nations of the world.

According to the law of roots and branches, the history of the Nation of Israel is actually a long and essential process of preparation for the correction of all humanity and actualizing the thought of creation. This is a projection of the lengthy inner process that the Point in the Heart must undergo in relation to the other desires within the person. We will follow with an extensive description of this process.

Everything began approximately four thousand years ago. In the year 3,000 B.C.E., most of the world population was concentrated in the area of Mesopotamia, in ancient Babylon. During that period, people sufficed with a roof over their head and basic food; life was managed in a natural, cooperative and peaceful manner, until suddenly - everything changed.

One bright morning, the Babylonians awoke to a feeling that their simple life in the pasture or under a tree was becoming gray and dissatisfying. The human ego (the concern for self-benefit at the expense of the benefit of others) burst out and caused them to seek more sophisticated ways to exploit each other.

With lightning speed, modern agriculture began taking shape and the initial foundations were laid for the means of commerce and utilization of money and taxation. In parallel, methods of ruling and governing developed, instilling classic procedures of order and management for the first time. The social changes also bore social class distinctions. The ego, which pushed the Babylonians to develop, made them more concentrated on themselves and also separated them, like a knife. At the peak of the ego's eruption, the Babylonians began to think that it was in their ability to control the forces of nature governing the world. They wanted to reach beyond the heavens and built the famous tower.

However, within the chaos of the erupting ego, one Babylonian, Abraham was his name, refused to accept the situation and decided to go against the flow. He began a different search after the force behind the scenes, causing life's events, until he succeeded in revealing it and developed a method for its revelation. He offered this method to all those interested.

This is how The *Rambam* describes it[44]: "Abraham was forty years old when he became aware of his Creator....He would go out and call to the people, gathering them in city after city and kingdom after kingdom... until thousands and myriads gathered around him and these are the people of the house of Abraham. And he planted in their hearts this great fundamental principle, composed texts about it...This concept proceeded and gathered strength among the descendants of Jacob and those accompanying them, and there became a nation in the world which knew G-d."

The next step in the development of the Nation of Israel is the traverse of Abraham and his group of students to the Land of Israel. The Land of Israel, as the Nation of Israel is a corporeal branch of the spiritual desire for connection with the Creator. The matter is alluded to within its name: "Land" (*Eretz* in Hebrew), from the word

---

[44] Rambam, "*Mishneh* Torah", the Book of Science, Laws of Idolatry, 11-16.

"desire" (*Ratzon* in Hebrew), and Israel (*Yisrael* in Hebrew, from *Yashar El* (straight to the Creator), a desire straight to the Creator. A person whose point in the heart has awakened will inevitably feel an unexplainable pull to the Land of Israel and a strong connection to it. From here, it is understood why all the Kabbalists throughout all the years of exile have yearned to return to the Land of Israel and many of them has even done so, in practice. We will expand on the special connection between the Nation of Israel and the Land of Israel in the next part of the lesson.

In order to draw Israel another step towards revealing the connection with the Creator in all its depth, a new degree of ego is revealed and Israel goes down to Egypt. In Egypt, the ruling of the will to receive is revealed to Israel more powerfully and in order to rise above it, a new method of correction is required. This method is the *Torah*, given to the Nation of Israel at the stature of Mount Sinai.

In essence, "Egypt," "Moses," "Pharaoh," "Torah" and "Mount Sinai" are also inner discernments of the will to receive of each one of us and in the internality of the desire, we need to reveal them. In parallel, similar to the Nation of Israel and the Land of Israel, they, too, manifest in our world. Regarding the story of Exodus from Egypt in its deep spiritual meaning and other parts of the history of the people of Israel, whose spiritual roots are not explained in this book, you may read on the site kabbalah.info and other books from Laitman Kabbalah Publishers.

The people of Israel who became a nation in Egypt, return to the Land of Israel and establish the First Holy Temple. Though the spiritual root had to touch the corporeal branch in the form of a physical structure, it is more valuable to think of the Temple, like other significant events in the history of the Nation of Israel, as a spiritual discernment, as well. Correcting the will to receive with the intention of in order to bestow is called "The Holy Temple" (*Beit HaMikdash* in Hebrew) in the wisdom of Kabbalah. Holiness in spirituality is bestowal; holy, *Kadosh* in Hebrew, comes from the term "separate" or "different." *Beit* (House of..) in spirituality symbolizes the will to receive. Thus, the state called "The Holy Temple" is the will to receive corrected with the intention of in order to bestow.

In the days of the Second Holy Temple, the entire Nation of Israel attained the highest spiritual degree as one body. It is told that even little children felt the spiritual reality. In the Babylonian Talmud[45] it is written that "from Dan unto Beer Sheba, no boy or girl was found who was not thoroughly versed in the laws of purity and impurity." Meaning, the entire Nation of Israel, from old to young, knew how to use the will to receive correctly, with the intention of in order to bestow (purity in the wisdom of Kabbalah - using the will to receive with the intention of in order to bestow. Impurity – using the will to receive with the intention of in order to receive).

It would seem that the whole story should have ended here. However, in actuality, this is where it just begins. The Nations of the world are not yet corrected. They are not even aware of the necessity for correction. We can check for ourselves and see how many desires within us can simply do without spirituality because they find adequate fulfillment in other pursuits. So, it is in humanity that only a small number of people feel they must know and attain the purpose of life. But, as abovementioned, the purpose of creation is to do good unto all the created beings. It goes without saying that this is beyond considerations of religion, sex or nationality.

In order to correct the Nations of the world as well – those desires that do not yearn for the purpose of life - it is necessary to mix them with Israel. Consequently, the will to receive is revealed once again in the Nation of Israel, this time in full force, causing the Nation to lose its spiritual degree and the destruction of the First and Second Temples. The Nation of Israel goes into a long exile of two thousand years. From a state of unfounded love, it deteriorates to unfounded hate and its connection with spirituality is disconnected.

---

[45] Babylonian Talmud, Sanhedrin 94:72.

Only at the end of exile, during these very days, is it possible to begin correcting all parts of the desire, correcting all of humanity.

Test Yourself:

What is the order of correction of the Nation of Israel and the Nations of the world?

From Exile to Redemption

It has been told of Rabbi Akiva and his three friends, who stood mourning outside the destructed Holy Temple. When they saw a fox running out of the ruins of the Holy of Holies, the three friends burst in tears. Rabbi Akiva laughed. His friends asked him "Why are you laughing?" He answered them, smiling: as long as the prophecy of exile hasn't taken place, the prophecy of redemption hasn't taken place. Now, when the prophecy of exile has been fulfilled, it is certain that the prophecy of redemption will also be fulfilled.

Rabbi Akiva was a great Kabbalist. From the height of his spiritual attainment, he saw what his friends could not see. Rabbi Akiva knew that the destruction and exile are imperative stages on the path to correcting the entire will to receive (what is called "redemption"); that the good, promised us in the thought of creation can be revealed only when every person in the world is qualified to receive it, including the Nations of the world. In order to enable the correction of the Nations of the world, the Nation of Israel has to go into exile and mix among them.

These stages of correction are enrooted in the spiritual structure of the desire. The will to receive is comprised of two main parts: a pure desire, closer in its nature to the light, and a coarse desire, farther in its nature from the light. The coarse desire cannot be corrected as is; it is completely opposed to bestowal. In order to correct it, sparks of bestowal need to be instilled in it and through them, be corrected, as well. That is why the purer desire, called "Israel," is corrected first and after its correction, it is shattered and mixed with the coarser desire, called "Nations of the world."

Similar to spirituality, so it is in corporeality. The Nation of Israel achieves spiritual attainment during the times of the First and Second Holy Temples and in order to bring the Nations of the world to correction as well, it loses its spiritual degree, goes into exile and mixes among the Nations of the world. Exile is an essential stage for revealing redemption. From the moment it is revealed, there is no more doubt that redemption will come, as well. That is why Rabbi Akiva laughed.

The loss of the Nation of Israel's spiritual degree and its exile are, as abovementioned, a certain sign that spirituality will be revealed to every person in the world as soon as the exile ends. Hence, immediately after Israel's exile, the spiritual force is revealed in the world, destined to draw all of humanity to spirituality at the end of exile - "The Book of Zohar."

Although the conditions for writing the "Book of Zohar" have ripened, conditions for its widespread revelation amongst humanity have yet to be revealed. The "Book of Zohar" will be revealed to all people only when necessity for it is revealed in the world, meaning, only when the will to receive is revealed in its full force and exhausts its development in this world. Thus, the "Book of Zohar" is written and immediately hidden for two thousand years, until there is a need for it.

The "Book of Zohar" is the most important book in the wisdom of Kabbalah. It is charged with tremendous spiritual force, only through which, is it possible to connect and correct all parts of the single desire and bring all of humanity to the end of correction. The book was written in the 2nd century ACE, by Rabbi Shimon Bar Yochai and his nine students, and hidden immediately upon its completion. In the book itself, it is written that only when all of humanity is ready to begin the correction in practice, will it be revealed. Indeed, in our days, the "Book of Zohar" is being revealed.

After the destruction of the Second Temple and the fall from unfounded love (spirituality) to unfounded hatred (corporeality), the Nation of Israel goes into exile and begins slowly and gradually mixing with the nations of the world, throughout thousands of years,. As abovementioned, the mixing of Israel with the Nations of the world is in essence, a process where the pure desire in creation mixes with the coarse desire. The coarse desire is slowly and gradually revealed and as long as it is not entirely revealed, exile (in externality) and the mixing of the vessels (in internality) continue. (see drawing #10)

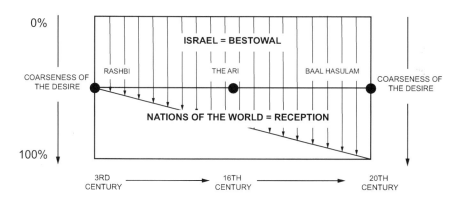

In the 16th century, approximately 1,300 years after writing the "Book of Zohar", the coarsest, most developed desires begin to be revealed, and for the sake of their correction, the "Book of Zohar" was written. The revelation of the developed will to receive brings the entire world to an unprecedented whirlwind. The scientific and industrial revolution and a series of civil rebellions and wars taking place in Europe are only a part of the extreme changes to occur in the following years. In parallel, at the end of the 16th century, the first Kabbalist since the writing of the "Book of Zohar" is revealed, who knows to interpret the "Book of Zohar" and draw the wisdom of Kabbalah closer to the will to receive that is being revealed at a new coarseness. The name of this Kabbalist is Rabbi Isaac Luria, also known as the "Holy *ARI.*"

The *ARI* symbolizes the beginning of the days of the Messiah. "Messiah" in the wisdom of Kabbalah is the force that draws all of humanity from corporeality to spirituality, from receiving to bestowal - Messiah, from the word "Moshech" (pulls/draws in Hebrew). From the time of The *ARI* onwards, the pulling force begins to be revealed, opposite the coarsest and most developed desires, on the greatest level of coarseness, also beginning to be revealed. The more these desires proceed to be revealed, so the need for the wisdom of Kabbalah proceeds and increases as the method of correcting the will to receive.

The process of development of the will to receive reaches its end in the 20th century, along with the exile of the Nation of Israel. There is no more need for it. The will to receive has been revealed in its entire force and within it all, the sparks of bestowal have been mixed. Now it is possible to begin correcting it. After two thousand years of exile, the Nation of Israel returns to the Land of Israel, in order to pass the wisdom of Kabbalah on to the entire world. The world is already prepared for it.

Humanity is ripe for the revelation of the wisdom of Kabbalah and indeed, the wisdom of Kabbalah is revealed. Baal HaSulam, Rav Yehuda Ashlag and his eldest son and successor, Rav Baruch Ashlag, act to bring the wisdom of Kabbalah to whoever desires it. They adapt the wisdom of Kabbalah to our generation, so that even a simple person can study it and reveal spirituality.

After over five thousand years, at the end of a lengthy process of preparation, the Nation of Israel (the group of students with an awakened Point in the Heart) is ready to begin to realize its true destiny: to pass the wisdom of Kabbalah onto the whole world (the rest of the desires, which have yet to awaken). We will learn about that in the following lesson.

Test Yourself:

Why does the Nation of Israel go into exile?

Lesson Summary

Main Points

- The relation between the coarse part of the desire and the pure part of the desire in the spiritual world dictates the development and correction of the Nation of Israel and the Nations of the world in the corporeal world, as well. If in spirituality, the purer part of the desire is corrected first and then the coarser part, the same order of correction is maintained in our world as well: first Israel and then the Nations of the world. If in spirituality, the will to receive and the will to bestow need to mix with each other, in order to enable the correction of the desire to receive, as well, so it takes place in the corporeal world; the Nation of Israel goes into exile and mixes with the Nations of the world.

- The main stages in the development of the nation of Israel: a) The ego erupts in ancient Babylon. Abraham the Patriarch reveals the method of rising above the ego and connecting in bestowal; b) A new degree of ego is revealed and the Nation of Israel goes down into Egypt. Moses receives the method of correction adapted to the new ego (Torah), and the Nation of Israel returns to the Land of Israel; c) The Nation of Israel corrects the will to receive at the new degree of coarseness and constructs the First Holy Temple and the Second Holy Temple. The ego erupts again. The Nation of Israel goes into exile and begins to mix with the Nations of the world.

- The exile of Israel is a sure sign of the revelation of spirituality to every person in the world at the end of exile. Consequently, immediately after Israel's exile, the spiritual force which will draw all of humanity to spirituality at the end of the exile is revealed- the "Book of Zohar."

- The mixing of Israel with the Nations of the world is in essence a process in which the pure desire in creation is mixed with the coarse desire. The coarse desire is revealed slowly and gradually, and as long as it is not entirely revealed, exile (in externality) and the mixing of the vessels (in internality) continue. In the 16th century, the coarsest parts of the desire begin to be revealed and in parallel the Holy *ARI* appears, the Kabbalist who knows how to draw the wisdom of Kabbalah closer to the new desire that is being revealed. In the 20th century, the process of the growing will to receive ends along with the exile. The Nation of Israel returns to the Land of Israel. Baal HaSulam and Rabash pass to us the method of correction of the will to receive.

Concepts

Land- Desire.

Land of Israel - A desire straight to the Creator, a desire to bestow.

House- Will to receive.

Holiness- Bestowal.

Holy Temple - The corrected will to receive with the intention of in order to bestow.

Purity – Using the will to receive with the intention of in order to bestow.

Impurity - Using the will to receive with the intention of in order to receive.

Messiah- The force drawing all of humanity to correction.

Answers to the Questions

Question: What is the order of correction of the Nation of Israel and the Nations of the world?

Answer: According to the law of roots and branches, first the Nation of Israel is corrected and then the Nations of the world. In order to correct the Nations of the world, the Nation of Israel goes into exile and mixes among the Nations of the world.

Question: Why does the Nation of Israel go into exile?

Answer: The will to receive is comprised of two main parts: coarse and pure. In order to correct the will to receive, sparks of bestowal have to be instilled in it. Thus, according to the law of roots and branches, the Nation of Israel goes into exile in corporeality as well and mixes with the Nations of the world. Exile continues in externality as long as the coarse desire to receive (the aspect of the "Nations of the world") continues to be revealed in internality. In the 20th century, when the will to receive is revealed in its full force, the Nation of Israel returns to the Land of Israel, in order to begin to correct itself and transmit the method of correction to the world.

Pass it Forward

We will end the third and last study unit as well as the entire course with an explanation of the importance of dissemination of the wisdom of Kabbalah in our generation, as "last but not least." The topic might sound marginal, but it is of great importance, as an inseparable part of the study of the wisdom of Kabbalah. Dissemination is an action that is spiritually beneficial for a student even if one does not understand exactly how it impacts one's spiritual development.

When we study the wisdom of Kabbalah in general and the importance of dissemination in particular, it is very important to discern the essential difference between the study of the wisdom of Kabbalah in previous generations and the study of the wisdom of Kabbalah in ours. The wisdom of Kabbalah is an ancient wisdom of over five thousand years, accompanying humanity from its first days. It has always been around. However, from the point of view of actualizing the wisdom of Kabbalah, all those thousands of years have only been preparation for its revelation in our time.

The wisdom of Kabbalah was given to all human beings as a method for correcting the desire and revealing spiritual reality. Yet, only in our generation, the conditions for its revelation have ripened for the first time to reveal the wisdom to every person in the world. Throughout thousands of years of the wisdom's concealment, humanity has undergone a process of development which prepared it for the revelation of the wisdom in our days. In parallel, the wisdom of Kabbalah has also gone through a process of development, in order to be able to be revealed to humanity. The time has come: The "bride and groom" can finally meet.

Baal HaSulam writes about it in the article "The Teaching of Kabbalah and Its Essence:" "Happy am I that I was born in such a generation, that it is already permitted to advertise the Wisdom of Truth. And if you ask me how do I know that it is permitted? I will reply, since I am given permission to reveal, meaning, that until now it has not been revealed to any sage, those ways that are permitted to engage in for every people and nation, and to explain every word according to its manner... and that is what has been granted to me from the Creator in its full measure, as it is accustomed, that it does not depend on the sage himself, rather on the condition of the generation, as the sages said, "And the little Shmuel was worthy etc, rather his generation is not worthy for that," thus I have said that I have been granted on the path of revelation of the Wisdom, is due to my generation."

It follows that we can understand the essential difference between the study of the wisdom of Kabbalah up to our times and the study from our times onward. Up to our times, the wisdom was studied in hiding, only in small groups. Even in the days of the First Temple, when the entire Nation of Israel actualized the method and was in spiritual attainment, the wisdom was only revealed to them. The whole of humanity still had no need for it. In our times, especially starting from the year 1995 (as Baal HaSulam stated), all of humanity is proceeding to reveal the need for the wisdom of Kabbalah.

We are the ones who need to reveal the wisdom to humanity. Every person whose point in the heart has awakened is obligated to pass the wisdom onwards to every person in the world, according to one's desire.

There are two ways to disseminate the wisdom: Internal dissemination and external dissemination. Internally, we disseminate the wisdom in every thought, desire, and intention that we add to the study of the wisdom of Kabbalah. As parts comprising together the single soul, the Soul of *Adam HaRishon*, every inner effort that we exert in the study of the wisdom of Kabbalah inevitably affects all parts of the soul and the soul as a whole. The results are not felt instantaneously, yet it is specifically our inner effort that is most effective.

We need to remember that when we study the wisdom of Kabbalah. In our individual effort, we influence the general public and draw the people closer, step by step, to the revelation of the Creator in our world. We need to study the wisdom of Kabbalah out of the intention to correct the whole of humanity. Indeed, we study that things will not be good for any of us, so long as there is a suffering person in the world. While studying and preparing for the study, indeed, we need to attempt to focus the study to the correction of all of humanity.

Of course, it is possible to disseminate the wisdom of Kabbalah in externality as well, to bring the wisdom of Kabbalah and its teachings to whoever is already prepared to receive them. The organization Bnei Baruch publishes dozens of books annually on the topic of the wisdom of Kabbalah, manages a web site for the study in dozens of languages, holds studies within the framework of dozens of branches of the "Kabbalah Campus, and produces Kabbalah conventions throughout the world. Each of us, according to one's desire, can participate in this expansive dissemination activity and offer the wisdom of Kabbalah to whoever is interested in it.

An important rule in the dissemination of the wisdom of Kabbalah is "there is no coercion in spirituality," meaning a person is not to be forced to study the wisdom of Kabbalah. The wisdom is open to all; everyone is invited to take from it as they wish. The Rabash would describe it as such: "Every morning I get up to open the store; whoever wishes to enter is welcome, the door is open." All we need to do is to make sure the material is accessible, and the study is available to every person. All the rest is according to the desire.

Dissemination of the wisdom of Kabbalah is one of the most important tools we have at our disposal for expanding the corrected loving and connected part within the single general soul of us all. The more the corrected part of the Soul of *Adam HaRishon* proceeds to grow, so does its influence upon us, the value of spirituality continues to increase in our eyes and as a result, we become closer to it.

The truth is that whether we are aware of this or not, our entire life is dissemination, because inside of us, in our desires and thoughts, we are all connected in one net. At each given moment, we pass each other covert and overt messages; conveying information to each other and influencing one another. Therefore, if we are participating in the "game" anyway, it is preferable to convey something good, the best upon one another, the method of how to truly love.

The book you hold in your hands has been written from this desire.

Test Yourself:

Why is it important to disseminate the wisdom of Kabbalah?

Lesson Summary

Main Points
- We are the ones who need to reveal the wisdom to humanity. Each person whose point in the heart has awakened in him is obligated to pass the wisdom of Kabbalah onward to every person in the world, according to one's desire. There are two ways to disseminate the wisdom: internal dissemination and

external dissemination. Internally, we disseminate the wisdom with every thought, desire and intention that we add to the study of the wisdom of Kabbalah. In externality, it is possible to participate in the general effort to bring the wisdom of Kabbalah and its teachings to whoever is already prepared to receive them, by means of all possible media: tv, radio, books, organized study, etc.

Concepts

There is no coercion in spirituality- The wisdom of Kabbalah is studied only according to the desire. It is impossible to force a person to study it.

Answers to the Questions

Question: Why is it important to disseminate the wisdom of Kabbalah?

Answer: There are several reasons for that: 1) Humanity is ready for the wisdom of Kabbalah; 2) Our role as a nation is to bring the teachings of the wisdom of Kabbalah to every person in the world; 3) In disseminating the wisdom of Kabbalah, we expand the single corrected vessel of the Soul of *Adam HaRishon*, and as it proceeds to grow, so it influences us further, raising the importance of spirituality in us and advancing us more towards it.

Logical Sequence
(Order of course development)

We learned that the wisdom of Kabbalah is the method of revealing the Creator to the created beings in this world.

We learned that in order to reveal the Creator, we need to change the intention from in order to receive to in order to bestow.

We learned that in Kabbalah books, a special spiritual force is embedded called the Light that Reforms and it is in its power to change our intention, from in order to receive to in order to bestow.

We learned that only in discerning our attitude towards others, can we create inside us a genuine request to the Light that Reforms.

We learned that only by choosing the correct environment for spiritual development can we discern our attitude towards others precisely.

We learned that the points in the heart are the shattered parts of the Soul of *Adam HaRishon* and that in building a spiritual environment with other points in the heart, we formulate the request for correction, for connecting the shattered parts and summon the Light that Reforms.

We learned that the basis for a genuine request of the Light that Reforms is "There is none else beside Him," meaning to attribute all the states being revealed to the single Creator, the source of all causes.

We learned that in revealing the control of the will to receive (the intention of in order to receive) we build within us a genuine request for correction.

We learned the order of correction: the purer vessels ("Israel") at first, and the coarser vessels ("Nations of the world") in the end.

Something for Dessert

That's it. The course "Introduction to the Wisdom of Kabbalah" is complete. Throughout the course, basic knowledge in all the areas of study of the wisdom of Kabbalah has been acquired, and as importantly, the correct approach to the study of the wisdom has been understood. The acquired knowledge and the correct approach to the study grants us a solid, deep and stable foundation to proceed and delve into the study of the wisdom of Kabbalah.

We hope you have enjoyed it. At the end of the day, the purpose is to derive pleasure. We will savor something sweet from the book "A Glimpse of Light" of Rav Dr. Laitman, which will leave us with a good taste in mouth and heart.

"Imagine seven billion people being in a state of love, unity, *Arvut* (mutual concern). You don't need to look for guarantors for the bank in order to get a loan, there's no need to hide anything from others. No one has to safeguard what he owns, to set boundaries.

There's no need to legislate laws for each and every detail, exactly like there's no need for laws in order to explain to a woman how to treat her newborn baby. Love directs her naturally. When there is love, there is no need for any other law besides one law – the law of love.

It is hard for us to accept how everything could become so simple, if we acquired the property of love and bestowal. We wouldn't need to guard anyone, to mention anything to anyone. Each one would only look for ways to benefit others and would receive infinite, spiritual pleasure in return."

Course Book

Study Unit #1 - The Foundations of Kabbalah

Part #1 - What Is The Wisdom of Kabbalah?

Lesson #1 - What do we really know about the Wisdom of Kabbalah?

Task #1:

Read the following excerpts from Rav Dr. Michael Laitman's Blog and answer the following questions:

- List at least two reasons for the numerous misconceptions regarding the wisdom of Kabbalah.
- Why is the wisdom of Kabbalah being revealed in our times?

The wisdom of Kabbalah was concealed for many years, thus arousing a desire in humanity to know what the wisdom is. Many thought that being concealed, it surely contains dark powers that must not be activated. If it were to be revealed, it would be accessible to evil people who would use it to harm others, as in the example of the curse "*Pulsa de Nura*" (Pulse of Light) and such.

As silly as it may seem today, there are still people who are convinced that by such actions, it is possible to harm the world by such actions and that it all resulted from Kabbalah.

Moreover, Kabbalists themselves were interested in distancing the people from the wisdom of Kabbalah, in order to give them the opportunity to reveal their own powerlessness as much as possible. They gave people the opportunity to clarify their own inner confusion and reveal their limitations. People have to attain the truth on their own, reveal it themselves, through personal experience, rational scrutiny and common sense!

The truth is that throughout all of human history, human beings dealt only in scrutinizing the truth. Still, the truth has yet to been discerned. Indeed, it is common knowledge that even our sciences develop by means of the imagination.

Only the wisdom of Kabbalah does not develop by means of the imagination, since it is impossible to imagine anything belonging to the spiritual world from the corporeal world.

Therefore, after a person exhausts everything he imagines, he comes to the only wisdom that has nothing imaginary about it. It is a wisdom where everything is revealed, not out of theory and hypotheses, rather from practical experience!

Over thousands of years, Kabbalists were interested in people thinking that the wisdom of Kabbalah is everything except what it truly is! That was so people could discern for themselves what the wisdom of Kabbalah actually is, beyond this confusion and denial, and come to its revelation specifically in our times, when we are in such need of it.

From Rav Dr. Michael Laitman's Blog, June 28, 2009

Question: A person who comes to study the wisdom of Kabbalah brings along baggage of mistaken, imaginary descriptions and finds understanding the matter confusing. How can they set that confusion straight and understand sooner?

Answer: The student needs to be accepted as he is. Aspiring towards revealing the Creator is the only thing affecting spiritual progress.

The truth is that in false methods there is great benefit. According to the law "a peel guards the fruit," The best will be revealed to us later on. We come to the wisdom of Kabbalah, loaded with a huge load of stereotypes and misconceptions we received in childhood and throughout our lives, and everything we have heard creates a basis of "facts" for us.

As long as a person does not acquire new attributes, operating within him with the same force as "slogans and facts" he heard and internalized in childhood innocently, which govern his life, he will not be able to rise above them, or feel the spiritual world!

However, a person is incapable of ridding himself of the previous imagery and descriptions which need to be replaced with new ones. Only studying the wisdom of Kabbalah can do that.

Question: To what extent does the knowledge we internalized in childhood limit us?

Answer: When a person receives spiritual strength, rises above corporeality and begins to see his material self from the side, he is amazed to discover the extent to which he is full of stereotypes with no hold in reality! He has simply accepted them in faith at some point. It permeated his childish brain and was embedded there, as information that cannot be erased and nothing can be done with it.

That is why every person can come and begin to study, and with time, meaning under the influence of the material he studies, he will gradually release the false stereotypes and previous misconceptions. Whatever a person acquired at later stages in life is easy to change, but the education he received during childhood is difficult to change. Still, by studying the wisdom of Kabbalah, a person very slowly cleans out and removes the whole "peel" and begins to use the spiritual fruit, when the fruit truly ripens.

From Rav Dr. Michael Laitman's Blog, April 9, 2009

Task #2:

In the following excerpt from Rav Yehuda Ashlag's "Writings of the Last Generation, Baal HaSulam describes who a Kabbalist is. Read the excerpt and answer the following question:

- How does Baal HaSulam's description add to the perception of the term "Kabbalist?"

Contact with the Creator[46]

The public imagines that whoever has a connection with the Creator should be feared and not spoken with, not to mention be in his presence. For this is human nature that fears anything outside of the nature of creation and infrequent things like thunder and lightning.

Although it is not actually so, because on the contrary, there is nothing more natural than attaining a connection with the Creator, for He is the Master of nature, and truly, every created being has contact with the Creator, although one does not know or feel it. Whoever merits connecting with Him acquires not only the knowledge. It is like a person who knows nothing of a treasure in his pocket and someone comes along and informs him of what he has in his pocket, then he really becomes wealthy. Nevertheless, there is nothing new for him and nothing to be excited about, because in actuality, nothing was new at all.

Accordingly, even more so, the person who has merited that connection also thus becomes more natural... and there is none more natural and closer to the public than him, who should only be loved, for they have no brother closer than him.

Baal HaSulam, "Writings of The Last Generation"

Task #3:

Read the following excerpt from the book "A Taste of Light" and explain in writing how the wisdom of Kabbalah's definition of the term "Creator" differs from the commonly accepted perception of the term "Creator."

---

[46] Originally "Contact with Him." The excerpt has been lightly edited for the book.

Question: I was taught that the Creator is in the sky, just like a type of kind grandfather; is that correct?

Answer: That approach has been part of humanity for generations past. It speaks of some force... but who knows which force? So, a person attributes to this concealed force an image based on his understanding.

The truth is that the Creator is the general force of nature, as explained in the wisdom of Kabbalah.[47] However, since the wisdom of Kabbalah was concealed for thousands of years, we have developed false perceptions.

It seems to us that if we ask the Creator nicely, he will reward us well; we want to use the Upper force for our pleasure. We tie our hopes on Him, as if he were someone in our world. "I will give Him something, and He will return a favor." It seems to us that in such a way, we can bribe Him, and everything will turn out for the best.

This is a common approach that was enrooted in us over the long years of exile, years of disconnection from attaining the Creator and feeling the Upper world. Exile is a state of concealment, disconnection from spiritual attainment.

Nowadays, the wisdom of Kabbalah is being revealed once again, clarifying the correct approach to the concept of "Creator."

Rav Dr. Laitman, "A Taste of Light"

Task #4:

Read the following excerpt from Rav Dr. Michael Laitman's Blog and detail at least 3 characteristics for the transition from a person's corporeal development to a new development.

The corporeal development of a person ceases and makes room for the new development.

---

[47] For expansion, see Writings of Baal HaSulam, article "The Peace".

In all areas of our life, despair and emptiness are exhibited. We do not know how to behave with our children. We thought we brought them into a good life, yet nothing like that is seen on the horizon. A person does not understand why he needs a family commitment if he does not see that any good will come of it. He feels that he is putting himself into a limiting, suffocating obligation.

Being tied to a certain place, or even a certain country is disappearing as well. The simple person wants to live better. Wherever such an opportunity exists, he is willing to go.

In such a manner, we are erasing all borders, breaking all limitations, ripping off all the old "wrappers" within which we developed for thousands of years.

In the past, a person knew that he belonged to a certain nation, a certain place and culture, connected to his family, children to parents and to everything that was once the foundation of life. Fathers passed their professions to their sons from generation to generation. A smith's son became a smith and the shepherd's son became a shepherd. Every young man knew who he would marry, whether a woman from the same village or from neighboring villages. All life flowed according to these laws.

In our times, everything has changed. All over the world, people are leaving the previous way of human existence. In other words, our ego, our inner desire and our awareness are changing sharply and quickly. Why? - We do not know the answer, ourselves.

In our times, the will to receive pleasure is what directs us. It is destroying all the old borders and barriers that used to maintain us in the accepted framework. These days, the old framework and connections have loosened and comfort is the determinant factor.

People have risen above the limitations in which he lived throughout all of history. The boundaries have been erased; people feel at home in any country. Whether we want it or not, Earth is becoming common area. Even if the new trend is just beginning, it is already irreversible.

Along with that trend, a new emptiness is being revealed, that we never knew. It doesn't matter where we go and what we do, we will not be able to fill that emptiness with anything. Rising above the old borders and the willingness for new forms of development will not enable us to fulfill the new increasing desire in any case, which has lifted us above the old world straight to the vortex of change. The fulfillment it is demanding of us is so vast, that it simply does not exist anywhere.

Humanity is in trouble. Since a new way of fulfillment has not been found, people calm themselves with alcohol, drugs and antidepressant pills. Despite growing and expanding use, the feeling is that it is not the solution. Therefore, sooner or later (preferably sooner), we'll realize that it is time to replace corporeal fulfillment with spiritual fulfillment.

From Rav Dr. Laitman's Blog, March 23, 2011

Task #5:
Read the following excerpts from the book "The Point in The Heart."

Let's try to imagine for a moment waking up in the morning being familiar with the general law of reality, the law defining everything.

We understand what we should do and what to avoid, in order not to render a negative response. Everything is clear to us and we awaken to life like children - with a huge desire and yearning, without so much fear or inhibitions. This is exactly the state we are worthy of living.

In actuality, why not? Why should we not always succeed? Why should we constantly have to bump into walls, take blows and encounter problems? Why should we be in the dark?

If we reveal this general law, we will have no problems; we will know exactly how to manage in life, how to be succeed, big time.

Rav Dr. Michael Laitman, "The Point in the Heart"

The wisdom of Kabbalah is a science which reveals the Upper governance over all of creation.

All of reality is governed by one general law, called the law of nature, or the law of the Creator. This is the general law of love, harmony, and benevolence. The method of Kabbalah grants us the opportunity to reveal this law and build our life accordingly.

Just as it is important and essential to study the laws of physics, chemistry, and biology in order to exist properly in our world, so it is important and essential to become familiar with the wisdom of Kabbalah. Knowing the general law of creation and living in accordance with it will save us suffering, wars, and natural disasters, bringing us to a state of balance and harmony.

Rav Dr. Michael Laitman, "The Point in the Heart"

Lesson #2 - Who can Study the Wisdom of Kabbalah?

Task #1:
Read the following excerpt from the book "The Tower of Babel-The Last Story" and answer the following question:
- **What is the difference between the different degrees of the will to receive?**

Studies of the various elements in nature show that the basic aspiration of any matter or object is to maintain its existence. However, this aspiration is expressed uniquely in each element. There are solids whose form is defined and permanent making it difficult to "penetrate their borders," while others actually maintain their existence through motion and change. As such, the question is: what causes each matter to behave in a certain way and be distinguished from other matter? What dictates each object's behavior?

The wisdom of Kabbalah calls the inner force found within each matter or object the "will to receive joy and pleasure" or in short the "will to receive" and in its essence, it is the desire of any matter or object to exist. This force is what forms the shape of the matter and defines its qualities and behavior. The will to exist has infinite options of forms and combinations and is at the foundation of all matter in the world. Every higher degree of matter is an expression of a greater desire to exist. The different desire in each of the degrees of matter - the still, vegetative, animate, and speaking (man) - forms the various processes occurring within it.

The desire to exist acts in accordance with two principles: (1) To keep its existing form, meaning to continue existing; (2) To add what it feels is necessary for its existence. The feeling of the desire to add something to itself is what differentiates between the various degrees of matter.

At the degree of the still, the smallest desire for existence can be found. Since the desire of the still is small, it does not need to add anything external to itself in order to exist. Its only desire is to maintain its existing form, structure and characteristics, such as an atom, a molecule, a crystal, etc, whereas anything other than that is repulsed.

At the vegetative degree, the desire to exist is greater and differs in essence from the desire of the still. The vegetative changes-it is not "satisfied" with maintaining its existence like the still; rather it undergoes certain processes of development. The relation of the vegetative to its environment is active. Plants move towards sun rays and send roots in the direction of the source of water. The life of the vegetative depends on its environment: the sun, rain, cold, heat, moisture, dryness, and the like. The vegetative receives what it requires to exist and develop from the environment, breaks it down and uses what it needs, secretes whatever is harmful, resulting in its growth. The vegetative depends on its environment much more than the still does.

The greater the desire of the matter, the more dependent the object is on its environment and the more sensitive it is to it. Such a connection is more apparent at the level of the animate, whose desire is greater than that of the vegetative. Animals belong to packs. They are mobile and have to move from place to place in order to find food and appropriate conditions for their existence. Animals need to eat other animals or plants and receive them as the force of their existence.

At the animate level, a certain development of personality is already apparent. By that means, the animal senses individual sensations and feelings, and it develops its own personality. Each animal senses its environment individually, approaches whatever is beneficial and distances from the harmful. The life cycle of animals is individual: each one is born and dies in its time, unlike plants, which act according to the season.

The largest degree of the desire to receive is the degree of man, the speaking. Man is the only creature whose development depends completely on others and has a sense of the past, present and future. Man himself affects the environment and the environment affects him. He continuously changes, not only because he himself feels bad or good in his current state; but also resulting from the feeling of others, causing him to desire whatever others possess. Moreover, man wants to have more than others, or for others to lack, so that one's relative sense of self and sufficiency improves. As a result, man's will to receive is called "ego," the "desire for pleasure," or the "will to receive joy and pleasure."

The development of the desire for pleasure causes a person to sense the constant necessity to develop that which exists, in addition to discovering and inventing new things. A greater desire means greater needs, which lead to the development of the intellect and ability for sharper perception. The growth of the desire for pleasure is what has brought about the evolution of humanity throughout its existence and is what has marched us forward.

A scan of human evolution in the areas of culture, education, science, and technology, in light of the understanding that the desire leads it all, brings us to the conclusion that the evolving desire is what has born all new ideas, inventions and innovations. All those are actually only "technical" tools, as servants, which developed solely to fill needs born of the desire. We will mention that this process of development of the desire has taken place not only in humanity over history, but over the individual life of each and every one of us. These desires awaken in us one after another in various sequences and direct the path of our lives.

Hence, the inner engine pushing us forward and causing the entire process to take place in the individual person and human society is the desire for pleasure. The development of the desire is incessant and is what forms the present and the future towards which we are proceeding.

Rav Dr. Michael Laitman, "The Tower of Babel-The Last Story"

Task #2:
Read the following excerpt from the book "The Tower of Babel - The Last Story" and answer the following questions:
- **Describe the mechanism which develops the will to receive.**
- **What is gained by the desire increasing to such a state where it no longer finds satisfaction?**

When we study our various pleasures from attaining knowledge, control, honor, or wealth, along with pleasure from food and sex, we see that in all cases, the greatest pleasure is felt in the initial and brief interaction between the desire and its fulfillment. From the moment of fulfillment, the pleasure gradually decreases. Pleasure from satisfying the desire may continue for minutes, hours, or days – yet it inevitably dissipates. Even if a person exerts efforts for many years to achieve something, such as an honorable job, or a prestigious academic degree, indeed after its attainment, the sense of pleasure is lost. It turns out that the pleasure fulfilling the desire, also cancels it.

Moreover, the entrance of pleasure into the desire and its disappearance builds in us a desire for pleasure doubly intense. What has satisfied us today will not suffice tomorrow. We want more than that. Much more. Hence, we see that satisfying our desires increases them and forces us to invest greater efforts in order to fill them.

The sense of life and vitality of whoever does not wish to attain anything dwindles. That is why human society constantly supplies each and every one with new desires, reviving us for another brief moment. Yet, again and again, we are filled for a moment and instantly emptied, so frustration increases.

Society today pushes us to acquire more and more products, enabling us to buy almost anything, even if we don't have the necessary money for it. Aggressive marketing, the need to keep up with social standards and the availability of credit cause us to purchase more than our actual financial capability allows. After a short period of time, excitement from the purchase ceases as if it never existed. Yet, the payments will accompany us for years. In such cases, disappointment from the purchase is not forgotten with time; rather it actually continues to accumulate.

From all the above mentioned, we find that our nature, the desire for pleasure, puts us in an impossible position, by definition. On the one hand, our desires continue to increase; on the other hand, their fulfillment, which involves much movement, meaning actions and great effort is felt only briefly, vanishes and leaves us with double emptiness.

Throughout all of history, humanity believed that better times await us; that we would develop science, technology, culture and education, and they would make our life better and happier. That is beautifully illustrated at places like "Spaceship Earth" found in Epcot Center, one of the Disney amusement parks, built at the beginning of the 1980's.

Visitors on site are led through stations describing historical landmarks regarding the evolution of humanity. The journey begins with cave drawings, continues through all landmarks of human development, such as the first use of paper and ends with the conquering of space. The attraction was designed according to the popular approach several decades ago as praise glorifying the greatness of man succeeding in all. The entire history of humanity is presented as endless progress towards happiness: Look, tomorrow is out there! And if not tomorrow - the day after. If not for our kids – for our grandchildren.

Several years have passed and these days, it's all over. Each of us has everything a person could only dream of a century ago: we have entertainment, traveling, rest, sports and the like at our fingertips, yet we no longer believe that tomorrow will be better. We are at a turning point, where we are starting to wake up and realize that no joyous future awaits us. It seems that our children's life will be worse than ours.

The sense of crisis in all areas, starting with the individual and ending with the collective is the result of realizing that whatever we have developed and are familiar with has not brought us happiness. Sensations such as meaningfulness and emptiness stem from that realization. That is also why depression and drugs are modern illnesses. These are expressions of our helplessness, resulting from not understanding how to fill our desire for pleasure, which has increased and no longer suffices with anything we are familiar with.

From now on, no known solution can help us improve our situation. Only if we are familiar with the fundamentals of nature, according to which all live bodies and nature in general exist, will we be able to learn where we have gone wrong and understand what the perfect method for satisfying our desire for pleasure is, which will lead humanity to a life full of content, security, and peace.

Rav Dr. Michael Laitman, "The Tower of Babel-The Final Story"

Task #3:
Read the following excerpts from the book "A Glimpse of Light" and write in your own words:

- What is the point in the heart?

From the start, I was created in my corrected form, in a state called "the world of *Ein Sof*" (Eternity). I descended and fell from there to the state called "this world" - the opposite, flawed form. Precisely in the same way I descended, I am supposed to ascend.

When do I begin to feel that I am ready for the path and how do I know what the path is anyway? Here, we have a combination of two components. On one hand, I feel misery in this life; not necessarily corporeal misery. It could be that from a materialistic aspect, I have the best of everything, yet I still feel somewhat empty. On the other hand, I feel a sort of attraction, inclination, yearning, to attain the source of life. This is already the awakening of "the point in the heart."

This point is like a spiritual gene embedded in me, a drop of spiritual semen from which my soul should evolve. A chain of states that I will undergo on my way back to *Ein Sof* is defined in my "point in the heart." Then, want it or not, I feel that I must come to a solution. Want it or not, I encounter the wisdom of Kabbalah, even if I am an Eskimo, African, American, Russian, or live in Israel, whoever I may be. Some examples of people's whereabouts and how they came to the wisdom are simply incomprehensible.

How does that happen? Our world is a spiritual field, just like a magnetic field and "the point in the heart" leads a person to the place where he can nurture and fulfill it.

Rav Dr. Michael Laitman, "A Glimpse of Light"

All of the spiritual development takes place inside "the point in the heart." We need to develop it, "inflate" it until it grows like a balloon. Within it, we will reveal Upper worlds, spiritual life.

The difference between feeling it as a small point and sensing the entire world within it depends on our level of discernment. We'll illustrate it as such: Suppose that looking from space to a certain place on Earth, it seems like a dot. As we draw closer, we see an entire city. We draw even closer and can distinguish buildings, cars and trees. The closer we get, are we able to discern more details.

Our level of noticing the details within the point develops through the work with the "Light That Reforms" found in Kabbalistic writings. It turns out that we do not need to yearn for some spiritual place "above;" rather only expand the point within us. It is the beginning of the soul.

Rav Dr. Michael Laitman, "A Glimpse of Light"

Task #4:
Read the following excerpts from the book "An Interview with the Future" and answer the following questions:
- Why wasn't the "Book of Zohar" revealed immediately upon its composition?
- What is the uniqueness of the ARI?
- Why was Baal HaSulam able to write a commentary of the writings of the ARI and RASHBI?

Rabbi Shimon Bar Yochai (RASHBI), was the author of the "Book of Zohar" in the 2nd century. It is the most prominent book in Kabbalah. Rabbi Shimon Bar Yochai is considered to be a great scholar of the Upper world. He is also listed among the most important of the Talmud elders and mentioned in the Talmud many times. He knew both Talmudic and Kabbalistic languages, through which he described the system of Upper governance, which is concealed from us: the spiritual worlds and forces that are included in this system, how all events in the present and future are born, all the innovations and changes, how they descend from there to our world and are revealed, being clothed in matter of this world.

Before RASHBI began writing the book, he formed a group of students around him, such that each soul of every student would match a certain spiritual degree in the Upper world. Together, they composed a group of nine and he was the tenth. Their bonding into one soul was in full compatibility with the complete spiritual structure existing in the Upper world, called "Ten *Sefirot* (Spheres)."

Rabbi Shimon Bar Yochai stated that he could not have written the book on his own. The book was meant to be written for the last generations, passing through all the generations in the interim, for it to be revealed only in the 16th century. Accordingly, in order to write this book in hiding, so that intermediate generations would pass it onwards, he was assisted by his student Rabbi Abba. As he listened/ studied the "Book of Zohar" from his teacher, Rabbi Abba began writing the book, in such a way that when people read it, they would only perceive the external layer of the book.

Even during Rabbi Shimon Bar Yochai's lifetime, the book was hidden immediately upon completion. The reason was that humanity as a whole and the Jewish people in particular were still not at the same degree of development, which would enable the "Book of Zohar" to be used correctly, for its spiritual goal, for the benefit of mankind and the entire world.

Rav Dr. Michael Laitman, "An Interview with the Future"

The ARI received the "Book of Zohar" in the 16th century. He was a great Kabbalist and taught from all the Kabbalistic sources existing before him. Later on, all those sources emerged as a single Kabbalistic book called "Tree of Life." It is a book of studying the path to the spiritual world, where he explains to us how we may ascend and attain eternity and wholeness.

The appearance of the ARI brought a new era of human development. New souls started descending into our world, awakening an aspiration for spirituality in the bodies in which they were clothed along with a desire for spiritual knowledge and attainment of the Upper One. This is what caused the Middle Ages to end and the Renaissance to begin; an era of development, leading to the technological and industrial revolutions.

From Above, the ARI was allowed to renew the method, which had already existed from the time of *Adam HaRishon*; so it would shift from a method for individuals with unique souls, to a method appropriate for the masses, numerous souls that had previously developed in this world and are now ready for spiritual ascent.

In addition to "Tree of Life," the ARI wrote around 20 other books. They are very difficult to understand, but today they are the main and most fundamental books upon which the entire method of Kabbalah is constructed, since he detailed all the laws of creation in those books as a clear, scientific method. Thus, his books differ from the "Book of Zohar" and can be used as study books. The main portion of his books is divided into eight sections called "Eight Gates." In each one of them, he describes a specific topic in Kabbalah in a purely scientific way: the laws of the Upper world, the influence of Man on these laws and the reincarnation of souls.

All of the ARI books are written with a new approach and on a completely new level. What guided him was the development of souls in his time. Then, many Kabbalists appeared who relied on his work; hundreds of Kabbalists from all over the world, especially in Eastern Europe: Russia, Ukraine, Belarus, and Poland.

Many were drawn to Kabbalah, upon which a popular non-Kabbalistic movement of many was founded, called "*Hassidut*." Those are people who were drawn to contact with the spiritual, Upper world. They began to see that in their lifetime, in this world, a sublime purpose exists.

The study of the ARI books raises a person above the degree of our world. In the preface to his books, the ARI said that whoever feels the desire of the Upper world can study them, unlike during the period preceding the ARI. Before the ARI, a unique soul of a Kabbalist would descend and then, seemingly at the right time, an appropriate book for that generation would be revealed as well. However, from the time of the ARI, whoever is somewhat drawn or aspires towards spirituality, can already study his Kabbalah books. We can suffice with studying the books of the ARI, in order to emerge into the spiritual worlds.

Starting with the ARI, the final stage of human development begins. From the 16th century, throughout the following centuries, spiritual souls begin to be born anew and attain complete emergence into the spiritual world while still in corporeal bodies. Kabbalah's flourishing period continued until about 1920. Without ARI's method, the spiritual world would not be accessible to such a large number of souls. It flourished particularly in Eastern Europe, where Kabbalists, Hassidic teachers and Rabbis appeared, many of which would be the origin of the future various streams in Judaism. There were many Kabbalistic groups and others, as well.

The ARI also had a group of students, yet before his death, he allowed the study only to one student, Haim Vital. Vital began his study with the ARI at a very young age and only for 18 months - until his death. Still, the words of the ARI, which Haim Vital wrote verbatim, were numerous, until they filled entire cabinets. Some of the writings were buried along with the ARI, others were concealed in a crate at ARI's relatives and Haim Vital began working on the rest. Thus, gradually, the books started to be published.

Rav Dr. Michael Laitman, "An Interview with the Future"

In the end, both the "Book of Zohar" and the books of the ARI were not intended for the methodical study of the wisdom of Kabbalah. Although Kabbalah is a science, there was no true study book until our century. In order to fill the lack of Kabbalistic literature, the great Kabbalist, Rabbi Yehuda Ashlag, who lived in Jerusalem from 1922 until his death in 1954 wrote a commentary of the "Book of Zohar" and all the ARI books. He developed the method of studying Kabbalah in writing, and published his most prominent book called

"*Talmud Eser Sefirot*" which is considered the main Kabbalistic study book of our time.

Only in our time, did the great Kabbalist, RabbiYehuda Ashlag create the comprehensive and precise method, suitable to every soul descending to this world. Rabbi Yehuda Ashlag was born in Warsaw at the end of the 19th century. In 1922 he arrived in Jerusalem and became a Rabbi of one of the neighborhoods. In 1933, he began writing his book "*Talmud Eser Sefirot.*"

When studying the book "*Talmud Eser Sefirot*" under special conditions, meaning in the correct fashion and with proper guidance, the Upper world opens to a person (There is a special approach to the material in this book and a special key how to read it, which opens the material correctly.) The person begins to sense the universe (the entire universe, the spiritual world and this world, along with all the souls existing in the Upper worlds - all consist of Ten *Sefirot*); one begins to see and feel in all of one's senses what truly exists outside the range of one's senses, because our senses are cumbersome, limited and incapable of perceiving anything out of our range of perception.

Rabbi Yehuda Ashlag, also called Baal HaSulam writes in the preface to the book "*Talmud Eser Sefirot,*" that due to the approval granted to him from Above to write this book, everyone in our world can attain the most sublime point of his soul's development. Everyone is able to attain equivalence of form with the Upper force, the Creator, and attain the highest spiritual states specifically while existing in this body, because the body is no longer a barrier between the soul and the individual. It does not matter if one lives in a body or not: one emerges freely between worlds, exists in all the worlds simultaneously and emerges to a state of eternity and wholeness, without time, motion or place.

Baal HaSulam writes that with his method, it is possible for every person to reach all of these states, with no exceptions. Other than "*Talmud Eser Sefirot,*" he wrote a commentary of the "Book of Zohar" and the ARI writings. Baal HaSulam writes about himself that he is an incarnation of a soul stemming from *Adam HaRishon* through Abraham, Moses, Rabbi Shimon Bar Yochai, the ARI and to him. That is why he was able to take all of the writings of those Kabbalists, process them and present to us in a way suited to our generation.

Although Baal HaSulam lived in our time, the same that happened to the "Book of Zohar" and the writings of ARI happened to his writings as well: some of his writings were hidden in cellars, some were collected, others were burned and now they are all emerging and being revealed.

Rav Dr. Michael Laitman, "An Interview with the Future"

Task #5:
Read the excerpt from the book "A Glimpse of Light."

If "the point in the heart" has not yet awakened in a person, he will not feel any connection to what the wisdom of Kabbalah speaks of. Those things will not attract him and will appear unimportant to him. But, when the point in the heart already awakens, a person simply feels, even if he doesn't really understand it, that there's something particularly in this wisdom that touches him deep inside, where he will find the source of pleasure for his spirit.

Rav Dr. Michael Laitman, "A Glimpse of Light"

Lesson #3 - The Order of Development of Creation

Task #1:
Read the following excerpts from the book "Kabbalah, Science and the Meaning of Life" (the book describes a series of meetings between Rav Dr. Laitman and a group of scientists) and answer the following questions:

- Who created the will to receive and why?

- Is the process of creating the will to receive part of the formation of matter in this world, or prior to it?
- How can we understand the formation of matter in our world?

The wisdom of Kabbalah is a method of revealing the reality which is concealed from us; that range of reality unperceivable by our five senses. Meaning, Kabbalah develops a new sense within us, which perceives the reality beyond our attainment at the moment.

The wisdom of Kabbalah states that all of reality is comprised of a substance called the "will to receive" - a desire to be filled with enjoyment and pleasure. We generally call this desire "egoism." This applies to all levels known to us: inanimate, vegetative, animate and speaking.

Dr. Wolf: A desire for what? A desire for the Creator? Where does this desire appear in our universe? Is it a basic desire like matter?

Rav Dr. Laitman: This desire is the matter of all reality.

Dr. Wolf: If so, is matter desire?

Rav Dr. Laitman: No. This is not about atoms. The atoms were formed afterwards. Everything created, whatever exists at the foundation of reality is the desire to enjoy, the desire for pleasure. At every level of reality, this desire takes on different forms.

Dr. Wolf: Do all Kabbalists agree that the matter of creation is the will to receive?

Rav Dr. Laitman: All Kabbalists, without exception, from Abraham to the last great Kabbalist Rabbi Yehuda Ashlag, believe that all matter of creation is the will to receive. A Kabbalist is a person who attains the Upper world and speaks from his attainment, not theoretically. "Attainment" refers to the ultimate level of understanding. All Kabbalah writings refer to the same thing, and the Kabbalists agree on this issue.

This desire for pleasure is the foundation of creation. The desire for pleasure was created by the expansion of the Upper Light. The term "Light" in Kabbalah means giving, bestowal, love and is called

287

"Creator." Hence, the Light created a desire for pleasure that wants to be filled with what is in the Light. This desire for pleasure is also called a "vessel."

Dr. Wolf: Does the desire create everything?

Rav Dr. Laitman: The desire to give creates the will to receive; meaning, the Light wants the vessel to receive from Him what He wants to give it.

Dr. Wolf: Is the vessel already matter?

Rav Dr. Laitman: The desire for pleasure is the beginning of matter. In Kabbalah, it is called the "primal matter," that is, initial material. It is not the final matter yet, since it is entirely a result of the Light's action.

Prof. Tiller: Does this process already exist at the quantum level? Does this stage take place prior to what is called "space time" in physics? In quantum mechanics, everything is already under constraints of space and time.

Rav Dr. Laitman: This process exists prior to the formation of matter as we know it, long before the formation of our universe in its material form.

Rav Dr. Michael Laitman, "Kabbalah, Science and the Meaning of Life"

The wisdom of Kabbalah describes all stages of development of the will to receive, from the first phase of creation up to our world. From the described stages, we understand how the material world was formed with dimensions of time, motion and space and how the will to receive would evolve in the world. Our entire history has been determined by the evolution of the will to receive. From here, we can understand the way in which man and humanity evolve. All processes taking place in reality, without exception, are the result of the development of the ever-increasing will to receive.

After the spiritual structure "descends" and materializes, the matter from which our world is built is created. So far, the world has undergone several periods of development and in our current stage, we are reaching the understanding that spiritual development must begin.

In our times, humanity has experienced a series of crises on all fronts, in various social and scientific domains. Humanity is in the midst of a global crisis and many signs attest to its poor condition: drug abuse is increasing and beginning at younger ages; depression is spreading like a malignant disease; global terrorism is getting out of control and striking us mercilessly.

The goal of all these is to bring humanity to the understanding that the root of all misery is the intensification of the egoistic will to receive in a person, which we need to correct. These issues were already written by Kabbalists thousands of years ago. They explained that when humanity reaches such a state, the time will be suitable for the revelation of the wisdom of Kabbalah as an instrument for correcting the ego.

Rav Dr. Michael Laitman, "Kabbalah, Science and the Meaning of Life"

Task #2:

Read the following excerpts from Rav Dr. Laitman's Blog and from the book "A View of Kabbalah" and answer the following questions:

- Why does the Creator conceal himself from the created being?
- What does it mean to resemble the Creator?
- Why does the created being need to be independent in order to actualize the thought of creation?

The Creator created man as a "desire for pleasure" in such magnitude, so that He may fill man's desire with everything He intended to give him. However, for this purpose, the Creator needs for man himself to desire to receive the bounty, rather than the desire descending to man from above, for then the desire isn't man's will, but the will of the Creator. If man doesn't feel that the desire comes from within him, he will not even receive the pleasure as his own.

What is that pleasure the Creator intended to grant unto man? Genuine pleasure is the stature of the Creator, nothing less. This is because the Creator is in perfection and eternity, and this stature alone is complete. If the Creator's will is to delight the created being, He can only do so by granting him the same complete and eternal stature, the only one that exists. In other words, in order to bring the created being true pleasure considered the Creator "giving," the Creator has to bring the created being to His own degree in all; to that same degree of power, understanding, feeling and fulfillment.

The Creator does this in a very special way; He does it so that the created being himself wants to attain the degree of the Creator and not for the attainment to come as an obligation from the Creator's force. For this purpose, the created being has to undergo many discernments, while he is in a state of concealment from the Creator and acquire a desire for spirituality specifically from the darkness in which he dwells. Afterwards, he has to yearn to resemble the Creator from the contrary state.

This is a gradual process taking place over many lifetimes that the created being undergoes throughout his life in this world. Progress occurs only while man lives in this world, until he reaches the end of correction, i.e. when he corrects himself completely and becomes similar to the Creator in all.

Then he receives the complete filling, that is, the same stature as the Creator, which is called the "end of correction." This condition must be attained, as mentioned, during a person's lifetime in this world. Then he won't have to reincarnate into this world, rather he will be able to separate from his body and not return here in another physical incarnation.

Rav Dr. Michael Laitman, "A View of Kabbalah"

Each of us exists in Nature and yearns for comfort. Balance is the solution of the equation, discovering the formula for your most comfortable situation: what warmth I need, what humidity, food, shelter, family and children, a secure place of livelihood and so on. This is called to achieve balance with Nature in our world, to satisfy all your desires.

Nature develops me so that this balance is constantly broken. Again and again I have to try to find it, from progressing forward. We constantly seek balance. Even when one craves for control or millions of dollars; one does so because one feels within oneself this necessity for fulfillment, to reach balance in order to calm oneself.

That is why the development that Kabbalah refers to is the most normal and natural in every person in this world, although each one has his own formula for achieving balance. Balance means that I'm so content that it could not be any better! It is called the end of correction, when all the desires are corrected, meaning completely filled with what each desire wants!

I do not have to look for any sophisticated formula of Nature! If I achieve a state of complete comfort, where I would not want to change a thing; that means that I have revealed the general formula of balancing Nature! I discover that I can be great and successful, and this form in which I now find myself is called "Creator" or Nature. It's as if I have grown very much until I became a king and I see: here is my palace, here is the army, here are the people. When a person feels that he has attained complete fulfillment, it means that he has discovered the formula of resembling the Creator.

From the Rav Dr. Michael Laitman's Blog December 8, 2010

The Creator is the force of bestowal and love, and whoever loves, suffers from the lack of opportunities to delight the object of their love.

Suffering from unrealized bestowal is much greater than suffering from not receiving, as it is said that more than the calf wants to suckle, the cow wants to nurture! When the big one cannot give the little one from his wholeness, because the little one is incapable of receiving anything - that is great suffering.

The Creator is a desire to bestow, grant, love. That intention should not be thought of as a deficiency! The deficiency to bestow and love does not come from lack of fulfillment, rather from undivided wholeness! Thus, the Creator creates a desire for pleasure, in order to fill it and express His love for us.

In our desire, all preparations have already been made in order to receive all the Light of the Creator and His love. Yet, in order for us to understand what He does and sense what He is giving us, we have to become like Him to match His qualities.

Therefore, only one element is missing here - our independence, our independent desire to feel His love and accept Him as one whom we love. If this aspiration does not emerge from within us, it will not be love. Can love be bought with money? - No. With money, I can only purchase services: I pay at the hair stylist, health clinic, restaurant, and everyone takes care of me because they need the money, not because they love me. What can I do so they love me? That we do not know...

Indeed, true love is possible only if I am completely independent of the other, as written regarding the Creator: "I am the first, I am the last." Therefore, the Creator's problem is how to create us while making us (seemingly) totally independent of Him, and at the same time for us to grow the love for Him within us. Regarding that, it is said: "I am the first, I am the last, and without me there is no Creator."

From Rav Dr. Michael Laitman's Blog Feb. 16, 2010

Task #3:
Read the next section of the book "A Thousand Questions on Kabbalah" and summarize the main points in your own words.

The desires grow frequently and a person feels a constant necessity, a constant need, to develop existing things, invent new things - discover and actualize within him the desires arising in him. The development of mankind over thousands of years of existence is parallel to the development and actualization of the desire's different levels. Finding the methods to satisfy the desire leads to the advancement of humanity in the fields of science, technology, culture and society. Due to desires that are constantly growing and improving, humanity moves forward.

The wisdom of Kabbalah divides the structure of development of man's desires into five stages:

- The primary basic desires are sex, food, and family;
- The second stage of the development of the desires is striving for wealth;
- The third stage of development of the desire is striving for control and glory;
- The fourth stage of development of the desire is thirst for knowledge;
- The fifth stage of development of the desire is the aspiration for spirituality, the Creator.

The need for sex and food is defined as beastly desires and is also felt by animals. Even when a person is in total isolation, he continues to feel hunger and aspires to continue the species, meaning sex. Desires for wealth, control and knowledge are human desires, and in order to satisfy them, one has to live among members of his own species - human society.

When a person is born, he undergoes a process of development of beastly and human desires; yet at a later stage he finds that their actualization does not satisfy him. This is because his hidden but true desire is beyond the limits of our world; except that he cannot yet recognize or formulate it.

A person receives the desire from above. It is not granted to him by Nature as a beastly desire and does not develop from the influence of society, like human desires.

The wisdom of Kabbalah calls this level of desire the "desire for spiritual light," or "man's soul."

The wisdom of Kabbalah investigates the spiritual structure called the "general soul" or "the first Adam." This structure consists of 600,000 parts, each of which is divided into many more particles clothed in material desires.

Rav Dr. Michael Laitman, "A Thousand Questions on Kabbalah"

Task #4:

Read the following excerpts from the book "A Taste of Light" and answer the question:

What is the purpose of the wisdom of Kabbalah?

The wisdom of Kabbalah has been concealed from the general public to this day, because it was necessary to wait until we evolved and reached a state where our lives no longer looked so good to us. Until a few decades ago, people still felt that due to science, wisdom and culture they were achieving achievements, prosperity and development. Life seemed promising, as if our children could expect a finer world.

Nowadays, we seem to have reached a dead end. Dangers from all angles and the ecological situation seem very threatening. The hope for a better life is fading. Out of a sense of deadlock, we are maturing enough to perceive the explanation that Kabbalah offers regarding the source of problems and their solution.

Kabbalah explains that at the end of thousands of years of egoistic development, the world has reached a state, where on the one hand we are all inter-connected; on the other hand, we hate each other - imprisoned in one cell and there is nowhere to escape. It is clear to us that we are suffering from this, only it is not clear to us how it is possible to stop the deterioration. This situation is not coincidental, but rather a deliberate pre-planned step in the development plan of creation. Its purpose is to advance us to the next degree of our existence.

Rav Dr. Michael Laitman, "A Taste of Light"

We are living in a very special time. After thousands of years of concealment, the authentic wisdom of Kabbalah is being revealed once again to all - to each and every human being, without any restrictions or preconditions.

People are beginning to realize that the purpose of the method of Kabbalah is to elevate us to the highest degree of Nature, up to the degree of the Creator. In other words, Kabbalah does not come to teach us any magic, tricks, remedies, talismans, medicine and blessings to improve our corporeal existence; rather it is intended to elevate us to a new degree of existence.

By means of Kabbalah, we become aware of the supreme plan of creation, understand the purpose of our existence on earth and what we must do to actualize the potential embedded in us. This is the special sublime state that all of humanity is supposed to attain in our times.

Rav Dr. Michael Laitman, "A Taste of Light"

Part #2 - Perception of Reality

Lesson #1 - What is reality?

Task #1:

Read the following excerpt from "Opening the Zohar" and briefly describe the approach of the wisdom of Kabbalah to the perception of reality?

The most complex and fascinating subject related to the "Book of Zohar" and to life in general is the perception of reality.

We are surrounded by many waves that we do not currently feel, although there is an all-encompassing field of information. This is a field of sublime information called "Sublime Nature" or "Creator." We can connect to that field and receive everything from it - feelings and understanding, knowledge, love, a sense of eternal life, and a feeling of the wholeness of the field, which fills everything around us.

The entire purpose of the wisdom of Kabbalah is to teach us how to develop within us a vessel of reception for that field of sublime information. It can only be done through our inner change, so that when we achieve it, we, ourselves, become as that field - as the Creator. There is nothing simpler than that. The field is here, all around us, yet we are blocked and do not perceive it.

We are unaware of the Creator, of true reality. Just like a person in a dream, experiencing all kinds of events where he is seemingly awake, so we are in this world.

In the "Preface to the Book of Zohar," Baal HaSulam compares this situation to a worm born in a radish, thinking that the whole world is the radish in which it was born. That is how we live in our world, without feeling that there is a great, enlightened, wondrous and beautiful world around us. That is where the Kabbalists are, people who have already awakened from the dream to the genuine reality. According to them, what we feel now is called the "imaginary world" and only when we rise above it, can we truly understand that the "Book of "Zohar" is being revealed to explain to us how to perceive reality correctly. It is not at all coincidental that science has also been indicating that reality is much greater and richer than what we are capable of perceiving at this time. Scientists say that there is a certain black energy, all kinds of white or black spots in the universe along with additional dimensions which we cannot feel in our senses or develop instruments to perceive them.

We have also been researching other creatures and see how their perception of reality is different from ours. Bees, flies, bears, frogs, snakes and even dogs and cats in our surroundings perceive reality differently. A dog, for example, perceives the world mainly as clusters of smells; the bees' image of the world is the sum of sights perceived in each one of the numerous units comprising its eyes.

Different beings perceive reality differently, yet they all end up perceiving reality. Which reality? That's a good question ... And another one: If a person lacks one of the senses, he will perceive a lesser reality. What if he doesn't lack a sense; rather has an additional one - will he see a larger and broader reality? It could be. The question is which sense that would be.

Now we feel the world and we can say that we lack glasses or hearing aids, because we know what it means to see or hear better, more or less. However, if we do not know which other sense we lack, how can we acquire it? Just as we do not feel a lack for a sixth finger on our hand, so, we cannot feel that we lack a sixth sense. Hence, we live in our world without the need to feel the true reality.

But let's stop for a moment and observe ourselves from the side: we have been living in the world for several decades; we do not know what was before or what will happen afterwards. We also do not know what is happening in between - throughout our lives. We have no idea what will happen in a moment and where our desires and thoughts come from. It can be said that we are in total darkness, except that within it, we have a sort of false feeling that we understand and control events.

In previous generations, man's life was simple. People made sure there was food, tried to spend their lives in maximum comfort, bore children and bequeathed them their ownings. The children continued on the same path, likewise generation after generation. When we lived like that, there really was no need to know what was happening around us.

However, nowadays, questions about life are arising within us. These questions shake us from the inside, until we can no longer relax and continue to flow with life as before. We are beginning to feel that without knowing what we are living for, things have no point and this is what requires us to reveal the true reality.

In order to be able to better understand the novelty of the wisdom of Kabbalah on the issue of perceiving reality, we will briefly review the way science has evolved over the years in its approach to the subject.

The classic approach represented by Newton was that the world exists in and of itself without any connection to Man and that the form of the world is fixed. Then, Einstein came and discovered that the world is much broader than what we perceive. Our perception is relative and depends on our senses; thus we cannot say what the world outside of us exactly is. It all depends on the observer investigating reality.

The modern scientific approach to the perception of reality, based on quantum physics maintains that Man influences the world and as a result affects the image he perceives. The image of reality is somewhat of an average between the characteristics of the observer and the characteristics of the object or phenomenon he perceives.

To understand these things better, we will take a look at a familiar example. In a spacious hall, a speaker stands at the podium and gives a lecture to the audience. They listen to his words through waves coming from the loudspeakers to their ears and through them to their eardrums. Then, the waves pass through an electrical and chemical mechanism. Following, the brain examines whether something similar exists in memory and decodes that electrochemical phenomenon accordingly.

Thus, according to the modern scientific approach, the image of reality is depicted within us. We have no way of saying anything about what exists outside of us, because we never perceive what is outside us. The wisdom of Kabbalah advances us a step further. Thousands of years ago already, Kabbalists revealed that the world actually has no image.

In order to illustrate these things, we will compare a person to a closed box with five entry channels: eyes, ears, nose, mouth and hands. These organs represent the five senses: sight, hearing, smell, taste, and touch, through which a person perceives something that is seemingly outside of him.

Through these five openings of the box, all kinds of stimuli enter. They all undergo various processing related to the information stored in the memory of that person and his desire. The result is a certain image of reality, which is projected on a type of "cinema screen" found in the back of the brain.

We were deliberately created such that our senses create an illusory picture of a world that is supposedly outside of us. Why? In order to enable us to gradually learn what the external image truly is.

Rav Dr. Michael Laitman, "Opening the Zohar"

Task #2
Read the following excerpt from "Opening the Zohar" and answer the following question:

- How does the will to receive affect our perception of reality?

If we want to begin moving forward from our present state, expand our reality, know where we exist and for what purpose, we need to deal only with what exists within us – the desire. Deep inside, the desire sits and activates all our vessels of perception, as well as our intellect and thought.

Sometimes, we are in a situation where we do not seem to see the world, we go inside ourselves, closed, not paying attention to what is taking place around us. What's happening to us? Our desire is detached, as if unconscious. At times, our desire is so great that it makes us truly swallow the whole world with our eyes and other times, our desire dies. Why do people get old? Because they no longer want to perceive the world. It is difficult for them, and as a result, the body stops working. The truth is that from the middle of our lives we already begin to fade and gradually die. It is our desire that fades and loses its force to move forward, not the body. People who begin to develop spiritually receive energy and desire to advance and feel like children - always full of desires, getting up every day with renewed strength.

It is the desire that arouses needs in us and determines what we will or will not see around us. For example, a person who has become a parent begins to notice the presence of stores for baby products on every street corner. The stores were there before, of course, yet since he did not need them, he did not really notice them.

Naturally, our desire is egotistical and directs us to perceive only what is good for us (or what might cause us harm). As the ego develops alongside the intellect, we understand more, perceive more, control more and accordingly, our perception of reality expands.

However, no matter how much it expands, in the end this perception is very limited, since after all, it depends on the five senses that give us the feeling of physical life. Our body is no different from that of all animals, thus this perception is defined as the perception of reality at the animate degree. How can we perceive the broader reality, which is not limited by our ego? This is precisely what the "Book of Zohar" deals with - the perception of reality at the degree of Man.

What we now perceive by our desire, our memory and our five senses are called "this world." Since our desire and memory are ours alone, we are limited as single cells. In order for us to feel all of reality, the sublime field of information, we need to connect to the desires of others, who are supposedly "outside of us," but in fact are parts of us. In other words, in order to grasp the true reality, we have to change the desire: to shift from our inner-egoistic desire to the external one.

Rav Dr. Michael Laitman, "Opening the Zohar"

Task #3:
Read the following excerpts from the books "Kabbalah, Science and the Meaning of Life" and "A Glimpse of Light" and answer the following question:

• What does the revelation of the Light depend upon?

The only difference between vessels for perceiving corporeal reality and those for perceiving spiritual reality is the intention. In corporeal vessels, the intention is egoistic and in spiritual vessels, it is altruistic. This intention is the attitude of a person to the use of his desires.

In fact, the only existing situation is the state of "infinity." In this state, the Light exists inside the vessel. This state is under concealment, which does not enable us to sense the state of infinity. The intensity of the altruistic intention gradually removes the concealment and exposes the Light constantly filling the vessel. The purpose of this illustration is to emphasize that we never reveal lights outside of the vessels. When Kabbalists say that lights enter or exit vessels, they want to emphasize the way a person draws closer to attaining the permanent state.

The state of infinity exists constantly, or in "complete rest" as the Kabbalists say, meaning unchanged. One has to gradually prepare one's vessels of perception to perceive this state. Hence, the only change taking place is in the ability to perceive.

When Light comes and "clothes" in a person and he feels how it gradually enters, indeed this is the way in which the permanent situation becomes clear, through the awakening of the person to feeling it. However, in fact, the Light neither enters nor exits at all. It only becomes clear within the person, meaning it is revealed from concealment.

The person reveals that he exists in an infinite world in a constant state and he has only to reveal his unique state. The Light that created the vessel filled it immediately, so that there was no difference between the creation of the vessel and the filled Light within it. When they say that Light emanates from the Creator, Kabbalists mean that there is already a vessel being filled by the Light.

We need to understand that spirituality is beyond time. Our language is related to time, which is why we say that "first" a vessel was created and "then" it was filled with Light. But in spirituality these things are together; the beginning and end are found at one point, inseparable by time. In our imagination, we distinguish between the Light and the vessel and assume that the Light inside the vessel is probably outside the vessel as well, whereas "outside the vessel" means outside of our perception.

This can be illustrated by the following: There is a vessel in which I perceive all of reality; in another vessel I perceive a little of reality and there is another vessel in which I am unable to perceive anything. Correcting the vessels means expanding my vessel from a small vessel to a larger and larger one. If I say that the Light comes and fills my vessel, it does not mean that it was not filling it before, but rather that is how the reality is now being revealed to me.

This is similar to an unconscious patient in the process of gaining consciousness. Everyone is standing around him, gazing at him and waiting for him to awake. He slowly opens his eyes and begins to recognize where he is. As far as he is concerned, reality is "coming to him" and filling his vessel of sensation, since everything is measured only in relation to the receiver.

Rav Dr. Michael Laitman, "Kabbalah, Science and the Meaning of Life"

The Upper Light is all around us in complete rest. It is a field of infinite information, eternity and wholeness. Yet we do not feel it because we are all closed- each one inside oneself. Our ego closes us inside, as if unconscious.

In order to feel the Light, we need to construct within us a quality like It, a quality of love and giving. It is just like a radio receiver that formulates within itself the same wave it wants to receive from the outside.

The entire wisdom of Kabbalah is actually the wisdom of perception. It is a scientific method for constructing a quality that enables us to receive within us the information found in the field surrounding us. Then, we no longer feel closed inside ourselves, but rather truly flowing in the Upper, complete and eternal Light, the wave of the infinite.

Rav Dr. Michael Laitman, "A Glimpse of Light"

Suppose my computer only has Word software installed and I get an email with an Excel or jpeg file. I try to open the file using Word, but it does not open. There may be something in this file that is very beneficial to me, but my software refuses to open it. I have no choice but to install new software on my computer's hard disk, which can receive the data and display them for me. A new data format requires new software.

In spiritual development, we undergo a similar process. By means of the wisdom of Kabbalah, we acquire new software that rides upon our desire and then we can perceive new images, new information. So far, we've only had the original software with which we were born, all of which is directed towards self-love. Now we are upgrading ourselves by acquiring new software that comprehends what love of others is. With the new software, the new "files" we receive "open up" just great!

Rav Dr. Michael Laitman, "A Glimpse of Light"

Task #4:
Read the following excerpt from "A Glimpse of Light."

Up until now, it seemed to us that "I" and the "world" were two separate things. However, now, at the end of human development which has lasted for tens of thousands of years, we are required to understand that "I and the world" are one whole, that Nature is truly global and that all of the inanimate, vegetative, animate and man constitute one whole.

Furthermore, we are coming closer to realizing that there really is no world outside us, but rather everything takes place within us, which is a higher perception of reality. We are facing exciting revelations in the Upper dimension. This is the entrance to a new life, an awakening from the dream we have been living so far, from the illusory feeling that we live in a reality which is divided and separated into parts.

As we look back at the past, we will begin to realize that the egotistical attitude we have applied to each and every detail existing around us has actually been detrimental to us. We have hated ourselves, exploited ourselves, lied to ourselves and stolen from ourselves. It will become clear to us that we have simply been living in a lie, a bitter mistake.

However, each and every such revelation will specifically take us a step closer towards complete unity and harmony with all of reality, which will be revealed to us as our actual selves. Moreover, as we reveal that we belong to the whole of reality and that all of reality belongs to us, we will also reveal the Upper force residing in all, the force of love and giving.

Rav Dr. Michael Laitman, "A Glimpse of Light"

Lesson #2 – The True Reality

Task #1:

Read the following excerpt from the book "Kabbalah in Simple Terms" and answer the question below:

- **What is the correction we need to perform?**

The will to receive is the driving force behind all progress and change in human history. However, the will to receive was always a desire to receive pleasure for one's personal satisfaction. Although there is nothing wrong with wanting to receive pleasure, the intention for pleasure in order to satisfy ourselves puts us in opposition to nature, to the Creator. Therefore, when we want to receive for ourselves, we separate ourselves from the Creator. This is our flaw and the cause of all problems and suffering.

Correction doesn't take place when we stop receiving, but rather when we change the reason for receiving, our intention. As mentioned in the previous unit, the attributes of the Creator are wholeness, connection and giving. Hence, when we receive for ourselves, it is called "ego" (egotism), meaning "separation" and when we receive in order to unify, connect with the Creator and act in accordance with His attribute of giving, it is called united with the Creator, with nature.

I'll explain: Would you enjoy eating the very same food every day for months on end? Probably not. Yet, this is exactly what babies need to do. They have no choice in the matter. In fact, the only reason they agree to it is that they don't know anything else. Certainly, they can derive very limited pleasure by eating, beyond filling their empty tummy. Now, consider the baby's mother. Imagine how her face glows when she feeds her baby. She's in seventh heaven just seeing her child eat his fill. The child is calm, at best, but the mother is truly happy.

What is actually going on here? Both Mother and baby are enjoying the baby's desire to eat, yet while the baby is focusing on his hunger, Mom is enjoying her ability to give. She isn't focused on herself, but rather on the baby. She is united with him, so her pleasure does not diminish as the baby eats, which is what happens with the baby, but only continues to increase.

The same thing happens with nature. If we knew what nature wanted from us and actualized it, we would feel the pleasure in unity and giving. Moreover, we would not feel it on the physical level, as mothers experience naturally with their babies, rather on the spiritual level of our connection with nature, with the Creator.

Thus, the correction we need to perform is choosing the correct intention which we will use with our desires. In return for performing this correction and attaining the intention, we fulfill the last and greatest wish - our desire for spirituality, for revealing the Creator. When this desire is fulfilled, one becomes familiar with the system controlling reality, participates in its operation and eventually receives the keys and sits in the driver's seat. Such a person will no longer feel life and death the way we do, rather will flow effortlessly with pleasure and infinite wholeness, united with the Creator.

Rav Dr. Michael Laitman, "Kabbalah in Simple Terms"

Task #2:
Read the following excerpts from Rav Dr. Michael Laitman's blog and answer the questions below:
- Why do we need the will to receive?
- What is an "inclination," what are the "good inclination" and the "evil inclination?"
- How is the valve to *Ein-Sof* (Infinity) opened?

The will to receive for oneself does not constitute a barrier between the Creator and the created being. The obstruction is the egoistic form of the will to receive, which is in opposition to the Creator. The 'will' itself is actually the matter for receiving the light.

If not for our desire for pleasure, we would not be able to reveal and feel the Creator! How could I possibly attain Him? Indeed He, the Creator, exists outside of me and in order to attain Him, I need to receive Him within myself, feel internally and that is only possible with my matter, through equivalence of form with the Creator!

I will never be able to feel the Creator outside of my own matter, because I am the created being and I only feel what is within me. My matter is not my obstacle; to the contrary, it's specifically within my matter that I receive the light. In this respect, I am akin to a radio receiver, made of metal, plastic and silicone (semiconductors) receiving the radio wave, since it is able to generate a wave of the same frequency within. That is why it is necessary to think not about the matter itself, but rather about my intention! This intention is the form we need to set upon the will to receive.

Excerpt from Rav Dr. Michael Laitman's Blog, January 31, 2010

We, the matter of creation, the desire for pleasure to fulfill ourselves, can only receive. If the intention of the will to receive is to receive for oneself, then this intention and not the will to receive itself, we call "evil." Indeed, the desire is unchangeable matter, which is why it is impossible to say whether it is good or bad. That is determined by the intention, whether it is good or bad. That is our free choice.

Regarding desires on the degree of the inanimate, vegetative and animate, where we have no free choice, we are incapable of changing anything. More and more scientific studies are proving that. The only possible change is on the degree of Man (speaking), in an intention above the desire.

The will on its own was created by the Creator and given to us in an unchanging form. The initial egoistic intention upon the desire was given to us from the start, "for my own benefit." We need to determine that this intention is evil, since it is directed against unity, against bestowing to others, against bestowing to the Creator. However, the intention can be reversed, "for the benefit of others," to bestow unto others and then it is called "the good inclination."

Meaning, the "evil inclination" and the "good inclination" are determined by the intention, whereas the inclination is a desire that does not change. The intention belongs only to the degree of Man. The intention to become similar to the Creator is called "good" and the opposite is called "evil." The intention is expressed in unity with others or separate from them.

Therefore, out of all my intentions, I need to choose only those, where I have free choice, to connect with others with a single intention of mutual bestowal. In that, we are similar to the Creator. Only there I determine good or bad, either relative to my egoism or relative to the Creator.

Excerpt from Rav Dr. Michael Laitman's Blog, May 18, 2010

In order to win at this game called "life," we only need to change our intention, from the intention to swallow everything only for myself and at the expense of everyone else - to the intention of love and giving, like the Creator. The wisdom of Kabbalah is the means to correct the intention and when that happens, the valve opens and all the abundance comes to us from *Ein-Sof* (Infinity).

Excerpt from Rav Dr. Michael Laitman's Blog, February 19, 2008

Task #3:
Read the following excerpts, from the books "A Glimpse of Light" and "Unlocking the Zohar" and answer the question:
  • **Where are the spiritual worlds found?**

We are in a perfect system created by the Creator. The matter of creation is all "the will to receive," and the perfect system is actually the collective desire that was created. That desire is also called "The collective soul" or "The soul of Adam HaRishon." (Editors Note: We will expand on the study of the soul of Adam HaRishon in the second and third study units.) But the Creator shattered the collective soul into numerous particles. There is only a shattered particle of the collective soul in each of us.

As a result of the shattering, in our world, each one's desire (Kli-vessel) is divided into two main parts: Internal vessels and external vessels.

I feel my internal vessels as "I," myself, hence, I care for them. I feel my external vessels as foreign, meaning not mine. The internal and external vessels are contrary to each other – the more I love my internal vessels, the more I hate my external vessels.

Why? Because "the boundary of the shattering" passes between both types of vessels – a type of partition causing me to look aside only in a way of: "How can I benefit from that situation? What do I get out of it?" It forces me to treat others egoistically, out of a desire to exploit them.

Rav Dr. Michael Laitman, "A Glimpse of Light"

The natural course of things, the different parts of our desire (internal and external, me and others) collide with one another. The wisdom of Kabbalah assists us in correcting the connection between them, in joining them until they become one and we feel no difference between them. This is the longed-for change in our perception of reality. This is how we discover the upper world, also known as "the next world."

It is not that we prepare ourselves here and subsequently reach some other place. Rather, the more we show love toward others instead of hatred, the more we begin to feel what is called "the upper world" or "the next world." All the worlds are here in the connection between us including what currently seems to be outside of us, remote from us.

Desires that seem to us as others are divided into several circles with respect to our ego. In the closest circle are family, relatives and friends. In the next circle are people who help us and who benefit us by their existence, such as doctors. Then there are the people that we only want to use, harm, yet to keep them alive. And the farthest are the people who we truly hate and may even be prepared to kill. However, they are all our own desires… When we reconnect them to ourselves, we will become the general soul that the Creator created and will return to the world of Ein Sof. That is the "trick of the trade" defined as "The world was created for me."

It is important to stress that the process of correcting the perception of reality is not meant to be carried out artificially. If my neighbor were to yell at me tomorrow, I would not reply with something like, "Relax, my friend. After all, you are only my will." It is also not a simplistic shift of "inward instead of outward." It is about a profound transformation. In order to execute it we need Kabbalah books to help us build the new perception within us, as well as the company of people who will support us in the correction process.

Rav Dr. Michael Laitman, "Unlocking the Zohar"

Task #4:

Read the following excerpt from Rav Dr. Michael Laitman's blog and answer the question below:

- **What is the difference between love that is felt within the ego and love that is felt out of the ego?**

Question: I try to love others, but people around me only look to do me wrong! What do you do when one tries to love and the other doesn't?

Answer: Even when you think others aren't being so good, that still doesn't justify you doing what they do. It's not advisable to learn from bad examples, because each one has their own calculations.

The mutual love to which we aspire is not possible within the ego. Within the ego, I love another only because he's beneficial to me and in essence, I would like to take advantage of him. Love within the ego is like "love of fish" - I love fish because I enjoy eating them. In the same exact manner, as long as I derive pleasure from someone, I feel good with him and I "love" him. However, as soon as I don't feel good anymore, I reject him.

But there is another kind of love we aren't familiar with, as yet. Above our egoistic calculations, above our nature - where we see the extent to which we're all parts of one, general system and interdependent. When this image is revealed to us, we surrender under its power and love towards others awakens within us.

Beyond this love, there is even a more supreme love - where even without the calculations of mutual dependency, the attribute of love itself attracts us, because we realize that being loving and giving is the most sublime in reality.

Love is what enables us to rise above our regular vessels of perception and begin to feel a different reality. When our natural aspiration to absorb everything into ourselves is replaced with the aspiration to love and give, then instead of the small and limited reality we sense now, the true reality external to us opens before us. This reality is called the "spiritual reality."

A person who attains the feeling of spiritual reality is no longer affected by the response of others to his love towards them. One understands it is how people treat each other, because the ego controls them by nature and not because they are bad. One understands that the Creator did this intentionally, in order to enable them to finally reach the independent realization of the worthlessness of the ego and emerge from it to a reality of love.

Excerpt from Rav Dr. Michael Laitman's Blog, April 3, 2008

Task #5:

Read the following excerpts from Rav Dr. Michael Laitman's blog and the book "A Glimpse of Light."

Suppose I only have the Word program installed on my computer, and I get an Excel or jpg file attached to an e-mail message. I try to open the file using Word, but it doesn't open. It could be that there is something very good for me in that file, but my program refuses to open it. I have no choice but to install a new program on the hard disk of my computer, which will be able to receive the data and present them to me. A new format of data requires a new program.

We go through a similar process in our spiritual development. Using the wisdom of Kabbalah, we acquire a new program which rides on the back of our desire, and then we can receive new images, new information. Up until now, we only had the original program with which we were born, that is totally directed to self-love. Now, we are upgrading ourselves – acquiring a new program that understands what the love of others is. With the new program, the new "files" we are receiving "open" just great!

Rav Dr. Michael Laitman, "A Glimpse of Light"

Question: What is "intention?"

Answer: Intention is what you want from your situation. It doesn't matter what you say or do, rather what's important is specifically where you are headed, what result you expect from your or our, current state.

In other words, how would you like to see your next state? How do you imagine it right now? What will you do: bestow unto the Creator, receive, for yourself, gain something, pass it on, share? The way you imagine yourself in your next step - that is your intention.

That is why only humans can have intentions, since they are the only ones in all of creation existing beyond time. Intention doesn't operate in 'corporeal' time, but in spiritual time, which exists above our desire.

Excerpt from Rav Dr. Michael Laitman's Blog, March 20, 2011

Part #3 - The Language of Kabbalah
Lesson #1 - The Law of Branches and Roots

Task #1:
Read the following excerpt from the book "The Wisdom of Kabbalah According to Baal HaSulam" and answer the following question:
 • **Why is spiritual attainment no less and even more real than the sensation of this world?**

The question that arises regarding the attainment of spirituality that spirituality is intangible compared to corporeality stems only from the lack of understanding and lack of feeling spirituality. It implies that spirituality is comprised of forces with which one cannot connect and attain, as anything else one can attain and grasp, see, taste, breathe or smell. People cannot conceive that it is the very same attainment. Baal HaSulam actually says here in the article that the attainment of spirituality and the attainment of corporeality are exactly the same.

Suppose everyone lost their sense of sight and a new generation were born not knowing what sight was, with no one who knows and tells of what it is, or could remember and tell. Even if possible, it would be to no avail, since they didn't have the sense of sight, which is just like how an ordinary person is in comparison with a Kabbalist. In that case, they would learn and know how to manage. They would use their other senses and write down their observations, sharing with each other their impressions of what they felt, other than through their sight.

Nothing else would happen; rather, they'd have their own world lacking only the impression from one sense. Albeit a very important sense, through which our main impression from the world and reality is received, but they would manage. They would live from revealing their senses' response to their surroundings. If we observed them, we would see how they examine the world, study it and how they manage without the sense of sight, creating all kinds of other signs and language, with no awareness of their lack of a sense. To us, people who have that sense, they would appear lacking in their knowledge and wisdom.

Except that it is not about the height of attainment, even though that difference exists between spirituality and corporeality, where Kabbalists possess another sense that we do not have. But the actual attainment of spirituality is just like corporeal attainment, with or without the sense of sight, similar to the feeling of spirituality or not. That is because even without the sense of sight, a person studies the world, things that happen to him when encountering things. Just as we see how blind people relate to their environment: When meeting someone, they touch his face, thereby become familiar with him. Meaning, what do they sense? They sense their response. The blind person can remember how certain matter responds. He doesn't know who he is, rather how he responds to that matter.

What happens with all of a person's senses is the same in spirituality: One never attains the object itself, but rather only an impression of it, according to how we are constructed. In the world itself, there is no inanimate, vegetative, animate or speaking; rather only a force. A single force divided into many forces that affect us. A person operates with his forces in resistance to those forces, feels and examines them. He can examine and study them in such a way that he doesn't know what is actually in front of him, rather how it responds to him.

The person then notes these responses, collecting his attainments, which provide him with an image of the world. Meaning, the world doesn't exist outside the person; rather it is an image the person constructs from his responses to the forces operating upon him. If his senses, feelings and sensitivity were to change, he would sense a different image; perhaps larger or a bit smaller, if his sensitivity increases quantitatively. If it increases qualitatively, he will feel what stands out more and less, meaning the changing relation between the phenomena, and accordingly how the world changes into different forms. If he acquires additional senses, another image will be added to the previous one.

In other words, the wisdom of Kabbalah's tangibility, relating to an additional sense is the same tangibility as in this world. By acquiring the additional sense, a person examines and studies additional phenomena, just like a blind person receiving the sense of sight. Even with an additional sense, a person examines, lives and sees only his responses to something unattainable.

That is why Kabbalists say that only matter and form clothed in matter can be studied, whereas abstract forms are just our pure imagination, not existing is reality, rather in potential. It is similar to the worlds before attainment of the souls, which have no form, rather exist in potential. The essence, that same reality outside of our contact with it is unattainable to us altogether. It is "Atzmuto" ("His Essence"), with which we have no contact. Yet, what we attain is exactly on the same degree of reality and tangibility as attained in this world with our ordinary senses.

Hence, those who acquire an additional sense and advance to a much broader image of the world ascend in their attainment. It's not that they enter a new plane, where confusion or intangible phenomena are sensed. Meaning, Kabbalists acquire more tangible knowledge than this world, which are revealed in this world in the end. They feel the forces operating upon this world. This ascent in the degree of knowing reality is called "attaining the roots of this world." However, even these roots, which the Kabbalists attain in a very real sense, are attained only in relation to themselves, according to that same law called "the law of equivalence of form."

Meaning, a person's sense operates such that to the extent of the equivalence of form of a sense with an external phenomenon, the sense feels it. However, it does not feel the external phenomenon, rather feels the form itself. Let's take hearing for example: One hears something because one's sense receives a form of something external, but the person measures the form the sense received and not the "thing" external to him. So it is with all the senses. All of man's senses operate in accordance with the equivalence of form.

With the spiritual sense, this principle is even more pronounced, because in the spiritual world, we speak only of forms. Naturally, in our world, with our senses, language is mistaken and deceptive. What is expressed is as if what is external to us is attained and felt. This is not the case, rather such expressions in the language stem from our life. That is how a person is born and how he feels. That is why it takes a long time to convince and teach him that he can't attain anything external to him, but attains according to the forms existing within him, according to the equivalence of form.

Humanity still does not understand this fact. Although a few scientists have already revealed and agreed with it, the rest still do not comprehend it. Whereas with Kabbalists, this process is obvious and simple, since with every new spiritual attainment, they must first work diligently on constructing the appropriate form for that attainment. Meaning, the Creator presents something, indicating the person should attain it. He gives the person starting points, "Reshimot", examples of forms that if one creates the same within himself, he attains and feels that external phenomenon. In such a way, the Creator teaches us of what we do not yet know or see.

Rav Dr. Michael Laitman, "The Wisdom of Kabbalah According to Baal HaSulam"

Task #2:
Read the following excerpt from Rav Dr. Michael Laitman's Blog and answer the question:
  • **Why is the law of Branches and Roots so important?**

Question: In the wisdom of Kabbalah, we have a law of Branches and Roots. Knowing various laws in this world helps us in our daily lives. In what way can knowing spiritual laws and the law of Branches and Roots in particular, be of help to us?
Answer: The law of Branches and Roots is the main and most important for us in the wisdom of Kabbalah. According to the rule of Branches and Roots, all that exists in our world descends from above to below in a definite one-way order and manner!

It's written: "There is no blade of grass below which does not have an angel above it, striking it and telling it to grow." In the wisdom of Kabbalah, an angel is a force. Every action, thought, desire, event, phenomenon, from the most elementary particles and up to the largest planets and galaxies, everything on all levels is operated and governed by a supreme force from above. This force splits and includes numerous forces on different levels of inanimate, vegetative, animate and speaking - physical and biological forces on different levels. All this comes into being from above.

Hence, the law of Branches and Roots is a very important one; since by means of the wisdom of Kabbalah, by learning the law of Branches and Roots, we will be able to rise from the branches in our world to the roots. We will begin seeing our world as "transparent," and behind every object we will see a force governing it and leading it to action.

We will begin feeling where thoughts come from, where desires come from; we'll begin to understand the reason for events happening to us and others. We will begin seeing how a network of forces operates in the world and how, as in the theater, it organizes everything taking place here! In such a way we will begin a dialog with the Upper force, with the root governing our entire world through its individual forces.

We will begin to understand the point from which we can enter a connection with these forces and the Creator behind them, in order to respond in some manner, participate in some way, change and intervene with awareness, understand what remains for us to do with this entire network of forces, operating us externally and internally.

We do not understand nor attain it, but at every given moment, we are in a certain image, which was prepared and designed for us by these forces. We need to understand where, within this image, we can actively participate in governing our lives and fates.

Rav Dr. Laitman's Blog, March 6, 2009

Task #3:
Read the following excerpt from the book "An Experience Called Kabbalah" and answer the following questions:
   1. **What is the Language of the Branches?**
   2. **Why can't Kabbalists use other words to describe spiritual roots?**

Kabbalists do not invent a language of their own. They share a sense of the same feelings of the spiritual world. They see what name they should give each sensation they feel in spirituality as a spiritual object. These words cannot be replaced. For example, in the creation of the world there are twenty-two properties, qualities which are signified respectively as letters in our language, and their various combinations provide a spiritual feeling of a physically-looking object in our world.

Describing the spiritual world is a description of the soul of man, describing its degrees of closeness to the Creator and how it senses Him more and more. The more it senses the Creator, the closer it is to Him. Kabbalah divides the general soul into parts, giving each part an accurate name according to its properties and describes its actions. This is a language of feelings, yet it is accurate. Kabbalah is the "engineering of the soul." However, how can we use such research and accurate descriptions if our language is inaccurate, limited and corporeal? That is why Kabbalists chose a special language for their science and called it "The Language of the Branches."

Everything in creation: inanimate, vegetative, animate and speaking, whatever has taken place, is taking place and will take place, all objects and their governance -everything descends from the Creator and passes through all of the spiritual worlds up to the state where it is no longer revealed in our world. Yet, their governance is constantly renewed with the Upper force, from above downwards to our world. Everything existing in our world inevitably begins in the Upper world and then descends to our world, slowly and gradually. Thus, all that exists in our world is an outcome of the world above it. There is a precise connection between objects of our world to their source in the spiritual world by a connection of cause and effect.

Kabbalists see this connection between the Upper object and the object in our world accurately. All that exists in our world is an outcome and under Upper governance. Accordingly, Kabbalists can accurately tell what pertains to what, and call objects, the roots in the spiritual worlds, by the names of their corporeal outcomes, "branches." This is the origin of the name "The Language of the Branches." Moreover, this connection between spiritual roots and corporeal branches is not permanent. There is always a process of development and renewal. From the beginning of creation of the world up to its end, a process of creating, correcting, ascending, etc. is activated. This process takes place accurately like a set program, which descends with all its details to our world, determining everything. Nevertheless, each object goes through its own path, yet interacts and connects with others, without ever disappearing and all remains as is, with its own essence. Of course, that is why it is absolutely impossible to exchange these names with other words.

In order to find an accurate and secret language, we always need to use only those words which express the Upper spiritual root, as shown to us by Kabbalists. The Kabbalists, who revealed this language, depict the spiritual world to us with precision, in our own words. There simply cannot be any other language. How is it possible to use words which are clear and common to both worlds? We need to learn from this that we should follow the most important rule in our relation to the Torah and Kabbalah. We should always remember that whatever we read in Kabbalah and the Torah are only words, not objects of our world. What stands behind these words are only spiritual objects, roots which under no circumstance have any connection to our world. This must not confuse us! The entire Torah is the Holy Names of the Creator. It is called "serving the Creator," hence naming something or someone expressing something. Similarly, in our world, we name objects. The Torah is a description of the degrees of closeness to feeling the Creator and how the Creator reveals Himself within our feelings.

The Kabbalists used this language to explain, share information with one another and put it into writing in their books, in the form of words and symbols of our world. Just as mathematicians use formulas, two Kabbalists, the one writing and the one reading, both feel what it is about, implied in these words in the language of Kabbalah.

In summary, a word is a symbol expressing a certain spiritual object, expressing a certain feeling and while reading a word, another Kabbalist can replicate it, just as a musician senses music. He doesn't need intellectual words in order to understand the language of music the composer indicated.

Rav Dr. Laitman, "An Experience Called Kabbalah"

Lesson #2 - The Light that Reforms

Task #1:
Read the following excerpt from Rav Dr. Michael Laitman's blog and answer the following questions:
  - **What condition is necessary for understanding the teacher of Kabbalah?**
  - **What is the benefit in reading Kabbalah books, before having reached spiritual attainment?**

Studying the wisdom of Kabbalah poses a problem for the student: In order to understand what the teacher is talking about, the student must be of a certain spiritual degree. His teacher may be speaking from very high degree, butt since all the degrees are identical by nature and have the same elements, even if the student is on a lesser spiritual degree than his teacher, he can still understand his teachings in accordance with his degree.

If one has not yet ascended to the first spiritual degree and exists only in this world, one is incapable of understanding the language of branches. Indeed, understanding the language of branches means attaining that which exists in this world - the "branches" - and on the spiritual degree attaining the "roots." Consequently, the connection between them is clear and one is capable of understanding what the teacher is saying.

However, if one does not attain the roots, one cannot attain what the teacher is saying. Indeed, he uses words whose hidden meaning is not understood. Just by understanding this world, we do not even attain the branches, because we do not know their roots. After all, branches are what descend from the roots. There is no branch without a root and no root without a branch. Hence, if we do not attain the branches' spiritual essence - their roots, we do not even have a point of contact with the language of branches.

It clearly follows that a student will not be able to understand the teacher, as long as he has not attained the spiritual roots. Unfortunately, that's the way it is. Thus, the study of the wisdom of Kabbalah is only for those who are in spiritual attainment. As long as we have not attained spiritual attainment, it should be clear to us that we are not learning the wisdom of Kabbalah; rather only using its "wondrous quality," the remedy embedded within it in order to reveal the "roots." That is our sole purpose in studying.

That is why the student is not asked to exert effort in collecting information; it suffices to concentrate on the fact that what we need is the Light that Reforms, as soon as possible. If we attain the roots by means of this Light, we will begin attaining wisdom. If we don't, we will remain in the dark.

Do not delude yourself that by learning the definitions written in the book, you are learning the wisdom. You are not, because you are not familiar with the connections between the branches and the roots; you have not yet attained the roots.

This explains why the wisdom of Kabbalah begins with spiritual attainment and not before. Prior to spiritual attainment, studying is only yearning to summon the influence of the Light upon us.

From Rav Dr. Michael Laitman's blog

Task #2:

Read the following excerpt from the book "The Wisdom of Kabbalah according to Baal HaSulam" and answer the following questions:

- What is the problem of the beginning student of the wisdom of Kabbalah?
- Why is it necessary to be familiar with the material while studying the wisdom of Kabbalah?

One who begins to study the wisdom of Kabbalah needs to know that most of the Kabbalah writings, including *Torah* and *Talmud* are written in the language of branches. Even in the language of Kabbalah itself, which speaks of *Sefirot, Partzufim* (faces), including all their details, the language of branches is also used, and those spiritual terms are called by their names in this world, such as: "head," "inner", "end," etc.

Thus, these words need to be translated into spiritual terms first, since we are not familiar with the spiritual object behind each and every word. One can only imagine a corporeal object, action or force in its regard, but cannot describe the spiritual objects. A word like "screen," although we know what it means in corporeality and it can be translated into other languages, what it means in spirituality is still not known. Without being familiar with the spiritual concept itself, it can be described as a wall, television screen, a concealing screen, or even a revealing screen. The same is true for each and every word learned in Kabbalah.

Those who do not achieve knowledge of the language or feel the spiritual character of each and every word are not studying the wisdom of Kabbalah; rather, they are still in preparation. Therefore, a beginning student's whole aspiration should be to acquire the language of branches, in order to ascend from the branches to the roots. When he knows what he should feel, know, see and understand regarding the spiritual character behind each and every word, he has begun studying the wisdom of Kabbalah. Before that, prior to attaining from branches to roots, one is not studying the wisdom of Kabbalah, rather is in preparation.

The problem is that beginning students want to grasp matters right away, without self-correction. A person who does not learn in order to attain correction, progresses incorrectly. Rather, "his wisdom is greater than his actions." He studies *"The Study of the Ten Sefirot"* technically: how, where and when the *"Reshimot"* (Reminiscence) emerge and what actions take place there. He becomes familiar with them and knows all the pages by heart, yet without understanding or attaining the internality of the writings.

Rabbi Baruch Shalom Ashlag (The Rabash) told his students that in the "The Study of the Ten Sefirot," it is enough to attain one line, in order to enter inside the entire Torah, for the entire wisdom and the Torah are found in a person's heart. Otherwise, the study is only memorization and oral knowledge, without being able to describe the terms with their correct spiritual character. That is also in complete contradiction to the teachings of Baal HaSulam regarding the order of study. Baal HaSulam says that first of all, the definition of the spiritual term of each and every concept needs to be repeated and acquired. Afterwards, within the written text, one needs to attempt and desire to construct and arrange what is written in a correct way, spiritually and emotionally. Then out of this demand, the Surrounding Light will come and begin to draw a person closer to the internal feeling of those words.

That is why there are few scientists of Kabbalah, since people crave for knowledge and wisdom, without self-transformation, which requires them to attain equivalence of form with the roots, through studying the branches. The study of branches is with the intellect and the aspiration is to attain the roots with the emotion.

Could the study of abstract terms in the language of Kabbalah distant a person from the need for self-correction? Could it be that particularly the study of rules and laws in the Bible and Talmud languages awaken the person to correction from seeing the extent to which he does not observe them?

It seems that one might think that through the study of laws and corrections as explained in the language of the Bible or Talmud, one would see that one does not observe what these laws require. The resulting regret would lead one to demand corrections and attain them through the study of the wisdom of Kabbalah. This is not the case with the study of the wisdom of Kabbalah in the language of Kabbalah.

In the language of Kabbalah, one studies dry technical material, which seems to be irrelevant to him. The technical study of the mechanical actions of "screens," "lights," "vessels," "mating while striking," "beating," "clothing," "*Reshimot*," perhaps distract him from being aware of evil, prevent him from seeing the extent to which he is not in equivalence of form with those holy conditions Torah study demands from the person.

However, in the article "The Essence of the Wisdom of Kabbalah" Baal HaSulam describes the four languages (the language of the Bible, the language of Laws, the language of Legend and the language of Kabbalah), and asserts that the language of Kabbalah is the most useful one. That is because modern man, with his ego, is incapable of extracting the Light that Reforms, other than through the wisdom of Kabbalah, since specifically within it, the most powerful Light for reform exists. One can easily be awakened by studying the Kabbalistic writings, written in the language of Kabbalah.

The language of Kabbalah is not learned in order to study *Sefirot* and *Partzufim*; rather the study is only a means. That is why it does not matter what a person knows. Knowing the material is intended only to cause the person to adhere to the study material and demand Light during the study. That is not because it is important to know the details presented in "*The Study of the Ten Sefirot*." Knowledge is only an external sign of engaging in the material, and it is enough to have superficial understanding, rather than deep understanding. It is unnecessary to force yourself to remember the material. You should study in order to adhere to the source of the study and life.

Even Rabash's students did not engage in the tiny details of the wisdom, nor were they proficient in all parts of "*The Study of the Ten Sefirot*," compared to other students who studied and memorized entire pages, for it is a completely different approach. Baal HaSulam also did not achieve his knowledge by memorizing pages, but rather from attainment. The smallest spiritual attainment is worth more than mounds of superficial knowledge memorized from the books. This difference between knowing what is written and knowing the internality of what is written is called "the opinion of Torah is opposite the opinion of homeowners."

In Kabbalah, people cannot be judged by their knowledge. A person who has a sharp mind and a good memory, or sleeps well before the lesson and has time to review the material learns well and is well versed in it. Those who are confused, unable to concentrate while studying due to internal problems or discomfort with themselves do not perceive the material because they have other questions. Then, they use the study out of despair and anticipate the Light that Reforms to stem from it, rather than the knowledge itself. As Baal HaSulam describes in "The Preface to *The Study of the Ten Sefirot*," the bat anticipates darkness, knowledge, and the rooster anticipates light - faith.

Rav Dr. Michael Laitman, "The Wisdom of Kabbalah According to Baal HaSulam"

Task #3:
Read the following excerpts from the book "The Point in the Heart" and summarize the main points in your own words:

From day to day, we reach the conclusion that as long as the ego continues to rule, the end of the world is getting closer, for we must choose life and love. However, without assistance, we will not be able to rise above the ego. That's how we were born. For that purpose, we need an external force which does not exist in our world. That is why we have been given the method of correction – Kabbalah.

A special force is embedded within the wisdom of Kabbalah, one that can create a new attribute in us. Authentic Kabbalah writings describe the nature of the Creator, the Upper world and the processes taking place therein. When we learn from the writings about states contrary to our world, actions of love and giving, we draw strength from them towards us.

This projection of Upper states towards our present state is called the act of the Correcting Light, the Surrounding Light. In the end, the Surrounding Light causes us to yearn for the attribute of the Creator.

Baal HaSulam explains this as follows:[48]

"Stemming from the strong desire and will to understand what they learn awakens upon them the lights surrounding their soul, which draw the person very much closer to reaching His wholeness."

Rav Dr. Michael Laitman, "The Point in the Heart"

Nature, the supreme force, the force of love and giving is found in the connection between all parts of creation that He Himself created, existing in harmony and absolute mutual connection.

We feel bad because we have emerged from that integral system. If we want to feel good, we need to try to return to this system called "wholeness."

How do we return? When we desire and exert efforts to return to the system, we awaken a force from it that influences us. It is called that we awaken upon us the "Surrounding Light," the "Light that Reforms," the force that brings us back to the general system.

This force operates in accordance with the intensity of our desire, meaning, to the same extent that we are capable of awakening, requesting and demanding it from the system.

---

[48] Introduction to "The Study of the Ten Sefirot," Letter 155

Rav Dr. Michael Laitman, "The Point in the Heart"

Who can explain how a baby grows and matures? Why did he not remain as he was yesterday? Science can say what takes place within matter, but it does not see the cause found outside matter, pushing it to develop.

I left science decades ago, because that's exactly what I wanted to know - where does the vital force come from? Where is it found? In atoms? In molecules? In systems within the cells? However, I discovered that science does not investigate those. So, if we do not know the main thing and do not even try to discover it, what is it worth?

According to Kabbalah, the force activating the baby is the same one that activates every other part of creation and develops it. This is the Light of life, the Upper force operating in creation and developing from still matter the degrees of vegetative, animate and speaking. Otherwise, matter would have remained dead without any change.

The Light of life cannot be perceived and measured by any instrument. We only see the outcome of its action: the baby develops from day to day, from moment to moment. In our world, this light acts as natural evolution. The locomotive of evolution crawls at its own speed, meaning, the Upper force acts within matter and pushes it to a predetermined goal.

When entering the spiritual world, every stage of evolution can be investigated, even the era of dinosaurs, if you suddenly have an interest in that. Indeed, all previous forms are known beforehand and must clothe in their form, according to the different combinations of forces of receiving and giving.

The wisdom of Kabbalah describes the following situations in our development. When we study it out of a desire to develop, we summon the Light of life to act upon us consciously. In such a case, an act of the light of life is defined as the act of the "Surrounding Light." Nowadays, the possibility of doing so is open to each one of us.

Rav Dr. Michael Laitman, "The Point in the Heart"

Task #4:

Read the following excerpts from the books "Kabbalah, Science and the Meaning of Life" and "A View of Kabbalah" and answer the question:

- **What distinguishes Kabbalah from the other holy languages?**

Kabbalists are scholars of the Upper world found outside Man's regular range of perception. Descriptions of their attainment refer to the Upper world, but since we are unaware of the fact that apart from our world, an Upper spiritual world exists, we attribute their words to our world. This phenomenon is called "materialization of things."

In the past, the people of Israel had attained the spiritual world. The two thousand years of detachment from the feeling of the spiritual world are called "exile." That period had us think that Torah deals with historical stories or codes of conduct between man and friend in our world. However, that is not the case. Among the details of each and every world, a relation of root and branch exists. Based on this principle, Kabbalists developed a language based on the parallel between the Upper world and our world. They describe processes taking place in the spiritual world by using the names of the branches taken from our world.

Kabbalists use four different languages in order to explain to us how man can reach the Creator's degree and how he can draw the force of correction to him, in order to correct his nature from egoism to altruism. Those are the languages of the Bible, Laws, Legend and Kabbalah. In his essay, "The Teaching of Kabbalah and its Essence," Baal HaSulam says that even though all four languages serve the wisdom of truth, and "the internality of the wisdom of Kabbalah is no different than that of the Bible, Talmud, and Legend," indeed the Kabbalah language itself is the most convenient and suitable one to use.

The difference between the languages is evident in their accuracy. The language of Kabbalah is more accurate than the other languages in describing the connection between the root in the Upper world and the branch in the lower world. The more precisely a person ties himself to his upper root, the greater the correcting power he attains. The language of Kabbalah uses terms nonexistent in our world, such as: "worlds" and "spheres," and makes use of diagrams and formulas. It makes it easier for students not to get confused, helps them not materialize the things, and enables approaching the study in a clear and orderly manner. The main difference between the language of Kabbalah and other languages is clearly and unequivocally expressed in the way the purpose of creation is described: resemblance of the created to the Creator, reversing egoism to altruism.

The main textbook of Kabbalah in our generation (alongside the Book of Zohar with the Sulam commentary) is Baal HaSulam's "*The Study of the Ten Sefirot*," a six-volume book based on the ARI writings. In over 2,000 pages, it depicts the structure of the Upper worlds, including diagrams, a glossary of terms and Q&A for reviewing the material. In the introduction to the book, Baal HaSulam elaborates on the reasons for the priority of the language of Kabbalah over the other languages, especially in our generation.

In our times, humanity is situated at the end of the final stage of development of the will to receive. Accordingly, Baal HaSulam appeared and adapted the ARI's method to the structure of the souls of our generation, so it would be accessible to each and every person.

Rav Dr. Michael Laitman, "Kabbalah, Science and the Meaning of Life"

In the language of branches, there are four types of books, written in
a. the language of the Bible
b. the language of Legend
c. the language of *Talmud*
d. the language of Kabbalah

The holy books are all written in the language of branches, yet each one of them expresses a different depiction of the impression from Above. All the books are intended for people to read and yearn to ascend emotionally through them to the same story the book tells, hence, to reveal the Creator.

However, of these four languages, the most effective one for us is the language of Kabbalah, whose influential force over a person, through which he is drawn to spirituality is enormous, powerful and most efficient. Accordingly, Kabbalists advise whoever wishes to attain spirituality to read their books and attain the revelation of Divinity, meaning to meet the Creator.

Why then, did the Kabbalists not write all their books in the language of Kabbalah? Because in each and every language there is another possibility to reveal the details of the spiritual state where the Kabbalist feels the Creator. Kabbalists can write about the same feeling in four ways, four languages. The language of Kabbalah is the most effective in its ability to bring a person to that status, but the other languages are better suited to convey all the details of the encounter, all the possibilities and approaches to it and are very helpful to the Kabbalist who is on the way to that same feeling, to that same revelation of the Creator.

Even regarding the language of Kabbalah itself, a question arises: Does a person who reads Kabbalah books study with the aim of drawing the force that will correct him and lead him to the same feeling, or does he want to obtain knowledge from the study, only understand intellectually what the book is about? If his goal is only intellectual, he does not yearn to attain spirituality, rather he reads what is written in the book, simply learns the text and knows it, without sensing what the the Kabbalist tells and feels.

Unfortunately, this is how most of those interested in Kabbalah books study. People, who for various reasons do not feel the need to enter a spiritual feeling and do not understand that there is a spiritual aspect, read the other languages. Meaning, holy books written in other languages and not in the language of Kabbalah, for their perception of the language of Kabbalah is of a dry, technical language which explains nothing.

One has no reason to open holy books other than in order to reach the goal of his life. The fact that most of humanity is not engaged in the correct study and the correct approach to these books is what burdens us, makes our lives so difficult and causes the decline of the generations, and leads to the fact that eventually, humanity will understand through suffering that these books must be accepted and opened correctly.

Rav Dr. Michael Laitman, "A View of Kabbalah"

Lesson #3 - Kabbalah books

Task #1:
Read the following excerpts from the books "An Experience called Kabbalah" and "The Open Book" and answer the question:

- What does a person acquire by reading Kabbalah books?

A person cannot change himself forcefully. If we are not changed from Above, we do not change. If we are not given new qualities from above, such as intellect, analytical abilities or sharp vision, nothing will help - neither my words nor your desire. Therefore, all we have to do is invest in our efforts. We will already be changed from Above and perhaps the changes occurring in us will not be at all like those we would like, but rather the opposite. There - Above – they know better...

Hence, the first stages in learning and advancing is constantly reading and rereading all the existing written material. Reading the books of Baal HaSulam, Rabbi Baruch Ashlag (The Rabash) and mine, especially the sections to which we feel drawn. In the written material, the Upper Light is concealed, which operates within you and gradually begins to change you. Just being filled with what is written in these books will give you the ability to analyze, discern and make decisions from a perspective other than a corporeal-beastly one. Then, the studied material in which the Upper Light is embedded will start operating within you, gradually penetrating and affecting you in a concealed way. As result of this process, internal knowledge and the ability to discern what is closer to spirituality and what is further away from it will appear.

Rav Dr. Michael Laitman, "An Experience called Kabbalah"

True Kabbalah books describe exactly how the mechanism operating reality functions. They describe the control room of all reality, accompanied by sketches and formulas, like operating instructions. These teach a person how the laws work in spirituality and how one can act on them by means of one's desire and thought, thereby influencing the outcome descending back to the person.

The "Book of Zohar" is written in the form of stories and legends. It was deliberately written as such and the book itself mentions that only people who already live in spiritual reality can know what is written and see what is truly described in the book. They can see the pictures and identify the image and the story as one. Whereas we cannot do that, because we still do not have spiritual vision, so the "Book of Zohar," which is a prominent Kabbalah book, seems to us like a book of stories and legends. That is why we do not begin learning Kabbalah from the "Book of Zohar" nowadays. There are introductions and books of Baal HaSulam which teach us how to understand what is written in the "Book of Zohar."

"The Book of Zohar" is not a book through which one can succeed in entering spirituality; rather it is intended for people who are already in spirituality. In order to understand the "Book of Zohar," one must first study several books and introductions, such as: "Introduction to the Wisdom of Kabbalah," "Introduction to the

Book of Zohar," "Preface to the Book of Zohar." Without acquiring clear and correct knowledge from these books, the "Book of Zohar" remains completely obscure to us.

On the other hand, The Ari writings are intended for more developed souls, later incarnations, so they seem foreign to us. The most suitable compositions for us are the writings of Baal HaSulam, which were intended for our generation. That is why they look like any other scientific systemic textbooks, university textbooks. They contain questions and answers, definitions of words and issues, along with being divided into clear sections regarding what it is about and how it is implemented. The books are also accompanied by specific articles on how one should relate to this study, on a personal level.

Accordingly, in our generation, even an uneducated person can approach the wisdom of Kabbalah, with no delay. It is a wisdom that does not require prior learning, as opposed to all other sciences and disciplines. It is enough for a person to feel that his life is full of misery, that he has no peace of mind, that there is no point in his life, in order to begin studying the books and advancing in them.

In the introduction of the "Talmud of the Ten Sefirot," which is the most difficult book in the study of Kabbalah, whose writing is dry and topical, Baal HaSulam writes in the first section for whom the book is intended. Only a person within whom the question of one's purpose in life burns should study that book. In section 155, one of the last in the introduction, Baal HaSulam adds that by studying, even though one does not know what he is studying, rather only wants to know what is written in order to escape his misery, the writings open up to him and he begins to reveal how to behave in order to have a better life.

While studying Kabbalah, one actually learns about one's inner structure, how one's feelings are constructed, how one's soul is formed. Within it is the key to understanding this science, and studying genuine Kabbalah books will suffice in order to reveal what is already embedded within him.

Even if one does not understand anything of this science, the moment he opens a book, his heart and soul begin to open up. He receives knowledge of spirituality in a natural way, just as we feel bitter and sweet, hot and cold. In order to feel such things, one does not have to go to school or university.

The study itself is intended only to help us open the soul; open the spiritual senses that are still blocked. When the heart and soul open up, we enter a state of inspiration, excitement, a completely natural recognition of our reality. It is similar to a person in our world who feels his own reality, regardless of whether he is a peasant or a professor.

This is all about clear, tangible attainment, which does not require a person to be wise and scholarly or philosophically inclined. This is a method which develops the feeling of the heart. It is a method for the revelation of the spiritual world, attaining inspiration by the laws that truly exist in Nature, except that we do not see or feel them yet, yet these laws act upon us incessantly, even without our awareness of them.

Rav Dr. Michael Laitman, "The Open Book"

Task #2:
Read the following excerpt from "Journey to the Upper World" and answer the question:
- What should we desire while reading in Kabbalah books?

The more a person's qualities draw near the attributes of the Upper force, the more the imaginary picture of "my world" draws closer to the truth on the one hand, and is less distorted by the selfish qualities of a person, on the other hand. Since the quality of the Upper force is altruism, indeed the person who acquires this quality unites with the Upper force and senses reality as it is. The only way a person can draw close to the correct view of reality is by studying

Kabbalah, since only Kabbalah deals with the structure of reality, which man has not yet attained.

However, it is not enough to only learn the text, for it is reading the unknown. One must also focus on true vision, be prepared to draw close to a more genuine sensation, which is concealed from us in the meantime.

Everything is within a person, inside him. Outside him is only the Upper force, the Creator, Who is not felt in any form. What a person feels is only the effect of the Creator on himself, his sense organs. Only by the consequence of these feelings, can one guess the essence of the Creator; more precisely meaning not His essence, rather how He appears to a person, how He desires to be felt.

Therefore, the study of Kabbalah must be properly focused, meaning, our thought must be focused on the idea that the inner qualities of a person are being studied, which are still concealed from him.

All the worlds, all those *"Partzufim"* (faces), *"Sefirot,"* names, whatever is described in Kabbalah, all exists within a person himself and will be revealed to him according to the degree of his correction. A person will reveal Moses and Aaron, King David, along with the angels, the wicked and the righteous within him, degrees of attainment called "Jerusalem," the "Holy Temple," etc. All the words of the Torah speak of the person's forces and the degrees of sensing a person has of the Creator.

That is all the Torah speaks of and that is all we speak about in our daily life. After all, we speak of our feelings and, as mentioned, we only feel the Creator's influence. Everything around us is nothing more than the influence of the Creator upon each one of us.

Hence, in order to feel the true picture of the world, we need to aspire, while reading Kabbalah books, to find within ourselves what we read about in the book, since everything written already exists within us, but has yet to be revealed.

According to the degree of a person's spiritual change, he begins to feel within him everything described in the book from which he studies. Hence, the great importance attributed to the study from authentic Kabbalah sources: the "Book of Zohar" (Rabbi Shimon bar Yochai), The Ari writings (Divine Rabbi Yitzchak Luria) and the writings of Rabbi Yehuda Ashlag (Baal HaSulam).

The spiritual change a person undergoes is one of the topics Kabbalist scholars wrote about quite extensively. Only through them is it possible to attain correction of sensations, feelings and qualities in the safest way and attain spiritual ascension.

The only means for progress is to study while thinking, that everything in the book is about me and all this exists somewhere inside me. All these worlds, *Partzufim*, all those are my qualities, which I need to reveal within me.

The more I acquire control of these qualities, the more I will feel more concretely how the Creator operates within me. Indeed, "Outside of me" I will never be able to feel Him, only through His actions within me; "From Your actions we know You."

Since we all sit together and study our true qualities, which are not yet revealed to us, we all investigate the Creator's action within us together. That is, we have one common goal, one thought and one field of experimentation - ourselves.

Therefore, a partnership of purpose, thought and aspiration is created, from which a sense of a common body and shared characteristics is born; a feeling that there are no separate entities, rather one entity called "Adam" and its single Creator.

Only from the internally directed thought toward changing our qualities, toward seeking the Creator within us, the reading of the Torah reveals the "Torah as a spice," the Torah as a method with the force of correction, called "the elixir of life," since it leads to the sensation of the Creator, the eternal and complete Light to flow in a person.

Studying true Kabbalah books draws the Light, the "Light that Reforms," and then the Creator is exposed, and the purpose of creation revealed.

Rav Dr. Michael Laitman, "Journey to the Upper World"

Task #3:
Read the following excerpt from the book "Opening the Zohar" and in your own words, summarize the five rules for studying Kabbalah books (the text refers to the study of the "Book of Zohar," yet applies to the study of all Kabbalah books.)

The "Book of Zohar" is a wonderful tool, capable of opening up to us a world of vast and surprising revelations.

The "Book of Zohar" is sort of gateway to the true reality, currently concealed from our senses. However, in order for us to be able to efficiently use the power of revelation embedded in it, we need to internalize the correct form of reading the Zohar. The following five rules will summarize all the contents of the book and will help you prepare for the great journey on the path of the "Book of Zohar."

The first rule: "The heart understands" - do not look for intellectual understanding.

The "Book of Zohar" is studied with the heart, through desire and emotion. What does that mean? Unlike the usual forms of studying in our world, based on intellectual processing of facts and data, here we have to develop a completely different approach. The study of the "Book of Zohar" is intended to awaken inner change in us and to prepare us for the perception of the concealed reality.

The degree of success in the study depends only on the extent to which we yearn to reveal and feel this reality. That is why there is no need for prior knowledge, talent or special wisdom! All that is required is to develop a simple and genuine desire, open your eyes wide, open your heart and "swallow" everything.

Second rule: "Man is a small world" - interpret the words correctly.

The "Book of Zohar" contains many descriptions and terms familiar to us from the corporeal world, such as: sea, mountains, trees, flowers, animals, people, trips and journeys. It is important to understand that all the details, figures and events mentioned in the book do not speak of the external world around us, but only of what is taking place within us.

Therefore, as we read the "Book of Zohar," we should try to interpret its written words as an expression of those inner actions taking place in the soul; view the text as a bridge leading to our deepest desires and qualities.

Third rule: "The Light in it (in the Torah) reforms" - seek the light.

Many times, we hear that there is a special remedy in the "Book of Zohar.". The remedy is the law of natural development operating in all life processes, not an imaginary mystic force.

Kabbalists explain that our corporeal world is controlled entirely by the egoistic desire to exploit others, whereas in the spiritual world, the only intention operating is to love and give. That is why we were given a unique means, whose function is to connect opposite worlds, or in other words, to direct our attributes according to the attribute of love and giving of the spiritual world - "the Light that Reforms."

The form of the Light's influence is concealed from our understanding for now; hence we call it "remedy" or "miracle." But from the Kabbalists' perspective, being familiar with the spiritual world, there is no "miracle" here, rather a completely natural process.

They emphasize that all we have to do is to read the "Book of Zohar" and desire for its embedded force to operate upon us while studying. We will gradually begin to feel an inner change taking place within us due to that Light. The spiritual world will open and what initially seems to be a "remedy" will become a clear and comprehensible rule.

Fourth rule: "Nothing stands in the way of the desire" - everything depends on the desire.

We all know what efforts are required of little babies in order to take their first steps in the world and with what admirable perseverance they do that. They do not give up and try again and again until they succeed. In the same way we too need to continue studying the "Book of Zohar" with patience and perseverance until we begin to "walk" on our own and reveal the spiritual world. The entire system required for progress has already been prepared for us. The only thing we have to provide is the desire to grow.

Fifth rule: "As one man in one heart" - connection is the key.

The "Book of Zohar" was written by a group of ten Kabbalists, who assembled a complete "vessel," a unified desire to reveal the Upper force of reality - the Creator. Only their internal connection and love enabled them to break through the boundaries of the material world and ascend to the level of eternal existence described in the Zohar. If we want to follow in their footsteps, we need to try to build a similar relationship among us, seek the force of connection that existed between the disciples of Rabbi Shimon bar Yochai. The "Book of Zohar" was born out of love; thus, its renewed revelation in our time will only be possible out of love.

For this chapter which summarizes the book, we have selected special sections for you from the "Book of Zohar." Between them, we have added explanations, guidance for the correct intention during the reading, etc., in order to help you connect to the light embedded in the Zohar.

We recommend you read this chapter slowly. The "Book of Zohar," our guide on the path of spiritual development was not intended for skimming, rather relaxed reading accompanied by a deep inner search.

Rav Dr. Michael Laitman, "Opening the Zohar"

Task #4:

Read the following excerpts from the books "Journey to the Upper World" and "An Experience called Kabbalah" and answer the following questions:

- What is the connection between the writings of Baal HaSulam, The Ari and Rabbi Shimon bar Yochai?
- Why is it recommended to study Kabbalah from the writings of Baal HaSulam?

In every generation, the Creator sends unique souls to our world, who are destined to correct this world and transmit knowledge of the Creator to humanity, as it is written: "The Creator saw that there are not enough sages, divided and shared them with each generation." Thus, in each generation there are spiritual leaders and teachers who adapt the wisdom of Kabbalah to the unique characteristics of their generation.

From the first source of the wisdom of Kabbalah - the book "The Angel Raziel" written by *"Adam HaRishon"* and the second book *"The Book of Yetzira* (Creation)" written by Abraham and up to the most recent ones, hundreds of books have been written over the years on the wisdom of Kabbalah. However, the third book, the "Book of Zohar," written in the 2nd century ACE by Rabbi Shimon bar Yochai is the most prevalent.

The contemporary Kabbalist, Rabbi Yehuda Ashlag (1884-1954), wrote a commentary to the "Book of Zohar" and all the books of The Ari in a language formulated and adapted to the souls of our generation. These days, and according to the type of souls descending into the world, only the "Book of Zohar" and books of The Ari, with Rabbi Ashlag's commentary, along with the books of Rabbi Ashlag himself, are the most effective sources that can help each and every one of us emerge into the spiritual world.

Rabbi Ashlag's commentary to the "Book of Zohar," after which he was named "Baal HaSulam," is called "The *Sulam*" (ladder), since a person who studies according to the "Book of Zohar" ascends spiritually as if on a ladder. His commentary to the book "The Tree of Life" composed by The Ari is called "Talmud of the Ten Sefirot." In addition to these books, Rabbi Ashlag wrote many reference books, such as 'The Giving of the Torah," "The Book of Introductions," "*Bet Sha'ar HaKavanot*," "Fruits of Wisdom," "*Shamati* "(I heard), "*HaOr haBahir*" (The Bright Light).

It is recommended to read the books of Rabbi Yehuda Ashlag in the following order: "The Giving of the Torah," " Introduction to the Book of Zohar," "Inner Observation," the first part of "Talmud of the Ten Sefirot," "Preface to the Wisdom of Kabbalah" and "Introduction to the Talmud of the Ten Sefirot."

Furthermore, it is recommended to study the wisdom of Kabbalah specifically from the books of this great Kabbalist, as they are written in simple, clear language and one can understand all the concealed insights of the "Book of Zohar" and other preceding sources of Kabbalah. It is also recommended to study the books of Rabbi Baruch Ashlag (Rabash,) Rabbi Yehuda Ashlag's eldest son and successor along with additional books such as this one, based on the writings of Rabbi Yehuda Ashlag and The Rabash.

After a student has acquired the basics of the wisdom of Kabbalah according to Rav Ashlag's books, he is capable of reading all the available Kabbalah literature. He will already be able to realize which of the books he is reading are truly spiritual, understand exactly what is written there, distinguish between true and false sources of Kabbalah, and discern between the various authors, faiths, and movements.

Rav Dr. Michael Laitman, "Journey to the Upper World"

Question: Why are the "Book of Zohar," the writings of The Ari and of Ashlag the only or main ones studied?

Answer: Since the authors are actually one author - one soul stemming from the soul of the *Adam HaRishon*, Abraham, Moses,

Rabbi Shimon Bar-Yochai, the Ari and Rabbi Yehuda Ashlag - a soul that descended specifically in order to teach humanity the path of correction. Although there are Kabbalists who know even more, they have not yet been given permission to write books designed to teach and correct people, especially books for beginners on the spiritual path. Throughout all the generations of Kabbalah, thousands of books were written. My Rav instructed me to study and teach only these sources:

- The writings of Rashbi (Rabbi Shimon bar Yochai).
- The writings of The Ari (Rabbi Yitzchak Luria).
- The writings of Baal HaSulam (Rabbi Yehuda Ashlag).

I suggest everyone starts studying from these three sources, and afterwards, after you have internalized the material, you can read and understand all the rest. In that way, you will have a foundation and be able to review other sources and realize if they also suit you. Surely, I have no intention of belittling other sources. The thing is that many Kabbalists, who were even at a higher spiritual degree than Rabbi Shimon bar Yochai or The Ari, were not given permission to write, and if such permission was granted, it was only to write mere intimations for those who were already in the Upper worlds, As Rabbi Yehuda Ashlag writes in his essay "Disclosing a Portion, Covering Two:"[49]

"Permission was not granted to write a book in this wisdom; hence they abstained from writing explanations belonging to the essence of the wisdom, rather sufficed with mere intimations, which seem not to be connected to each other at all."

Question: The articles studied rely heavily on the "Sulam" Commentary." What is that commentary?
Answer: Rav Yehuda Ashlag called his commentaries of the "Book of Zohar," "*HaSulam*" (The Ladder) since reading the "*Sulam*"

---

[49] The Writings of Baal HaSulam, p. 9

commentary helps a person ascend the ladder of "man - Creator," from the degree of man in our world up to the degree of the Creator, which is the purpose of creation. The "Sulam" commentaries can be understood only after studying all the prefaces to the "Book of Zohar," written by Rabbi Yehuda Ashlag, and the most prominent of which is "Preface to the Wisdom of Kabbalah." For many years, I have been gradually collecting all the unique and interesting sections of the "Book of Zohar," and I hope it will soon be possible to compile them into a separate book.

Rav Dr. Michael Laitman, "An Experience called Kabbalah"

Task #5:
Read the following excerpts from Rav Laitman's blog.

The Rabash described and recorded our entire spiritual path and explained what we need to do with ourselves in order to receive the correcting and fulfilling light. There is no other Kabbalist in history who has done anything similar. Of course, this became possible due to him being the right person at the right time.

It is impossible to describe how we could have advanced without the detailed guidance we received from him. Without his explanations, we would not be able to implement Baal HaSulam's method. Now, as we approach the practical application of the wisdom of Kabbalah, we better understand how much we need Rabash's detailed explanation.

There are thousands of Kabbalah books, high and sublime way beyond evaluation, yet they cannot be used practically in our times. The Torah, for example, is only understood by those who are already in spiritual attainment. Whoever wants to enter the spiritual world can be assisted only by the books and works of Rabash.

From Rav Dr. Michael Laitman's Blog, Sept. 12, 2010
The Rabash wrote nearly 400 articles, one per week, in which he interpreted all the wisdom of Kabbalah regarding the inner work of

man. By means of his articles, The Rabash enabled us to enter the feeling of the spiritual world in a systematic, simple and logical way, close to a person.

In his articles, he frequently quotes the Torah, the Talmud and other sources, wishing to connect us with authentic sources, as well as explaining the way of thinking of their Kabbalist authors, who expressed their feelings to us specifically in that manner.

Without the Rabash's books, we would not have been able to find the connection to Baal HaSulam's work, and without his explanations, those books could not have been "opened."

I am grateful to the Upper force for sending me such a teacher, through whom we received the wisdom of Kabbalah. In his lifetime, he caused a spiritual breakthrough to a new degree and revealed to us the method of Kabbalah.

Although Baal HaSulam described this method in his articles, they still remained concealed. Whereas, The Rabash took his father's articles and rewrote them so that they would be understood by the world and he also transmitted them to his students orally.

From Rav Dr. Michael Laitman's Blog

Study Unit # 2 - Freedom of Choice

Part #1 - Receiving and Giving
Lesson #1 – Good and Evil in Creation

Task # 1:
Read the following excerpts from Rav Dr. Michael Laitman's blog and from the book "Kabbalah, Science and the Meaning of Life" and answer the following questions:

- What do the wisdom of Kabbalah and science have in common, and how do they differ?
- Unlike ordinary sciences, what type of research does the wisdom of Kabbalah enable us?

Question: Can you present the axioms upon which the wisdom of Kabbalah is based, similar to what is practiced in other sciences?

Answer: There are no axioms in the wisdom of Kabbalah, rather laws that were revealed by Kabbalists. Whatever has not been revealed cannot be used in any form!

Question: In your opinion, is the definition of a "science" more suitable for Kabbalah, simply because the masses associate "mysticism" with magic or something "vague?"

Answer: Kabbalah appeared before all the sciences. It is light, information, descending from above and constructing our world. We only reveal it partially through our five physical senses. However, before it is clothed in the matter of our world, the light is a bodiless force, without matter, as written in Baal HaSulam's essay "The Essence of Kabbalah."

Kabbalah is a science of the Upper Light, even before it is clothed in objects in our world. That is why Kabbalah is the root of all sciences, through which we can understand everything taking place in our world. Meaning, we cannot attain all of our sciences without this comprehensive science that explains all of creation. That is why we are witnessing a growing crisis being revealed in the corporeal sciences nowadays.

Kabbalah can also be called wisdom, but all this is rather vague. The term "science" is more accurate. The whole difference is that Kabbalists study by means of a special sixth sense they developed, by means of the soul, the quality of bestowal, whereas scientists research from the quality of reception. The form of attainment does not change in essence in both cases of ordinary science and the wisdom of Kabbalah. The guiding principle in the research is "studying only what is attained." Therefore, Kabbalah cannot be associated with mysticism.

Scientists have yet to understand their limitations and will inevitably become Kabbalists– they will correct themselves and as a result, will be able to explore the Upper world. In order to understand how Kabbalah reveals all of creation as a single system of all the worlds together, we must first understand the principle of perception of the world and the entire universe, and only then will it be possible to understand where we truly are.

From the blog of Rav Dr. Michael Laitman Aug. 13, 2008

The wisdom of Kabbalah is a scientific method of revealing the Upper force in all its forms of revelation, in all generations, until the end of our existence in this world. It does not just explain to us the purpose of creation and tells us what is happening and what will happen; rather it also elevates us to the degree of revelation!

Other sciences do nothing with us, rather just explain how something can be done with them for our own benefit, to somehow improve the world around us. However, the wisdom of Kabbalah is a method of raising a person from our world to the Upper world.

When studying the wisdom of Kabbalah, one begins to ascend, change one's shape and essence. You begin to see yourself, the whole world, and truly elevate yourself to the next degree. This is not about a regular science that teaches you what is happening outside of you, but rather a method for self-change and ascension. This is undoubtedly Kabbalah's main quality.

We see that today every science is limited within its narrow field, and in each and every science there are thousands of different niches, where many scientists do not understand how to communicate with each other. The wisdom of Kabbalah is intended to unify all the sciences, provide them with a common basis and raise them all to the single purpose, to the one and only knowledge. This is its entire uniqueness. In the end, man will relate to the world in which he exists as a single, global and integral entity. We should already aspire to reach this realization now.

From the blog of Rav Dr. Michael Laitman, Feb. 2, 2011

When a scientist studies Nature, he takes certain matter, performs various actions upon it, such as heating or cooling, and measures the matter's reaction to the changes he conducted. He seemingly observes it from above. Man can perform such actions upon the lower degrees of Nature – the inanimate, vegetative and animate, but not upon themselves.

We cannot truly rise above ourselves and explore ourselves from above. In order to study who man is, we have to observe him from a degree above man. That's why psychology and psychiatry, which investigate one's inner problems, desires and thoughts, are not a science like the natural sciences. As much as we may progress in these domains, things will remain obscure. Although, we may know a little bit more, we still will not be able to truly penetrate the depths of the heart and brain. Entering these depths and understanding them are impossible without the inner wisdom, the wisdom of Kabbalah.

Kabbalah deals with the internality of a person, observing the matter from which we are made and revealing to us how we are activated, react and operate. Kabbalah enables us to recognize the forces activating us, rise to their degree and from there to study ourselves.

Rav Dr. Michael Laitman, "Kabbalah, Science and the Meaning of Life"

Task # 2:
Read the following excerpts from Rav Dr. Michael Laitman's blog and the book "Light at the End of the Tunnel" and answer the question:
- What is the benefit of the contradiction being revealed in how Nature relates to us?

When we observe reality around us, we can see a contradiction in how Nature treats us at different stages of development. On the one hand, we see goodness and nurturing, especially in childhood when we are under the supervision of our parents and environment. On the other hand, as we get older, this good and positive treatment of Nature disappears. Once we become independent, an endless struggle of survival begins. That same Nature which had previously worked for the good of man shows him its rough side.

To explain this contradiction, a number of theories have been developed concerning the conduct of the world:

The first: Nature is blind. The Creator Who created the world is devoid of feelings and lacks reason, otherwise He would not let people suffer so. The rigid laws of Nature govern everything; Man has no one to be angry at or pray to.

The second: Two rulers. Two forces manage the world: the good and the evil. In other words, there are two gods, the wise and the tough.

The third: Multiple divinities. Since we witness many phenomena in Nature, each of them has its own creator: the creator of the moon, sun, wind, and so on.

The fourth: Nurturing has ceased. The Creator is wise and omnipotent and from His greatness, the world is but a grain of sand to Him, unworthy of His attention. This is the reason for chaos and disorder in our lives.

These theories stem from a lack of understanding of the laws of Nature. Attempts by humanity to reduce the gap between good and evil have not succeeded; torment and suffering are only increasing. The main law of Nature is bestowal to society, to others. Until we begin to fully observe this law, Nature will not stop punishing us. The laws of Nature have a purpose, which is to direct us to correction, to the correct connection among us and to the correct connection with Nature, based on principles of love and bestowal.

From the blog of Rav Dr. Michael Laitman Nov. 21, 2010

Initially, Nature, which is good and benevolent, envelops the person in an environment and then this embrace gradually distances from him. From the state in which the womb and cradle were formed for him, he them moves to a room of his own, later to kindergarten and school, until the door opens to the wide world, where struggles and blows begin. Why?

Providence is the law of Nature, pushing all parts of Nature to the "pre-determined" purpose, which is "the revelation of Godliness to Man in this world." This law is called the law of Providence and it operates upon every individual.

In his article "The Peace," Baal HaSulam asks why Nature's treatment is divided in such a way, what the reason is and if there is a reason for Man starting from something minuscule and then born, and as he grows up, he suffers more and more. Meaning, the question is about the reason for such a development and the different treatment of Nature towards children and adults. What should Man learn from it, is there any causality in this?

Baal HaSulam explains that there is causality, and furthermore, when we study the differences in Nature's treatment of Man, we understand what the general goal and the general process are that we all need to go through. That is why this point is very important. From this simple point, Baal HaSulam begins his research.

If Providence did not change towards a person from childhood to adulthood, one would not think of anything beyond one's own life and would exist in supposed goodness and no more. Rather, this opposition shows a person the source treating him differently.

Rav Dr. Michael Laitman, "Light at the End of the Tunnel"

Task # 3:
Read the following excerpt from the book "Tower of Babel - The Last Storey" and answer the following questions:
- What can we learn from how cells in the human body function, regarding the spiritual work we need to do?
- What is the principle which constitutes the basis for the existence of life?

At first glance, Nature appears to be an egoistic arena, in which individuals confront and struggle with one another and the strong survives; hence the need for researchers to develop various theories to explain the direct or indirect motive of an individual to altruistic action. However, deeper observation and a comprehensive view show that all the struggles and confrontations operate specifically to maintain balance in Nature and mutual existence support, for greater health and more successful development of Nature as a whole.

An example of the cycle of balance in Nature was seen in the early 1990s, when the North Korean government decided to get rid of street cats that had become a nuisance. A few weeks after the extinction of most cats, there was an increase in the number of mice, rats and snakes, to the point where cats from neighboring countries had to be imported.

Another clear example is presented by wolves. We are used to treating wolves as harmful and cruel animals, but when the wolves began to become extinct, their great contribution to the balance of deer, wild boars and various rodent populations became obvious. It turns out that unlike humans who prefer to hunt the healthiest animals, wolves hunt down the sick and weak animals, in particular. In this way, predators contribute to the health of other animals in the wild.

Thus, as scientific research progresses, it reveals the extent to which all parts of nature are inter-connected as parts of a single comprehensive system. Although when we learn from our emotional world towards nature, we believe that there is cruelty in nature, but in fact the preying of one creature upon another is an action that ensures the continuation of harmony and health in the comprehensive system of Nature. It is no different from the fact that in our bodies, billions of cells also die at any given moment and billions of cells are renewed, which specifically assures the continuation of life.

In every multicellular organism, an interesting phenomenon stands out: if we observe each cell in itself, as a unit of its own, it seems to function as an egoist and "thinks" only of itself. Yet, when we look at it as part of a system, as a cell in the body, we see that it receives only the minimum necessary for its own existence and all the rest of its activity is directed towards the body. It acts as an altruist, "thinks" only of the good of the entire body and functions accordingly.

Among all the cells in the body, there must be full harmony. In the nucleus of every cell in the body, the same genetic information is embedded; every cell in the body must be aware of the whole body; it must know what it needs and what it can do for it. Otherwise, the body cannot survive. The existence of a cell in the body depends on its "consideration" of the whole body. All the actions of the cell - the beginning and ceasing of cell division, acquisition of expertise and moving in the direction of a specific point of the body - all that takes place according to the needs of the body.

Connection creates a new level of life - although each one of our cells has exactly the same genetic information, each cell activates a different part of that same hereditary information, according to its location and function in the body.

In the early stages of embryonic development, all cells are identical, but over time they undergo a process of differentiation, in which each cell acquires characteristics of a certain cell type. Each cell has its own "intellect," yet the altruistic connection among them enables the creation of a new creature, an entire body; the intellect of the body belongs to a higher degree and is not found in one cell or another, but rather in the connection among them.

An egotistical cell is a cancerous cell - healthy cells in the body function under a wide range of laws and restrictions, whereas cancer cells do not consider these restrictions at all.

Cancer means a condition in which the body is degraded by its cells which have begun a process of uncontrolled self-proliferation. In the process of proliferation, the cancerous cell divides incessantly. It does not consider its surroundings or even respond to the orders of the body. The cancerous cells destroy their surroundings, thus making room for their own growth. They stimulate their adjacent blood vessels to germinate into the malignant tumor in order to nourish it, thus enslaving the entire body for their own benefit.

Cancerous cells lead to the death of the body by their egoistic activity. They do so even though it does not bring them any benefit; for the opposite is true - the death of the body is also the death of its "murderers." All the cunningness implemented by cancerous cells in the process of taking over the body only leads them to their own extinction. Thus, when egoism nurtures itself, it leads everything to death, including itself. Egoistic behavior and lack of consideration of the entire body lead directly to doom.

The life of the individual versus the life of the public - a cell in the body "concedes" its own continuation of life in favor of the body's life if necessary. When genetic disruptions occur in a particular cell that could turn it into a cancerous cell, the cell activates a mechanism that leads to the end of its life. The fear that it will become a cancerous cell and pose danger to the entire body causes the cell to concede its own life for the benefit of the body's life.

Everything in Nature moves towards unity - the evolution of Nature proves that the process of transforming the world into a small global village is not coincidental, rather a natural stage in the development of civilization in the direction of general harmony. At the end of the process, a single balanced system will be created, whose parts are all inter-connected in mutual relations and cooperation, according to biologist Dr. Elisabeth Satorius.

In her lecture in November 2005, Satorius explained that every process of evolution includes stages of individualization, conflict and competition, and ultimately the individuals merge into one harmonious system.

She contends that the evolution of life on the planet proves this. Billions of years ago, the planet was inhabited by bacteria. The bacteria multiplied and competition began over natural resources such as food and habitat. As a result of the competition, a new entity, more adapted to the conditions of the environment was created - a colony of bacteria, which is actually one community of bacteria that function as a single body. Exactly by the same stages, single-celled organisms evolved into multicellular organisms, creating complex living bodies of plants, animals, and human beings.

Every individual entity in itself has a personal interest. The essence of evolution is that individuals with personal interest unite into one body and operate for its overall interest. Satorius sees the process that humanity is undergoing today as a necessary step towards the formation of one human family, a community that will provide the interests of us all if only we function as healthy parts within it.

Indeed, deep observation of the elements of nature shows that altruism is the basis for the existence of life. Each living body and system consist of a group of cells or parts that work together, complementing each other by giving and mutual assistance, conceding to one another and living according to the altruistic principle "one for all." The more we explore nature, we discover more and more examples of the fact that all of its parts are inter-connected and that the general law operating in Nature is a connection among egoistic parts altruistically, or in short, the "law of altruism."

The force of Nature has shaped life so that every cell must be altruistic towards the others in order to build a living body. It created laws, according to which the glue keeping the cells and organs together as a living body is the altruistic relations among them. It follows that the force creating and sustaining life in Nature is an altruistic force, a force of love and giving. Its purpose is to create life based on the existence of the law of altruism, a harmonious existence balanced between all its parts.

Rav Dr. Michael Laitman, "The Tower of Babel - The Last Story"

Task # 4:
Read the following excerpts from Rav Dr. Michael Laitman's blog and the book "Light at the End of the Tunnel" and answer the questions:
- Why does globalization seem to perpetuate the oppression of the weak?
- How can one succeed in the global world?

The world is revealing that it is connected from the inside, and in this connection people are not free to act as they please. It will not help people to isolate themselves, because they will still find that everyone is connected with each other.

For example, Russian leaders have repeatedly declared that they need nobody because of the oil they possess, and that they can control others by shutting down the oil pipelines. In fact, when the Lehman Brothers Investment Bank collapsed in America, Russians began to be concerned. All over the world a great change was taking place, as the mutual connection among everybody was revealed. When this connection is revealed within the souls, it draws humanity without the possibility of disengaging from it. So it is now, through the banking system, humanity is already revealing this connection and will continue revealing it through other phenomena to take place in the future. The only solution is to act according to the principle of the law of "bestowal;" there is no other solution.

Solutions such as selling or buying a bank will not help. Now, although that is what they are doing in order to remediate the situation, it will result with a greater blow and then with even a greater one. These blows are intended to make us realize that not only America, Europe, Russia, China or any other country are bound together, but that even the last individual, even in Africa and the most faraway places will have a feeling of its dependency on these changes.

Until everyone realizes that they are inter-connected with each other, only through misery are they shaken up. For humans exist in a faulty system, in which they do not act in harmony with each other. This situation of lack of harmony among people what is to be revealed.

It is already beginning to be revealed in the global crisis and later we will see the hastening of pace of its revelation.

Rav Dr. Michael Laitman, "Light at the End of the Tunnel"

Question: I am interested in knowing what the spiritual root of globalization is. On the one hand, it seems to be contributing to the world, but on the other hand, it seems to perpetuate the oppression of the weak by those in power.

Answer: You're right, but it seems so because today's globalization is based on us being great egoists. On the one hand, we are increasingly discovering how interdependent we are in the general system; on the other hand, the huge ego is causing people to hate each other.

The situation of the world today is similar to what sometimes happens in families. Spouses are together in a small apartment, they cannot stand each other, yet the external conditions oblige them to share their living quarters.

The wisdom of Kabbalah is a science that explains to us how to maintain correct globalization, to be based on balance. For this purpose, we have to be familiar with the "law of equivalence of form," the law of balance. When we are familiar with the law of balance and aspire to live by it, love will prevail among us. As a result, interdependence will not cause anyone any harm. On the contrary, we will all feel secure, prosperous, mutually responsible, calm and peaceful.

So what is actually missing? Revealing the general force of Nature, which is one of love and giving, that can pull us out of the ego and connect us all in a balanced and harmonious way.

From the blog of Rav Dr. Michael Laitman, April 1, 2008

We do not perceive the world as "round;" we still think it is flat and that through egoism we can succeed in it. Meanwhile, the world has already "changed plans:" now one can succeed only through unity. It is a completely different algorithm, and we, as usual "do not understand."

For thousands of years, man has achieved success according to the size of his egoism, yet in the past fifty years this trend is at its end. We are advancing towards an integral world, in which whoever is more connected with others is the one who benefits most. We see that the more connections one creates, the more successful one is. People feel it instinctively and are drawn to reaching integral decisions.

However, we still do not understand that being saved from misery requires us to be connected at the human level as well, beyond the banking system, global industry and other global mechanisms. This situation began after World War II, when the United Nations, UNESCO, and other international organizations were founded. However, they also continue to operate with egotistical methods, rather than adopting a complete and comprehensive approach.

If everybody is important, if all countries demand equal treatment, why do some countries have veto power over any decision and others do not? The size of the country should not give it superiority. In the "round" system, particularly the great ones should concede more; otherwise they only take care of themselves.

Our egoistic approach is completely distorted, yet we do already feel that the world is truly becoming "round," integral and interconnected.

From the blog of Rav Dr. Michael Laitman, May 11, 2011

Lesson #2 – From Love of People to Love of the Creator

Task #1:

Read the following excerpts from the books "The Last Generation" and "A Glimpse of Light" and answer the following questions:

- Why does a person's relationship with one's environment enable emerging from the boundaries of one's will to receive?
- How do our actions become similar to those of the Creator?
- What is the meaning of the phrase "ascending spiritual steps?"

The Creator created Man, and for a person to be able to be independent and resemble the Creator from the point of free

357

choice, one must disconnect from the Creator. Only from within the concealment can a person build a relationship of two partners between himself and the Creator. Such a relationship will not be influenced by the Creator-created connection. Concealment includes two levels:

- Concealment of the good, meaning the feeling of suffering.
- Concealment of the source of this feeling, meaning the concealment of the Creator as the cause of suffering.

A consequence of the concealment is that people suffer; not knowing the origin, what it depends on and how it can be stopped. Stemming from the concealment, a person needs to rise above the feelings of good and evil, and aspire to resemble the Creator. This is the only way to solve the problem of independence. Only then, will a person begin to see that all the terrible situations and torments he underwent in all incarnations become a type of receiving vessel, above which a correct relationship between himself and the Creator can be built.

Although the Creator is concealed, He built society for man. Society should serve people as a laboratory for conducting attempts to construct a correct relationship and attitude towards the quality of bestowal. A person should relate to society as he would like to relate to the Creator concealed from him.

As mentioned, if the Creator were revealed, a person would never be capable of emerging from the will to receive. The relationship with society enables emerging from the boundaries of the will to receive, since society is unable to fulfill a person's will to receive. Hence, a person performs work towards society and receives his reward from the Creator. Since the payment comes from another source, a person can gradually attain the degree of bestowal towards society.

Rav Dr. Michael Laitman, "The Last Generation"

Nowadays, more and more people are sinking into depression and despair, escaping to drugs, alcohol, sedatives, and so forth. This is an unprecedented global phenomenon. Why is it happening? Because of the lack of satisfaction.

What causes lack of satisfaction? Our desire for pleasure constantly grows and demands more and more fulfillment which we cannot provide, so it remains empty. This emptiness is felt inside us just like physical hunger. This lack of satisfaction is the darkness of the 21st century.

The wisdom of Kabbalah offers a solution to this helplessness. It explains that there is no way to fulfill the desire for pleasure directly. The solution is to rise to another level of fulfillment, derive pleasure from fulfillment that is always available to us - the pleasure from love and bestowal.

There is a contradiction here: Particularly, when I attain the love of others, I become free. Why? Because I can always love others and bestow unto them. No one limits me in that. In such a state, I can always enjoy my actions.

At this point, a question immediately arises: Suppose I really want to love others and give to them, would I have something to give? Indeed, I barely provide myself with what I need in order to live...

Well, Kabbalists, those who have already gone through the process of emerging from self-love to the love of others say that as soon as I begin to be concerned with love and giving to others, I begin to be filled with sublime abundance, the Light of the Creator and then I can convey to others limitlessly.

In this spiritual state, pleasure fills me, since I want to fill others by its means. I exist in true goodness, without any restriction and my sole concern is to bestow unto others. My action becomes like the Creator's. I become His partner in action, in creation and enjoy wholeness and eternity similar to Him, which is the most supreme feeling possible in reality.

From here we can already begin to see that "Love your neighbor as yourself – a great rule in the Torah "[50] is not just a fine slogan that speaks of being good children, but rather a means, lever, springboard by which I leap to the degree of the Creator.

Rav Dr. Michael Laitman, "A Glimpse of Light"

Every cell in our body exists only in order to provide life to the entire body. No cell or organ in the body thinks of itself. Each body organ operates only to satisfy the needs of the body and due to that, the body lives.

If we communicate as cells in the body, out of awareness and realization, we will begin to feel the life of the "general body" of which we are all parts. The system of connections that are then built among us will be called the "general soul" in which we will feel spiritual life.

Just as scientists study our world, Kabbalists study the Upper world and its revelations; they reveal the spiritual world. According to them, the "spiritual world" means that we are all connected to each other, not in our bodies, but in our internality.

From that same internal part that connects us in the spiritual world, we now have a little spark, drawing us back to spirituality; a spark that wants something higher than this world. This spark is deep within us and is called "the point in the heart."

For the time being, the spark is wrapped in an egoistic heart, which is why we do not feel that it wants to connect with others. However, if we corrected our ego and began feeling the spiritual world, we would find that ascending the spiritual steps means an increase in the intenseness of the inner connection among us. This connection creates a common vessel in which more and more Light is felt.

Rav Dr. Michael Laitman, "A Glimpse of Light"

---

[50] Talmud Yerushalmi, Nedarim 30:72

Task #2:

Read the following excerpt from the book "Opening the Zohar" and list at least three reasons why it is necessary to study the wisdom of Kabbalah in a group.

One of the necessary means for spiritual development is the group.

In order for us to be prepared for spiritual development, the Creator awakens in us two sensations; the first is emptiness towards this world and the second is being drawn to attain the source of life - the awakening of "the point in the heart."

The point in the heart connects us to the place where we can nourish and fill it - to the group. We truly see that people whose point in the heart awakens are drawn to one another, naturally. As always happens in human society, people of similar desires are drawn to each other and assemble together.

The group enables the genuine connection with others, according to the new principles of love and giving instead of hatred and separation. Therefore, working in a group is an essential means of attaining the revelation of the Creator. It enables a person to measure his attitude towards others accurately and prevents him from mistakenly fantasizing about his spirituality and his personal connection with the Creator. Indeed, the Creator is the attribute of love and giving that dwells in the corrected relationships among us.

Such groups have been established throughout history. By changing people's attitudes in the group into one of connection and mutual love, they created the necessary conditions for feeling the genuine reality. Out of the rich experience they accumulated, they wrote about the world which opened before them. The books they left us after them enable us to attain the new life in the shortest and most efficient way.

Such a group is called "a group of Kabbalists" and they have one purpose - to connect among themselves in the spirit of what is written in the Torah: "as one man with one heart," "all Israel are friends," "what is hateful unto you, do not do to others," "love your neighbor as yourself," etc.

Correcting relationships in the group, from self-love to the love of others can only be done by the same Upper force that created our egoism. Only it can turn the evil inclination into a good inclination.

Even now, we are in the corrected and appropriate reality - in close contact among us as parts of one body, in mutual love, connected to the bountiful Upper force that created us, except that we have not yet awakened to be aware of this state. This awakening, this vital power, the Light that Reforms, can be achieved when assembling together.

In the group, Kabbalah books are read together. These books speak of our connected state, and as a result, joint reading, with the intention of attaining unity and love awakens the Light that Reforms. Gradually, we begin to rise above our natural egoistic feelings and begin to feel that same bond of love is found among us, within which we feel the Creator. This is the way to reach realization of the essence of the wisdom of Kabbalah, revealing the Creator to the created.

In our generation, all of humanity needs to become one large group and correct itself. Therefore, Rav Baruch Shalom HaLevi Ashlag (the Rabash), son and successor of Baal HaSulam, wrote dozens of essays on working in a group. He gave the world the doctrine of connection with detailed guidance on all situations existing in the relationship within the group. According to his writings, we study and develop spiritually.

It is impossible to progress spiritually without a group. Advanced technology existing today enables us to convey the method of correction via television and the Internet to everywhere in the world. Lessons in the wisdom of Kabbalah, the "Book of Zohar," the essays of Rabash and others are broadcast live daily on the "Kabbalah for All" channel (Channel 66 –HOT and the www.kab.co.il website), by which tens of thousands of people have been joining the group of students. Some gather in study centers of "Kabbalah for All" in Israel and abroad and others connect to the group virtually.

Nowadays, a variety of possibilities of connecting to a group are open to anyone interested in developing spiritually and even the physical distance between people all over the world is no longer an obstacle. We are talking about creating an internal connection among us and it turns out that it is possible to connect very well to others through the media, because it is not the bodies that need to connect but the hearts...

In this large group, extending all over the world, although people are very different externally, they are very similar internally. Everyone wants to feel a part of one world of love, security and prosperity, and to ensure a good life for their children – that is why they connect.

Ultimately, the wisdom of Kabbalah will become a universal education system, offering all of humanity a way to be saved from all evil. Israel will become a central point, from which the method of connection will emerge to the entire world. We will thus fulfill our destiny and spread the Light to the world - the new bond which will connect people, one of mutual responsibility, giving and love.

Rav Dr. Michael Laitman, "Opening the Zohar"

Task #3:
Read the following excerpts from Rav Dr. Michael Laitman's blog and from the book "A Glimpse of Light" and answer the following questions.

- What is the correct attitude toward the ego, according to the wisdom of Kabbalah?
- Can any ethics not be motivated by egoistic considerations?

When one delves into understanding the perception of religions and various methods developed throughout human history, we find that they are based on ego reduction. A person needs to "calm" himself as much as possible, be nice to people, accept everything submissively, and so on.

The wisdom of Kabbalah, on the other hand, says exactly the opposite: do not destroy the ego. Throughout history we have developed it, so why should we suddenly destroy it now? I want to take advantage of the whole world, beat everyone, be the smartest, the most successful, inflate myself with all kinds of lust and various fulfillments. Good! In that regard, it has been said: " He who is greater than his friend, his inclination is greater." [51] If we destroy the ego, we have nothing to correct, because we are no longer "we," as if we have vanished. Any spiritual ascension is only over hatred and this is what "Mount Sinai" symbolizes - all the hateful thoughts inside us. The more we reveal the hatred and the ego embedded within us and learn to use them correctly, our ascension will be higher. However, this ascension depends on seeing our ego as a helpful force, "help against him."

In summary, the true work is to use everything created, all the intensity of the ego. It is not without purpose that man was created as the most egotistical creature in nature, and it is not by chance that the people of Israel have the most developed ego among the nations. We merited begin the first to receive the wisdom of Kabbalah, the method of correction, because we have something to correct...

Rav Dr. Michael Laitman, "A Glimpse of Light"

Ethics relates to drives arising in a person, such as: envy, hatred, rage, the desire to steal or cheat etc. as evil forces operating in a person, like "demons and ghosts," which one needs to oppress and eradicate from within. Conversely, the wisdom of Kabbalah explains that even such impulses, just like everything else that exists, come from the Creator [52] in order to teach a person what his true nature is - egoism.

---

[51] Talmud Bavli, Sukkah 52:71.

[52] See the essay "There is none else besides Him" The Writings of Baal HaSulam, Shamati Essays, p. 513

Baal HaSulam writes: "I am joyful and happy with those revealed faults and those being revealed." [53] In other words, he is happy to see the revelation of egoistic qualities in man, because this indicates his preparation for correction. Whereas according to doctrines of ethics, all negative traits must be suppressed! This opposition stems from ethics being based on human relations in our world, while Kabbalah speaks of the development of egoism and its correction up to attaining the degree of the Creator.

Thus, according to ethics, a better person is one whose egoism is not revealed. Ethics appreciates little, naïve people who respect the fanatic "righteous," submissive and undeveloped. Kabbalah develops the person and is not afraid to arouse in him the most painful questions and answer them.

Ethical-religious answers do not convince a person to be better through psychology or the temptation with rewards such as a peaceful life in this world and the next world. No. Kabbalah says that if you do not attain the Upper world during your life here - you will return again, as if you have never been in this world. You have lived in vain, even if you were considered as a highly virtuous person in this world.

"If a person learns the entire Torah, and is well versed in the Talmud and commentaries, and is also filled with virtues and good deeds better than all his contemporaries, and he has not learned the wisdom of Kabbalah, he must reincarnate and come again to this world."[54]

Why? Because the purpose of ethics is for a person man to look good in the eyes of society and the purpose of Kabbalah is for a person to look good in the eyes of the Creator.

From the blog of Rav Dr. Michael Laitman

---

[53] The writings of Baal HaSulam, "Letters," Letter 5.

[54] The Writings of Baal HaSulam, Preface to "Mouth of the Sage"

Question: If the method of ethics and the method of bestowal are opposite each other, why did the Ramchal, who wrote many Kabbalah books, also write *"Mesilat Yesharim"*, one of his well- known books of ethics?

Answer: The Ramchal was one of the greatest Kabbalists in all the generations and he only wrote of the wisdom of Kabbalah. That was why he was exiled and banned. If not the *Gaon of Vilna*, they would have killed him! And when the *Gaon of Vilna* said that the Ramchal was great, the anger toward him turned immediately into kindness.

Ramchal's books do not deal with ethics. Their only concern is the wisdom of Kabbalah! Yet often, in order to protect themselves, Kabbalists say they write about ethics, It has even been said about the Book of Zohar, that it is ethics written in the language of Kabbalah. The Rabash also wrote in his essays several times: "and now let's look at the matter in terms of ethics," and immediately afterwards writes about pure spiritual work. That is how Kabbalists hid themselves for centuries from "ethics lovers."

From the blog of Rav Dr. Michael Laitman June 22, 2008

Question: I have been asked - what is the difference between Kabbalah and the method of ethics? It's hard for me to answer, because in my opinion, giving and bestowing is very ethical and the ego is very unethical. Adhering to the Creator is adhering to the quality of bestowal and love, and this, too, is very ethical to me. So, is the entire goal of Kabbalah to be as ethical as the Creator? Is the method of correction of Kabbalah equivalent to the method of ethics? Or perhaps I don't understand what ethics is.

Answer: We are all in a huge ego, like an inflated balloon. There is nothing else in this world other than this attribute, in our consciousness, desires, drives and attributes - nothing! Even the best morality is ultimately egoistic, for our own sake.

The spiritual world, however, is the attribute of giving that is contrary to us in e-v-e-r-y-t-h-i-n-g! The attribute of giving without any self-interest. This is a one-way relationship. It is not enough for the recipient not to know that you gave to him, but rather that you yourself (your ego) will not know that you are taking this action. It is possible only through the correct study of the wisdom of Kabbalah, when you summon the sublime light of correction and as a result of its influence, the possibility of bestowal is revealed within you.

From the blog of Rav Dr. Michael Laitman April 29, 2008

None of us really loves others. Though we can attempt to believe we do, it will not change the fact that we were created with the nature of self-love. And here the wisdom of Kabbalah explains that we must not coerce ourselves and forcibly try to love someone else. All we need to do is open the writings of Kabbalah and study.

Stemming from the learning process, we gradually begin to feel a new world. The connection among all people reveals itself, as if from out of the fog. Suddenly we feel and see how we are all connected together. We begin to reveal that all are our own inseparable parts. We cannot cut any part out - it's not in our power. The same as in our body, no part is superfluous. We begin to feel that this is an eternal network of connections in which we are all bound together forever.

A special bond is revealed compelling us to love naturally and we can no longer avoid loving others. It is much stronger than any bond we know of today. In our world, for instance, a person can disconnect from his family and in effect delete them from his life, but now this is incomprehensible. The image of the bonds that unfolds is placed before us, within our heart and emotions, and brings us to the love of others.

In summary, the wisdom of Kabbalah does not require us to do anything artificial. If this method is used correctly, true connection among us is revealed and true love is born within us.

Rav Dr. Michael Laitman, "A Glimpse of Light"

Part #2 - Free Choice

Lesson #1 - Do We have Choice?

Task #1:
Read the following excerpts from the books "The Tower of Babel - the Last Story" and "Kabbalah in Simple Words" and answer the question:

- What internal software is our basis for making decisions?

Pleasure and suffering are two forces governing our lives. Our inner nature, the desire for pleasure compels us to act according to a formula of behavior inherent in us from the start: the will to receive maximum pleasure in exchange for minimal effort. Hence, a person is always obligated to choose pleasure and escape suffering; in that, there is no difference between animals and us.

Psychology realizes that it is possible to change the order of priorities of every person and teach how to calculate feasibility and benefit in a different way. It is possible to raise the importance of the future in every person so that one agrees to undergo difficulties in the present for the sake of future profit. For instance, we are prepared to put out great effort and invest in studies in order to acquire a profession, because the effort is expected to yield a high income or respected status.

It all depends on our calculation of profits. We subtract the effort required to do something from the anticipated pleasure to be gained. If the balance is positive, we work to achieve it. There is nothing here but a calculation of the price we have to pay compared to our future profit. That's how we're all built.

In this regard, the difference between Man and animal is only in Man being able to look ahead to a future goal and agree to experience some degree of difficulty, suffering and agony for the future reward. When we observe people, we find that all actions stem from such calculations, and the person actually only executes them with no choice.

Rav Dr. Michael Laitman, "The Tower of Babel - The Last Story"

All of Nature obeys only one law, the "law of pleasure and pain." If the only matter in creation is the desire to receive pleasure, then only one principle of behavior is needed in order to govern it - attraction to pleasure and avoidance of pain.

We humans are no exceptions. We are driven by internal software which dictates every step we take; we want to receive as much as possible, invest as little as possible, and preferably for free! Therefore, in everything we do, even when we are not aware of it, we always try to choose pleasure and avoid pain.

Even when it seems to us that we are sacrificing ourselves, we are actually receiving more pleasure from this "sacrifice" than any other possibility we can think of at that moment. The reason we delude ourselves and think we have altruistic motives is because deluding ourselves feels better than telling ourselves the truth. The witty essayist Agnes Repplier summed it up with the words: "There are few nudities so objectionable as the naked truth."

Everything we do stems from calculation of profitability. For example, I calculate the cost of a particular product compared to the future enjoyment I expect from it. If I think that the pleasure (or lack of pain) I'll derive from the product is higher than the price I have to pay, I say to the "inner trader" in me: "Buy!"

We can change our priorities, adopt different values of good and evil, and "train" ourselves to become fearless. We can even make a goal so important to us that any difficulty on the way of achieving it becomes meaningless, unnoticed.

If, for instance, I want to achieve the social and economic status of a well-known doctor, I will study and work very hard for years in medical school, then a few more years of chronic lack of sleep during the internship, hoping that it will end up rewarding me with wealth and fame.

Sometimes the calculation of immediate pain in return for future profit is so natural that we do not even notice that we do it. For example, if I became very ill and found that only a certain surgery could save my life, I would happily go through that surgery. Because even though surgery itself may be very unpleasant and even dangerous, it threatens me less than does my illness. In some cases I may be willing to pay large amounts of money (if I have it) to do so.

Rav Dr. Michael Laitman, "Kabbalah in Simple Words"

Task #2:
Read the following excerpts from Rav Dr. Michael Laitman's blog and from the books "The Tower of Babel - the Last Story" and "Kabbalah in Simple Words" and answer the following questions:
- How do we choose what to enjoy?
- How can we hasten our development by means of the environment?

Apart from the fact that the desire for pleasure obligates us to escape pain and suffering and always choose the pleasure facing us, we cannot even completely choose the quality of pleasure. The decision regarding what to enjoy does not stem from our choice and free will, rather it is influenced by the desires of others. Every person lives in an environment with its own culture and laws. Not only do these determine our rules of conduct, they also build in each of us our attitude towards all areas of life.

We do not really choose our way of life, areas of interest, leisure activities, the food we eat, the fashion trend of our dress, and so on. All of these are chosen according to the will and taste of the society around us, not necessarily according to the desire and taste of its elites, but of the majority. In fact, we are bound by the etiquette and tastes of society, which have become the rules of behavior in our lives.

Society's appreciation is the motive for all our actions. Even when we want to be different and special, do something that no one has ever done, acquire something that no one has ever purchased and even retire from society and seclude ourselves, we do so in order to gain the esteem of society. Thoughts like "What will they say about me?" "What will they think of me?" are the most important thing to us, yet we generally tend to deny and repress it, because admitting this seemingly eliminates our "I."

Rav Dr. Michael Laitman, "The Tower of Babel - The Last Story"

Question: How can we explain that equality is a good thing?
Answer: Equality is necessary, not to create a perfect human society, but to be in balance with the force of nature, to fill oneself with a sense of wholeness.

Today, under the influence of the environment, we value money. One person has a million, and the other has ten million! You start looking at him, as if he's finer, healthier, and smarter than others. And if someone has a billion, then he's a king altogether...! As if he is no longer an ordinary person, flesh and blood, but someone unattainable...! That's how we're built. You can hate him, or appreciate and respect him, because it all depends on the appreciation of the environment! In the end it all depends on the scale of values of the environment!

From the blog of Rav Dr. Michael Laitman June 30, 2009

Our actions are not implemented by themselves, but under the influence of the surrounding society. The next best situation can be arbitrary, but we choose it under the influence of the environment. In such a way, the society in which we live shapes us and our future. A person is given intellect and is given a feeling of lack, and by means of the environment he can direct himself toward the next situation he himself has chosen.

We evaluate a person according to the action he takes in relation to the environment, in order to invite within him a defined direction of thoughts and desires in anticipation of the new situation to be revealed to him. Hence, we need to create around us an environment that will accurately determine our future state, that same state to which we aspire, in accordance with the future image depicted in our imagination. Then our movement forward will be quick and the thoughts that appear in us will be realized and embodied immediately.

From the blog of Rav Dr. Michael Laitman January 19, 2011

Nature does not only "condemn" us to a constant flight from suffering and an ongoing pursuit of pleasure, it also prevents us from the option of determining the kind of pleasure we desire. In other words, we cannot control what we want; desires pop up within us without any prior notice and regardless of our opinion on the matter.

Moreover, Nature not only created our desires, it also gave us an indirect way to control them. If we remember that we are all parts of the same soul, the soul of *Adam HaRishon*, we can easily understand that the way to control our desires is by bestowing upon the whole soul, that is, humanity, or at least part of it.

Let's look at it this way: if one cell wants to go to the left, but the rest of the body wants to go to the right, the cell must go to the right as well, unless it convinces the entire body, or the overwhelming majority of the cells, or the "government" of the body, that it is better to go to the left.

So even though we are unable to control our desires, society can and does control them. We, on our part, can choose the kind of society to influence us in a way that we think is the best. Simply put, we can use social influences to control our desires. By controlling our desires, we will be able to control our thoughts and, ultimately, our actions.

The "Book of Zohar" already described the importance of society, its role in relation to us and our role in relation to it, two thousand years ago. However, since the twentieth century, when it became clear that we depend on each other to survive, the correct use of our interdependence has become vital in order to advance spiritually. The supreme importance of society is the message that *Baal HaSulam* conveys very clearly in many of his essays, and if we follow his line of thought, we will understand why.

Baal HaSulam says that the greatest wish of every person, whether he admits it or not, is to be loved by others and receive their approval. Not only does it give us a sense of security, it confirms our most precious possession - the ego. Without society's approval, we feel as if society ignores our very existence, and no ego can tolerate being ignored. This is the reason for people often performing extreme acts in order to gain attention from the environment.

And since our greatest wish is to win society's approval, we are obligated to adapt ourselves to environmental laws and adopt them. These laws not only determine our behavior, rather also shape our attitude and approach towards everything we do and think.

As a result of this situation, we are incapable of choosing anything - not our way of life, interests, the way we spend our free time, or the food we eat and the clothes we wear. Furthermore, even when we rebel against the fashion trend and dress otherwise, we are still referring to a particular code of clothing that we did not choose, unlike society around us that did. It follows that the only way to change ourselves is to change our social environment.

Rav Dr. Michael Laitman, " Kabbalah in Simple Words"

A person is born with forces and qualities he received from his parents. Later, he integrates with the environment and continues to develop according to what the environment imprints in him, the way it "sculpts" him. The "database" built this way in the first 15 years of his life, becomes part of his nature.

Throughout life, the environment constantly causes a person to absorb whatever is in it. In this way, Nature pushes one to develop: when one is a child, one wants to know everything, observes those around him, learns from them and imitates them. A person in one environment or another copies all that into himself in addition to what he received from his parents. The impact of the environment is also imprinted in him, similar to the innate nature, and afterwards, over his lifetime, he'll implement everything he acquired in his first 15 years, with no choice.

Meaning, we have an innate nature and an acquired nature. It is not by chance that we specifically provide education to a person in his early years. A person does not choose the education he will receive. Education is chosen by one's parents, the environment, state and world. That's how we have evolved over the course of tens of thousands of years.

There are people who follow what they received in childhood. They cannot resist it. They follow the flow of the radio and television channels, along with the human society from which they take an example. And there are other people who ask the question of the meaning of life: "What am I living for?" They rise above the nature they received from education and the environment, and then also break the innate nature they inherited from their parents: the will to receive.

In such a way, we need to ascend from one degree to another. The first degree is the degree of the masses, where we were born and whose education we received. It is the inanimate degree, spiritually speaking, from which everything begins. Then, we rise to the degree of individuals, the chosen.

From the blog of Rav Dr. Michael Laitman 11.2.2011

Task #3:
Read the following excerpts from Rav Dr. Michael Laitman's blog and answer the following questions:

- In what stage, if any, is up to our choice, in the development of creation and personal development of each one of us?
- What is the point of "I" according to Kabbalah?

In our existence, life, nothing takes place without a purpose. There is nothing accidental in creation. We are in a comprehensive, closed reality, in *Malchut* of Infinity, where everything takes place according to a predetermined plan, from the beginning of creation to the end. Everything is there, arranged and signed in advance, except for our free choice, the measure of our personal participation.

However, your participation or non-participation does not change the plan; you can only hasten it, for you and for others. It's the only thing that can be done, and in fact, it is the only thing that can occur. Either we progress according to the plan ("in its time,") or we hasten the program ("Hastening"). Whoever tries to hasten this plan by self-participation in accordance with the thought of creation contributes to the hastening of the development of other people, since we are all one soul.

Today's world is in crisis, in states of recognition of evil. Gradually, from day to day, human beings are revealing what our nature is, what brings us the bad, why we do not have the tools to cope with it. Even an ordinary person in the world begins to hear, digest these things, talk about them. The more we intervene in this process and give people an explanation of what is taking place, we thus hasten development.

The program remains the same, but we have the option of fast forwarding its progress.

From the blog of Rav Dr. Michael Laitman July 3, 2011

Question: When I look around me, I don't see any free choice. Someone determined the initial situation and the final situation, and we are only running from start to finish, so where is our free choice?

Answer: That is totally true. We are unable to choose - not the very states of creation, nor the stages of our progress from the first stage to the last, because everything is predetermined.

I was born with the qualities set in me and have to implement the software that was inserted into me. I, the faulty, need to attain the end of correction. And I know how faulty I am and how corrected I need to be. Even the whole path to my correction is known, step by step. And when the path to my correction is clear to me, I understand how everything is connected and tightly linked, like an engine in which one part must continuously move after the other.

"Torah" alludes to the word "teaching" (*Hora'ah*), meaning that you are given clear directives and instructions; no choice is possible here, except one! Do you want to do all of this by your own choice, your free choice, or will you be forced? Now decide whether you will go yourself by your own will or be beaten until you want to go. This choice is not in order to avoid suffering. When you choose to progress by your own will, you proceed towards attainment, development; you attain the greatness of spirituality, so it is revealed to you as something of eternal supremacy.

That point in you that willingly chooses to reveal the spiritual world by rising above your egoistic corporeal desire, is what is called your "I". It is not in your power to avoid this state, but you can choose by yourself how to reach it.

From the blog of Rav Dr. Michael Laitman January 7, 2011

Lesson #2 - Choosing an Environment

Task #1:
Read the following excerpts from the books "The Tower of Babel - The Last Storey" and "Interview with the Future" and answer the following questions:

- In your own words, describe the four factors which define the development of every created being.
- In which of the four factors do we have freedom of choice?

Where, if at all, do we find free choice? In order to answer this question, we first need to discern what our essence is and understand the factors from which we are composed. In Baal HaSulam's essay "The Freedom" written in 1933, he explained that in every object and in every person there are actually four factors defining them, which he explains with a description of how a seed of wheat develops. The process of its development is convenient to observe and helps understand the essence.

1. The initial matter - the inner essence

Initial matter is the inner essence of any object. Although its shape changes, it never changes. For example, wheat rots in the soil and its external shape completely vanishes; nevertheless, a new germ emerges from its inner essence. The first factor, the essence - the foundation, our genetic code – exists in us from the outset; hence, clearly we are incapable of affecting it.

2. The unalterable properties

The laws of development of the essence itself never change, stemming from which the immutable properties of the object are derived. For example, the seed of wheat will never produce grains other than wheat; it will not produce oats, rather only the previous form of wheat, which it lost.

These laws and characteristics derived from them are predetermined by Nature. Every seed, every animal and every human being contains within them the laws of development of their own essence. This is the second factor we are composed of which we cannot influence.

3. The properties that can be changed by influence of the environment

The seed remains the same type of seed, yet its external shape changes according to the external environment. Meaning, the outer covering of the essence changes, affected by external factors and according to defined laws, undergoing qualitative change. The influence of the external environment causes additional factors to be integrated in the essence, together producing a new quality of the same essence. These factors could be the sun, soil, fertilizer, moisture, rain and more. They determine what difficulties in growth may occur, as well as the quantity and quality of wheat that will grow out of that same given wheat germ.

So is Man: his external environment can be his parents, educators, friends, colleagues, books he reads, content he absorbs from the media and so on. Thus, the third factor is the laws according to which the environment affects a person and changes his alterable properties.

4. Changes applying to the environment that affects the object

The environment affecting the development of wheat is also affected by external factors, which may change, even to the extreme: for example, there might be a drought or flood, and all wheat will die. Regarding Man, the fourth factor is actually changes in the environment itself, which cause changes in the way it affects a person, or more precisely, his alterable properties.

The general state of each object is determined by these four factors. These factors define our character, way of thinking and conclusions and even determine what we want and how we act at any given moment. In Baal HaSulam's essay "The Freedom," he discusses each of these factors at length and reaches the following conclusions:

Man cannot change his roots, his genetic code - his essence.

Man cannot change the laws according to which his essence itself evolves.

Man cannot change the laws by which external factors affect his development.

Man can change his environment upon which he is completely dependent. He can replace it with another environment, one which will better suit his progress towards actualizing his life's purpose.

In other words, we are incapable of influencing ourselves directly, since we do not determine our essence and the way it develops. We also cannot change the laws of influence of the environment upon us. Yet, we can influence our lives and destiny by means of improving our environment. Our only free choice is in choosing the correct environment. If we change external conditions around us and improve our environment, we will change the effect of the environment on our alterable properties. This way, we can determine what our future will be.

From all levels of Nature - inanimate, vegetative, animate and Man - only Man can consciously choose the environment that defines his desires, thoughts and actions. Therefore, the process of correction is based on the individual's relationship with the environment. If we have an environment which constitutes a suitable space for development, we can thus achieve wonderful results.

Rav Dr. Michael Laitman, "The Tower of Babel - The Last Story"

We receive the first factor, "platform," foundation, essence, spiritual object, our spiritual gene directly from the Creator; Therefore, it is clear that it cannot be affected in any way. This factor includes the origin of man, his level of thinking, his ancestors' mindset as well as the knowledge they acquired, which in future generations are revealed as physical and mental traits and personality tendencies, of which we are unaware. In Man, they can be embedded as tendencies towards beliefs, critical thinking, physical or spiritual assets, stinginess, or shyness etc. These qualities are similar to the seed of grain that lost its physical shape in the soil. They are handed over to us without a body

- a physical carrier by natural heredity, and as a result, some of them appear in us in opposite form, contrary to the parents' characteristic.

The second factor is laws according to which our essence develops. These laws are predetermined by the Creator and do not change - because they are drawn from the nature of the essence and its predetermined form, towards which the essence aspires to attain as the purpose of creation. Every seed, plant, beast, every human being, contains within them, in their internality, the plan and the laws of their development. This is the second factor, and we cannot influence it.

The remaining two factors, the third and the fourth - belong to our development, yet are "external" to the soul itself – these are the external conditions that make voluntary changes in me out of choice, or exert pressure upon me that is independent of me, at times even against my will. Meaning, the third factor in our development is the external conditions, which can partially change our path of development, towards the "good path" or towards the "bad path."

Let's go back to the seed of grain, because its process of development is convenient to observe and it will help us understand the principle we are discussing. For example, if in both parts of a field we sow the same kind of grain but treat each part differently - say, we conceal one part from sunlight, not giving it enough water, not cutting the weeds, whereas for the second part we'll provide the best conditions for growth, it'll become clear to us the extent to which external factors affect the process of development. Though at the end of the process the same kind of grain will grow, the question is what growing difficulties it suffered, and what its quality will be.

The fourth factor is change in external conditions. We cannot affect ourselves directly, but if we change the external conditions around us, we will be able to determine our future, future thoughts, desires, aspirations - in one word, the quality.

The first factor, the "platform," and the other, the laws by which our essence develops, can be expressed negatively in the framework of what we call heredity: physical or mental, psychological and spiritual weakness. Hence, if Man, like the seed of the grain, finds a suitable space for his development, by submitting himself to the positive influence of an environment, he is capable of achieving marvelous results.

Rav Dr. Michael Laitman, "Interview with the Future"

Task #2:
Read the following excerpts from the books "The Tower of Babel - The Last Storey" and "The Last Generation" and answer the following questions:

- How can we transform our attitude toward others from egoistic to altruistic?
- Can society force a person to change his nature from egoistic to altruistic?
- What exactly can be acquired from the environment?

By summing up these four factors that shape a person, it is revealed that the bottom line is that we are activated by two sources. One source is the internal data embedded in us from birth and the other is the data we absorb from the environment throughout our lives.

It is interesting to note that science has reached similar conclusions on this matter. Since the 1990's, the field of behavioral genetics has consolidated in science. This field deals with finding a connection between genes and personality, cognitive and behavioral characteristics, from anger, adventurism, shyness and violence to sexual desire of people. One of the first researchers in this field in the world is psychologist Professor Richard Ebstein, who maintains that genes determine about half of character traits, while the rest is determined by the environment.

Since we cannot change the internal data, we need to turn to the second factor upon which our development depends - our environment. All we can do in order to advance towards actualizing life's purpose is to choose an environment that will push us towards that. In Baal HaSulam's article "The Freedom" he explains as follows: "... he who strives to continually choose a better environment is worthy of praise and reward.... it is not because of his good thoughts and deeds, which come to him without his choice, but because of his effort to acquire a good environment, which brings him these good thoughts and deeds."

A person who invests his strength in choosing and creating the environment required for correct development can thus actualize his innate potential. Understanding and actualizing this principle requires a high level of awareness, still it seems that many of us are already there.

If we want to transform our relationship to others from egoistic to altruistic, we need to bring ourselves to a state where our desire to care for the benefit of others and to connect with them is much greater than our desire for any other egotistic possessions. This can only happen if our environment's scale of values sets altruism as a supreme value.

We were created as social and egoistic beings and from our point of view, nothing is more important than the opinion of those around us. Actually, our life's purpose is to gain the appreciation and praise from society. We are completely and involuntarily controlled by society's opinion and are willing to do whatever we can in exchange for appreciation, praise, honor and glory. That is why society can instill in its members different values and forms of behavior, as abstract as they may be.

Society also builds in us the standards by which we measure our self-respect and self-esteem. Therefore, even when we are alone, we act according to the values of society. That is, even if no one knows about a specific act we have performed, we will carry it out in order to feel positive self-esteem.

In order for us to begin building the desire to care for others and create connections among us as parts of one system, we need to be in a society that supports it. If those around us value altruism as a supreme value, each of us will naturally have to obey and adapt it to ourselves.

Optimally, a person's environment should convey to him: "You have to treat others well, the single system of which you are a part, for us to achieve balance with nature." When the desire for altruism is evident in our surrounding society, we will absorb it. If we encounter reminders and appreciation of the importance of altruism wherever we turn, our attitude towards others will change. Gradually, the more we think about it, the greater our desire will be to become healthy parts within the single system.

We are unable to change ourselves directly, but we have the power to improve our environment. We are absolutely capable of that. When the influence of the environment on us changes, we change. The environment is the lever which elevates us to a higher degree. Consequently, the first step that each one of us can take is to think and examine which environment is most worthwhile to be in for advancing towards life's purpose.

As above mentioned, the power of thought is the strongest force in nature. Hence, if we strive to be in a better environment, our inner strength will lead us over time to people, organizations, guides, books, or, in one word, to an environment where we'll be able to develop. The more we focus on the idea of improving the environment and try to implement it in our lives, the more possibilities will open before us to actualize it.

When our environment is comprised of people who are also drawn to equilibrium with nature, they will be able to set an example for us, with encouragement and reinforcement. They will understand that we want to treat them lovingly, and will enable us to learn how to do it. That is how everyone will learn the meaning of resembling the force of Nature in one's qualities and will feel how good it is to be immersed in love. Whoever resembles the altruistic force of Nature does not feel any pressure, so in such an environment we will feel protected, content, safe, happy and free of worries. This is the kind of life towards which Nature is directing all of humanity.

Rav Dr. Michael Laitman, "The Tower of Babel - The Last Story"

The rule "there is no coercion in spirituality" means that it is impossible - thus forbidden - to directly influence a person's desire. Society cannot force a person to change his will, since it is contrary to his nature; rather it can offer him the possibility to demand of himself, by means of the society, the future form he desires.

If society's pressure obligates a person to act according to its laws, it won't be of one's own free choice. Although one may be able to fulfill the demands of society forcefully, it will not lead one to an inner request from the Upper force to change one's desire from receiving to bestowal. Kabbalists have said in that regard: "There is no coercion in spirituality." A person cannot be forced by any external pressure to want to correct his nature. Only through the recognition of evil and the craving for good, meaning, to become the bestower, one summons the action of the "Light those Reforms" which corrects every desire a person feels bad about, for the good.

The desire to correct egoism can be acquired from the environment. After one receives from the environment correct examples of desires to bestow and desires them, one turns to the Upper force and merits a response, namely, correction of the will to receive. As a matter of fact, only one request coming from a person to the system of Providence receives a response and answer - the request to correct one's desire from "receiving" to "bestowing." Any other question, request, or prayer from a person does not merit any response.

Now we shall detail the stages of the process of changing the desire. In the first stage, a person understands with his intelligence that he needs to raise his degree of development, meaning, his degree of bestowal. This is an intellectual-external understanding - not the heart's inner desire. Although his heart does not yet desire that, he is still able to increase the intensity of feelings of bestowal and love found in his surroundings, by means of external actions. As a result of these actions, society will project upon him an example of bestowal, from which he'll be impressed not only externally, i.e. in action only -but internally as well, meaning, in the feeling of the heart. Now the person already wants the example of bestowal that society presents to him, to come to him naturally. A person's desire to be more in bestowal is called "prayer" or "*MAN*." This is the only request for a truism, and the only one the Creator answers.

Rav Dr. Michael Laitman, "The Last Generation"

Task #3:
Read the following excerpts from Rav Dr. Michael Laitman's blog and from the book "A Glimpse of Light" and answer the following questions:
- How does choosing the environment help attracting the Light that Reforms?
- Indicate at least two benefits of group work.

In our progress on the spiritual path, we begin to appreciate the quality of bestowal, egoistically. It gives freedom and fulfillment, enabling us not to be dependent on anything. This attitude towards the attribute of bestowal is called "Not in Its Name." Afterwards, under the influence of the Light, the quality of bestowal turns into a value of its own for us. This attitude towards the attribute of bestowal is called "In Its Name.

In order to achieve that, we need to carry out the advice of Kabbalists. The point in the heart brings us to a new environment, the group, so that whether we want to or not, we begin uniting with others. Due to the act of uniting, we immediately summon the Surrounding Light, which always surrounds us, but in the act of uniting we draw it intentionally.

The more I invest increased efforts in uniting with others, the more the Light affects me and I start to receive new impressions. In the end, I come to appreciate that bestowal is good. That's how it looks to me now: elevated and special, and that's called the influence of the environment.

Our common efforts and desires make it possible to summon the Light that Reforms. We are all in an ocean of Light and can draw it towards us. A correct environment is one that helps me draw the Light.

The Light acts and influences us even if we do nothing, except that then the process flows slowly, at the natural rhythm of the development of "*Reshimot*" (Reminiscence). However, if we start to summon the Light through studying and uniting with friends, we arouse the influence of the Light upon us.

From the blog of Rav Dr. Michael Laitman Sept. 29, 2010

The Jewish people originated from a group of people whom Abraham gathered in ancient Babylon. They joined together in order to attain the spiritual world, by using the method of Kabbalah that Abraham developed. The principle of connecting to a group is at the foundation of the method of Kabbalah, hence over the course of history, Kabbalists connected in groups.

If we were alone in the world, we could not emerge from ourselves and attain spirituality. That is why the Creator divided the single soul into numerous parts. A reality was created where we live in a world with many people around us. From this state, if we want to attain spirituality, we need to connect with other people who want it as we do.

A special part in the wisdom of Kabbalah explains how to act within a group, what the mutual spiritual work that we have to perform is and how to help one another. A single person does not have enough power to emerge from himself and needs additional forces. Within the group, he finds people who provide him with their own awakening. They push him, he pushes them - they all work together.

Rav Dr. Michael Laitman, "A Glimpse of Light"

A group is a type of laboratory, within which we sharpen our intentions. The lab includes friends, original Kabbalah writings and a Kabbalist teacher with spiritual attainment. We learn what the power of love and giving is, what the Creator's force is and try to actualize it in the group. Not alone, in our imagination, but with other people who are in the same process.

Together we receive guidance about what it is to be more influential, loving and giving, more like the Creator. Our constant attempt to build the Creator's attribute "before our own eyes" and the development of our yearning for this quality to rule us is the "work with intentions."

Rav Dr. Michael Laitman, "A Glimpse of Light"

Task #3:
Read the following excerpts from Rav Dr. Michael Laitman's blog and answer the following questions:
- What is the angel of death and what is the angel of life?
- Why only by resembling the Creator is it possible to reach eternal life?

Baal HaSulam, "The Freedom" essay: "The sages said, "'Harut (carved) on the stones,' do not pronounce it Harut (carved), but rather Herut (freedom), for they have been liberated from the angel of death."

It is said: "I created the evil inclination; I created for it the Torah as spice." So what is the Torah? It is the vessel in which the Light that Reforms resides. In such a way, we can attract the Upper Light, and it reforms us, so that the evil inclination will become the good inclination. This is how we move from the desire to receive called "angel of death" to the desire to bestow called "angel of life," and this is called the freedom from the angel of death.

In our will to receive we can only feel this world, the beastly existence, nothing more. We live, suffer and eventually die. We cannot even imagine how low, flawed and defective this existence is. Until we attain bestowal, our whole life here is an escape from suffering for the sake of such minor pleasures, which have no place in spirituality. The lowest spiritual level is a billion times greater, fuller and more complete than all the pleasures of our world in all times. We cannot even imagine it.

In order to maintain such great spiritual pleasure, it is necessary to prepare a vessel with the intention of in order to bestow. In any case, only with the attribute of bestowal can we transcend the angel of death.

From the blog of Rav Dr. Michael Laitman June 24, 2011

Question: Who is the Angel of Death?
Answer: The state opposite to the Creator, the state we are feeling now is what is gradually killing us. Accordingly, advancing towards the revelation of the mutual relationship among us is called "freedom" and "liberation from the angel of death." The liberation from the angel of death is the entrance to eternity.

The question of why we die is not a philosophical one, but rather seemingly the most difficult and essential question for us. Do we die because the physical body dies and all physiological processes cease? What happens when an organism dies, altogether? That's very strange, is not it?

The whole issue is the ego, whose attribute is to swallow everything into itself instead of passing it on. True Nature exists in a sea of Upper Light, which passes through it and never extinguishes, because it has no ego to extinguish it. Indeed, in spirituality I receive in order to bestow unto you and you receive in order to bestow unto someone else. The Light that passes through you is not intended for you, rather for others, and you are constantly in the process of recycling the Light.

This Light never ceases nor diminishes, because no one takes it in. In this entire chain, no resistance appears, thus super-conductivity is achieved. If I have no inner resistance, whatever enters me passes through me and I do not obstruct it from passing on.

Moreover, in the spiritual world, we increase the amount of Light that passes through us 620 times, since we operate above our egoism. Thereby, eventually, we benefit much more.

From the blog of Dr. Rav Michael Laitman Feb. 25, 2011

Part #3 - Worlds and Souls

Lesson #1 - The Spiritual Worlds

Task #1:
Read the following excerpts from the book "Kabbalah in Simple Terms" and in your own words, describe the order of emergence of the will to receive in the four phases of Direct Light.

In order to actualize His thought to bestow pleasure, the Creator planned a creation of the will to receive the specific pleasure of resembling Him, the Creator. If you are parents, you know that feeling. There are no words to warm a proud father's heart like "Your son is a carbon copy of you!"

So, as we said, the thought of creation is to bestow pleasure unto the created being and is the root of creation. Thus, the thought of creation is called the "Root Phase" (in Hebrew, *Bechina* "phase" as used here is from the word *Havchana*-"discern") and the will to receive that pleasure is called "Phase 1."

Kabbalists also call the Creator the "will to bestow," meaning, "desire to give abundance." They call the created being the "will to receive enjoyment and pleasure," or simply the "will to receive." We will speak more of the way in which we perceive the Creator, but at this stage it is only important to understand that Kabbalists always tell us what they perceive. They do not tell us that the Creator has a will to bestow; they say that what they see in the Creator is that He has a desire to bestow, which is the reason why they called him "will to bestow." Since they have also revealed within themselves the desire to receive the pleasure He wishes to bestow, they have called themselves the "will to receive."

So the will to receive is the first creation; it is the root of all created beings. When creation (the will to receive) feels that pleasure coming to it is from someone who is giving, it grasps that true pleasure is in giving, not in receiving. As a result, creation begins to want to give. It is a completely new phase, which is called "Phase 2."

What turns it into a new phase? If we look at the vessel itself, we see that it does not change throughout the phases. Meaning, the will to receive receives to the exact same extent as before. Since the will to receive was programmed in the thought of creation, it is eternal and unchangeable.

However, in Phase 2, the will to receive wants to receive pleasure from giving and not from receiving and this is the significant shift. The major difference is that Phase 2 is in need of another to whom it can give. In other words, Phase 2 must relate positively to someone or something else, outside itself.

Phase 2, which obligates us to give, despite our basic drive to receive is what makes life possible. Without it, parents wouldn't care for their children and social life wouldn't be possible at all.

Now, we can understand why the law of nature is the law of giving and not a law of receiving, although the will to receive is the basic drive operating in every created being, just like in Phase 1. From the moment creation has both the will to receive and the will to give, everything happening to it will stem from the "relationship" between these two attributes.

As mentioned, the will to give in Phase 2 obligates it to communicate and seek someone who needs to receive. Therefore, Phase 2 now begins to examine what it can give to the Creator. After all, at this stage, there is still no one else to give to.

Yet, when Phase 2 attempts to give, it reveals that the Creator only desires to give and has no desire whatsoever to receive. Besides that, what can the created being give the Creator?

Moreover, Phase 2 reveals that deep within it, meaning in Phase 1, its true desire is to receive. It reveals that its root, in essence, is the will to receive enjoyment and pleasure and that there is nothing within it, not even an ounce of true desire to give. Yet, and this is a very important point, since the Creator wants only to give, the created being's will to receive is precisely what it can give to the Creator.

Confusing? Perhaps. But, if you recall the example of the mother and the pleasure, she receives from feeding her baby, you will understand that in essence, the baby gives pleasure to his mother, simply by wanting to feed.

Therefore, in Phase 3, the will to receive chooses to receive; thus, it gives back to the Root Phase, the Creator. Now we have a perfect cycle, in which both players give: The Root Phase (the Creator) gives to the created being (Phase 1) and the created being, after having gone through Phases 1, 2 and 3, reciprocates the Creator by receiving from Him.

As we can understand, our egoistic intentions are the reason for all problems we see in the world. Here too, at the root of creation, the intention is much more important than the action itself. It seems that we now have a perfect cycle, in which the Creator has succeeded in making the created being resemble Him, the bestower. Furthermore, the created being enjoys giving, thus reciprocating pleasure to the Creator.

However, does it complete the thought of creation? Not really. The action of reception (in Phase 1) and the understanding that the sole desire of the Creator is to bestow (in Phase 2), cause the created being to desire to be in the same state, which is Phase 3. Yet, the fact that the created being became the bestowal doesn't mean that it has attained the state of the Creator, thus completing the thought of creation.

In order to be in the state of the Creator, the created being not only becomes a giver, rather, it has the same thoughts as the Giver, the thought of creation. In such a state, the created being will understand why the cycle of Creator-created being was created altogether and why the Creator created creation.

The desire to understand the thought of creation is a completely new stage. It can only be compared to a state of a child who wants to be both as strong and as wise as his parents. Clearly, that can only happen when the child truly "steps into his parents' shoes."

In the wisdom of Kabbalah, understanding the thought of creation, the deepest degree of understanding, is called "attainment." That is what the will to receive longs for at its last phase of development, Phase 4.

The desire to attain the thought of creation is the strongest force in creation, found behind the entire process of development. Whether we are aware of it or not, what we all truly seek is understanding why the Creator does what He does. That is precisely the drive that motivated Kabbalists to reveal the secrets of creation thousands of years ago and as long as we do not attain it ourselves, we will not have peace and quiet.

Rav Dr. Michael Laitman, "Kabbalah in Simple Terms"

Task #2:
Read the following excerpts from Rav Dr. Michael Laitman's blog and the book "Kabbalah, Science and The Meaning of Life" and answer the following question:

- Under what conditions is the will to receive worthy of being called a created being?

Rav Dr. Laitman: The desire for pleasure is the beginning of matter. In Kabbalah, it is called "primal matter," meaning the initial matter. It is yet to be the final matter, since it is all an outcome of the Light's action.

Professor Tiller: Does this process already exist on the quantum level? Is it about the stage taking place, prior to the creation of time and space? Here in quantum mechanics, everything already exists under constricts of space and time.

Rav Dr. Laitman: This process has existed before any formation of matter as we know it, much before the formation of our universe in its material form.

Since this will to receive stems from the action of the Light, it feels the Light, meaning the pleasure, only in a miniscule form. It has no independent desire for the Light. In order to develop this will to receive to become independent, another component has to be added. That is why the Creator gives the will to receive the feeling of its own existence, the feeling that there is a "Giver" granting it the pleasure it feels. In other words, after the will to receive receives the pleasure, it begins to feel the "Giver of the pleasure" within the pleasure.

It is like after we receive a gift from someone, we begin to feel the giver's attitude towards us, beyond the present itself. We should remember that in mentioning the concept "Creator," we mean the concept of the Giver. The created being now begins to feel a certain gap or clash between the pleasure and the feeling of the Giver of the pleasure. This dissonance creates a response in him; he wants to be like the Creator. This reaction is born in him since the Creator is higher than the pleasure itself. Here, the will to receive already develops to the next degree.

The will to receive chooses by itself to be as the Giver and also to give. This is the first response of the created being, although it is not yet a genuine response from within. It is the created being's response stemming from its feeling of the Giver; hence it is an inevitable response. It is entirely a result of the Giver's appearance before him and there is still no choice here.

The created being begins to think: what can I give to the Creator? The Creator gives because He is the source of pleasure, but when the created being wants to give, he has nothing to give to the Creator. Thus, from his need to give, the created being reveals the Creator's nature. He reveals that the Creator loves him. If the Creator loves him and wants to give him pleasure, it follows that the Creator has a will. The Creator has a "deficiency." The created being understands that the Creator's deficiency is His desire to give the created being pleasure. While the created being receives pleasure, the Creator derives pleasure. When the created being does not receive pleasure, the Creator is in sorrow.

Thus, in order to realize the created being's desire to give to the Creator as He gives to him, the created being decides to receive pleasure from Him. The issue somewhat resembles a good child who eats in order to please his mother. It follows from all the above mentioned that even when he receives everything from her, his action is considered as bestowal unto his mother. Now it can be said that the created being resembles the Creator. He receives everything the Creator wishes to give him only to give unto the Creator. He gives precisely the way the Creator Himself does, yet the process does not end there.

After the created being performs a similar action to the Creator, he feels additional pleasure – one of being at the status of the giver.

This pleasure creates in him an additional desire, a desire to enjoy the status of the giver. Thus, a new desire is born in him, constituting an added desire to the one created initially by the Light. This desire is new and does not come from "Above," which is why it is worthy of being called a "created being."

The root of the word "created being" (*Nivra* in Hebrew) stems from the term "*Bar*," which describes extracting something, external to the Creator's desire. This process of development thus includes five phases.

Rav Dr. Michael Laitman, "Kabbalah, Science, and The Meaning of Life"

The desire isn't revealed as long as it hasn't passed through all 4 phases of development by means of the Light, and reaches an awareness, a sense of self and then it can already make decisions and respond to the Light in some way.

Everywhere in creation, wherever you meet the Root Phase, it means bestowal of the Creator Who wants to summon a response from the created being in "existence from absence." From this Root phase, which is called the "edge of the *Yod*," we are to undergo all 4 phases of *HAVAYAH*, or the phases of Root, 1, 2, 3, 4 and only in the Phase 4 the response is created from the desire.

Everywhere in creation, in all the worlds, wherever we may turn, we will reveal the Root Phase: the Creator's attitude towards the point of "existence from absence." From within it, under the influence of the Light, the desire already begins to evolve, needs to go through the 4 phases, for the created being to be formed and begin to feel the actions of the Light and respond to them.

Then everything begins from the "edge of the *Yod*," from "existence from existence" - from the thought of creation. Afterwards, it begins to act and bears Phases 1, 2, 3, 4, until we reach Phase 4, which already feels itself as existing.

There is a leading force, and a force that is being led here, and each of them is in potential and in practice. The first 3 Phases (Root, 1,2) are still attributed to the Creator; phases 3, 4 already belong to the created being.

The Upper One is *Keter* (Root Phase). Its attribute of bestowal is *Hochma* (Phase 1). The form in which it wants to bestow is *Bina* (Phase 2). The way in which it relates to the lower one is *Ze'ir Anpin* (Phase 3). *Malchut* itself (Phase 4) is the matter that absorbs within it all of the previous forms, wanting to receive them and create within it, in order to acquire the same form as the previous phases.

Thus, *Malchut* actualizes this action within itself, which is why it must feel all of the previous Phases, receive impressions from them, agree with them and want to be similar to them. Then, on its part, it reacts by building the same approach to the Root, and becomes the Root.

It is impossible for the created being to be revealed if it hasn't passed through the four previous phases. Only from the last phase of development, Phase 4, when I already have both the desire and the intention, meaning everything emerges from me, only from that point onward, is it possible to speak of the created being. Before that, only the attributes of the Creator exist, by which He builds the created being.

From Rav Dr. Michael Laitman's Blog May 26, 2011

Task #3:
Read the following excerpts from the book "Kabbalah, Science and The Meaning of Life" and "The Point in The Heart" and answer the following questions:
- **What is the role of the spiritual worlds in the realization of the thought of creation?**
- **Where are we located in relation to the spiritual worlds?**

The first thing the created being must attain in order to resemble the Creator is the correct environment that will enable him to develop. This environment is called "worlds."

At the beginning of the chapter, we said that the pattern of the four Phases is the foundation for all that exists. Hence, the worlds also develop in the same pattern that operated in the process of creating the phases: *Adam Kadmon* is considered the Root Phase, *Atzilut* - Phase 1, Beria –Phase 2, *Yetzira* –Phase 3 and *Assiya* – Phase 4.

From everything we have learned so far, we still don't know which of the five above mentioned worlds is ours. Actually, none of them are. Remember that in spirituality there is no "space," only states. The higher the world is, it represents a state of higher giving. The reason our world is not mentioned here anywhere is that the spiritual worlds are worlds of love and giving and our world is like us, a world of ego (of the will to receive for ourselves). Since the ego is the opposite of giving, our world is disconnected from the system of spiritual worlds; hence, Kabbalists did not mention it in their description of the structure.

Moreover, the spiritual worlds do not really exist, unless we create them by becoming similar to the Creator. The reason we speak of them in past tense is that Kabbalists who have climbed from our world to the spiritual worlds tell us what they have revealed. If we also want to reveal the spiritual worlds, we need to create these worlds anew within us.

We can imagine the system of relationships between the worlds and the created being as a group of construction workers, with one worker who doesn't know how to work. The worlds exemplify to the created being how to perform each one of the tasks: how to drill, how to use a hammer, splitter, and so on. In spirituality, they show the created beings what the Creator gave them and how to work in the correct form. Thus, gradually, the created being learns to use his desires correctly, as they float and rise from the smallest to the strongest ones.

Rav Dr. Michael Laitman, "Kabbalah, Science and The Meaning of Life"

The wisdom of Kabbalah teaches us that we live in a multi-layered reality. It is divided into two basic levels: our world and the Upper, concealed world. The Upper world is built of 125 different degrees of existence, erected one upon the other, just like a ladder of 125 rungs. As of now, we exist beneath the bottom rung of the ladder. "The Point in the Heart" awakens us to climb to its top rung. When we reveal that there is a higher degree, a drive will awaken in us to attain it and climb up the ladder, until we reach the top. This form of development will lead us to *Ein Sof* (Infinity).

Rav Dr. Michael Laitman, "The Point in the Heart"

Task #4:

Read the following excerpts from Rav Dr. Michael Laitman's blog and the book "A Journey to The Upper Worlds" and answer the following question:

- **How is the next degree in the spiritual worlds revealed?**

Question: Why did Rabbi Shimon write the "Book of Zohar" in allegorical language, thus concealing the fact that it actually speaks only of the connection between the Light and the desire?

Answer: Has Rabbi Shimon truly concealed anything? At the beginning of the Holy Ari's book "Tree of Life," he states that before all the worlds and created beings were created, there was only simple, eternal Light. Later, the first point in the heart appeared and when that desire evolved, the worlds and all that filled them were revealed within.

Other than the desire to receive Light, there is nothing. The development is only in the connection between the Light and the desire. The Light remains unchanged, only the desire changes as it resembles the Light. This connection is described by the wisdom of Kabbalah in general and in the "Book of Zohar," in particular.

When a person is at a spiritual degree, he succeeds in viewing the connections in the picture of our world, through which he sees his current degree. When I enter the spiritual world, I am suddenly able to see the picture of this world, as it is depicted to me from a higher degree along with how it is divided to different degrees. This vision enables me to automatically name all the forces and attributes descending to the world, as they manifest in this world. The names of the attributes and forces in all 125 degrees remain names of our world, yet behind each name, a spiritual root exists.

The search amounts to the correction of my attributes, revelation of all the forces, attributes, and connections. According to the extent of the correction, the image of the upper degree becomes clear to me and I ascend to the next degree.

The picture of our world remains unchanged until the end of correction, until the ascent to the state where everything connects into one: all forces, all Lights, all desires connect into one and express the complete merging with the Creator.

When I reveal the connection between the picture of this world and the next degree, and I succeed in connecting both polarities: Above - the Creator, below - me, then I will be able to reach a state of unity and merge with the Creator; I will attain complete equivalence with Him and thus attain the world of *Ein Sof*. In the world of *Ein Sof*, all desires, images and forms together merge into a single reality, which is called "He and His Name is One," one single desire.

From the Blog of Rav Dr. Michael Laitman January 14, 2010

All five worlds: *Adam Kadmon, Atzilut, Beria, Yetzira* and *Assiya* are parallel to one another. Let's try to imagine five rings with a shared center, and there is nothing besides them. Now, we'll copy the same picture five times, one beneath the other. We will have received five parallel areas, within which are five circles. These areas are worlds called *Adam Kadmon*, *Atzilut*, *Beria*, *Yetzira*, and Assiya. Beside these areas, we will place an additional area, within which there are five circles, and call it the world of *Ein Sof*. On the other end, we will exhibit an additional area within which there are five circles and it is Man. Between Man and the world of *Ein Sof* are five worlds. Man is capable of connecting himself gradually, by means of his attributes, with all the worlds, to attain equivalence of form in attributes, with the world of *Ein Sof*. In accordance with the change in his attributes, Man feels himself traversing (internally) from world to world, from only feeling himself in this world, to feeling himself in a completely similar fashion with the world of *Ein Sof*, the Creator.

Rav Dr. Michael Laitman, "A Journey to The Upper World"

Task #5:
Read the following passage from Rav Dr. Michael Laitman's blog.

Question: Why is it that the more you explain the structure of the spiritual worlds, the more I feel confused?

Answer: Imagine I go to a doctor and detail all my aches and pains to him. He performs a variety of tests and discusses the outcomes with another doctor. While they are consulting, I don't understand a thing, although they are talking about me, my feelings and sensations, my health, because they are discussing me on a much more internal degree, taking place within me. After that, they give me a pill, whose chemical component I am not familiar with either, yet I believe them that the pill will help me, which is why I take it. It is clear the doctors have confused me with all the medical information and it would have been better for me not to hear them altogether. However, in our world, the pill they gave me helps and it makes no difference whether I understood the doctor or not.

Here, I am reading about what the Kabbalist doctors wrote about me; one Kabbalist writes to the other about whatever is taking place within the souls in the system, where they need to correct themselves. Of course, I do not understand anything of it! Yet, since I include myself in this story, I want to understand and feel it; I connect with them and draw closer to it.

If I want to become a Kabbalist like them, I use the connection with them and learn how to do it. If I feel confused, but still want to penetrate the truth, I feel that the book is talking about me, correcting my soul, so I have no choice, I have to learn their language and understand what they speak of (similar to studying Latin throughout medical studies).

Kabbalists wrote these books for Kabbalists like themselves. They speak amongst them in a language they understand, for they speak of another world, of spiritual concepts. Although I don't understand what is being said in Kabbalah books, yet if I yearn to understand what they teach, I long to live it, feel it, I open these books and try to enter them. It doesn't matter how much I understand, I need to desire to enter with my sensations and feelings inside and not understand with my external intelligence.

I need to ask for revelation! I must see what they are talking about. Indeed, they write of what they see and feel, and I also want to feel it! Therefore, whatever I do not see, understand, or feel should motivate me to proceed onward.

From Rav Dr. Michael Laitman's blog, April 4, 2010

Lesson #2 - The Soul of Adam HaRishon

Task #1:

Read the following excerpts from the books "The Arvut" and "The Wisdom of Kabbalah According to Baal HaSulam," and answer the following questions:

- In this world, how is the connection among souls as parts of one vessel- "The Soul of Adam HaRishon expressed?"
- In your opinion, how can the connection among souls be used for the benefit of spiritual development, as it expressed in this world?

Adam HaRishon is the state of wholeness, constructed from above. We need to attain this state of wholeness by ourselves, from below in this world, in our lifetime. All laws come to us from that state. We, who are on the last degree, the most distant from that state, need to gradually actualize, observe and implement them upon ourselves, and thus advance until we return to that same state.

Rav Dr. Michael Laitman, "The Arvut"

A person desires to boast before his society. Not necessarily before his closest society around him; but rather before all of humanity. A person would like not only to merit the recognition of his own generation, but of all future generations. For that purpose, a person is ready to do anything.

This is how a person's ego naturally feels, since we come from one vessel and receive all the abundance, not in each one's vessel, but in connecting each one's vessel with the other vessels. Meaning, a person exists in other vessels, within which he feels fulfillment. Therefore, what is acceptable for one person and most important to him is everyone's appreciation felt in their vessels, since they are the true vessels, in which he can feel something other than the physical pleasures necessary for life, to be filled according to the body's biological demands. All the various human pleasures: money, honor, knowledge, with all the wealth in each of them, a person does not receive in his own vessels, rather in the vessels of society. That stems from the connection of all the souls into one vessel.

What a person has at his foundation and what he will ever have is only what will be in this general vessel, which in our life is called "what they will think of me." Meaning, the fulfillment of a person is the honor and respect he receives from everyone. Whether he wants to or not, a person lives under this condition, unless the importance of the Creator and the connection with Him are raised above society's opinion.

Then, although a person does not emerge from the control of this law and doesn't naturally care about the society, he begins to use the society, in order to attain the Creator. It is more important for him to be connected with the Creator, to be impressed with, connect with and be accepted by the Creator. It is as if he replaces the society with the Creator. However, even then, he does not receive fulfillment in his private vessel, rather in the vessels of society. Within the vessels of society, he receives the reasoning of the Creator, equivalence with Him, connection with Him.

We are all the general vessel of *Adam HaRishon* and each of us is a part of the six hundred thousand souls, which today are eight billion people. Each of them at his source, at the spiritual degree in which we all exist, does not receive within his vessel, rather feels life and his livelihood within the vessels of others. Then, people also feel connected to one another in the desires of this world, in fulfillment derived from money, honor, knowledge.

Everything stems from the spiritual construct. If, in the spiritual construct we weren't connected together and felt pleasure specifically in the general vessel, dependent on fulfillment and feeling of what exists in the other vessels, then in this world, we would also not yearn for money, honor, and knowledge. Why is it important for a person to know that he has a million dollars and someone else has a hundred? Because the difference between them enhances one's sense of fulfillment. The gap is the person's fulfillment.

A person who works for two billion dollars instead of one billion, clearly feels the difference between a desire for a billion and a desire for two billion, compared to one who has not yet reached these desires and doesn't feel any difference at all. He feels the difference because others see it as more respectable and accepted. He feels himself more important than them, that his filling is more important than what they have. Meaning, all social fulfillment is based on the gap between the person himself and others. It is either for his own benefit, in order to receive, before the screen, or for the benefit of others, after the screen.

Rav Dr. Michael Laitman, "The Wisdom of Kabbalah According to Baal HaSulam

Task #2:
Read the following excerpts from the blog of Rav Dr. Michael Laitman and the book "A Glimpse of Light" answer the following question:
- **What is the shattering and what is its benefit?**

The general force of nature is the force of love and giving. In the wisdom of Kabbalah it is also called the Creator or the Upper Light and we study that from the very beginning, He created one reality called *"Adam HaRishon"*(The First Man). One "Man" - a single desire (the meaning is not one human being, like ourselves, rather a spiritual construct.)

As our body is comprised of billions of parts, so the single desire includes billions of desires. They are all connected in a wondrous system. Just imagine how many components and connections there are in this system…

In the beginning, all the parts of this system operated in harmony and were as one. However, this harmony was actually caused by the Upper Light. At the next stage, an action took place called the "shattering" and the Light withdrew from the single desire He had created. The desire remaining without the influence of the Light is considered shattered. To be more exact, each of its parts, in and of itself, seemed to remain whole, yet the connection among the parts was broken. That is a system collapse; suddenly one part doesn't work with the other, it is impossible to receive, impossible to give, the system stops functioning.

What have we gained through the shattering? We have gained our ego.

What does that mean? On one hand, the more we hate one another and are distant from each other, so we lack Light. On the other hand, only from this dark state will we be able to understand what Light is, what the Creator is. This is written as "The advantage of the Light from the darkness."[55] Only from the difference, out of the opposition between those two states, can we begin to understand the Creator and attain Him.

Rav Dr. Michael Laitman, "A Glimpse of Light"

The origin of all souls is in a single soul, the soul of *Adam HaRishon*. Everything takes place within it. When a desire entered it which opposed unity, it was divided into numerous parts.

Similar to a king who decided to transfer his wealth across the sea and in order to assure that the messengers would not be tempted to steal the treasure on the way, he gave one coin to each of his subjects and commanded them to transfer the coin across the sea, so the soul of *Adam HaRishon* corrects itself (traverses from our world to the spiritual world) in parts. The work of each soul is overcoming the force of division and separation and connecting its part of the general wealth to the single mutual connection. When a person corrects himself, he returns to the parts of the soul of *Adam HaRishon*, meaning, acquires a mutual intention for all the parts, for the entire

---

[55] Ecclesiastes 2, 13.

force of separation which permeated the system and shattered it into 600,000 souls.

Correction occurs from the light to the heavy, according to the repulsion felt in one's attitude towards others. It is only upon a person to actualize his free choice by means of connecting with all the others, with the general system.

From the Blog of Rav Dr. Michael Laitman Feb. 11, 2010

Why did the Creator shatter the single created being He created, the general soul? Actually, we also act that way towards our children sometimes, when we want to enable them to develop. For example, in order to create a puzzle for them, we first paint a complete picture and then break it into small pieces. The children try to fit the pieces of the puzzle together themselves and that is how they develop. According to the same principle, only by us, human beings connecting ourselves anew into one complete Man, will we be able to understand creation.

It is important to realize that there is a huge qualitative difference between the general soul before its shattering and after its correction. We will illustrate this through another example, this time of a television. The television is a complex device; nevertheless, everyone knows how to operate it. Suppose the television broke into small pieces and I have no choice, I have to fix it. How smart I become after fixing it!

I have to be familiar with its structure, the plastic and metal parts, cables, wires and connections and their laws of connection. After all, we are talking about a complete shattering. I have to know everything in order to fix it. When I understand how it is built, I also begin to become familiar with the one who planned and created it. Indeed, he invested his entire being in its creation, which is why by mimicking his actions, I understand and attain him.

Thus, instead of a basic understanding of "how to push buttons," I, myself, assemble all of creation and the entire creation becomes mine. Hence, I acquire the intellect of the Creator, His stature.

Rav Dr. Michael Laitman, "A Glimpse of Light"

The single soul divided into numerous souls in order to give each and every one of us an opportunity to resemble the Creator. The Creator has a "desire to give" and we are constructed from a "desire to receive." It is our nature.

What is wrong with being the one to receive? When I receive, my desire is canceled by the pleasure. We see it in our life. For instance, I can work several years for something, in order to purchase a fancy car. I buy the car, sit in it, enjoy it... I have been waiting for this moment for so long! Every button in the car brings me pleasure.

Yet, with time the pleasure fades. I have become used to the car, which seems to have lost its charm. We all understand that. This is how the will to receive is built. I chase pleasure, each time after a different pleasure, until I grow tired. And then what? Then I die. Yes yes, it is truly like that. People die when they grow tired of life.

The feeling of eternal pleasure means eternal life. Is it possible to lead the created being to that-to a degree where he becomes like the Creator - eternal and whole? For this, the created being has to receive unlimited fulfillment and for that pleasure to constantly increase more and more. Not from a feeling of lack, rather from good to better, and even better than that. We cannot imagine such a possibility, of not feeling that something is lacking between one good to another. This is something that cannot be sensed in our ordinary life.

How can this be done? For this, the Creator took the large vessel He created, the will to receive, and divided it to myriad parts, every one of which seems to be closed within itself and does not feel connected to the other parts. This process is called the "shattering of the vessels." Consequently, each part has a feeling that he is the only important one and that all the others exist only for him.

Why was it done like that? So that now, with my own strength, I will change my attitude towards others and behave like how a mother treats her children. I have to reach a state where I feel all the other desires, for them to be as my own. Then I acquire the entire great vessel the Creator created: all are like my children; I love and fulfill them. Endless lights pass through me and they fill the great vessel I sense as my own, as me. In such a way, I will have attained an incessant stream, unlimited and thus I resemble the Creator. I have reached His stature; I have become like Him - good and benevolent.

Rav Dr. Michael Laitman, "A Glimpse of Light"

The wisdom of Kabbalah explains that the perfect state, where all human beings and all the details of reality connect together as one in complete harmony, already exists. However, each of us is at different stages of development and attains a different part of the same state.

The degree of closeness each person goes through on the way to his perfect state, through acquiring the attribute of bestowal is called different names in Kabbalah books, such as: "*Malchut*" (Divinity) and *Zeir Anpin* (The Creator or The Dweller). The degree of closeness of *Malchut* to *Zeir Anpin* is the degree of closeness of a person to the perfect state.

The matter is similar to a house (*Malchut*) that is shared by all people, yet the degree of use and dwelling in it, depends only on his desire. The house seemingly ""waits" for us to be ready and want to come and use it.

To the degree of the person's desire to identify with the attribute of bestowal more than his natural attribute of reception, he enters that same "house," or in the language of Kabbalah: "raises *Malchut* to *Zeir Anpin*." Although "*Malchut*" already exists in its perfect state, only the demand of Man allows him to enter it. Meaning, to the degree a person acquires the attribute of bestowal, he attains the perfect state of *Malchut* to a greater degree.

Thus, a person corrects the "shattering" - the corporeal perception in which he feels his desires and lives for them alone. To the degree a person acquires more of his perfect state and attains more of the attribute of bestowal, he "enters" and senses that he is in one perfect "house," in which all the desires of people exist in harmony. Then, he transitions from a restricted life focused on self-fulfillment, to eternal life and pleasure from the ability to fill others.

From the Blog of Rav Dr. Michael Laitman Jan. 11, 2009

Task #3:
Read the following excerpts from the books "Light at the End of The Tunnel," "A Glimpse of Light" and "The Open Book" and answer the following questions:

- How is the shattering of Adam HaRishon corrected?

In what way is the shattering of Adam Rishon revealed in our time?

The soul we learn of in the wisdom of Kabbalah is called the soul of "*Adam HaRishon*" and is the single soul that exists. "Soul" is called desire, the will to receive. This will to receive is full of Upper light, the light of pleasure which fills it. When the soul exists in a way of being full of light, it exists in a state where it does not feel a thing in and of itself, like a drop of semen. Since it still exists under the control of the light that fills it, in that form, there is no entity.

This desire to receive is not yet called a created being, for it exists under the governance of the Upper light. In order to give the created being a feeling of an entity, a feeling of independence, a feeling of free choice, in which he will resemble the Creator, the Light, it is necessary to add to that will to receive the intention of "in order to bestow." In order to add to this desire to receive the intention of "in order to bestow," the soul of *"Adam HaRishon"* undergoes shattering. It was shattered into about seven billion parts. The number of parts is less important, because at different times there can be more or less parts, according to the specific egoistic desire existing in each part.

The shattered soul is the current shattered state of humanity, which is called this world. From this state, it is necessary to ascend independently back to that same perfect state as of the single soul of *"Adam HaRishon."* In other words, in the state of this world, correction has to be actualized, meaning, to understand that the purpose of man is to become that single soul as *"Adam HaRishon."* How can this correction be actualized? Only by that same light which filled the soul, and that which we need to draw to us. This light is called the Light that Reforms or the Light of *Torah*, or the Surrounding Light. The Light that Reforms is drawn while studying Kabbalistic writings, when we desire to reach a state, where there is not only receiving and the vitality of life of this world alone, rather yearning to feel the eternal, Upper life.

Meaning, when existing in this world in a state of shattering, in a state of egoistic connections with one another and hating one another, if we desire to correct this connection, we draw the light against the ego. As written: "I created the evil inclination, and I created the Torah as a spice," as "the Light within reforms." Each person draws this Light upon his ego, then corrects himself and ascends through five worlds: *Assiya, Yetzira, Beria, Atzilut, Adam Kadmon*, until he returns to his place in the world of *Ein Sof* (Eternity). When he ascends, he is already connected with all the other souls, as they were connected in a single desire and now, once again, the desire becomes one.

The egoistic desire among people remains and above the egoistic desire, they connect to each other in ties of "love your friend as yourself." Meaning, on one hand, each person's ego remains. On the other hand, mutual love exists among people. The gap between hate and love creates the new vessel, in which the person who creates this vessel begins to feel a new reality of *Ein Sof* and reaches a state of resembling Divinity, resembling the Creator. That state is the purpose of creation.

There is no difference between the general soul of "*Adam HaRishon*" and all the people in this world. It is only necessary to understand that we are all in a closed system, where each person exists within his ego as the other seven billion parts. Each person's specific ego has increased until our special times, when the shattered connection between each and every one of us is being revealed, in the billions of everyone's connections. As we reveal today in the world that by means of six people, every person knows everyone. We will soon reveal that every person is connected to all.

However, this connection is a bad one. That same connection among people, in which each person relates to the other in his ego, only that needs to be corrected. The ego of people is received from the start, no one is at fault. Yet by being revealed today, it must be corrected and other than that correction, there is no need to do anything else in life. When everyone reveals the connection among them, in this relation of mutual connection, that same world of *Ein Sof* is revealed.

That same world of *Ein Sof* is revealed, without the necessity to change a thing. Rather, to the extent a person begins to reveal the correct connection with others, he begins to feel, within the correct relation to others, the Upper force, the force of giving and love. Then, he emerges from the perception of his inner world and begins to see the world in a way as if he exists outside of it. In the world outside him, he reveals the Creator.

This world is never felt outside a person. Rather in the wisdom of Kabbalah, we learn about the perception of reality, according to which everything is perceived within, inside the brain, according to the inner Reminiscence revealed inside. When we enter a correct relationship with others, we begin to reveal the system of *Ein Sof*. We should attain it in our generation. All the conditions for it have been revealed, as Kabbalists who founded the entire method write; we only need to actualize it.

Rav Dr. Michael Laitman, "Light at the End of the Tunnel"

Let's imagine that all the people in the world are connected, that we are close to one another, as family relatives. How would we relate to one another? Everything would suddenly work out.

Before that, I hated you and you hated me. I had to keep my distance from you. But now I reveal in my senses that we are truly connected, one body. In such a state, to cause harm to others is to cause harm to oneself… it may be difficult to describe, yet this is the revelation the wisdom of Kabbalah brings a person, revealing the system of "*Adam HaRishon*."

In the revelation of this system in our world there are two states: "Face" and "Back." During our times, the system has already begun to be revealed, although only from its "Back for now." As a result, the connection between countries and people is being revealed. We all live in one small village, where everyone influences everyone. Except that now rejection, hatred, fear, distance, problems and struggles are being revealed – revelation of the "Back."

If we were to reveal the system of *Adam HaRishon* by its "Face," all the evil would cease, just like that, all at once, and we would all feel as one. In such a state, you are incapable of doing anything, other than actions that you would do for yourself. You do not feel that "others" exist; everything becomes one body; everything is you. That is the revelation the world needs and for this purpose the wisdom of Kabbalah is being revealed in our days.

Rav Dr. Michael Laitman, "A Glimpse of Light"

The corrected system which we are supposed to reveal is a combined system. All its parts are interconnected with one another, connected to each other. The law maintaining the system is love, bestowal and mutual responsibility.

Today we are in a shattered system and we need to advance towards the corrected system. It serves us as a measurement, to which we want to adapt ourselves. At the end of the process, the shattered system returns to being the corrected system, meaning both systems unite.

The corrected system is described in Kabbalah writings. When we study it and desire to move towards it, then our efforts awaken a special force which acts upon us, a force called "The Light that Reforms." This is the force of correction projected onto us from the corrected system, and its intensity depends on the degree of our desire to push ourselves in the correct direction.

Rav Dr. Michael Laitman, "A Glimpse of Light"

The soul of a person exists to the degree of the recognition and knowledge of its root. Therefore, one's soul has to return to its root after emerging from it as a branch stemming from the root.

Within each person is an inner readiness, his desire develops from physical pleasure to human pleasure: lust for money, control and honor, and knowledge. All of these grant a person an ability to begin to draw nearer to his root independently; yet, a person is not able to awaken independently prior to the awakening of the point in the heart, that same inner point which is hidden and concealed within every person.

When will a person awaken and under what circumstances? All of that does not depend on the person. However, if one already received the inner awakening, he is obligated to focus on it, invest his full attention in it, in order to continue and develop it himself. It can be said, that after a person has received an awakening, from there on, the obligation to aspire and yearn to actualize that inner point in him is upon him alone. That already refers to questions about the essence of life and one's goal in it all.

Thus, every thought of a person about something found outside the borders of this world, any yearning towards something more sublime, which is not around us in this world, awakens in him from that same inner point, our root. From now on, every connection formed is already mutual.

Rav Dr. Michael Laitman, "The Open Book"

Study Unit #3 - The Work of Man

Part #1 - There is None Else besides Him

Lesson #1 - One Force

Task #1:

Read the following excerpts from the books "The Open Book" and "Kabbalah at a Glance" and answer the following questions:

- What is the single purpose of all events in creation?
- What is the connection between that purpose and the feeling of good and evil in the world?

In the study of the comprehensive law of creation, words such as "G-d," "Creator," "Emanator" are used as technical names for forces, lights, or degrees. For example, each Upper degree, in relation to a lower degree is called "Creator" since the superior creates the inferior, controls and develops it. The "Creator" is also everything that exists, other than the soul which is called the "created being."

"Creator" is a single general force which oversees the entire system of creation. In Kabbalah, there is only one major law: the law of the Creator to bestow maximum pleasure upon the created being. All the other laws stem from that law and everything taking place in reality is its actualization. The sole purpose of any occurrence at any given moment in creation is to obligate a person to come to the point of the greatest pleasure of being filled with the Light of the Creator.

The act of the Creator is similar to that of the law of gravity. In the center of creation is the Creator. The souls were distanced from Him by a range of five worlds: *Adam Kadmon, Atzilut, Beria, Yetzira, Assiya*, to the farthest point called "our world." From that point, He draws us to Him.

Rav Dr. Michael Laitman, "The Open Book"

The Bible speaks of many "trials" the Creator places before a person his entire life. What is the Kabbalistic approach to that and what is the purpose of these trials all together, if the result is already predetermined?

First, we need to understand the system in which we exist. A person's life is no more than his relationship with the Creator, through the image of this world which appears to him as "me", family, nation, world, nature. While, in fact, he should see all of these as only a wrapping, behind which one Upper, unique force stands, performing all actions upon a person, in order to draw him closer to the purpose of creation.

Nowadays, this concept is accepted by all those who engage in the research of reality and everyone already refers to it: scientists, philosophers, religious clerics. The only question is - what is the result of this beautiful saying which claims that the Creator governs the world and manages us all?

Thus, we should perceive the complete, general image of reality, in which each and every individual in reality is an actual part of this mosaic, with no exceptions. Hence, if a person receives any beatings or experiences illness and even fatal blows, he should see them as forces acting upon him, in order to bring him to a predetermined goal.

Accordingly, these forces are not negative or positive; rather they all act with determination, as written: "He gave a law and it shall not be transgressed," and "I the Lord have not changed." That means: "I do not change my governance and supervision, for I have a predetermined goal to bring all of reality, the whole of humanity to equivalence of form with Me, to My degree, so you return to Me. I will do so in good or in bad towards you, that is, in how it may appear to you."

It is similar to a parent-child relationship. We punish a "bad" child, while a "good" child advances on his own. However, laws are laws, and they all work as one. Thus, when parents pressure a child, in order to bring him to the good, if the child understands their pressure and agrees with them even before pressure is applied, he feels good, progresses nicely and acknowledges their love for him. And vice versa; to the extent that he does not accept or understand their pressure and even disagrees with it, seemingly trying to escape it, so they increase their pressure upon him and the child's life troublesome.

Thus, first a person should agree to accept the general system, in which he feels trapped in a kind of whirlwind of forces, whether it is external pressure from the environment, family, work, or internal pressures arising from within his body and thoughts. A person needs to realize that all that comes from a special and unique force operating in reality, which is called the "Creator."

The Creator is a force whose field passes through all the bodies and activates them, just as electricity enters the electric system and activates it. If there is no electricity, the apparatus with all its systems and electric circuits is lifeless.

The wisdom of Kabbalah is unique in that it opens the general system before a person, and then one sees the Creator, Who stands behind the image of this world. He sees all the forces operating, knows why things happen to him the way they do, the goal these events lead him to, and he learns how to respond to them. Thus, the whole purpose of the events in our life is to reveal what stands behind them – the system of leadership and Providence. This revelation is called to "return to the Creator," draw near to Him, understand Him and adhere to Him.

Rav Michael Laitman, " Kabbalah at a Glance"

Task #2:
Read the following excerpt from "A Glimpse of Light" and answer the following question:

- If the Creator is the cause of all events in creation, what can we add to the process of creation of our own?

The Creator is the force operating in the world, "the force that acts upon the enacted." He maintains creation and renews it.

He creates me, now constructing in me a heart and a mind, a feeling and vision, filling of the senses. When I see something or speak to someone now, the force that gives me an image of reality and stabilizes me within it, in emotion, mind and everything is what is called the Creator.

And if He does everything, what do I have of my own? I only need to understand that this is how it happens, from Him. If I want to grow, then from this little point of recognition my "I" can grow. The development is in being able to recognize Him in return, on my own; the way He builds matter, the forces and the operating system.

"From Your deeds we have known You," asserts the wisdom of Kabbalah. In other words, when I reveal His actions in me, I attain Him, Who stands behind me and constructs this whole image for me."

Rav Dr. Michael Laitman, "A Glimpse of Light"

Task #3:
Read the following excerpt from Rav Dr. Michael Laitman's blog and from the book "Kabbalah at a Glance" and answer the following questions:
- If you desire to change, what do you need to do?
- What should we ask for?
- How can we reach true connection with others?

The Light is the Creator – the Light is the first, always and in everything! In the beginning, the Light created the created being, which is why the Light controls the created being. The created being would not exist without the Light. The Light generates every movement and change in the created being.

1. A minimal force of illumination of the Light keeps the created being in an "inanimate" state and to the extent that the Light increases its force, the created being changes in its quality. It transforms from "inanimate" into "vegetative," which can already absorb and feel.

2. The Light is the Creator – the Light is the first, always and in everything! That is why it is written, "There is none else besides Him." The Creator is your shadow; you need to find the Creator in all your situations, as a force creating that situation for you.

3. You can direct the Light – if you long to change, you need to summon the influence of the Light upon you, so that it will change you. The Light will influence you and your *Reshimot* (Reminiscence) with the goal of drawing you closer to the purpose of creation. In other words, you can do only one thing on your own – hasten your spiritual development, or the opposite- cause the Light to depart out of the lack of desire for correction ... The Light's departure is felt as suffering and misery. Indeed, the Light is Life!

It is important to understand: since the Light is the source of all your desires, you will not be able to influence it with those desires. You need to obtain a desire for development, not for the Light. Only with a new and free desire, will you be able to influence the Light, summon further enlightenment, and thus shorten the path. You will find and obtain this desire only from the correct environment.

From the blog of Rav Dr. Michael Laitman, Dec. 6, 2008

Science has reached the conclusion that there is one comprehensive law in Creation, which the wisdom of Kabbalah calls "Creator,"

"Upper Force" or "Upper Light." Yet, unlike an ordinary scientist, in the study of the entire system of creation, the Kabbalist feels the part that we do not feel, since he has developed an additional sense. This force has an unaltering intent: to bring the entire system of Creation to wholeness. In other words, from his point of view, everything that exists in reality is already in the state of the most supreme wholeness.

As a result, the Upper Force operates upon whoever is not in this state of wholeness, accordingly, pushing and hastening it to attain wholeness. This process operates equally upon all parts of creation and its action is felt as misery in us.

Our uncorrected initial state was deliberately created from Above by the Creator, in order to give us the option of choosing wholeness as something we desire and attaining it ourselves. The only form of advancement that exists is turning to the Upper Force for help. Since nature did not imprint this force in us, when we turn to the Upper Force, we are not violating its law, rather performing the only correct action that can be performed.

Except that turning for help should be out of awareness. Why are we asking for help? Is it for our own sake, in order to fulfill our desires in this world, or in order to ascend spiritually? We should remember to whom we are turning, who gave us this misery that causes us to cry out. We need to remember that it was given to us in order to attain crying out, so we will turn to Him out of no choice.

The Creator feels what is in our hearts long before we do. It follows that as long as we are not whole, His governance is also felt in us as incomplete. Therefore, we should ask Him not to change His governance, but to change us, so that we can feel His complete governance.

We pray to Him because we feel bad; meaning, out of an egoistic motive, so that we will feel good. However, if we ask to change ourselves not because we feel bad, but because we are suffering from the fact that we curse the Creator in our hearts, that is already a request that is not for our sake but for His sake. The Creator responds to such a request immediately.

Rav Dr. Michael Laitman, "The Open Book"

We forget that we do not have to do anything, but only to ask the Creator to do so! You think about how you obligate your heart to open up, how you connect with others, how they will connect to you ... we do not need to think about that at all! We imagine the connection within our egoistic mind, but it is not at all the way we think it is! It is the degree of the Upper world; a new reality is revealed to us! We just have to ask to be corrected; nothing else!

We learn that everything takes place as a result of the request. It follows that the Surrounding Light comes and corrects everything, and we are found in the time of correction. Everything comes from Above. On our part, only the demand, the request, the craving are needed. The problem at this point is whether we are turning to the Creator or trying to do everything on our own. It is precisely at this point that we err and remain stuck for many years. We are not able to change the direction even slightly and realize that there is nothing other than a request, a demand!

In order to attain this request, all we have to do is try. If we attempt to build a correct global system based on love and brotherhood on our own, it will be a long way until we are led to the realization that we are drawing distant from the goal. We will find that we are not genuine, that we hate each other and are not drawing closer to unity.

The wisdom of Kabbalah should lead us to a very accurate conclusion: Do not try to connect with others; you are egotistical and so are they. Only the Supreme Light can make it happen. It will come and connect you, only the Light! Therefore, do not seek connection among yourselves, for it is said, "When a man and a woman merit, Divinity is between them," meaning you, the friend, and the Creator between you, "making peace in His high places, He will make peace upon us." All of our relationships with one another without the force that connects us are false. When we embrace, we do not really want to, or do so only at the level of this world. Do we demand mutual love, connection, unity? We do so only at the level of this world. Who can be a guarantor for the other or for oneself? Where do we have such strength? We may long to connect amongst us only through the Supreme One that fills all the space between us. If we demand that He fills the void, connects us and dwells among us on a regular basis, it will happen and easily so.

The wisdom of Kabbalah was intended to lead us to the correct attitude towards the connection with others, whereas we, by our egoistic nature always run away from it. Let's not forget that "there is none else besides Him!" The Creator performs an action, but in order for it to take place, we need to precede His action with our desire. This is called "to forge a covenant;" we sign an agreement with the Creator, we demand, and He executes. Just as little children pull adults along, thus we draw the Supreme Force to correct the nature that He created and then we'll be in equivalence with the Creator.

We cannot attain mutual guarantee or even truly want it. As soon as we start talking about uniting, we need to remember the condition "Israel, Torah and the Creator – are one." You, the others and the Creator, only the three of you are capable of attaining true peace and wholeness. It is specifically the craving for connection that will bring our awareness that we need to turn to the Creator for help.

From the blog of Rav Dr. Michael Laitman, Nov. 15, 2010

Task #4:
Read the following excerpts from Rav Laitman's blog and answer the question:

- Give two definitions for a situation called "other gods" and explain what is beneficial in such a situation.

Man was created in such a state, with such a perception of reality, where it seems to him that other human beings exist and a great world surrounds him. However, all of this reality is his inner desires, which he cannot yet connect together, in order to finally see that only he exists and faces the Creator. All the distortions, disturbances, thoughts, and foreign desires that are seemingly "coincidental" events happening to him, he should attribute not to the numerous imaginary sources and reasons which for the time being are depicted to him out of the imperfection of his work, rather only to the Creator.

This is what the inner work is composed of, because indeed everything that a person attributes to other forces: other people, all kinds of reasons or destiny, and even to himself, rather than to the Creator – all those are called "other gods." That is because it turns out that he considers himself dependent on something other than the Creator, as if there is any other force that could be a source of influence upon him: good or bad.

We must actualize this principle that "There is none else besides Him," above all the disturbances that deliberately confuse us, so that we'll learn to direct ourselves to the single force, the single source.

This work has various stages:

To discern the uniqueness of the source: Are there other sources, or is it the only one?
To discern the nature of the source: Is it good or bad?
To discern my relation to the source: is it "for my own sake" or "for the sake of bestowal?"

A person performs the work related to the source out of his personal spiritual vessel, out of the desires, by connecting with all the others and as a result feels himself as the only created being. He also unites all the forces operating upon him, all the different sources, into one source. In other words, the work is divided into several types, depending on how the person and the Creator connect.

From the blog of Rav Dr. Michael Laitman July 7, 2011

Man as a created being is divided into numerous parts, into the entire huge creation. The Creator is divided into numerous sources of influence upon Man, good and bad, and the world surrounding Man is divided into good and bad. That is why the relationship between the Creator and the created being is also divided: between a person who has already united everything into the unique created being or who has not yet succeeded in doing so and between the single Creator or the Creator composed of numerous disconnected sources, at times good and at times bad.

Similarly, the relationship between them is also divided: for my sake or for the sake of bestowal and a person is supposed to understand what is required of him: why he must act only for the sake of bestowal and attain it despite all the confusion and the burdensome ego. He learns to connect within him the intention of in order to bestow with the will to receive. At the end, he unites all these conditions into one and in a way that even he himself ceases to exist as a source of thoughts, forces and actions; rather he is merely an inverse "copy" of adherence to the Creator, of the only state that exists.

One needs to reproduce, find, and imagine this sole state! If a person is constantly in a search for this point of union, to the extent that he disappears into it or is totally integrated equally, then it means that he is working above "other gods."

Thus, he discerns his relationship with the Creator: meaning, whether in all his thoughts, reasoning and actions another power exists besides the Creator, influencing his thoughts and decisions, within him. Then the person sees that he is participating in the work of all the forces of thought and desire, together with the Creator. He becomes like a glove on the Creator's hand, who knows all the movements of that hand and agrees to all those actions, despite all its opposite qualities and performs them in union and agreement with the landlord, with devotion. That symbolizes the attainment of the only true existing state.

This entire great world and all the Upper worlds join in this union. Therefore, we need to constantly work on "exposing" the other gods. Any reason, which shows us that we are not in union with the one and single force, including ourselves, is called "other gods." This is how the principle of "there is none else besides Him" is applied.

From the blog of Rav Dr. Michael Laitman, July 7, 2011

Task #5:
Read the following excerpts from Rav Dr. Laitman's blog and from the book "Kabbalah in Simple Words" and in your own words, write two definitions for the concept of faith, according to the wisdom of Kabbalah.

In almost every religion and method in the world, faith is used as a means of compensating for what we are unable to see or perceive clearly. In other words, since we are incapable of seeing the Creator, we have to believe that He exists. That is called "blind faith".

However, faith serves as compensation not only in religion, but in everything we do. For instance, how do we know that Earth is round? Have we ever flown into space to examine it for ourselves? We believe scientists who tell us it is round, because we think scientists are reliable people who can be trusted if they say they've examined this issue. That is also faith -blind faith.

So, in every place and situation that we are unable to see for ourselves, we use faith to fill in the missing parts of the picture. But it is not solid information – just blind faith.

In the wisdom of Kabbalah, the word "faith" is exactly the opposite. Faith is a perception of the Creator (of the Law of Life, the Law of Giving) in a tangible, clear, vivid, absolute and irrefutable way, or in one word – "attainment". Hence, the only way to acquire faith in the Creator, attain Him, is to become just like Him. How else can we know beyond any doubt who exactly He is and if He even exists?

Rav Dr. Michael Laitman, "Kabbalah in Simple Words"

"Faith" is the force of bestowal. Faith is not that I believe something is revolving in space because someone told me, and I believe the person who told me and he also believes someone else who told him. Faith in the wisdom of Kabbalah is the force of bestowal of *Bina* – *Bina* is called "faith." It is not the faith in our world when I believe someone's rumor. In science it is not acceptable to believe in rumors and in the wisdom of Kabbalah, we do not use the term "faith," the way it is commonly interpreted in our world.

In the wisdom of Kabbalah, there is no blind faith; it is not enough for someone to tell me something and I believe him, rather I need to believe what Kabbalists write for me in order to summon the Surrounding Light. They tell me to do so and so and explain to me why, why it happens this way and I learn this system. In the wisdom of Kabbalah, I have no force of faith, except at the beginning of the study, when I believe the way a person believes a teacher at school or his parents who tell him "you should do this and shouldn't do that." The young must believe the elder regarding how to ascend to a greater degree, because he has not yet risen to a greater degree. That's why he has to rely on what he is being told from the greater degree. Yet, no more than that.

In the wisdom of Kabbalah, we need to scrutinize everything that Kabbalists tell us and ultimately validate that it is true. In the wisdom of Kabbalah, I ask and receive an answer, only in order to ascend the spiritual ladder, check the answers myself and understand. This is completely different from the common faith in this world, where I close my eyes and proceed fanatically with it and someone's words are facts for me. However, in the wisdom of Kabbalah, I do not accept these things as fact, I am going to actualize them and test them on myself, as we develop in all research and science. I believe whoever tells me about the multiplication table, Newton's law, or any other law. I have to acquire it from someone who knows; I have to believe him at that moment, that he knows and that what he is telling me is true, but after I have accepted his teachings, I examine them for myself. Moreover, from the entire body of evidence and information I have acquired, I have the ability to continue researching on my own.

In popular faith, based on what I have been told and accepted without any objection, it is commonly call innocent faith, but in the wisdom of Kabbalah "innocent" means "complete," meaning that I have reached absolute bestowal, that all my vessels are in bestowal. This is called "complete faith".

From the blog of Rav Dr. Michael Laitman, Sept. 11, 2009

Lesson #2 – The Landlord and I

Task #1:
Read the following excerpts from the books "Journey to the Upper World", "A Glimpse of Light" and "The Wisdom of Kabbalah According to Baal HaSulam" and answer the following questions:

- How does the created being remain independent while attaining equivalence of form with the Creator?
- How is a person's feeling of independence expressed?

Our desire to drink, eat, sleep, marry, have children are all from Nature created by the Creator. We cannot ignore that, let alone change it. However, I can build the intention upon my will to receive, formulate a correct manner to use this desire and the degree and depth of that intention depends only on me and is called a "created being." I need to look for a correct method of using my nature, my desires. Nature is from the Creator and my job is to know how to use it. The point in the heart is a person's attitude towards his nature, its use as a corrected desire with an intention of giving, which is called "bestowal" in Kabbalah. The heart itself is a person's desires, an aspiration for pleasures alone.

Everything outside the Creator is called the created being, limited within the framework of Nature and divided into four degrees according to the magnitude of the will to receive: inanimate, vegetative, animate and speaking (man). Of these four degrees, only man is capable of using Nature by means of a special intention he creates himself and that quality is called the point in the heart.

The first stage, the stage of the fetus begins when a person completely annuls himself and dissolves into the Creator. Afterwards, the created being has to gradually elevate himself to the degree of the Emanator and overcome the gap existing between him and the Creator.

By means of the intention, a person seemingly builds the Creator within himself, yet he feels his "I" because his "I" is the Creator. By attaining the Creator, achieving equivalence of form with Him, we attain our own "I".

The Creator wants to create the created being such that the created being, while attaining the Creator, remains truly independent, thereby attaining the degree of the Creator twice, so to speak: once attaining the Creator, and once attaining himself, as operating like Him.

The created being's will to receive is completely equivalent in size to the Creator's will to give (the will to bestow). The will to receive is not exhaustible or lost and the created being remains independent in that he uses all his desires in order to bestow upon the Creator. That is how they become equivalent. The goal is for the created being, though he remains as is as the will to receive, to achieve true wholeness.

Rav Dr. Michael Laitman, "Journey to the Upper World"

What is a person's primary investigation?

Our only investigation with which we should begin and end is the study of the oneness of the Creator. A person needs to constantly reveal his true state. In order to do so, the Creator sends him disturbances, confusion and concealments keeping the person from seeing and understanding that the Creator is One.

A person is in a state of "me and Him" and nothing else. Except that this state is seen by him as the whole world, as the word "world" (*Olam* in Hebrew) is derived from the word concealment (*He'alem* in Hebrew.) What is concealed? The specific existence of a single force, one governance facing the person. That is to say, regarding the Creator, even the person does not exist as a force or governance, rather only He. A person seemingly thinks, feels and determines. He does not determine anything with his own force and governance, only with his intellect, in his regard.

It follows that the investigations and examinations a person conducts are all about how to reach the discernment that there is a single force and one governance facing him, regarding all the disturbances. He feels that there are many forces and varied governance both external and internal to him. It seems to him that he exists and is capable, that he does good and bad; meaning attributing to himself certain independence and being an entity. That is no longer "there is none else besides Him." If he attributes independence and being an entity to various forces and people, it is already idolatry, of which it is said, "You shall not make for yourself a statue or figure." For idolatry means that there are additional forces other than the Creator, Who is One.

Hence, all the work is about concentrating only on the single force and how it takes on various forms clothing a person while working upon him. We need to reveal that this work comes from a single source. From the revelation coming to a person that the work comes from the Creator, he should attribute all the good and bad things to Him. Afterwards, he makes calculations not towards himself, but towards the Creator. In other words, all of the person's revelations are in order to delight the Creator, thus attaining equivalence of form.

Rav Dr. Michael Laitman, "The Wisdom of Kabbalah According to Baal HaSulam"

The wisdom of Kabbalah teaches us that everything comes from the Light. Within the Light, one small point is created, from which all of reality then develops. This point is the matter of creation. The point begins to expand within the Light, concealing it, receiving various shapes from the Light, distancing from the Light at various levels and degrees. "Worlds" are created from the point, which leads to concealment and reduction of the Light.

The point reaches a state within which a discernment called "Man" (*Adam* in Hebrew) is formulated – a desire that understands himself, has a sense of himself and is about to recognize Who created him. It is a type of replay regarding the Light that created and shaped him. He asks "why" and "how." That is surely how the Light awakens him, yet this desire begins to feel he exists, is independent and that he is returning towards the Light, forming himself.

This can also be seen in the development of life in our world – from a drop of sperm, almost from nothing, a tiny body is created. Gradually, within this body, one's own individual development begins, with desires, thoughts, and independent opinions. That is also how we grow spiritually: that same black dot which was once formed in the Light begins to understand by itself and links itself to the Light. At the end, the point truly becomes as the Light.

Rav Dr. Michael Laitman, "A Glimpse of Light"

Task #2:
Read the following excerpt from the book "Tower of Babel – The Last Story" and answer the following questions:
- How can balance between receiving and giving be attained?
- Should we cancel the ego, restrain it or use it with all its force?

The ego creates imbalance, but that does not mean that it should be canceled, only that the way it is used should be corrected. Throughout history, humanity has tried to achieve equality, love, and social justice in various ways, by canceling the ego or attempting to reduce it artificially. Revolutions and various social changes have followed one another, yet they have all failed. The reason is that balance can be achieved only by the correct integration of the full power of the force of reception and the full power of the force of giving.

The general law operating in any living body is the connection between egoistic parts altruistically. These two fundamental opposite forces, egoism and altruism – receiving and giving – exist in all matter, phenomena, processes and created beings.

Whether on the material, emotional level, or any other level, there are always two forces, not one. They complement and balance each other and manifest in different ways: electrons and protons, rejection and attraction, minus and plus, acid and alkali, hate and love. Every detail in nature maintains in a reciprocal relationship with its system and in such a relationship, receiving and giving are integrated in harmony.

Nature aspires to bring us to wholeness and unlimited pleasure, which is why the ego was embedded in us – the desire for pleasure for us to enjoy. It follows there is no need or reason to cancel the ego. All we need to do is correct it, or more accurately, correct the way we use our desire for pleasure, from egoistic to altruistic usage. The correct development makes use of all the force of the desire for pleasure within us, but in its corrected form. Moreover, since the ego is our nature, it is impossible to go against it or limit it over time, for it is an act against nature. Even if we try to do so, we will discover that it is impossible.

Although our current state does not indicate that Nature aspires for us to derive pleasure, it is because unlike all other degrees of Nature, our ego as not yet completed its development, has not yet matured.

In fact, as long as anything in creation does not reach its final form and maturity, the wholeness of the force of Nature is not apparent in it. In our case of human beings, our present state is not yet the final and complete state; hence it does not look very good. However, just as with the growing fruit, there is nothing in us we should destroy; otherwise it would not have been embedded in us in the first place.

The force of the ego is a wondrous force. We have developed by it to this day and will likewise attain wholeness. It is the ego that pushes us forward and enables unlimited development. Without the ego, we would not have developed as a human society or been intrinsically different from animals. Due to our ego, we are no longer willing to suffice with familiar and temporary pleasure and nowadays aspire to achieving what is beyond them.

The entire wisdom is to understand the way to use the force of the ego wisely so that it helps us advance towards altruistic connections with others. The method that assists us in that is the wisdom of Kabbalah; hence its name ("Receiving" in Hebrew) – the wisdom of how to completely receive delight and pleasure. The wisdom of Kabbalah does not recommend suppressing one's innate natural egoistic forces and drives. On the contrary, it acknowledges them and explains to a person how to use them in a correct and efficient way to achieve wholeness. In the course of one's development, a person correctly assembles and harmonizes all his data and tendencies and harnesses them to the process.

For example, it is common knowledge that envy, lust, and honor are negative traits and everybody knows the proverb "Envy, lust and honor remove man from the world." What is less known is the inner meaning of the proverb which Kabbalah reveals to us: envy, lust and honor remove man from our world – into a higher world, a higher degree of Nature. That is on the condition that these natural tendencies are directed in a positive and beneficial direction, so as to push us towards attaining balance with the force of altruistic Nature.

Rav Dr. Michael Laitman, "The Tower of Babel – The Last story"

Task #3:
Read the following excerpts from Rav Dr. Michael Laitman's blog and from the book "The Wisdom of Kabbalah according to Baal HaSulam" and answer the following questions:
- What is the basis for achieving equivalence of form?
- From whom does the will to receive want to derive pleasure?

In our development, there is a law that stems from the relationship between the Light and the vessel. The Creator created within His Light a black dot, inversed from the Light. This point has to develop until it begins to feel itself. Out of the feeling of self, it begins to feel its desire. Out of the feeling of desire it begins to feel the filling of the desire and then the One filling the desire with pleasure. All these stages are called the development of the created being.

After this point recognizes its own desire, knows of the pleasure that can fill the desire and the One giving it pleasure, then from these feelings it needs to achieve equivalence of form with the One providing the pleasure. Hence, the matter of creation, the will to receive itself and the pleasure found within the will to receive are the basis for achieving equivalence of form with the One fulfilling it, the Giver of the pleasure. That is to say, the will to receive and the intention of in order to bestow are the conditions for the created being to attain equivalence of form with the Creator.

This law between Light and vessel is predetermined. Nothing seemingly remains for the vessel itself, the created being, to do. Since he cannot leap back to a state that preceded his creation and determine the nature of the Light, which would create its opposite, the vessel, and the shape of that vessel. This is how we should approach our reality. Man is incapable of changing Nature, thus he should not change it. Rather, he should only change his form of participation, the extent to which he develops, meaning, in resembling the One filling him, the Creator.

Rav Dr. Michael Laitman, "The Wisdom of Kabbalah According to Baal HaSulam"

The Creator wants us to receive pleasure from Him. That is the thought of Creation. Since He is "good and benevolent," his only lack is upon whom to bestow that goodness. That is why He created us from matter called "desire for pleasure."

What should we enjoy? What is specifically from Him, the Creator. When our desire feels the Creator as close, filling it and in adhesion with it, then it derives pleasure. When the desire distances from the Creator, it feels a cooling, even suffers and feels emptiness. In any case, we always only feel the Creator!

If our matter is sensitive to feeling the Creator and His presence and feels the Creator more, it perceives Him as pleasure. If it feels Him less, then it perceives Him as suffering.

The desire for pleasure proceeds to distance itself from the Creator until it completely loses contact with Him. Then the desire to receive pleasure finds itself in this world, a place where there is no contact with the pleasure itself and the Giver of the pleasure – the Creator.

Distancing from the Creator to the point of disconnection is necessary for us, in order to awaken in us a desire of our own to draw near Him, derive pleasure from Him and understand that there is nothing finer and better than being in adhesion with Him. This mutual act is called "coupling" (a spiritual connection), when we are so closely intertwined that we cannot be differentiated or separated. We need to attain such a connection. If we acquire the correct necessitation for it, we will begin to feel Him, connect with Him and feel His embrace.

From the blog of Rav Dr. Michael Laitman, Nov. 6, 2010

Task #4:

Read the following excerpts from the books "The Wisdom of Kabbalah according to Baal HaSulam" and "An Experience called Kabbalah."

From the start, one should behave as if he knows nothing and is the only one handling the situation, needing to do everything by himself – "If I am not for me, who is for me?" as written in Ethics of the Fathers, and then it says: "And when I am for me, what am I?" It is also said, "There is none else besides Him."[56] On the face of it, these sentences seem to contradict each other, yet at a closer look, one can see that they can coexist and even must do so.

The *Baal Shem Tov*, a Kabbalist from the 18th century who lived in Russia wrote that in the morning, a person should get up and look for a job, as if the Creator does not exist and he is on his own with no one from Above to help him. Even though he believes in the Creator, he must say that the Creator does not affect his behavior. That is: "I am my own landlord that of my future."

The landlord in the world can be a person or the Creator- one of them. At the point given to me to choose, I am the landlord, because the Creator is not there, so to speak. This is how one should act throughout the day. Except that in the evening, when he returns home with money in his pocket, in no way should one say that it was he who earned, found the job, or had been lucky. The Creator planned everything and even if you had slept all day in bed and not lifted a finger, you would have what you earned anyway.

However, our intellect cannot understand that, let alone combine those two perceptions, which seem to be opposite one another. It is only after acquiring spiritual attributes, is a person able to combine these fundamental and contradicting concepts.

---

[56] Deuteronomy 4:35.

It is the same the "following day," meaning the following moment. When one is faced with a choice, one must relate to it in one way: "Everything depends on me." After exercising choice, without expectations and faith in the Creator, regardless, one must say "Everything is done by the Creator." There should be a clear separation between the two perceptions, as if there are two different people: a believer and a nonbeliever, before and after the decision, with no religious or secular meaning. A believer and a nonbeliever are states of those seeking spirituality.

It is written in the Torah that on *Rosh HaShanah*, the New Year, we are written Above in a certain "book." Everyone is written there, what will happen to during the coming year, who will live and who will not, how much each one will earn, who will marry, divorce, become ill and so on. If everything is predetermined as we are told, why should we do anything in this life, why should we make an effort? Is a person capable of changing what the Creator has already done?

Only Kabbalah has answers to these questions. Philosophy and science do not deal with these questions, as they are the product of human intellect. A person's reward for his efforts is in the correct attitude towards what takes place.

A person should have a clear understanding of what he needs for his spiritual progress, and then this is his free choice. A person needs knowledge in order to have freedom of choice. As long as he has no knowledge, there is no freedom of choice.

Rav Dr. Michael Laitman, "The Wisdom of Kabbalah According to Baal HaSulam"

Question: It is said that at the beginning of each act one should say: "If I am not for me, who is for me?" And after the effort one should say: "There is none else besides Him." How to relate to emotions while taking action and where am I in my decisions?

Answer: Specifically since a person still lacks the feeling of equivalence between the "self" and the "Creator," he needs to forcefully awaken a state in which he is seemingly completely adhered with the Creator, as though there were no difference between him and the Creator and then there is no question: "Who is acting – I or the Creator?" By awakening this state of adhesion, by the will power and longing for the Creator, with time, he begins to actually feel that state.

But this is not all of a person's work, because progress is possible only out of opposition. Therefore, before and during the action, a person should ignore the Creator's existence and force himself to act. Not artificially, rather truly as if "He does not exist." These exercises are necessary because suddenly, at this stage, one begins to "have faith in the Creator," "be righteous" – even though he does not really feel the Creator.

Rav Dr. Michael Laitman, "An Experience called Kabbalah"

Baal HaSulam says that in every action a person is about to perform in his life, he should add his approach to life, to his existence. Despite his tendency to say that everything is in the Creator's hands, he should first say, "If I am not for me, who is for me?" That is to say, to make an effort to see himself as acting out of his own free will. To know with certainty that the Creator alone is the working force and with that in the background, assume his independence and act as if the Creator were not there, despite his knowledge of the first condition, "there is none else besides Him."

After a person has worked that way throughout the entire process and attained the goal; when reaching the goal, it is his duty to say that "there is none else besides Him." Meaning, that even if he had done nothing, even by his own free choice, he would have achieved the same result he merited. It is because the Creator determines everything, including the result. What is choice for? Choice is only in order to add effort, direction and longing for the Creator. Thus, by means of the conditions that the Creator creates before the person, at the degree of difficulty a person must work with, one must work with both these conditions: "If I am not for me, who is for me?" and "There is none else besides Him."

Rav Dr. Michael Laitman, "The Wisdom of Kabbalah According to Baal HaSulam"

Lesson # 3 – An Organ of Divinity

Task #1:

Read the following excerpts from the books "Interview with the Future," "Light at the End of the Tunnel" and "The Wisdom of Kabbalah according to Baal HaSulam" and answer the following questions:

What is the only creation that was created?

What is the condition for revealing the Creator?

How does the connection between the parts of the soul of Adam HaRishon manifest in our world?

In the system of creation, everything takes place within one soul that senses the Creator within, its "I" and the connection between them. The soul is the only creation that was created and other than the Creator, only it exists. This soul does not feel what is outside it, but only its internality, what is found within it. It is called "Adam" (Man) or "Adam HaRishon,"(The First Man) and is divided into parts; each part is an organ of "Adam HaRishon," from his body. The soul is actually that same "will to receive" pleasure and delight. Its parts are individual desires to receive pleasure and delight and are called "souls."

Rav Dr. Michael Laitman, "Interview with the Future"

It follows that Adam HaRishon's soul was divided into six hundred thousand souls and all of its parts mixed with one another, preparing the place for Man's correction. Therefore, no action can take place towards the Creator without connecting each and every part with all the other parts. We cannot depict any spiritual elevation without the connection among the parts of the soul of Adam HaRishon, meaning among human beings, in order to reconnect at the end with the Creator. For that purpose they were divided and distanced, and have to reconnect and bind together.

The wisdom of Kabbalah is the method, the study and the practice of how to correct this general vessel for the purpose of creation. In other words, the wisdom of Kabbalah teaches us how to relate to the purpose of Creation, the revelation of G-dliness, the infinite abundance which can be received only in a unified vessel.

Rav Dr. Michael Laitman, "The Wisdom of Kabbalah According to Baal HaSulam"

The phenomenon called the "butterfly effect," according to which the flapping of butterfly wings on one end of the world causes fateful consequences on the other end of the world is similar to Baal HaSulam's example of sesame seeds: When one adds a single sesame seed to the scales, he shifts the entire world from merit to demerit. Meaning, every person in the world is dependent on the side of the scales to which he adds his sesame seed, on the side of merit or on the side of demerit. If he thinks about the world and adds in his thought of the world even a very tiny seed, he already turns the world around to the side of merit. And if he does the opposite, the world turns upside down accordingly.

This is an integral, global system which must be explained to humanity. This explanation must penetrate people's minds and hearts, becoming the main and perhaps the only issue discussed by the media. In such a way, stemming from the power of society which we know operates upon the individual, one begins to accept everyone's thoughts and commands. The power of society has no problem operating like that since all of humanity comes from the spiritual system of "Adam HaRishon, " where all were dependent on everyone else and upon the entire system. This law continues to operate in this world as well, although people are not aware of it existing in any case.

Rav Dr. Michael Laitman, "Light at the End of the Tunnel"

Task #2:
Read the following excerpts from Rav Dr. Michael Laitman's blog and from the books "A Glimpse of Light" and "The Arvut" (Mutual Responsibility) and answer the following questions:

What is the connection between the individual soul and the general soul – the soul of Adam HaRishon?

How does the correction of the individual soul affect the soul of Adam HaRishon?

Every soul that corrects itself improves the state of the general soul, thus helping the rest of the souls to correct themselves and in its turn adds its correction to the general soul.

Everyone must attain the root of one's soul; that is to bring one's own "Reshimo" (Reminiscence) to the individual end of correction. The individual end of correction is the full integration within the general soul of Adam HaRishon.

What is the general soul of Adam HaRishon? Is it all me, or am I a part of it? The general soul is all me, as all others are already corrected. I take the desires I need to fulfill from them. I am like one small organ in a body, obligated to provide its part and role for the entire body and all of the parts. That is why the general body is revealed to me only to the degree of my filling.

I reveal the entire system of Adam HaRishon in relation to me. I connect myself to the immense desire of the general soul and like a mother caring for her children, like a cow that wants to nurse,

I completely change my attitude towards others, for I must fill them with the fruits of my work.

Hence, when I connect all the unfulfilled desires to me- unfulfilled because I have not done my job and left an empty space in each one of them – I begin to feel the system of Adam HaRishon. Indeed, it is my spiritual vessel, my desire. It seems to be in others, yet it's mine!

It turns out that I am operating like the Creator, Who wants to fill the created being. I appear as a bestower in relation to this foreign desire and for me they are the receivers. I connect with them and treat them with love, just as the Creator treats the general soul.

How do I attain the state where I feel like the entire Adam HaRishon and consequently reveal the Creator? By identifying with the entire system of Adam HaRishon, connecting with each one and adding my part to the work towards Him, I connect with all these parts in a corrected manner. Indeed, they are all corrected except me. It turns out that I reveal Adam HaRishon as is and acquire the life of the general soul.

So, each person needs to actualize himself, correct his personal attitude, his individual ego, bring the desires of others into it, feel them as his own, fill them and through them attain the entire system of Adam HaRishon and within it reveal the Creator.

From the blog of Rav Dr. Michael Laitman June 3, 2010

From the beginning, one soul was created, that of Adam HaRishon, which was divided into 600,000 Souls and each of them divides into numerous sparks. However, spirituality is not divided into parts. Therefore, in reality there is only one soul of "Adam" and it fully exists in each of us. What divides this soul into 600,000 parts is Man's egoism. Initially, the ego distances and pushes the soul away from its light. However, if the ego undergoes correction by means of the study of Kabbalah, the general soul illuminates in it.

Hence, regarding Man, several states exist:

He feels his individual soul but does not realize that it is the general soul.

According to the extent of unity with the souls, the light of the general soul illuminates in him.

In the complete correction of the ego, one feels that one's soul exists in every person and the general soul illuminates him with all its force, as in "Adam HaRishon."

Thus, three steps are created in Man's spiritual growth:

The soul's spark.

The individual soul that feels itself as part of the general soul, which arouses pangs of love.

Approaching wholeness, in bestowal upon the Creator, integrated with the general soul.

It turns out that even if one soul remains uncorrected, light is lacking in all of the souls. Likewise, in its correction, each soul awakens the light of the general soul, thus bringing correction to the souls of the entire generation. Hence all the souls are interdependent. After its correction, each soul makes efforts to raise its entire generation to the spiritual level it has attained. "The particular and the general are equal," so whatever all the souls underwent in all generations, every individual soul also undergoes when it connects with them – all the faults of all times and all of their corrections.

Even one with the smallest soul acquires the general soul when he yearns for love and giving. Even if only one person in the generation has attained the general soul, he is able to bring all of them to that state.

From the blog of Rav Dr. Michael Laitman Feb. 2, 2008

Even if we do not yet feel the meaning of the global world we have entered, the intenseness of the ties among us are about to become clear very soon.

In the meantime, it can thus be imagined: Each individual is holding everyone's oxygen tap in his hand. If anyone in the world does not turn his tap on for me, then I have no air. I'm dead along with everyone else.

What determines whether he opens or closes it? His inner attitude towards me. I cannot forcefully obligate him to open the tap, only with love ... In such a world we won't be able to survive without mutual concern.

Rav Dr. Michael Laitman, "A Glimpse of Light"

Mutual responsibility is attained through the work of each one and among all together, which is the condition for connecting all desires and souls together. Therefore, all the craving for individual work, any result from individual work has to be integrated with the general vessel, as an inseparable part including everyone, and everyone is included in it. The correction of all is in everyone's connection in their agreeing to mutual responsibility. If it is actualized, we become a vessel for the light.

The more the vessel becomes connected, the more the desire grows, the ego, yet mutual responsibility also grows, integrating with each other, being devoted to each other and the vessel becomes more useful, with a stronger intention for bestowal, according to which more light is revealed in it. This process is called ascending the ladder. From bottom to top there are no ascensions other than through revealing a greater desire among everyone, upon which further connection and mutual responsibility are revealed, from which the vessel is formed. Other than this connection, nothing else needs to be done.

Rav Dr. Michael Laitman, " The Arvut-Mutual Responsibility"

Task #3:

Read the following excerpt from Rav Dr. Michael Laitman's blog and answer the question:

What is the sorrow of Divinity?

Question: How can we explain the fact that Divinity is in sorrow? It is written in the article "There is none else besides Him" about "the sorrow of Divinity." Is it something that really exists, or should we just think that it exists and act accordingly?

Answer: The simplest explanation is in the example of the individual and society. There is suffering of the individual, and there is suffering of a group (family, relatives, society, nation). The sufferings of individuals in a group are not only connected, rather they create a new quality – a social one.

If people gather with the aspiration to reveal the Creator (the quality of bestowal and love) and unite through mutual support (mutual responsibility) in order to attain the revelation of these attributes within them, a common "sorrow" is created, a longing for the revelation of the Creator (the attribute of bestowal and love) in their united desire.

This common sorrow is called the sorrow of Divinity and the Creator Whom we wish to attain is called the "dweller" (the one fulfilling). "Divinity" is not a name that stands on its own but is defined according to the state of the readiness for receiving the filling, the dweller.

From the blog of Rav Dr. Michael Laitman April 11, 2008

Task #4:

Read the following excerpts from Rav Dr. Michael Laitman's blog and from the book "The Last Generation" and answer the following questions:

What is a person's uniqueness?
Where should we not look for self-realization and why?

Question: The total equality you are talking about is somewhat frightening. After all, if everyone is the same, then how is my uniqueness expressed?

Answer: Your uniqueness is expressed by everyone being included within you and you desiring to bestow unto all. What you can give everyone, no one else can give in your place. If you want to bestow unto others, you must first acquire all their desires, so that their desires become yours. Then, for them you will become a conductor of the Upper Light, which connects them to the Creator. That is your uniqueness – to be like the Creator!

From the blog of Rav Dr. Michael Laitman, May 15, 2009

Question: In the ideal state, where the whole world studies Kabbalah and develops spiritually, where is space for the individual expression of a person? Is there such an expression according to the wisdom of Kabbalah? On the one hand, I feel that the highest and most fulfilling thing that can be is spiritual development, yet I wonder where each person's creation is, his contribution to the corporeal world. Is it my ego that fears its loss of self?

Answer: Individuality is revealed specifically in spirituality because it is particularly in our souls that we differ. Each one attains his "Creator" stemming from his individual qualities, and each one becomes similar to the Creator in his own special way.

From the blog of Rav Dr. Michael Laitman, Feb. 8, 2009

The question is the extent to which we perceive that we are locked in a network of forces; do we feel that? We are not free, neither in thought nor in intention. Even in understanding this fact itself, we have no freedom. Even the lack of free choice, we reveal out of no choice. It's neither good nor bad. It is nature, but what can be revealed beyond that?

First of all, we need to ask why we were given the ability to grasp and understand our lack of freedom. Apparently, this ability was given to us so that we would still want to emerge from that situation. It seems that we have that option.

Here is the importance of the extent to which a person is sensitive to freedom, the extent to which he understands that he is governed by all sorts of drives; the extent to which he wants to be free of them, acquire a new force, look at himself from the side objectively and rise above his nature. The question arises once more, ascend where to? To another nature that will also govern him?!

There are not many people in the world who ask and are interested in these questions, attentive to them. According to this criterion, we can draw the precise line between "man" and "beast."

"Beast" is not a derogatory term, rather a level of development: A person lives as society dictates to him, which is not free either. Even the kindergarten teacher, schoolteachers, parents and the media shaping my opinion lack freedom of choice. All internal and external systems do not operate independently but are activated. That is why they are not worth discussing.

If I am looking for some kind of self-actualization that is above this forced flow, there is no point searching for meaning in its drift and turbulence. They of are no significance; I will not find anything in them other than the forces of nature governing humanity and all of creation, all its parts, all through history. No one has freedom of choice.

It's a shame to waste time studying futile things. Generally speaking, this is how the wisdom of Kabbalah relates to our world. It's not being contemptuous. It truly seems to us that we activate forces and laws, set the rules of conduct so that life will be more comfortable. We assume that enacting new laws and creating new machines will make the world better.

We do that without feeling that we are being governed. Indeed, the very desire to be free and somewhat improve our lives does not stem from freedom of choice, but from inner drives we have received from above.

Even when we realize that we are not free, we are forced to perform certain actions that appear to be free, but they are not.

From the blog of Rav Dr. Michael Laitman March 17, 2011

Man consists of two polar points that need to reach their maximum power. The highest point is the oneness of the Creator and the lowest is the egoistic nature of the created being. The intensification of these points is made by a person climbing the ladder of degrees from "below to Above," meaning from this world to the world of infinity. In the course of the path, a person activates an increasingly greater will to receive, while making correct use of his uniqueness.

The actualization of a person's uniqueness is expressed in the acquisition of a maximal desire to receive that acts "in order to bestow" unto the Creator. The acquisition of the intention to bestow beyond the will to receive makes a person independent. Just as the Creator is unique in bestowal, so does a person become unique in bestowal. The intention to bestow is the image of Man in man, where he is completely independent of the Creator's control, equal to Him, similar to Him and His partner.

Rav Dr. Michael Laitman, "The Last Generation"

Part #2 - The Path of Torah and the Path of Suffering

Lesson #1 - Two Paths – the Good and the Bad

Task #1:

Read the following excerpts from the book "The Wisdom of Kabbalah according to Baal HaSulam" and "The Last Generation" and answer the following questions:

- When is the benevolent purpose of creation revealed?
- What is the benefit of concealing the benevolent purpose of creation?

It is known that "The final act is in the initial thought," meaning, the action and its result already exist in the initial thought, similar to a person who wants to build a house and depicts it in his mind, thus determining his purpose. Based on that purpose, he sketches out the construction plan, so that the purpose, which he has set as his goal, will succeed.

It is the same concerning the structure of the worlds: after discerning the purpose, it is clear that all the orders of creation, in all its revelations are pre-defined only in accordance with the goal. Based on that goal, humanity will develop and rise in the attribute of bestowal until it is able to feel the Upper Providence, as well as others.

The Kabbalist scientists attain Upper Providence, the Creator, as the "absolute good." In other words, it is inconceivable that the Upper Force would harm anyone. Those who attain that define it as a primary law of creation.

It is common sense that the basis of all evil acts is egoism, man's desire to receive pleasure for his own sake, the will to receive. Meaning, the lustful pursuit of the will to receive for self-benefit is the reason for being bad to others, since the will to receive is eager to fill itself.

If the created being had not found satisfaction in self-interest, no creature in the world would have done evil to the other. If at times, we see a creature harming others, not as a result of the will to receive, indeed it does so only by virtue of habit, which was originally born of the will to receive and that habit is now the only reason for its action.

Since the force of Providence is a complete entity, which does not need anything for Its completion, it clearly has no will to receive, hence has no reason to harm anyone. That is simple and comprehensible. Moreover, if we look at the entire, vast creation that He created and set before us, indeed, it is proof that His will is only to bestow good upon others.

Whatever the created beings feel, the good feelings and the bad ones, are sent to them from the force of Upper Providence, whose only quality is the desire to bestow, the desire to do good unto His created beings. Since it is known that there is no evil in the law of the Creator, all created beings inevitably receive only good and He created them only in order to do good unto them. Therefore, Kabbalists define the force that created us and is our Providence us as "the absolute good."

Let's look at actual reality, which is found and governed under the Providence of the Upper Force and we will see how it bestows only good.

If we take any creature, even the tiniest one of the four types: inanimate, vegetative, animate, speaking, we see that both the individual and the entire species are subject to purposeful Providence, meaning a slow and gradual development based on cause and effect. It is just like the fruit on the tree, being watched over for a good purpose until the end of its ripening, when it will be sweet and tasteful fruit.

Botanists can explain how many stages the fruit goes through from the time we see it until it reaches its purpose, final ripeness. Yet, all the states prior to the final one not only do not contain a hint of its final, sweet and beautiful state, but on the contrary, as if to spite, it reveals states opposite to its final form. The more bitter and ugly the fruit is in its early stages of development, the sweeter it is at the end of the process.

The differences are even more pronounced at the animate and speaking degrees. The animal, whose mind remains very minute even at the end of its development, is not so deficient throughout its development. Whereas in man, whose mind grows considerably at the end of his development, many flaws are revealed throughout his development. For example, a newborn calf is already called a bull because it has the strength to stand on its own legs and walk and has enough intelligence to beware of hazards it encounters, while a newborn human lies as a creature with no developed senses.

It follows that the Providence of the Upper Force over reality It created is no other than a form of purposeful Providence, which does not take the order of stages of development into consideration. On the contrary, they were meant to deceive us, divert our eyes from understanding the purpose of their existence, stemming from the fact that they are in constant states contrary to the final state.

In this context, we say: "None is so wise as the experienced." For only a person who acquired experience, meaning, who has the opportunity to view creation at all stages of its development until it reaches the final and complete stage, is capable of remaining fearless when facing all the distorted images in his life during the various stages of development. Rather, he believes in the beauty and completeness of the end of development. The reason for this gradual order, which is necessary in every creature is well-explained in the wisdom of Kabbalah.

Thus, discerning the ways of Providence in our world indicates that Providence is only purposeful. Its benevolent approach is not apparent at all before the creature has reached its final form and the end of its development. On the contrary, until then the developing creature is constantly presented to the observer in an external shell of flaws.

Rav Dr. Michael Laitman, "The Wisdom of Kabbalah According to Baal HaSulam"

Many times, the question arises as to why the Creator torments human beings so much. What are they guilty of? Had a parent behaved this way with his children, it would be puzzling. How could it be that "the Good and the Benevolent" treats His created beings in this manner? If a person could understand why he had been struck, so be it; but even that is incomprehensible to him. What is the point in a person realizing that he does not understand what is happening to him? We are also incapable of understanding how it could be that the cruelest and the most cunning are most successful. The correlation between a person's actions and his success or misery is concealed from the eye. If a person understood the reason for the blow, he could immediately relate to the blow, the striker, and the one receiving it.

The purpose of misery afflicting a person regardless of his actions is to detach him from the will to receive. Baal HaSulam says that "if Providence were revealed before us, everyone on earth would be completely righteous."[57] The will to receive would never allow a person to perform an action whose direct result is being struck.

If the Creator's Providence were visible, a person would naturally listen to the advice of the will to receive and want to be at peace with the Creator. Yet, that way he would never be able to disengage from the will to receive. In order for a person to be free of the will to receive, not depend on what he has received or not received, rise above his original egoistic nature and acquire the nature of the Creator – it is necessary for the Creator's Providence to be concealed from him.

The Creator created man and for man to be independent and resemble the Creator from the point of free choice, he must disengage from the Creator. Only out of concealment, can a person build a relationship of two partners between him and the Creator. Such a relationship will not be influenced by the Creator-created being connection. The concealment includes two levels:

The concealment of the good, i.e. feeling suffering.

The concealment of the source of this feeling, i.e. the concealment of the Creator as the One afflicting suffering.

As a result of the concealment, a person suffers, not knowing the source of suffering, what it depends on and how it can be stopped. Out of the concealment, a person has to rise above the feeling of good and evil and yearn to be like the Creator. That is the only way to solve

---

[57] Introduction to Talmud of The Ten Sefirot, letter 43.

the problem of independence. Only then, will a person begin to see that all the terrible situations and torments he underwent in all his incarnations have become a type of large vessel, upon which a correct relationship can be built between him and the Creator.

Rav Dr. Michael Laitman, "The Last Generation"

Task #2:
Read the following excerpts from the book "The Wisdom of Kabbalah According to Baal HaSulam" and "The Last Generation" and answer the following questions:
- What mechanism is the driving force of the revelation of new states of development?
- What does the feeling of emptiness indicate on the spiritual level?

Kabbalah teaches that the Upper World is the source of everything that cascades into our world and that the last degree of the Upper World bore the matter existing in our world. Similar to the Upper World, built according to four steps of the propagation of Light, or in the language of Kabbalah, "the tip of the letter *Yod*," the root and the four-letter name "*HaVaYA*," matter in our world is divided into four degrees: inanimate, vegetative, animate and speaking. The inanimate matter is also divided into four degrees: solid, liquid, gas and plasma. So are the other degrees.

In the "Writings of the Last Generation," Baal HaSulam describes the gradual creation of Earth: At first, a ball of gas appeared, which, under the influence of the force of gravity, atoms were compressed until they ignited. Then, by the actions of the positive constructive force and the negative destructive force, the heat decreased and caused the formation of a thin, rigid crust, while an increase of the destructive force led to a renewed flare of the liquid gas which outburst and caused the crust to explode. Everything returned to its initial state. However, the continuation of the struggle between the forces once again led to the increase of the constructive force and the creation of a harder crust capable of sustaining greater pressure from within and for a longer period, while the power struggles gradually led to the development of further stable structures. Thus, in a gradual process which lasted for millions of years, characterized by alternation of eras, the constructive force gradually overpowered the destructive force and created a ball with a thick and stable crust full of liquid at its core and ideal conditions for organic life to come into being.

The law of gradual development in Kabbalah, according to which Earth evolved, is a law operating on all of Nature and is true for all its details. Kabbalah explains that just as the law of gradual development operates on matter, so humanity gradually evolves by the positive constructive force and the negative destructive force. Each stage or step comes as a result of negating the previous step. Every form of regime exists for a period of time, when its shortcomings are revealed to the extent that it is negated. The more we acknowledge the negative in the existing situation, so the transition to a new state draws near, one which is free of the previous disadvantages. These shortcomings, which are revealed at every degree and cause its death, are actually the reasons for the development of humanity.

Rav Dr. Michael Laitman, "The Open Book"

It is not enough that you love the Creator and yearn for adhesion with Him. You also have to hate the evil in you, your nature, the desire for self-pleasure, from which a person cannot escape on his own.

A person has to reach a state, where he observes his state and sees all the evil within him. He realizes how much he loses and knows that he cannot be redeemed from the evil by himself, while he is incapable of accepting his state. He senses all the losses the evil causes him and also sees that he himself will not be able to find the forces of redemption within him, since that attribute was cast in him by the force of Nature, by the Creator.

To emerge from our world into the spiritual world, a person has to feel a number of defined states, but first he has to sense that his state is completely intolerable. That can only happen when he feels, if only slightly, what spirituality is - which is the total opposite of his state, where all the goodness, abundance, serenity, perfection and eternity exist, and all is one force drawing one to it.

Here in this world there is the repulsive force that repels you from the state that has just become intolerable to you. When both forces, the one that pulls to the spiritual, and the other that repels him from his present state, reach their climax and a person also realizes his helplessness, as well as his inability to redeem himself from the evil within him. In the case when these three conditions exist, something shatters inside the person and the Creator redeems him.

If states of emptiness, indifference and bad feelings arise, it means that his state is already associated with his next level, which he has not yet corrected. Every state begins from the darkness, just as the day begins from the night. It starts from "vessels," from the "will to receive," one corrects them and receives light within them. Hence, whenever a new "bad" feeling is formed, one should rejoice, for the next step is receiving the light. Without bad feelings, there is no progress. Indeed, only the presence of two opposing states enables attaining the "middle line."

In Baal HaSulam's book "A Sage's *Fruit*," he defines such movement as breathing. First the lungs empty and then fill. In all matters, one should first feel a deficiency and only then fill the lack.

Rav Dr. Michael Laitman, "Journey to the Upper World"

Task #3:
Read the following excerpts from the books "A Glance at Kabbalah" and "The Last Generation" and answer the following question:

- How can we avoid misery on the path of actualizing the thought of creation?

What promotes a person is his desire to attain the thoughts and plans of the Creator in his regard and carry them out himself. It follows that what he has is only his voluntary participation, for whether he wants it or not, what is supposed to be done – will be done, i.e. either way the same thing will happen. Rather, if a person participates and desires it, proceeds towards it, he attains the degree, understands, learns the Upper Force and is together with It.

Acquiring the attribute of altruism is life's purpose, to which Nature's law of development propels us through egoism itself. The goal of Nature is to lead us to acknowledging the necessary correction, which will enable us to complete ourselves out of awareness and understanding and self-identification with the process of changing the attitude towards others. Hence, each of us faces choice between two paths:

- To promote ourselves in the process of development, meaning to acknowledge the egoistic nature within us as harmful and contrary to Nature's own attribute of altruism and learn the method to correct it.
- To wait until blows, pressure and suffering resulting from the imbalance will obligate us to seek a method to correct it out of no choice.

Correcting the ego resulting from escaping pressure and suffering is guaranteed, but we were given the option to choose the process of our development in advance, understand and control it. Thus, we will balance ourselves quickly and in a pleasant manner with the general law of Nature, the law of altruism, the law of love and giving. These two possible paths of development are called "the path of correction" (the path of Torah) and "the path of suffering."

There is no doubt that Nature will "win," namely, that ultimately we will abide by its laws. The question is which path we will choose to do so. If we prefer to march by ourselves towards balance prior to being subdued by suffering, that's fine. If not, suffering will push us from behind and provide us with its own motivation. It is interesting to note that in Latin "motive" is Stimulus, which means a sharp stick by which a donkey is pricked to hasten it.

Ostensibly, in order to experience the state of balance with Nature, the best state in reality, we first need to experience is its opposite state, the worst state in reality. For we perceive everything by its opposite: light versus darkness, black vs. white, bitter versus sweet and so on. Yet, there are two possible paths to experience such a terrible state. One is to actually be there and the other is to visualize it in our imagination. That's why we were created as feeling and reasoning beings.

We are capable of depicting in our mind the terrible meaning of complete imbalance between us and Nature even without experiencing it on our flesh, as it is said, "Who is wise - one who foresees the consequence of one's actions." This description will serve us as a force pushing us from the future evil to the good, ahead of time. Thus, we will avoid enormous suffering and accelerate the pace of our development. Disseminating knowledge about the cause of all the crises and problems and the way out of them into a new life was meant to hasten the march of humanity on the path of correction.

Rav Dr. Michael Laitman, "A Glance at Kabbalah"

Spirituality can be felt only in the same will to receive which has been revealed, developed, recognized the evil within him and has been corrected to goodness, to bestowal. That is the reason for the multiplicity of states taking place in a person's will to receive along the process of correction. The choice facing Man is to undergo the process in misery, or to undergo it quickly helped by means of an external environment providing him correct values.

Actually, the path of suffering is not a path at all. A person on the path of suffering stands in his place and waits, while misery accumulates. Suffering proceeds to increase up to the level where suffering is revealed in all parts of the will to receive at its current degree. Then a person feels that he is incapable of using the will to receive at all. The moment even a tiny fraction of the will to receive is awakened, suffering is felt instantaneously. In such a state, a person no longer has use for his will to receive and he "kills" it. He understands that "my death is better than my life," meaning that it would be better if he wanted nothing.

It is very difficult to assess the will to bestow out of the negation of the will to receive. Throughout the history of the human race, no one has ever achieved this naturally. Although the greatest minds of the human race have reached peaks in their exploration of Nature and Man, they achieved it with their corporeal desire within them. That is not the attainment of spiritual Nature. They haven't managed to find a method for spiritual development or even develop one.

The strength and intellect of Man found within the single nature - whose actions and thoughts are within corporeal nature are not able to imagine, invent or develop anything that is not found in it. Those researchers did not have a method of progressing out of suffering, and certainly not a method of progressing without suffering. Without an appropriate environment drawing the "Light that Reforms" to operate upon a person, the desire for spirituality and its actualization cannot be understood.

For thousands of years, humanity has been evolving in accordance with time, "in its time," on the path of suffering, but this progress is on the corporeal - human plain alone. If mankind has had enough of developing on that plain and desires to ascend from this world by the ladder of spiritual steps up to the "world of infinity," it needs to adopt a completely different approach to development. It has to shift from progressing on the path "in its time," to progressing on the path of "hastening" (the path of Torah). This is development beyond time, beyond place, with spiritual means and forces. This is development by means of the Light that Reforms. Development beyond time is possible only by the conscious participation of the person. The only means available to the person to change the course of his life is to change the scale of values of the will to receive by means of the environment. The wisdom of Kabbalah teaches us how to do that.

Rav Dr. Michael Laitman, "The Last Generation"

Lesson #2 - Recognition of Evil

Task #1:
Read the following excerpts from the books "The Wisdom of Kabbalah According to Baal HaSulam" and "A Glimpse of Light" and answer the following questions:

- List at least two definitions of "evil" according to the wisdom of Kabbalah.
- What is the benefit in revealing the evil?
- What is the ego according to the wisdom of Kabbalah and what is the connection between the ego and our desire to enjoy corporeal pleasure?

We were created connected in one vessel, as one body, "as one man in one heart," in a connection where each one completely fulfills the others. In such a vessel with those qualities, the Upper Light is revealed; the Creator Who fills it brings it to the highest state, to His own plain.

After the shattering, meaning, after the parts of the vessel disconnected from one another, each part only feels its own reality, not the others and is prepared to use them only for its own needs. The part itself feels only what fills it and only this filling is sensed as pleasure. Regarding the others, it feels the opposite, "a sorrow shared is a sorrow halved." The feeling that they have less filling than another has is sensed as added pleasure.

Our entire correction is to shift from this faulty state, from the lack of relating to one another, to the corrected state, to the relations that existed prior to the shattering. This is the whole development we undergo in recognition of the evil. In other words, by studying, feeling, becoming familiar with the Upper system, a person begins to realize how dependent he is on the others and how important he is to the others.

Therefore, the process of recognizing evil is the process of recognizing a person's own ego in relation to others. To the extent that a person recognizes his evil and that he lacks bestowal, or bestows evil unto others, one can correct oneself, be included in the general vessel as an inseparable part and add to the connection among the parts of the vessel, meaning the connection among the souls. To that extent one causes the general vessel to return to the corrected state and be filled with the Upper Light.

The recognition of evil, which at first is experienced as "feeling bad" like every small animal, later receives the form of "feeling bad from the Creator," since his attributes are contrary to the Creator. Correcting these qualities that cause the bad feeling is carried out by a person changing his attitude towards the other parts of the vessel, the rest of the souls and created beings, until they all return to the state of "as one man in one heart." The wisdom of Kabbalah helps us become familiar with and actualize all these stages of recognition and actualization.

Rav Dr. Michael Laitman, "The Wisdom of Kabbalah According to Baal HaSulam"

At the beginning of the path, one feels good or bad physically. Physically good is "I feel good," disconnected from the others. From there, one attains recognition of the evil, that evil is that I do not connect with the others in order to attain adhesion with the Creator, in order to reach wholeness. To the extent a person recognizes this evil, he disconnects and abstains from using his vessels naturally and it becomes important to him to connect with the others and build the general vessel.

Recognizing evil is not realizing what makes me feel bad within the will to receive, rather to recognize what is evil in reality. Evil is not what makes a person feel bad, but what disconnects him from the eternal and complete goodness. In other words, a person begins to measure filling or lack of filling, pleasure or misery, not in physical vessels, but in vessels of bestowal, in spiritual vessels, where the measurement is different.

Rav Dr. Michael Laitman, "The Wisdom of Kabbalah According to Baal HaSulam"

Nowadays, we have reached the state where the ego controls people, not enabling them to consider others. Even the rule of "what is hateful unto you, do not do to your friend" has lost its validity.

Up until now, this rule has served us in everyday life. We did not want to harm our neighbor, so that he would not harm us. Our ego warned us: "You'll get beat up, let it go, stay away." The neighbor felt the same way, so life went on in an orderly manner.

That's the way we have lived throughout the generations and although at times, a person felt this as a certain limitation of his internal drives, by and large, people realized that it was good. However, today the ego is increasing and overflowing beyond the boundaries we are able to create among us, beyond all the barriers and walls of defense. It's just bursting out and as a result, we can no longer control ourselves.

People will do anything to succeed. The excessive use of the ego has become a social norm and the media sanctifies these phenomena. Everything is allowed, as long as it leads to success.

Here we need to understand the process in depth. It's not about good or evil people, rather it is a development meant to force us to recognize the destructiveness of the egoism and the urgent need to correct it.

Rav Dr. Michael Laitman, "A Glimpse of Light"

The evil that we feel in our world is a force which advances us to the complete good.

As abovementioned, we are comprised of a desire to derive pleasure which wants to be constantly filled. In order for the desire to develop, it is given a direction, "there you can find fulfillment" and the desire runs there and fills itself. Yet once the desire is filled, the filling neutralizes it.

Let's take a look at our lives. If we have no desire for anything, we are in trouble and sink into despair. We have to desire something, chase after something – in order to feel alive and in motion. However, after attaining the filling, pleasure dissipates, and we become empty. That's how we develop, from chase to chase, moment after moment, generation after generation.

As development in this world reaches saturation, we are beginning to feel that nothing in this world will truly fill us anymore. Now we need to advance to the Upper world. It turns out that all the evil felt in this world is meant to lead us to the recognition of a different kind of fulfillment, one that does not dissipate after its attainment; an eternal spiritual fulfillment.

Rav Dr. Michael Laitman, "A Glimpse of Light"

When I want to eat, drink, spend time with the family, have a good job, go on vacation and so on, it is not considered egoism.

Our desire to enjoy all kinds of corporeal pleasure, everything I need in order to have a comfortable, safe, healthy life, etc., is not related to the precise meaning of the term ego, according to the wisdom of Kabbalah.

So what is ego? True ego is the person wishing harm to others. That is hatred of others, opposite the general law of reality "Love your friend as yourself."

Rav Dr. Michael Laitman, "A Glimpse of Light"

Task #2:
Read the following excerpts from Rav Dr. Michael Laitman's blog and the books "A Glimpse of Light" and "The Last Generation" and answer the following questions:
- Should we yearn for revelation of the evil?
- What should we do in order to reveal the evil inclination?

Question: Is revealing your evil inclination the most important thing?

Answer: We should not try to reveal our evil inclination, no matter what states we undergo. The most important thing, actually the only thing that we can do is draw the Light to us. Due to the Light, I will go through all the stages of which I now know nothing: I will reveal my evil inclination, continue to its correction and then to its fulfillment. On this path, only the Light can help me and nothing else.

I should yearn for the Upper Light to carry out all the actions upon me. What exactly it will do, in what form and order are not my concern at all. I do not need to think that now the Upper Light should reveal the evil in me. I do not know what it should reveal. True, so it is written, but I still do not understand what the "evil inclination" is. It is not worth diverting attention and concentration from the main thing: drawing the Light.

If we divert our attention from drawing the Light, we will begin to search the evil within ourselves and think that every evil attribute of ours is the evil Inclination. But believe me - we have not revealed it yet.

The evil inclination is an angel. When we reveal the evil, we reveal that the Creator is within it and He has given us that quality. Thus, in order to reveal the evil inclination, one should not think about hatred, but about connection among us! Due to my attraction towards connection, what interferes with that is revealed: the evil inclination.

I constantly long to connect with the other souls, until the Upper Light does all the necessary actions with me and eventually reveals to me who I am. I have to go through all the aspects of Root, A, B, C, and in the fourth aspect of the Light's action, I always feel that I have completed a certain degree and received new understanding. And then again: Root, A, B, C, and in the fourth aspect, another new understanding will be revealed to me.

I constantly yearn only for connection and do not think of anything else, no matter what states I undergo: good or bad. Whatever was revealed has been revealed. I am drawn forward, towards further connection and nothing will stop me on this path, be it good or evil, including any philosophical theory that is suddenly depicted in my mind and misleads me into thinking that I seem to understand what is happening. All my attention must be focused on one thing alone: connection. Then I can be sure that I am drawing the Surrounding Light.

Once you start being "wise" and determining what you should do on your own, you immediately lose the Surrounding Light. The Light is complete and you must long only for It.

From the blog of Rav Dr. Michael Laitman March 17, 2011

The first stage of development according to the wisdom of Kabbalah is the recognition of evil. It is written "In Your Light we shall see Light." In order to locate the evil, a person first needs light. We have to receive a great deal of Light from studying in order to reveal that there is something evil within us. Only after we reveal the evil and understand what it is, will it become clear to us how to transform it to the good.

Rav Dr. Michael Laitman, "A Glimpse of Light"

On my own, there is no way I can overcome my ego. Indeed, if every vessel of the will to receive is egoistic, surely I cannot extract myself from myself.

Here a system of correction comes into the picture, including studying, books, a teacher and a group. By means of this system, I draw the Light that Reforms me. It is a special force that influences and corrects me.

No one demands that I correct what the Creator has made faulty. The Creator said: "I have created the evil inclination; I have created the Torah as a spice." I'm the One Who created you faulty and I'm the One Who'll correct you. You just have to attain the realization that your inclination is evil and demand that I replace it with a good inclination. I'm waiting for you.

Rav Dr. Michael Laitman, "A Glimpse of Light"

Replacing the will to receive with the will to bestow is not possible unless a person adheres to the Creator. Only the Light that created man's desire can also change it. The language of the Bible describes this with the words of the Creator to Moses, "Come unto Pharaoh." He invites him to go unto "Pharaoh" with Him, since Moses is not able to do it by himself. "Pharaoh" refers to all of the uncorrected will to receive in a person. A person is incapable of doing anything against the desire, for the desire precedes Man; hence the greatness of the Creator is the condition for correcting the desire from receiving to bestowing.

A person's approach to reality is erroneous as he thinks that he is required to take action. Actually, he needs to awaken the Upper

Force to act upon him, and that is all he needs to do. This error misleads a person into thinking that spiritual work is very difficult, while Kabbalists say the complete opposite. A person tries to correct his nature by himself instead of summoning the "Light of correction" that will change it. In so doing, he wastes a great deal of energy and much time, fails, falls into despair and stops trying. Whoever succeeds is only one who follows Kabbalists' advice and concentrates on turning to the Creator with a request for Him to build a desire to bestow in him.

Rav Dr. Michael Laitman, "The Last Generation"

Task #3:
Read the following excerpts from Rabbi Dr. Michael Laitman's blog and from the book "The Open Book" and answer the following questions:

- What is the difference between Kabbalah and teachings of ethics?
- Is correcting the relationship among people in our world sufficient to bring human society to the perfect state?

Ethics relates to drives that arise in man such as envy, hatred, rage, a desire to steal or deceive, as evil forces operating in man, certain "spirits and demons," which he must oppress and get rid of. On the other hand, the wisdom of Kabbalah explains that such drives, just like everything else that exists, come from the Creator,[58] in order to teach the person what his true nature is- egoism.

Baal HaSulam writes: "I am joyous and happy with those faults that have been revealed and are being revealed,"[59] Meaning, he is

---

[58] See essay, "There is none else besides Him," The Writings of Baal HaSulam, Shamati articles, p. 513

[59] The Writings of Baal HaSulam, Letters, Letter 5.

very happy to see the revelation of the egoistic attributes in man, because it indicates his preparedness for correction, whereas ethics professes to suppress all of the negative traits! This opposition stems from Ethics being based on the human relations in our world, while Kabbalah speaks of the development of egoism and its correction up to attaining the degree of the Creator.

Accordingly, according to Ethics, it is better for egoism to not be revealed in a person. Ethics values small, naïve, submissive, undeveloped people. In Kabbalah it's the opposite. Kabbalah develops a person, with no fear of raising the most painful questions and answering them.

From the blog of Rav Dr. Michael Laitman, June 2, 2008

We are all parts of one general soul called "Adam," or "Adam HaRishon." (The First Adam) The goal of all of Nature is to bring this general soul to the most perfect state, which includes all the souls. This goal cannot be actualized unless every individual soul attains correction that brings it to wholeness. Every person has to correct his individual part which is found in the rest of the souls. Hence, the commandment "Love your friend as yourself" is the basis for progress. It's impossible to achieve any elevation without connecting with other souls and the joint correction with them.

Humane treatment of others is not genuine if it is not built on spiritual attainments. We see how the concept of the family is proceeding to disappear nowadays and in five or six years it will not exist at all. In many families in Europe, each spouse works in different cities and they meet only on weekends.

The "will to receive" (egoism) will grow to such an extent that even such a small cell as the family will no longer be able to exist. This disintegration will continue until humanity realizes and understands that it must exist in "equivalence of form" with the Upper system. Only then will it be content, only then will it understand and be able to do something for its benefit. Then, the family will become a family once more.

A family can only exist correctly on condition that it functions similarly to this spiritual structure. People will sink so deeply in their misery that they will decide to build their relationships on spiritual foundations. Such spiritual attainment will reveal wholeness to a person, so that he will be able to carry out a similar situation in our world. Until then, there will be no amiable relationships among people and within people.

The question arises if it is not enough for us to be good to others, not to curse or steal? Definitely not. That is not what the Creator demands of us. The spiritual qualities we need to attain are completely different from what our society considers as good qualities.

In our world, we have formulated definitions of acceptable behavior: "How not to harass each other." It is called a civilized society. The truth is that it is a more subtle use of group egoism, but these are not the spiritual qualities we need to attain.

We need to develop within ourselves spiritual qualities under the influence of the Upper Light, which enlightens us and affects us only through the study of Kabbalistic books, since those who wrote them were on a spiritual degree and in connection with the Light at that time.

We cannot correct anything in our world directly, rather only through the Upper World. If we attempt to do anything directly, we are affected from Above in such a way that we begin to feel more agony, futility and unhappiness.

Rav Dr. Michael Laitman, "The Open Book"

Part #3 - Israel and Nations of the World

Lesson #1 – Straight to the Creator (*Yashar-El*)

Task #1:

Read the following excerpts from the books "A Glimpse of Light" and "An Experience called Kabbalah" and answer the following questions:

- What are "Israel" and "Nations of the world" in a person's internality?
- According to the wisdom of Kabbalah, in what way do people differ from one another?

The point in the heart, the inner tendency that may awaken in each and every person to reach straight to the Creator's attribute of love and giving is "Israel." The other egoistic tendencies within our heart are called "Nations of the world."

Rav Dr. Michael Laitman, "A Glimpse of Light"

Kabbalistic sources always emphasize that a "Jew "(also called "Israel") and "non-Jew" (also called "Nations of the world") are a distinction between the corrected part (Jew) and the uncorrected part (non-Jew) of the soul of a person who longs for the Creator and spiritual attainment. A person who doesn't aspire to spirituality has no soul at all, meaning he has no desire to attain the Upper One by correcting his "I" and equating his attributes with the Creator.

The soul (the created being) has two parts:

A desire to be filled by the Upper One.
The filling itself.

As soon as a person begins to sense a desire for the Upper One, he begins to actualize that desire, seeks a way to fill it and works with the genuine sources of Kabbalah in the framework of a group and a Teacher-Rav. He begins to feel that he longs not only to connect with the Upper One, but also to fill himself, detached from the Creator and unrelated to Him. Hence, one can understand the internal division between "non-Jew" and "Jew:" whoever begins engaging in Kabbalah is of the aspect of a "non-Jew," meaning that a person who has an uncorrected desire, who only wants to fill his animate desire. However, gradually, throughout the learning process he becomes a "Jew" (*Yehudi*) - derived from the word "union," (*Yehud*) in the sense of being unified with the Creator, since he acquires a desire to be like the Creator.

Rav Dr. Michael Laitman, "An Experience called Kabbalah"

An uncorrected soul is called "non-Jew" and the corrected one is called "Jew" or "Israel." Kabbalah does not relate to a person's physical body, but to his eternal, unchanging part alone, the part called "Adam." Meaning, Kabbalah speaks only of the soul.

You need to adapt yourself to the language of the wisdom of Kabbalah and then all the concepts will be clarified in their true, eternal and spiritual meaning and there will be no confusion between body and soul. I encourage you to expand your reading, and gradually everything will become clear to you.

Rav Dr. Michael Laitman, "An Experience called Kabbalah"

Kabbalah relates to everyone as a created being. It divides all the people - the created beings - into a group of "uncorrected" called "non-Jews" (Nations of the world) and a group of "corrected" (those who have corrected themselves - Israel) also called a holy nation. Kabbalah compares people only according to their spiritual distance from the Creator, according to the extent to which a person has corrected himself in order to match his attributes with those of the

Creator, desires to be like Him and adhere to Him. Only in that do people differ from each other.

Rav Dr. Michael Laitman, "An Experience called Kabbalah"

Task #2:
Read the following excerpts from Rav Dr. Laitman's blog and from the books "The Wisdom of Kabbalah According to Baal HaSulam" and "An Experience called Kabbalah" and answer the following questions:
- What is the difference between correcting the desire called "Israel" and correcting the desire called "Nations of the world?"
- What is the result of the intermingling of desires from the aspect of "Israel" and "Nations of the world," in a person and in the world?
- .What is the work with the desires from the aspect of "Israel" and "Nations of the world" in a person?

The desire in a person called "Israel" (*Yashar-El*, straight to the Creator) is corrected in gradual stages, since it has to reach the understanding and attainment according to its internal demand. That is the difference between it and the other desires called "Nations of the world" which are corrected all at once.

The desire called "Israel" requires a person to clarify and attain the spiritual world, become familiar with it, delve into its details and become the Creator's partner, not simply connect to the system and receive all the prepared goodness from it. The person whose desire called "Israel" has awakened in him wants to connect with this system, work with it and derive pleasure from knowing it. As it is written: "Know your Creator and worship Him."

There are desires and people who do not yearn to know the Creator, even though eventually "everyone shall know Me from their oldest to their youngest," as the prophet says. However, the knowledge to which the scripture refers is the ordinary knowledge of a person living in the spiritual world. Just like in our world, not everyone wants to be a scientist or a researcher and derive pleasure from revealing creation and understanding cause and effect. These are two degrees of bestowal: to explore and recognize the Creator or to simply connect to the source of goodness.

Therefore, the souls belonging to Israel advance gradually, they suffer in stages and naturally so, since all of the attainment is based on a previous, unsatisfied demand, which needs to be increased. Souls belonging to "Nations of the world" - a lower degree arriving when everything is already seemingly "prepared." Surely, they also need to perform considerable work, yet it does not require an internal connection with the Creator as the connection between two partners.

A strong desire has to pave its own path and reveal the secrets of creation, whereas the weaker ones proceed according to each one's extent, or they simply connect to the strong desire and support it. The important thing is that each one attains the root of one's soul, which is the end of one's correction. There is no inequality in spirituality, which is another difference compared to the corporeal world. When a person is in the spiritual world, he acts out of his natural desires and cannot desire anything that is not embedded in the root of his soul.

Only in our world can one envy a neighbor for having a luxury car. In spirituality, one is unable to desire what the other desires, rather only what is embedded in one's spiritual genes, the "Reshimot" (Reminiscence) You can be inspired and motivated by a neighbor only to correct yourself, which is why there can be no division between "big" and "small."

From the blog of Rav Dr. Michael Laitman

Each and every one in the world has a mix of desires to receive and intentions to bestow, which generally manifest in the world as the people of Israel among the Nations of the world. Stemming from this intermingling, each and every person individually and the entire world in general are divided between pursuing the spiritual ideal or the corporeal one.

If we only had a corporeal ideal, everyone would proceed together from a place of understanding. We would work according to the will to receive in a simple way, similar to the inanimate, vegetative and animate and there would be no confusion. Everything would be organized simply according to one law, one rule, with clear connections, pleasures and the desire to receive those pleasures. A great will to receive would swallow small desires to receive and would receive more than them, both in general and in particular, in every person as well as in the whole world.

The problem is that as a result of the shattering of "Adam HaRishon," from the spiritual roots , both the spiritual ideal and the material ideal – both craving for spirituality and craving for corporeality are found in each and every created being, in each and every person. This split makes us restless. A person races and searches, not knowing why he constantly remains unfulfilled.

The reason for that is simple. He has an inner goal that he must attain with which he is not yet familiar. Therefore, he cannot rest until he reveals that in the will to receive there is an intention of in order to receive which must become an intention of in order to bestow. Only in the corrected will to receive will he receive fulfillment. Until people realize that they must change their intention, they will continue to tend to the desire, thinking that the desire is the problem. However, the desire itself is not subject to human control and correction, rather only the intention. Only the intention needs to be corrected to in order to bestow.

In other words, we have to correct the participation of the "people of Israel" in the "Nations of the world." The faulty intention of in order to receive, which serves the Nations of the world, must be disconnected from the will to receive and changed into an intention of in order to bestow.

Rav Dr. Michael Laitman, "The Wisdom of Kabbalah According to Baal HaSulam"

Whoever begins the spiritual path has thoughts that he should be more egotistical and increase the desire so that later he will be able to receive more Light from the Creator. But it should not worry him because everything he needs, he'll receive from Above. The desires to receive and the forces of evil will be revealed within him if and when he can confront them. This is how it takes place in the spiritual world and also in this world. That is why we have to think only of how to ascend.

There are very clear instructions for those who wish to belong to Israel. If a person wants to be corrected, he should in no way interfere with his natural attributes, the "non-Jews." One needs to resemble the Light, distinguish between good and evil, between those conflicting desires within a person.

Rav Dr. Michael Laitman, "An Experience called Kabbalah"

Task #3:
Read the following excerpts from the books "Light at the End of the Tunnel", "The Wisdom of Kabbalah According to Baal HaSulam", "The Open Book" and "The Wisdom of Kabbalah in Our Times" and answer the following question:

- Describe the interdependence between Israel and the Nations of the world.

There are two stages:

A. At the first stage, the more refined vessels are corrected and only Israel undergoes correction.
B. At the second stage, Israel, along with the Nations of the world undergo correction after the shattering took place before the last exile.

In any event, the correction begins with Israel, as Baal HaSulam explains at the end of the "Preface to the Book of Zohar" that Israel is to blame for the lack of correction of the world and must tend to the correction of the entire world.

Meaning, even if the correction of Israel were performed in the past, it does not mean that their role in this world has concluded. Rather, the entire shattering took place so that Israel could be integrated with all the Nations of the world, correct themselves, and then bring them the method of correction. Through the vessels that have already been corrected and are called Israel, abundance will flow to all the other vessels called Nations of the world. Thus, only in such a way will the world reach the desired correction.

The whole shattering occurred in order for there to be preparation for correction. The entire destruction of the Temple was as preparation for correction. After the intermingling took place in exile, among all parts of creation, among all the souls, now all reach a state where they are prepared for correction. Israel cannot correct themselves as long as they are not connected with the world. From the start, their whole job is to correct the world. It is impossible for them to correct themselves alone, with no connection with the world.

Rav Dr. Michael Laitman, "Light at the End of the Tunnel"

The matter of creation, the will to receive along with the Light filling it undergoes changes. A person can participate in the pace of the revelation of these changes, but not in the stages that matter must go through, since they already stem from the nature of the Light and the vessel that was determined even before Man. Whoever longs to go through this development with awareness, with the fullest possible participation on his part is called "Israel," who aspires "straight to the Creator." (*Yashar-El*)

This plan operates upon all of us so that each one must become familiar with one's own development and participate in it in full.

Hence, Baal HaSulam says: The rapid development of the nation of Israel as compared to other nations follows the laws of Upper Providence. That is because the obligation to reveal the Upper force through the wisdom of Kabbalah is upon this nation.

"The people of Israel" is the intention of in order to bestow and the "other nations" are the nature of the vessel, the desire for pleasure. Only when the people of Israel participate with the other nations, meaning, only when the intention of in order to bestow is upon the will to receive of all the matter of creation, only then will we achieve implementation of the wisdom of Kabbalah; only then will we be able to correct all matter with the intention of in order to bestow.

In other words, when is the wisdom of Kabbalah necessary? When, as a result of exile, the people of Israel intermingle with the Nations of the world. That is, within a person, out of desires for money, honor, and knowledge, there is already a willingness and desire to attain spirituality. All of one's desires have already been intermingled with the desire for spirituality, with the intention of in order to bestow, found in exile. That is how the work begins with the wisdom of Kabbalah in a person, for only then does one begin this scrutiny.

Therefore, according to the same law that the general and the particular are equal, regarding humanity in our world as well, as long as it does not reach the final stage, the wisdom of Kabbalah is not revealed. Likewise, regarding a person - as long as he does not attain a desire for spirituality, he has no need for the wisdom of Kabbalah.

Rav Dr. Michael Laitman, "The Wisdom of Kabbalah According to Baal HaSulam"

The purpose of the Upper Light is to fill the will to receive, the vessels of reception, which are called "non-Jews," or "Nations of the world." "Israel" (*Yashar-El* "straight to the Creator") are vessels with the intention to give. Their role is to transmit the Light to the Nations of the world; hence they are called "Light unto the nations."

The spiritual quality of "Israel," the intention "for the sake of the Creator" ("to give"), spreads in all nations, in all the desires to "receive" and consequently creation becomes corrected. The correction is that each and every desire of the Nations will have the intention of "Israel."

This is how a new, corrected creation is created: a desire of "non-Jew" with the intention of "Israel." Hence, "Israel" and the Nations specifically complement each other, and their existence is not at the expense of one another. It follows that the people of Israel will never be annulled.

So, we are told in the sources: In the beginning, the Creator turned to each of the seventy nations of the world, who represent the 70 desires to receive in creation and wanted to give them the "Torah" (the Light). But none of them agreed to receive it, which is why He offered His Torah to the people of Israel.

The Torah can only be received in the "will to receive" to which the intention "for the sake of the Creator" has been attached. Eventually, this desire is called "receiving for the sake of the Creator" ("receiving for the sake of giving"). That is how the Creator seemingly connected "Israel" with the other nations, with all the "desires to receive." For, none of the seventy "desires to receive" were created with the ability to "receive for the sake of the Creator." Therefore, only in combining their desire to "receive" with Israel's intention to "give," can this ability be attained.

Rav Dr. Michael Laitman, "The Open Book"

All of creation is the will to receive, which was originally given to us in its faulty form, as an intention of in order to receive. The matter of creation, the desire to receive itself does not change. Yet its intention, how to use the matter, is what is called "egoistic" or "in order to receive." It is what distanced this matter from the Creator at all five stages, in all the depths of the desires existing in matter. What is needed is to correct the use of this matter, these desires, to in order to bestow.

Simply put, it is called to correct the actions from receiving to bestowing, from unfounded hatred to love of others and love of the Creator. Since the Light of the Creator, the thought of creation, the main *HaVaYa*, the Creator's relation to the created beings do not change, then to the extent that the will to receive changes in its intention to bestow, it feels itself similar to the Light. This resemblance to the Light is felt in it as fulfillment. Thus, first comes the correction of the desire, then the feeling of redemption which exits the control of the will to receive, to complete redemption, to bestowal.

In this correction there are two main stages: absorbing the intention of in order to bestow. A stage called "correction of *Galgalta ve Eynaim*",(Skull and Eyes) "smallness," "internality." A stage of acquiring the attribute of bestowal, called "the correction of Israel," when Israel corrects themselves. For Israel does not belong to creation, but rather is the quality of bestowal, the intention of bestowal, which is under the control and in captivity of the "Nations of the world," called "desires to receive," "the matter of creation." These intentions of in order to receive are called "Israel in exile" and need to be corrected to in order to bestow.

With these intentions, the use of the matter of creation itself, the use of desires is corrected. That is to say, the matter of creation, the desires to receive which are called "Coarseness C" and "Coarseness D" are used in order to bestow. Then, it is considered attaining the implementation of the entire thought of creation. For the main thing in the entire process is to correct the externality, the coarseness, the desires themselves. Therefore, in the process of correction, the internality is corrected first, the correction of "Israel," and only after that, through them, the externality, "the Nations of the world," are corrected.

Rav Dr. Michael Laitman, "The Wisdom of Kabbalah in Our Times" (Issue No. 5)

Lesson #2 - The History of the Jewish People

Task #1:

Read the following excerpts from the books "The Last Generation" and "The Wisdom of Kabbalah in Our Time" and answer the following questions:

- What is the difference between the spiritual development of the Jewish people and the spiritual development of the Nations of the world?
- Describe the development of Israel and the Nations of the world according to the order of correcting the desire.

Many ask whether mankind could have evolved differently; could we have evolved "for the good," that is moving from degree to degree quickly and without suffering. This question is the kind of questions such as: "Can the Creator create a stone that He cannot lift." Our perception is limited. We live in dimensions of time, place, and motion; hence we are incapable of understanding the depth of the question, nor its answer.

On the one hand, it can be said that if the Jewish people had not fallen from its spiritual height, they and the world would not have been burdened with so much misery. The people of Israel would have advanced spiritually and spread its knowledge to the whole world. That is how humanity would have progressed and ascended to spirituality beyond the will to receive, which would have gradually increased to the highest level necessary. Thus, the problem lies with the people of Israel: Their downfall from its spiritual degree prevented them and the entire world from being able to be corrected in a good way and brought darkness to the world. Humanity missed the opportunity to know and adhere to the Upper Force and ended up with a multiplicity of religions and beliefs.

However, these things can be presented otherwise. The development would not have been actualized had the people of Israel and all of humanity not experienced the evil at each and every degree of the will to receive and if they had not digested it to its final degree. The revelation of evil must be felt in matter, namely, the will to receive. It was impossible to offer Kabbalah to the Nations of the world as a method of correction as long as they were at a negligible level of development, within a slight will to receive. Humanity would not have understood what it was about, because it would not have felt anything bad. It would lack the necessary discernments.

The path of Israel's development is very different from that of other nations. The development of the Jewish people takes place "from Above downwards," meaning from the outset, their will to receive was spiritual; Then it descended to corporeality and became enslaved to the will to receive of the Nations of the world; from there, it must emerge into spirituality once again. The development of the Nations of the world is completely different - it is in the corporeal will to receive alone, from the slightest will to receive to the greatest. Once the Nations achieve it, they will break through above the level of this world and reach equivalence with the will to receive of the Jewish people.

Abraham is the wource of the method of correction studied these days and he received it as a gift from Above. The method has been known to the sages of Israel for thousands of years and was passed from generation to generation. The Jew who lived three thousand years ago was tenfold wiser than the contemporary Jew; it was possible to learn from him the same wisdom of Kabbalah that is being taught nowadays. On the other hand, people from the Nations of the world knew nothing. Were it not for the development of egoism, there would have been no need for the method of correction, for there would have been nothing to correct - mankind would not have understood what it was that required correction. This development lead humanity to realize the necessity for correcting the ego and being willing to adopt the wisdom of Kabbalah as the method of correction. Only under such conditions, can the method be presented. The dissemination of Kabbala nowadays is meant to bring humanity to that realization, before it begins to use the will to receive with horrible cruelty and destroys itself.

Rav Dr. Michael Laitman, "The Last Generation"

"Israel" after the shattering constitutes attributes of bestowal that were included at the time of the shattering of vessels of reception and fell together. "Israel" are the internality, the intentions. For the vessels of reception, which are called "Nations of the world," desires are the most important, not the intentions, because within them intentions are joined with desires as a result of the shattering.

This principle can be illustrated historically. In the beginning, there was only an ancient Babylonian nation, as told in the Torah. Out of this one nation, one man emerged who revealed "Divinity," the intention of in order to bestow, who was called "Abraham." He organized a group around him, people who also wanted to increase the intention of in order to bestow within them. Thus, that group of Kabbalists was created, which proceeded to grow to such a dimension, called a "nation," even though it already appears in the Torah that there is no such nation among the nations.

Israel are only a means for correcting the world. The rest of the world continues to develop by its egoism. Only the nation of Israel proceeded to develop by the intention that developed within it. Until the destruction of the Second Temple, whenever the will to receive grew, accordingly, Israel would strengthen the intention of in order to bestow.

However, the time came for Israel to intermingle with all the nations, and then the "destruction of the Temple" occurred, the loss of the intention of in order to bestow and its replacement with the intention of in order to receive.

It is as told regarding Rabbi Akiva's twenty-four thousand disciples, who fell from the level of "love your friend as yourself" to unfounded hatred, causing the destruction of an entire nation. In other words, that group of Kabbalists called "Israel" fell from the spiritual, internal degree to the external, corporeal degree, becoming like all the nations. That is why Israel's emergence to the nations is called "exile." For similar to exile in spirituality, losing the intention of in order to bestow, the intention straight to the Creator ("land" *Eretz* is called desire, *Ratzon* and Israel is called "straight to the Creator") on the corporeal level, they also exited the Land of Israel and moved abroad. That is because the root is what determines what happens with the branch.

Thus, what takes place in spirituality takes place in corporeality. Israel intermingled with the non-Jews and "performed their actions." All the wisdom they could develop was given to the Nations of the world, and in return the Nations of the world gave Israel their ego until that intermingling and inclusion with each other reached an end in the twentieth century, as the Kabbalists had predicted and the time came for correction. In other words, that same group of Kabbalists must raise itself from the state of exile, the faulty state, to the corrected state and then correct the Nations of the world. For the whole breakage and falling to destruction and exile were only to connect with the Nations of the world for the purpose of correcting them.

The Nations of the world are incapable of correcting themselves on their own; rather they can only slightly desire the correction. However, correction itself has to come from Israel, which intermingled with the Nations of the world throughout exile. Now, upon the integration they acquired, they must bring themselves back to the corrected state. For, according to the order of correction, first, the "Israel" part of the people of Israel, called the "internality of Israel," corrects itself, thus the externality of Israel becomes corrected. The externality of Israel is connected to the correction of the internality of the Nations of the world. The externality of the Nations of the world will be corrected only at the end of correction. There are more details regarding this order of correction. After all, until the internality is corrected, the externality needs to apply pressure of desire and necessity for correction.

That is why Baal HaSulam states that even before the correction of Israel, there must be an expansion of the wisdom of Kabbalah among the Nations of the world as well, in order for the Nations of the world to obligate Israel to correct and carry them "on their shoulders" to Jerusalem, as written in Isaiah. For if the externality requires correction from the internality, if the Nations of the world feel a need for Torah, then it will also be easier for the people of Israel to carry out their mission as the chosen people. There are many more details in this process, but the process is the principle that the same group of Kabbalists who fell from spirituality must return to spirituality, correct itself and bring about the correction of the world.

Rav Dr. Michael Laitman, "The Wisdom of Kabbalah in Our Time" (Issue No. 5)

Task #2:
Read the following excerpts from the books "Opening the Zohar" and "The Last Generation" and answer the following questions:
- What is the connection between ancient Babylon and our time?
- What does receiving the Torah at Mount Sinai symbolize?

In all of human history, there was only one period when the wisdom of Kabbalah was open to all. It was in ancient Babylon, which was a "small village" where everyone could influence upon everyone's life. Society existed as one system, thus the wisdom of Kabbalah was needed, to teach how to implement the law "Love your friend as yourself."

Abraham, a resident of Babylon, called for keeping this law, but only a few listened to him. Only those whose "point in the heart" had awakened in them followed him and actualized the wisdom of Kabbalah. Due to their craving, they called themselves "Israel," from the term *Yashar-El* "straight- to the Creator", straight to the attribute of the Creator.

All the others preferred not to connect together, but to distance themselves from each other, so they scattered all over the world and actualized all the drives that the ego naturally aroused in them from generation to generation.

Abraham's group grew and developed to the dimensions of the people of Israel, until 2,000 years ago a great, huge ego was suddenly revealed in us and we fell from the degree of loving others to unfounded hatred. We lost the sense of living in a unified system, the sense of comprehensive love disappeared, and the Creator became concealed from us. Only outstanding individuals were drawn to revealing the Creator, engaged in the wisdom and developed it from generation to generation until all would need it.

Nowadays, the circle is closing and both paths which split in ancient Babylon are merging. The world is reaching a sense of unity, of a "small village" - Global Ego. Yet now there is nowhere to escape... the interdependence among all people requires the implementation of the law "Love your friend as yourself."

The wisdom of Kabbalah teaches how to attain love of others in order to survive. It is being revealed again today to everyone, in order to teach us how to live in the new world.

Rav Dr. Michael Laitman, "Opening the Zohar"

Abraham is the one who founded the method of correction that leads to adherence to the Creator. That is why Abraham formed a group of students around him and they progressed together toward the revelation of the Upper World. When the corrected will to receive with the intention to bestow reached its full minimal dimension called "seventy souls," Abraham's group received added will to receive. This addition led the members of the group to a state called "descending to Egypt."

The term "seventy souls" used in the language of the Torah[60] implies the degree of "Nefesh" the smallest degree of spiritual attainment. The lights filling the spiritual vessels are called *Nefesh, Ruach, Neshama, Haya* and *Yechida*. The light of *Nefesh* is the smallest light and the light of *Yechida* is the largest.

Accordingly, adding to the will to receive requiring correction of Jacob and his sons is called "descending to Egypt." The continued growth of the will to receive is described as the proliferation of the "seventy souls" who descended to Egypt, becoming an entire nation. During the exile to Egypt, almost no connection remained between the Israelites and the Upper Force, the attribute of bestowal. Throughout exile, the will to receive increased and developed to the next degree and its correction became possible only with "receiving the Torah."

It was impossible to correct the will to receive with its new power by means of acknowledging the Upper Force only, as in Abraham's period. The Israelites needed instructions clarifying to them how to conduct themselves and attain bestowal at the new degree of the will to receive. They were required to act as "one man in one heart," observe the rule of "love your friend as yourself" and be "responsible for one another." Only when all of these had been fulfilled, did the Israelites reach adherence to the Upper Force and the quality of bestowal prevailed among them.

After receiving an updated method of correction tailored to the will to receive added in Egypt, the people of Israel began to apply it and attained the spiritual degree called "the First Temple." In the period of the First Temple, the will to receive returned and grew to a higher degree, the Temple was "destroyed" and the people of Israel went into another exile, the exile of Babylon.

As mentioned above, in the time of Jacob and his sons, the power of the will to receive was minimal, thus the additional desire to receive was called "descending to Egypt." Yet, in the period of the

---

[60] Exodus 1: 5.

First Temple, the power of the will to receive was much greater, thus the additional will to receive was called "destruction."

During the exile of Babylon, there was an added will to receive in Israel called "Haman," as described in the Book of Esther. The return of Israel from the exile of Babylon and the establishment of the Second Temple symbolize the correction of the new will to receive. Yet this time the nation was divided into two: some succeeded in correcting their will to receive and others, whose will to receive was greater and they were unable to correct it. It was specifically the egoists who led the nation to corporeal development. They succeeded in their actions as a result of the growth of the will to receive among the people and even joined additional parts of the nation to them.

Gradually, more and more parts of the nation lost spiritual awareness, the quality of bestowal. Thus, the people entered a state of spiritual concealment along with the other nations and the Second Temple was destroyed. With the destruction of the Second Temple, the entire people of Israel lost their spiritual degree and were ruled by egoism.

It can be said that over all the periods, from the time of Abraham until the destruction of the Second Temple, the connection of the people of Israel to the Creator was not severed. However, since then, only a few outstanding Kabbalists remain, who have kept contact with the Creator over the generations.

In our time, the people of Israel and the Nations of the world are gradually reaching the awareness that the will to receive is the cause of suffering and the solution to our dismal state can only come about by correcting the will to receive. As long as they do not acknowledge that, human beings will not be able to demand correction from the Creator and the purpose of creation will not be actualized. In our times, the ego is being revealed in its fullest power, thus its correction with the intent to bestow will lead us to attaining the greatest Light, the "Light of *Yehida*." This correction will be called the "Third Temple."

Rav Dr. Michael Laitman, "The Last Generation"

Task #3:
Read the following excerpt from "A Glimpse of Light" and answer the following questions:
- What is the "Temple?"
- What is the "Third Temple?"

"House" is desire, and "sanctity" is love and bestowal. If someone has a holy desire, a desire to love others and bestow upon them, it is called that within him there is the "Temple."

In the past, this feeling prevailed among many people who were connected with each other. Then they discovered how to express their spiritual attainment in corporeality as well, and as a result the Temple was built in the corporeal world as well. These days, we need to concentrate on correcting the heart of all human beings and for this purpose the method of correction is being revealed in the world.

When all of humanity unites and all parts of the soul connect together with love, we will all reach the most sublime state in reality, the "Third Temple." The Light that will be revealed in us in this state will be the greatest light there is - the Light of "*Yehida*," the Light of the degree of "*Keter.*"

Rav Dr. Michael Laitman, "A Glimpse of Light"

Task #4:
Read the following excerpts from the book "The Wisdom of Kabbalah according to Baal HaSulam," "The Last Generation," and "Tower of Babel - The Last Story" and answer the following questions:
- What is the need for a spiritual state called "Exile," in every person and in the world?
- Why is the last Exile so long?
- What are the three main stages in the revelation of Kabbalah during Exile?

The people of Israel are called the intention to bestow, the forces of *Bina*, the attributes of *Bina*. It is written that Israel is not like other nations, that there is no such nation as "The people of Israel." There are only the seventy nations of the world and the people of Israel have no place in the world. Meaning, Israel is not found in corporeality. It is not a part of the seventy properties of matter, the will to receive.

In Kabbalah, we learn that the people of Israel are that same intention of in order to bestow which comes from the Light as the attribute of bestowal. This intention acts upon matter, shatters along with matter and penetrates matter as an intention of in order to receive. This state is considered that the people of Israel are in exile, within matter itself, serving matter in order to receive. That is to say, whatever way the matter desires pleasure, so the intention of in order to bestow, the attributes of *Bina* and the connection with the Creator serve matter.

Hence, we see this result in our world as well, that the people of Israel in exile are under the control of the Nations of the world. That is, serving them, giving all the nations everything they have and they have a great deal, since all the development of humanity comes by their means. In spirituality this state manifests in each and every one beginning to desire spirituality in order to receive, to derive pleasure oneself. That is a state called "not for Her name," (*Lo Lishma*), where a person is in exile.

Why do we need to be in exile? In order to insert the intention of in order to receive into matter, into the seventy properties of matter, which can later be corrected with the intention of in order to bestow. First the intention needs to be corrected, restricting the will to receive, only transforming the intention from in order to receive to in order to bestow. This is called bringing the people of Israel out of exile to redemption. Afterwards, with the intent of in order to bestow, to begin correcting all matter, all seventy attributes of matter, the seventy nations of the world.

This is what will hopefully happen in corporeality in all of humanity in our times. It can happen to every individual at any moment. The condition for the correction to occur is for all seventy attributes of matter, including numerous properties to be mixed with all the intentions of in order to bestow found in the people of Israel, who have the intentions of the Priests, Levites, common people and many other discernments. At the end of their intermingling, which is called "the end of the exile," the work of scrutiny begins, followed by the work of correction.

The scrutiny and corrections we work with at the end of the exile, both individually in each and every one, and in our times in the whole world, can only be performed by means of the wisdom of Kabbalah. That is not in a natural way by the intermingling of intentions and matter as in the time of exile, the time of darkness. Rather, the scrutiny and the request for corrections must include the person's participation.

Rav Dr. Michael Laitman, "The Wisdom of Kabbalah According to Baal HaSulam"

The cause of "exile" and "destruction" is the outburst of an egoistic will to receive in a person and this process is inevitable. After the "destruction" the will to receive controls Man. A person needs to realize that the will to receive is evil, since it prevents him from attaining the thought of creation - "the absolute good."

The Israelites time in Egypt did not bring about a sufficient recognition of evil, thus it was said that the premature termination of the Egyptian exile led to the other exiles. The essence of exile is the recognition of evil; A person must recognize that he is in exile, disconnected from bestowal. One is not in exile if one does not feel in exile.

As noted, during the period of the descent of the sons of Jacob to Egypt and even during the destruction of the First Temple, the people still remained with certain spiritual awareness. Only the destruction of the Second Temple brought the people of Israel to total detachment from spiritual awareness and the gradual entry into the greatest egoistic desire. Parallel to the development of the Jewish people, the intermingling between Israel and the Nations of the world also began, due to which the Nations of the world began to progress and develop.

The length of exile is determined by the feeling of the people that they are in exile. The last exile is so long because throughout this period, the egoistic will to receive needs to develop to its final degree. As long as the desires for physical cravings, wealth, honor, control, and knowledge are not revealed in full force, it is impossible to fully recognize the will to receive as evil.

Only in the twentieth century, did humanity begin to realize the destructive consequences of its actions. Humanity is beginning to fear the consequences of past actions and the approaching punishment. Like a child who is afraid of his parents, humanity is seeking a place to hide, and the future is no longer safe.

If it were possible to gather famous influential people who were willing to abandon their narrow worldview and understand that humanity is on the edge of an abyss, humanity could be brought into action. If we could come forward with a worldwide declaration, such as "Planet Earth is about to explode in a month's time," everyone would abandon their egotistical business and think of a way to be saved. It follows that what we lack is the view of our present fatal human condition.

Rav Dr. Michael Laitman, "The Last Generation"

Before going into the last exile, in the second century A.C.E., the "Book of Zohar" was written by Rabbi *Shimon bar Yochai* (*Rashbi*) and his group of disciples. "The Book of Zohar," which was written in Aramaic, details the method of correction and describes everything that a person who attains balance with Nature experiences.

Furthermore, it includes a description of all the states that humanity will undergo until the final correction of the ego.

It should be noted that even though the "Book of Zohar" was written prior to the exit of the whole nation into exile, it already said that it would only be revealed at its end and bring to an end the spiritual exile: "And since Israel are going to taste from the Tree of Life that is this 'Book of Zohar,' they will return from exile with mercy."[61] It is further stated that towards the end of the six thousand year period allotted for correcting the ego, the Book will be revealed to all humanity: "When the Messianic age approaches, even babies in the world will later find the secrets of the wisdom and know the formulas and accounts of redemption and at that time, it'll be revealed to all."[62]

Thus, immediately after its writing was completed, the "Book of Zohar" was concealed. Only in the 13th century it was published in Spain for the first time. About 1,400 years after the writing of the "Book of Zohar," in the 16th century, The *ARI* appeared in Safed. The same method of correction which had been presented in the "Book of Zohar" in a language full of allusions and parables, The *Ari* expressed in scientific and systemic language which described the stages of correcting the ego which lead to balance with all of Nature in great detail.

His writings include descriptions of the structure of the Upper World and explain to a person how to enter that dimension of reality. However, since at the time of The *ARI*, the ego was not yet revealed in full force, only a few were capable of understanding his teachings, for the more developed ego leads to a sharper ability of perception.

We are drawing close to the end of the allotted period of correction, bringing the ego to its last degree, a crisis creating the necessity for a method of correcting the ego. Nowadays, many people already need the method of correction and are capable of perceiving what only few people understood in the past.

---

[61] The Zohar with "*HaSulam*" commentary, section *Neso*, letter 90.
[62] The Zohar with "HaSulam" commentary, section VaYera, letter 408.

Therefore, at this time, the full method of correction is being exposed: *Baal HaSulam* (1884 -1954) merited interpreting the "Book of Zohar" and the writings of The *ARI* so that each one of us could understand them. That is why he said: "Happy am I that I was created in such a generation where it is already permissible to publish the wisdom of truth. And if you ask me how I know it is permissible, I will answer you, because I have been given permission to reveal[63]

His main essays are "The Sulam Commentary on the Book of Zohar," where he translated the book from Aramaic, interpreted the "Book of Zohar" and "Talmud of the Ten Sefirot," where he explained the writings of The *ARI*. In addition, Baal HaSulam wrote numerous articles explaining the way to establish a human society existing in balance with Nature. He explained that the generation's need for an orderly and clear system for correcting the ego enabled him to do so.

From the end of the twentieth century, as the Kabbalists had foreseen, a new stage in the development of humanity began: people started to be drawn to the wisdom of Kabbalah in droves. In the eighteenth century The *Gaon of Vilna* had already indicated 1990 as the year when the process would begin, in his book "*Kol Hator,*" and Baal HaSulam mentioned 1995 in a conversation with his students fifty years earlier.

Rav Dr. Michael Laitman, "The Tower of Babel - The Last Story"

Lesson #3 – The Role of the People of Israel

Task #1:

Read the following excerpt from the book "Tower of Babel - The Last Story" and answer the following questions:

- What is the condition for maintaining a normal life for the people of Israel in the Land of Israel?

---

[63] The writings of Baal HaSulam, Essay "The Wisdom of Kabbalah and its Essence."

- How is the return of the people of Israel to the Land of Israel after exile different from their dwelling in the Land of Israel before exile?

The return of the people of Israel to the Land of Israel is a predetermined course of Nature's plan. In order to understand it, it is necessary to understand the spiritual meaning of the concept of the "Land of Israel," which requires being familiar with the language used by Kabbalists.

When Kabbalists attained balance with Nature, they revealed that same part of reality found beyond the perceptual range of the egoistic person and named it the "Upper world" or the "spiritual world."

Having found that from every detail in the Upper world called "root," a force cascades into our world and bears a corporeal "branch" here, they used borrowed names from our world to describe the details, forces and actions of the Upper world. Thus, the "language of the branches" was developed, based on the parallelism between the Upper world and our world. In the language of the branches, land means desire, Israel means *Yashar-El* (straight to the Creator). Meaning, the Land of Israel is a term for the desire that directly focused on attaining the attribute of altruism of Nature.

The generations that lived in the Land of Israel before the destruction of the Second Temple were in spiritual attainment. At that time, the spiritual level of the people of Israel corresponded with their corporeal presence in the Land of Israel, thus they were worthy of being present there. Later, the people lost their spiritual degree and fell under the control of egoistic desires. The lack of correspondence between the peoples' spiritual level and their presence in the Land of Israel eventually led to the destruction of the Temple and even to exile from the Land of Israel.

Although in the past, the spiritual fall preceded the exile of the people from the Land of Israel among the nations, now the situation is reversed. The corporeal return to the Land of Israel precedes the spiritual return, yet the correspondence of the spiritual root with the corporeal branch must be constructed. The people of Israel have to return in the same way they "descended" in the past, only in reverse order: first the corporeal return, then the spiritual return.

Accordingly, it is incumbent upon the people of Israel to attain the spiritual level of the "Land of Israel," and for this purpose the method of correction is being revealed to them. As long as the people of Israel are not corrected, they will feel discomfort on this land. It is impossible to live in Israel without the spiritual ideal: the forces of Nature will not enable Man to exist in it at rest, without being spiritually suited.

In order to awaken the dwellers of the corporeal Land of Israel to rise to the spiritual degree called "Land of Israel," a reality is being revealed, creating a life devoid of security and full of concerns.

All the pressures put on Israel, both by other countries and by inner social crises - on the state level through the social level to the personal one - occur only for us to begin advancing towards the purpose of our existence in this world

The "Book of Zohar" and the Kabbalists of all generations have indicated the return of the people of Israel from exile as the time when the correction of the world must be carried out. Therefore, upon returning to Israel, the great Kabbalist *Rabbi Kook*, who was also the first Chief Rabbi of Israel after two thousand years of exile, declared: "Now the days are near, when all will realize and know that the salvation of Israel and the salvation of the entire world depends only on the appearance of the concealed wisdom of the internality of the secrets of Torah (Kabbalah) in clear language."[64]

Just as the people of Israel do not exist in the count of seventy nations of the world, but rather constitute a unique group meant to convey the method of correction to all mankind, so too, the Land of Israel does not exist upon the planet Earth unless it is a land in which a spiritual nation dwells.

---

[64] The Letters of The *RAAYA*, Part !, p. 82

Therefore, only to the extent that the people of Israel carry out their role, are they worthy of living in the Land of Israel. If they do not carry out their role, they are not called "people of Israel" and the land is not the "Land of Israel;" rather it becomes a land that rejects and ejects the people itself, a land that is incapable of bearing this nation on its soil, "a land that devours its inhabitants."

Rav Dr. Michael Laitman, "The Tower of Babel - The Last Story"

Task #2:
Read the following excerpts from the books "The Tower of Babel - The Last Story "and "Opening the Zohar" and answer the following question:

- Which connection cannot guarantee our existence in Israel and which connection can guarantee our existence in Israel?

If we want to be a free people in our country, in the words of the national anthem, we need to reach the same formula according to which we existed before the destruction of the Temple and our exile. Instead of separation, alienation and unfounded hatred found among us today, we have to return to the state where we were united as parts of one body and in balance with general Nature.

Actually, we have united from the external aspect in the Land of Israel mainly out of necessity. Nature's plan caused the Nations of the world to pressure and force us to flee from the Diaspora to Israel. For the most part, people came to Israel against their will for refuge, where they could be saved from the pressure of their enemies or improve their corporeal lives, not out of an inner drive to connect with love and create a united nation, in balance with altruistic Nature and lead all human beings to such a state.

In the long run, this type of connection does not enable us to confront other nations who rise up against us, whose inner connection is far more solid than ours. These days, they are clearly aware of this weakness of ours, as explained by Dr. Zeev Magen, head of the Department of Middle Eastern History at Bar-Ilan University:

"The Iranians and the other fundamentalists are convinced that we are a society with no foundation of uniform principles. Furthermore, they are convinced that we have also reached the conclusion that such a foundation cannot exist among us. Hence, the fundamentalists are certain that sooner or later they will defeat us and force us out of Israel, or at least put an end to our sovereignty, for certainty will always overcome uncertainty. We, in their eyes, are living on borrowed time.

A recent article in one of the Arab newspapers concluded with an excerpt from Khamenei's speech quoting the Koran: "The Jews will not fight against you as one man - you think they are united, yet their hearts are divided."[65]

Unity among us can be achieved only when we unite around the actualization of our role towards the world. This union is not intended to improve our situation over other nations or, G-d forbid, at their expense. National education for the ideal of the people of Israel, of which the wisdom of Kabbalah speaks is diametrically opposed to that.

We must not see ourselves as superior people, rather to the contrary - "the chosen people" means that these people have been chosen to serve all nations. Our role is to help them attain balance with Nature - the most flourishing degree of spiritual growth. We should view ourselves merely as a means and we can do this only by uniting amongst us.

Our return to the Land under external threat was surely directed by Nature's plan; thus, we have been given the opportunity to reveal for ourselves the internal need to unite in order to be built as a nation that leads humanity to wholeness.

---

[65] Dr. Zeev Magen is quoted in the writings of Zeev Galili, "How the Iranians view Israel," published on Aug. 10, 2006, in the newspapaer *Makor Rishon.*" On the Internet: www.makorrishon.net/show.asp?id=81041

It is not coincidental that we have not succeeded in creating a united society in Israel for so many years: religious vs. secular, left vs. right, The Ashkenazi vs Sephardi, native Israelis vs. new immigrants, and so on. All attempts and efforts that we have exerted to unite everyone have failed so far.

Our present situation requires us to reexamine what our roots are: where we came from, how we became the people of Israel, what the principles are by which the nation was founded in the past and for what purpose. Only on the basis of those eternal foundations of the spiritual idea can we now unite and bring to the unity of all human beings everywhere.

Rav Dr. Michael Laitman, "The Tower of Babel - The Last Story"

The study of the Book of Zohar and the wisdom of Kabbalah connect people from all over the world, without any difference of race, sex, nationality or religion. This wisdom bridges the gaps of mentality, character, age, economic or social status, even within our divided people, even between us and the entire world. This is an actual fact that has become evident in recent years, among two million students who study within the different frameworks of "Kabbalah for All" in Israel and abroad.

Rav Dr. Michael Laitman, "Opening the Zohar"

Task #3:
Read the following excerpts from the books "Opening the Zohar," "The Tower of Babel - the Last Story," "A Glimpse of Light," "The Wisdom of Kabbalah according to Baal HaSulam," and answer the following questions:
  • What is the reason for anti-Semitism?
  • What is the solution to the problem of anti-Semitism?

It is important for us to understand that we hold the key to happiness of all humanity, since we are the owners of the system. That is not to mean any ultranationalism, G-d forbid; we are not better than others, as some of us like to think out of pride. We only have a defined role in the general plan of Nature.

We need to remember that our people were not created on the basis of race or nationality. We are those same souls who already gathered around Abraham in ancient Babylon, in order to actualize the spiritual concept of "Love your friend as yourself" which leads to the revelation of the Creator.

Kabbalists explain that from the beginning, the method of correction was offered to all nations, but at that time, no nation was willing to accept it. Humanity still did not need it. That is why the method was given to the people of Israel.

We should begin to use the wisdom of the "Book of Zohar" and Kabbalah once more, to shift from unfounded hatred to brotherly love, return to our spiritual root and bring light to the world; to be "a light unto the nations." Actually, this is what humanity has always demanded of us, the inner wisdom, the light of life. Our excellence in high-tech is not enough …

The world is unaware of this, and so are we to a certain extent, yet this is the basis for anti-Semitism towards us. Subconsciously, everyone feels that we have something special that is concealed and we are withholding it from them. That is why they hate us.

The actualization of the wisdom of Kabbalah in our time is the only way we can truly merit being treated otherwise by the world and have a safe and peaceful life. Only by means of the spiritual wisdom that turned us into a nation, can we return to being "one man with one heart" and build a society and a prosperous state in Israel, being the spiritual center of the world.

Rav Dr. Michael Laitman, "Opening the Zohar"

Understanding the role of the people of Israel also makes it easier for us to understand the phenomenon of anti-Semitism and its solution. The root of anti-Semitism and blaming the Jews for all evil in the world stems from the purpose of Israel's existence - to convey to the world the method of correcting the ego. The fate of the people depends on the way it fulfills its mission.

As long as the people of Israel do not actualize the system of correction itself nor convey it to all other nations, humanity's imbalance with Nature will grow. As a result, the intensity and frequency of adverse events in the life in all humanity as well as in the life of every person has increased, until now, when this state already manifests as a global crisis.

In nations of the world, Anti-Semitism is being revealed in the world, according to the development of the ego. In their subconscious, the Nations of the world feel that their suffering depends on Israel, thus specifically the developed nations have developed a negative attitude toward the Jews. It is not surprising that Germany, the most developed country at the beginning of the twentieth century is where there was such a huge anti-Semitic outburst. As the ego of the nations develops, so hatred toward us is aroused in them-some with the sword, silently, or in consent and support.

These days, the development of the ego has led to objection towards Israel in most countries around the world. Even in countries that used to sympathize with Israel in the past, the attitude has changed for the worse, such as in North-European countries. Surveys conducted in the European Union show that Israel is the country most endangering world peace. Around 60% of the European population think so, while in the Netherlands, 74% of the public think so. It also turns out that the negative image of Israel increases among the educated people.[66] Small and marginal countries on the map of the world make public

---

[66] These data were taken in Oct. 2006 from the site: www.nfc.co.il/ NewsPrintVersion.asp?docId=20233&subjectID=1.

declarations against us and even nations with whom we have no direct connection show a negative attitude towards us. The negative attitude toward us from the western world is compatible with the negative attitude towards us from the Muslims; sharp hate speech is heard every day; Jews are accused of international scheming and blood libels appear again.

It should be noted that the attitude of the nations to each other is completely different from their attitude towards us. Even if two nations hate each other, indeed, at a time of common danger, they will agree to unite in order to be saved, like animals fleeing together from danger. However, the attitude towards us is different. Even in times of general danger, the nations will point a blaming finger at us and view us as the reason for their danger.

Many people in the world now think that the Jewish nation has no place in the world, not even in the State of Israel. These things are being said out of an inner sense, from an instinctive and deep feeling that we are the source of all the world's problems, except that people are incapable of explaining this to themselves or to us consciously and with awareness.

Actually, we are also incapable of explaining why everyone hates us and why we also cultivate a sense of guilt or liability towards other nations - as if we deserve this special negative attitude. However, these things derive from absolute natural laws which are unchangeable.

It turns out that anti-Semitism is not dependent on the Nations of the world, but solely on the functioning of the people of Israel. We must not rely on a particular nation to assist us and we shouldn't hope that the attitude of the world towards us will change for the better. On the contrary, even in countries where we are ostensibly supported today, hatred towards us will arise if we do not begin to actualize our mission.

Rav Dr. Michael Laitman, "The Tower of Babel - The Last Story"

In the end, all of humanity is supposed to attain actualization of the law "Love your friend as yourself." In order to make it easier for humankind to correct the nature of man, the method of correction was developed among a certain group of people within the people of Israel.

These days, we need to return to being a spiritual nation, engage with internality of the Torah, the wisdom of Kabbalah - implement the method of correction upon us and help the entire world ascend. It is called being "light unto the nations" and this is our whole destiny as a chosen people.

Subconsciously, the world feels that we hold the key to its happiness, that we have something special that we are hiding from all. According to the wisdom of Kabbalah, this sensation is the root of anti-Semitism. As the world's correction is delayed, suffering increases, along with anti-Semitism among the nations.

Simply put, the key to changing the state of the world and the negative attitude towards us is in our hands. As soon as we begin to implement the method of correction, we will immediately sense tremendous improvement and even our greatest enemies will suddenly become friends.

Rav Dr. Michael Laitman, "A Glimpse of Light"

According to the general law of Nature, at the end of one's development, every person in the world is obligated to reveal the sixth sense within himself and by its means, attain all of creation. This is the purpose of creation. Accordingly, the Kabbalists are obligated to teach the people the method of developing the sixth sense and ensuring that the people of Israel will convey the system to all of humanity.

The reason for anti-Semitism lies in the fact that the people of Israel are not carrying out this mission. The Nations of the world argue against the people of Israel and accuse it of erroneous conduct, preventing the world from receiving the good to which it is entitled. In truth, the feeling of covert guilt even exists among the Jews themselves. It can be argued, however, that the nations of the world's main religions- Christianity and Islam, actually developed from the Jewish religion, which was created on the basis of Kabbalah, after it had disappeared from the overt attainment of the Jews, leaving only the legacy of the past.

Since in the people of Israel *Reshimot* (Reminiscence) of the spiritual attainment of their forefathers remained, they replaced that lost attainment with the tradition of customs and external actions. Later, the term "spiritual attainment" also disappeared and they no longer understood that their ancestors lived on a different level of perceiving the world.

Baal HaSulam describes this situation in a parable of a man who arrived at a distant place and forgot his home. Then one day, a book about a distant and wonderful land fell into his hands and that was what led him to remember that he, too, must have come from that same country. Similarly, we must all return to perceiving the Upper world.

Rav Dr. Michael Laitman, "The Wisdom of Kabbalah According to Baal HaSulam"

Task #4:

Read the following excerpts from Rav Dr. Michael Laitman's blog.

We keep repeating that dissemination of the wisdom of Kabbalah is necessary for the successful study of the wisdom of Kabbalah. But I feel that it is not the suitable word, because in our time the word dissemination is related to trading. People might think it's about a salesman or an insurance agent who is offering everyone his policies. It could seem that we are disseminating the wisdom of Kabbalah, as if we want to give something to people.

When we talk about disseminating the wisdom of Kabbalah, there is a fear that people will think that we are dealing in commerce or business, as if we're selling something and making a profit from it. That is quite a "slicky" word.

Yet, actually, our whole lives are dissemination, because dissemination means drawing close to the Creator, development, revelation, attainment.

All of creation begins with dissemination - from one single point, created from nothing, from which suddenly something existing emerges, "substance from absence," and then spreads: four distinctions of direct light, spiritual worlds, down to our world and the last spiritual degree bursts into our world with the single small spiritual baggage.

All the matter of our creation, the entire universe, was born of that one spark in the Big Bang. It spread and developed into our solar system, Earth and everything that exists on it. All that has to do with dissemination - the expansion of the Creator in creation. The purpose of dissemination is to bring creation to equivalence with Him, out of the pressure of the Light, His quality of bestowal.

Every birth, every development is dissemination. Dissemination in its intrinsic and true quality symbolizes partnership with the Creator - assisting in the transmission of His idea, we help Him to be revealed in the world, act together with Him.

From the blog of Rav Dr. Michael Laitman, Oct. 28, 2009

We need to engage in dissemination to the whole world, accept the world in its entirety and provide everything necessary for the correction of each one wherever one is. Everyone in the world is sick with the same disease, egoism, which tears us out of the light of life. So, the cure is to arouse this light upon us and everyone needs it. That's what we think, which is why we disseminate this medicine to all.

It already depends on the person whether he wants to accept it now, or when he feels his illness more acutely. We need to meet not in one place, but with one intention despite the physical distance. This is the meaning of our world.

From the blog of Rav Dr. Michael Laitman

Made in the USA
Middletown, DE
20 September 2022